D1080109

CONFLICT
IN JAPAN

CONTRIBUTORS

JOHN CREIGHTON CAMPBELL
MICHAEL W. DONNELLY
TADASHI HANAMI
TAKESHI ISHIDA
ELLIS S. KRAUSS
TAKIE SUGIYAMA LEBRA
AGNES M. NIYEKAWA
SUSAN J. PHARR
THOMAS P. ROHLEN
PATRICIA G. STEINHOFF
TEIGO YOSHIDA

This book is based on a conference sponsored by the Joint Committee on Japanese Studies of the American Council of Learned Societies and the Social Science Research Council.

CONFLICT IN JAPAN

edited by
ELLIS S. KRAUSS
THOMAS P. ROHLEN
PATRICIA G. STEINHOFF

University of Hawaii Press *Honolulu*

Library of Congress Cataloging in Publication Data
Main entry under title:

Conflict in Japan.

  Includes index.
  1. Social conflict—Japan—Addresses, essays, lectures.
2. Social conflict—Addresses, essays, lectures.
3. Japan—Social conditions—1945-   —Addresses,
essays, lectures.   4. Japan—Politics and government—
1945-   —Addresses, essays, lectures.   I. Krauss,
Ellis S.   II. Rohlen, Thomas P.   III. Steinhoff,
Patricia G., 1941–
HN723.5.C67   1984   303.6'0952   84–108
ISBN 0–8248–0948–3
ISBN 0–8248–0867–3 (pbk.)

TO OUR PARENTS
Irving and Pearl Krauss
Karl and Frances Rohlen
David and Ruth Golden

Not the presence but the absence of conflict is surprising and abnormal, and we have good reason to be suspicious if we find a society or social organization that displays no evidence of conflict.

Ralf Dahrendorf

Contents

Acknowledgments

The editors would like to thank the many individuals and organizations who made this project possible and aided us in our endeavors over the years of this book's preparation. First, a special thanks to Gerald Curtis of Columbia University, the project's "godfather" who first conceived and encouraged it as chairman of the Joint Committee on Japanese Studies of the American Council of Learned Societies and the Social Science Research Council. Thanks too to the JCJS committee members who voted us the funds over the years to carry out the project. And thanks to the four successive staff members, Susan Pharr, Ron Aqua, Sophie Sa, and Ted Bestor, who lightened considerably the administrative burden of the project.

Our thanks too to the Center for Asian and Pacific Studies, University of Hawaii, which provided released time for Pat Steinhoff just at the time the manuscript was ready to be edited. We very much appreciate the manuscript typing and word-processing services provided by Geri Walker and her staff at the Bureau for Faculty Research, Western Washington University.

Numerous individuals participated in the planning meetings and workshops of the project and were invaluable in helping us to develop our themes and concepts: Lewis Austin, John Bennett, Ronald Dore, Scott C. Flanagan, Chalmers Johnson, Richard Johnson, Dan Okimoto, Herbert Passin, T. J. Pempel, and Kurt Steiner. We are also grateful to Sol Levine and two anonymous reviewers for their helpful suggestions on the manuscript and to Damaris Kirchhofer of the University of Hawaii Press for her pleasant and efficient handling of the production process.

Finally, we editors would like to thank our contributors, as well as the organizations that supported their research in various ways, for their patience in waiting for our collective efforts to reach fruition.

PART I:
Introduction

I

Conflict: An Approach to the Study of Japan

ELLIS S. KRAUSS
THOMAS P. ROHLEN
PATRICIA G. STEINHOFF

A book that examines Japanese society and politics through the study of conflict will strike some as an unusual, and even perverse, approach to adopt, given most previous English-language studies of Japan. Social science research on Japan for most of the postwar period has emphasized just the reverse, visualizing a hierarchical society with strong collective unity. To the outside world contemporary Japan was characterized as lacking both major schisms and as resolving its lesser conflicts with relative ease, thanks to a consensual decision-making process. In the prevailing paradigm Japanese institutions are effective and satisfying to their loyal and cooperative participants. This general image of Japan has been accompanied by microlevel studies of individuals and small groups that portray the Japanese as "polite" people seeking the social harmony idealized in traditional Japanese culture. Foreign social scientists have regularly portrayed modern Japan as alive with Confucian values. Rural villages as well as modern organizations have been described as valuing identity with the collective, hierarchically ordered interpersonal relations and decision-making by consensus.

That the qualities stressed in this model exist to a significant degree in Japan is beyond dispute; but the model is inadequate because it has virtually excluded serious consideration of conflict. Anyone who knows Japan will agree that it witnesses conflict like other societies, that it has known periods of extraordinary conflict, and that much of the dynamic of change stems from conflict.

Along with the dominant chord of harmony and consensus in many earlier studies, there were also some scholars who studied conflict and recognized its importance in Japan. In recent years, this minor chord has become more insistent and prevalent. It has become apparent, for example, that rapid economic change has created conflicts and dissension over the costs and benefits of industrialization.[1] Environmental and minority rights issues (*burakumin*, women) have intensified, and rivalries among government and opposition parties and within the policymaking process have been major concerns of observers of Japanese politics.[2] Follow-up studies of villages are likely today to discuss "harmony and its tensions" and to probe deep antagonisms beneath the surface of the apparent solidarity villagers maintain before outsiders.[3] Student movements and mass protests reflecting severe generational cleavages and political alienation have been a consistent and popular theme in studies by Western scholars.[4]

Yet, despite the frequent discovery of conflict in many studies, the older paradigm of Harmonious Japan remains. No alternative approach to the study of Japanese social and political life has yet emerged. Certainly almost no scholarship on Japan hitherto has adopted an explicit conflict approach or attempted to use Western social science conflict theory to understand Japanese society. Rather, the original model of Japanese society, albeit in a more sophisticated form, actually has been expanded and perpetuated. The field's most widely used and influential concepts have revived notions of unity, consensus, and harmony through visions of Japan as a "vertical society,"[5] as "Japan, Inc.,"[6] and even as "Number One" in effectively solving the problems of advanced industrial societies through group cooperation.[7] A gap between theory and empirical research is increasingly apparent in scholarly studies on postwar Japan.

With this in mind, we initiated this set of studies in 1975. An interdisciplinary project was formed under the auspices of the Joint Committee on Japanese Studies of the American Council of Learned Societies and the Social Science Research Council (ACLS-SSRC). The project held two major conferences and a number of smaller planning sessions and meetings between 1976 and 1979. Participants in the project were encouraged to undertake original research on conflict in a Japanese institution or, alternatively, to rethink their prior research from a conflict perspective. The essays in this volume are the result of these endeavors.

The Conflict Approach

For all their diversity, conflict theories share several distinctive characteristics.[8] The most fundamental of these is the assumption that conflict is ubiquitous, normal, and integral to the workings of every society. More explicitly, conflict is viewed as arising from the very structure of society itself, not as something alien which occasionally emerges to disrupt the normal order. Based on this fundamental assumption, most conflict theories also share four other characteristics:

1. the assumption that incompatible interests and goals are prime sources of conflict;
2. an emphasis on process and the dynamics of change;
3. attention to inequalities of power, status, and reward and to the functions performed by perceptions and ideologies; and
4. pursuit of conflict and its transformations across different levels of social life, from the social psychology of individuals to the organizational processes of major social institutions.

While not all the authors in this volume explicitly apply a particular conflict theory, these characteristics are apparent in their choice of subject matter, their interest in the dynamics of social relations, their attention to power relations and ideologies of harmony, and their concern with the connections among various levels of explanation. These elements of a "conflict approach" are applied to studies of the major institutions of Japanese society—family, village, school, workplace, bureaucracy—and to studies of the relations between institutions and organized groups in the political process.

SOURCES OF CONFLICT

Most conflict theorists, including Marx, Weber, and Freud, place the origins of conflict in incompatible interests and goals. Society is assumed to consist of individuals joined together in specific relationships with some degree of mutual interdependence. While certain aspects of such dependent relationships may be mutually advantageous, other aspects will benefit one party to the detriment of the other. Conflict theories assume that each person wants to advance or protect his own interest and, moreover, that this self-interest inevitably produces conflict when the interests are mutually exclusive or the goals are incompatible.

A generalized concept of "cleavages" has evolved from these theories. Cleavages divide society on the basis of some interest; that is, special interest groups organize to protect common interests or to pursue common goals. On a smaller scale, many anthropological and social psychological theories examine how individuals manage conflicts on a face-to-face basis in close relationships. Because individuals, groups, and organizations in conflict are mutually dependent on the outcome of the conflict, and since the means by which a conflict is terminated affects the interests of all those involved, the study of conflict is inextricably linked to the study of conflict resolution.

The essays in this volume demonstrate that structural conflicts pervade Japanese society. Some of the studies focus on the traditional conflicts of interest (economic and organizational, for example); others locate new sources of conflict and offer fresh interpretations of Japanese social phenomena.

The primary relationships of small groups, typically described by earlier students of Japan as unusually harmonious, are subject to structural conflicts of interest. Thus Teigo Yoshida traces the occult phenomenon of spirit possession in Japanese villages to prior conflicts of interest between the villagers. Similarly, by assuming that intimate, face-to-face relationships in Japan entail structural role conflicts, Takie Lebra and Agnes Niyekawa shed new light on both the form and content of interpersonal communication in Japan.

A number of these essays examine the highly structured conflicts of interdependent, organized groups with incompatible vested interests. Thus Tadashi Hanami looks at labor-management relations, Michael Donnelly at the complex world of agricultural politics, and John Campbell at the predictable organizational strains within and between the bureaucracy and the ruling political party. Three other studies, those by Patricia Steinhoff, Thomas Rohlen, and Ellis Krauss, examine conflicts that arise from structural role conflicts and the clash of interests in student protest, educational politics, and party politics in the Diet, respectively. In these cases, the usual conflicts of interest are exacerbated by a fundamental conflict of values: the polarized ideologies of left and right in postwar Japan. More than a clash of vested interests is involved here; participants are drawn to conflict on the basis of differing political worldviews. Fundamental identities, both individual and organizational, are involved. The contest is not only for power; it is also a moral struggle.

Susan Pharr and Takeshi Ishida examine yet another source of structural conflict in Japanese society, one based on status. New interest groups have emerged among urban residents dissatisfied with pollution and among women dissatisfied with their previously assigned roles. Both share a consciousness of victimization by modern society and particularly by the existing value system that assigns power, priorities, and roles.

THE PROCESS OF CONFLICT

Conflict theories begin with a notion of social structure based on interdependent relationships; the expectation that participants will pursue their own interests and goals implies that they seek change in the structure. Conflict implies action, and therefore conflict theories tend to be dynamic explanations of the processes of change. Yet conflict theorists diverge widely in their orientation to change. Some, such as Marx and Freud, assert the inevitability of certain developmental sequences of change. Others, such as Weber, Dahrendorf, Simmel, Coser, Kriesberg, and Lofland,[9] identify certain patterns of change and, without positing a unilinear development, try to specify the conditions under which they will occur.

Much of the study of conflict involves even more specific questions about variations in the conflict process itself. One of the great advantages of a conflict approach is that it focuses attention on the dynamic element of social relations. Here we want to underline three issues that are central to the study of conflict.

The first issue is *escalation*—namely, how and why conflict, once initiated, expands in intensity and scope. Some answers lie in such contextual variables as the number of actors and their relationship, the extent and accuracy of their communication, and the methods they use in attempting to resolve conflict. All the essays in this volume address the problem of conflict escalation, but the ones that contain case studies of particular issues (the chapters by Pharr and Donnelly, for example) or concentrate on general modes of conflict behavior in particular issue areas (the chapters by Hanami, Steinhoff, and Rohlen) offer rich analyses of how and why conflict tends to escalate in certain Japanese settings.

A second issue in the study of process is *how conflict is controlled*. Handling conflict is a result of the degree to which participants acknowledge the situation and the action taken toward resolution. There are several options, which can be viewed on a continuum:

Avoidance—Repression—Displacement—Management—Resolution

In avoidance, conflict is handled by denying its existence or by acknowledging its existence but attempting to avert conflictual behavior. In repression, too, conflictual interaction is averted, but by explicit action intended to punish its expression. Displacement involves avoidance by projecting a particular conflict with one party onto another party or onto a different issue with the same party. In conflict management, the pursuit of incompatible goals continues, but in a limited and orderly manner or with diminished intensity, by mutual agreement; in conflict resolution, by contrast, the conflict is terminated by adjustments that eliminate or drastically modify its causes. In the case of conflict management and resolution, the study of process involves particular attention to the specific agents and mechanisms used to handle conflict, such as bargaining, communication, mediation, and arbitration.

Some of the chapters in this volume focus explicitly on the left-hand side of the continuum: avoidance, repression, and displacement. Thus, Yoshida's essay is a detailed study of a unique type of displacement process in Japanese villages. Steinhoff studies the effect of repression on student protesters. Lebra (using the term "conflict management" in a broad sense) analyzes the various ways in which Japanese tend to respond to conflict situations without engaging in confrontation or without actively seeking resolution of the issue. Campbell, Krauss, Donnelly, and others focus on the techniques of management and resolution of overt conflict.

The third central issue in analyzing process is the relationship between *institutionalization* and *conflict*. [10] Institutionalization is the process whereby behavior in a recurring relationship becomes regularized through the development of a set of legitimized roles and formal and informal norms governing the expression of conflict. The changes brought upon Japanese society by defeat and the American Occupation created the conditions for considerable conflict in public institutions. The Americans encouraged a multiplicity of power centers and the democratization of policymaking and administration. Conflicts of interest and ideas were legitimized as long as they remained within the newly created legal boundaries of representative democracy. A long enough period has elapsed since the introduction of new values and organizations in the immediate postwar period to observe how these values and roles have become institutionalized.

Institutions and conflict are linked in a complex but integral manner. Conflict is structured by the institutional environment in which it takes place; conversely, the process of institutionalization is a response to the problems that institutions have in coping with conflict. The studies by Campbell, Rohlen, and Krauss dramatically illustrate this interconnectedness. Within an institutional arena, the parties to a conflict are involved in a continuous, interlocking relationship and thus have the opportunity and incentive, as Krauss's study of the Diet illustrates, to create new procedures and forms for handling their conflict. Institutionalization, however, does not necessarily prevent or diminish the incidence of conflict;[11] indeed. it can itself be the source of predictable conflict, as Campbell's analysis of the Japanese bureaucracy shows. Moreover, antagonisms themselves can be "institutionalized," becoming a recurrent element in the roles and relationships of organizational life, as Rohlen demonstrates for the case of education.

One mode of institutionalized or "orderly" conflict is conflict behavior that has become ritualized—that is, performed in a predictable manner (often implicitly expected and accepted by the adversary) primarily for the purpose of symbolically affirming the separate interests, identities, and goals of the participants. The annual rice-price demonstrations of farmers, discussed by Donnelly, or the spring labor offensive mentioned by Hanami and Ishida, are well-known examples of the ritualization of conflict in Japan. Steinhoff's chapter describes the rituals of conflict behavior engaged in by students confronting authorities.

POWER AND PERCEPTION

When conflict theorists examine the world from the perspective of conflicts of interests and goals, they observe that the structures which create such conflicts are rarely equal for both parties. Hence conflict theories tend to focus attention on inequalities of power,[12] wealth, and social status. These commodities are seen not only as interests that people pursue for their intrinsic value (that is, the goals of a conflict) but also as assets which can be employed to protect and extend the inequities of distribution. Pharr, Steinhoff, and Hanami, for example, discuss dissatisfied groups challenging entrenched authority. Krauss's essay on the Diet traces how conflicts changed as the relative power of the ruling party and its perennial opposition was gradually altered. Rohlen examines a deadlock between union and administrative power in public education. Campbell and Donnelly's studies of bureaucracy, parties, and interest groups, on the other hand, are cases of dominant groups that have sought to maintain their advantages in situations of fluid power and temporary coalitions.

A focus on unequal power relations also leads conflict theorists to a concern for the means by which such inequality is maintained. Lofland's exposition of labeling theory, Simmel and Coser's formulations on how groups handle internal and external conflict, Mills' work on power elites, Marx's theory of the relationship between ownership of the economic means of production and law, religion, politics, and culture—all reflect this concern.[13] A sensitivity to the coercive elements underlying much of social interaction, as well as to more subtle means of domination and control, thus also characterizes conflict theory. The assumption that conflicts of interest are integral to social interaction causes conflict theorists to question especially any attempt to present unequal relations as harmonious and beneficial to all parties; rather, they search for the functions that such ideologies of harmony perform for those in power and for the maintenance of organizational structure.

Even beyond a sensitivity to the functions of ideology, conflict theory inevitably involves questions of perceptions, motives, beliefs, and cognitions. The fact that it is individuals who perceive their interests and formulate their goals grounds conflict theories in a social psychological level of explanation. Hence Marx's theory of the historical transformation of whole societies was ultimately tied to the individual's experience of alienation and class consciousness, much as Weber's analysis of authority structures rested on individual followers' belief in their legitimacy.

The problem of perception and belief is crucial to the conflict approach in a number of ways. As Pharr points out in her essay, for conflict behavior to be initiated, parties with incompatible interests or goals must first perceive conflict. The perception that there *is* a conflict is thus a crucial early stage in the process of conflict interaction. The perception and interpretation of conflict is, in fact, involved through all stages of the conflict process. Individuals evaluate conflict differently, and they perceive its existence, intensity, and significance differently. They learn to ignore conflict under certain conditions and to be sensitive to it under others. The meaning people put on conflict affects how they promote their interests, how they respond to each step in a developing conflict, and how they attain conflict resolution.

In every culture, social phenomena such as conflict have unique configurations of meaning. Two conflicts may seem similar in one culture but not in another. In view of this problem of cross-cultural relativity in the perception of conflict, one should regard with great caution superficial comparisons of the cumulative level of tensions and conflict in different societies. Harmony may be observed where there is, in fact, deep-seated antagonism. The emotional, verbal, and behavioral cues for signaling conflict are so different between cultures that outside observers may easily misjudge the intensity and character of conflict. Hanami's essay is particularly interesting in this regard as he shows the different meaning given strikes and other dispute actions in Japan compared with Europe and the United States.

Generally, the cultural ideal of harmony is more notable in Japan than in the West. Conflict is not considered natural there; rather, it is regarded as an embarrassment to be avoided whenever possible. A fascinating issue in the perception and meaning of conflict in Japan, therefore, is the way in which ideals interact with the reality of a conflict-permeated daily social existence. The question is not simply one of contrasting the real with the ideal; it is a matter of examining rationalizations, self-explanations, coping devices, role strains, and attempts to redefine conflict situations and then determining how these in turn affect the conflict process itself.

Lebra's essay deals with this issue most directly as she analyzes how the cultural norm of avoiding confrontation gives rise to a large repertoire of conflict management techniques, many of which ironically increase latent hostility. Niyekawa's chapter demonstrates how cultural norms do not prevent conflict so much as create subtle cues for communicating it beneath the veneer of politeness and emotional restraint. Ishida's essay discusses how the ideology of solidarity could only be maintained in modern Japan, especially in the prewar period, by constant redefinitions of group boundaries and identities, bringing wider and wider segments of society into the ostensible harmony of the in-group. Other chapters, such as those by Campbell and Pharr, analyze how the ideologies of harmony and cooperation can structure the conflict process in bureaucratic organizations and become potent weapons for maintaining existing arrangements. Finally, the chapters by Rohlen, Steinhoff, and Krauss examine how organizations in a culture that values harmony cope with the infusion of ideologies of conflict. In short, all the authors in this volume see culture as part of the conflict process, not just as a policeman preventing conflict from occurring.

LEVELS OF SOCIAL INTERACTION

Conflict theory provides a means for studying the connections between levels of social life. The same behavior may have totally different meanings and consequences depending on the level of social interaction at which it takes place. For example, the murder of a wife and that of an enemy soldier—both "interpersonal acts"—are recognized as separate matters in the sense that they occur at different levels, and therefore in different contexts, of social life. The role of emotion, the degree of particularity, the amount of loss, the place of law, the issue of choice, and so forth are all different. Interactional levels can be distinguished by the conditions that limit conflict, by the institutional means available for resolution, and by the characteristic modes of interpretation and response in those conflict situations. In the same society, the very same people may be expected to be conflict initiators in a role at one level and avoiders in another role at a different level.

These simple points are easily forgotten when comparisons between whole societies are undertaken. When one is comparing Japan with other nations, for example, there is an inclination to generalize about "national character." Often this means that a behavior pattern operating at the interpersonal level in a rather circumscribed context is selected as typical of all conflict interactions in the society. Nearly every essay in this volume devotes some attention to interpersonal interaction, yet the authors seek to be precise about the degree and management of conflict and to respect differences in social context. Many demonstrate specifically how personal interaction processes are linked to the impersonal patterns of larger social units.

At the most basic level, conflict can occur within a single person or between two or more people. Five essays in this collection deal explicitly and in great detail with the relationship between personal conflict and interpersonal conflict. Lebra offers fresh interpretations of the subtle ways in which conflict is communicated in intimate relationships. Niyekawa, in her study of a popular television drama series, finds far more direct expression of personal and interpersonal conflicts than has previously been recognized in these intimate relations. Yoshida and Pharr show how resentments arise from frictions in role expectations and how their expression greatly affects close-knit small groups. Steinhoff demonstrates how the labeling of student radicals as "deviants" creates dilemmas of identity for individuals that then influence the behavior of protesting sects.

If the very intimacy of face-to-face relationships can add emotional intensity to conflicts at the interpersonal level, other essays show how these same relationships can be used to manage structural and impersonal conflicts in big organizations. At higher levels, as in large organizations, between organizations, and in the political process, the connection between levels is also a key issue. A classic example of linkage is the use of external conflict to overcome internal disunity; that is, conflict at one level—between groups or organizations—is pursued to limit it at another—within a single group or organization. Conflict can spread up or down in society: from the individual to the larger societal units or from the macrolevel down to the individual. Organizations may seek to extend their symbolic and impersonal conflicts to lower levels; lower units may seek to elevate their conflict to broader significance. Since conflicts call for allies and for tactics of maneuver, an expansion of the conflict to higher levels is often part of a struggle for power.

As conflict is expanded either up or down, it must be transformed, often in complex ways. Its character and intensity must be shaped to the new environment, and this change in turn introduces new limits and avenues for resolution. Some of the essays deal specifically with the transformation of a conflict as it moves into a different context. Pharr, for example, analyzes how the issues of the nationwide women's rights movement are handled in a specific environment dominated by personal relations and conventional modes of interaction. Rohlen, Donnelly, and Campbell examine how "top-down" or "bottom-up" conflicts change as they are handled at different organizational levels.

Social levels, on the other hand, also may be barriers to conflict. Most political conflict is confined to the organizations involved, for example, and most personal conflict is contained within dyadic or small-group relationships. For ideologically inspired conflict to become personal, unusual circumstances or efforts are required. The typical means employed in this case is the recruitment and socialization of individuals to an organization and cause, as Steinhoff relates in her essay on student activists. Conversely, personal conflict rarely assumes general ideological or political significance. What is typically required is the symbolic restatement of a particular issue into a universal matter. To cite an example from Donnelly's essay, farmers transform their individual economic grievances into collective appeals based on traditional rural values.

Questions and Aims

Applying these basic elements of conflict theory to Japan inevitably raises general questions about Japan and conflict theory. What does the application of conflict theory tell us about Japanese society? Is

Japan really as harmonious as it has been depicted? If not, where are the major sources of tension in Japanese society? Have the main arenas of relative conflict and relative harmony remained the same over the entire postwar period? To what extent are the patterns of conflict in Japan similar to or different from those in the West? And what do our findings tell us about the limitations of the harmony model of Japan? About directions for future research and the relevance of Japan to conflict theory? We will return to these questions in our conclusion.

NOTES

1. On the growing disenchantment in urban areas over rapid economic growth and its consequences, see Kurt Steiner, Ellis S. Krauss, and Scott C. Flanagan, eds., *Political Opposition and Local Politics in Japan* (Princeton: Princeton University Press, 1980).

2. See, for example, Taketsugu Tsurutani, *Political Change in Modern Japan* (New York: David McKay Co., 1977); Robert A. Scalapino and Junnoseke Masumi, *Parties and Politics in Contemporary Japan* (Berkeley: University of California Press, 1962); George R. Packard III, *Protest in Tokyo: The Security Treaty Crisis of 1960* (Princeton: Princeton University Press, 1966); Hans H. Baerwald, *Japan's Parliament: An Introduction* (New York: Cambridge University Press, 1974).

3. "Harmony and Its Tensions" is a chapter analyzing latent conflicts under the surface of harmony in a rural village in Robert J. Smith, *Kurusu: The Price of Progress in a Japanese Village, 1951–1975* (Stanford: Stanford University Press, 1978), pp. 229–241; see also Ronald P. Dore, *Shinohata: A Portrait of a Japanese Village* (New York: Pantheon Books, 1978), especially chap. 16.

4. See, for example, Packard, *Protest in Tokyo;* Ellis S. Krauss, *Japanese Radicals Revisited: Student Protest in Postwar Japan* (Berkeley: University of California Press, 1974); Yoshio Sugimoto, *Popular Disturbance in Postwar Japan* (Hong Kong: Asian Research Service, 1981).

5. Chie Nakane, *Japanese Society* (Berkeley: University of California Press, 1970).

6. The idea of "Japan, Inc." is a popular theme in American business and government circles and in mass media in the West. See Eugene J. Kaplan, *Japan: The Government-Business Relationship* (Washington, D.C.: U.S. Department of Commerce, 1972), especially pp. 14–17.

7. Ezra Vogel, *Japan as No. 1: Lessons for America* (Cambridge, Mass.: Harvard University Press, 1979). See Sugimoto, *Popular Disturbance,* pp. 3–13, for a more extensive review and critique of the "harmony model" in the literature on Japan.

8. For major contributions to conflict theory, including important reviews and critiques, see Lewis A. Coser, *The Functions of Social Conflict* (New York: Free Press, 1956); Georg Simmel, *Conflict* and *The Web of Group-Affiliations,* trans. Kurt H. Wolff and Reinhard Bendix (New York: Free Press, 1955); R. Mack and R. Snyder, "The Analysis of Social Conflict," *Journal of Conflict Resolution* 1 (1957); Clinton F. Fink, "Some Conceptual Difficulties in the Theory of Social Conflict," *Journal of*

Conflict Resolution 12 (1968); James T. Duke, *Conflict and Power in Social Life* (Provo: Brigham Young University Press, 1976); Louis Kriesberg, *The Sociology of Social Conflicts* (Englewood Cliffs, N.J.: Prentice-Hall, 1973); Ralf Dahrendorf, *Class and Class Conflict in Industrial Society* (Stanford: Stanford University Press, 1959). For a discussion of the essence of conflict theory that is related to our assumptions below, see Ralf Dahrendorf, "Toward a Theory of Social Conflict," *Journal of Conflict Resolution* 2 (1958).

9. See references in note 8 above and Max Weber, *The Theory of Social and Economic Organization,* trans. A. M. Henderson and Talcott Parsons (New York: Oxford University Press, 1947); John Lofland, *Deviance and Identity* (Englewood Cliffs, N.J.: Prentice-Hall, 1969).

10. On the relationship between institutionalization and conflict, see Mack and Snyder, "The Analysis of Social Conflict," pp. 30–31.

11. Ibid., p. 30; this point is somewhat similar to one made by Sugimoto, *Popular Disturbance,* pp. 190–191, that participatory integration may actually increase conflict.

12. Indeed, Duke argues in *Conflict and Power in Social Life* that conflict theories are really theories of power.

13. See references in notes 8 and 9 above. Duke discusses this relationship in the work of many conflict theorists.

2

Conflict and
Its Accommodation:
Omote-Ura *and*
Uchi-Soto *Relations*

TAKESHI ISHIDA

There are two opposing views on conflict situations in Japan. One characterizes Japanese society as harmonious; a lack of conflict is here of prime importance. The other, in contrast, stresses the extreme militancy of opposition parties and labor unions; judging from their pronouncements, they are dogmatic, inflexible, and unwilling to make any concessions to the existing system. Both views are partly correct; only their emphasis is different.

Paradigm for Conflict Accommodation

These seemingly contradictory depictions of the same society may be reconciled by using Takeo Doi's concepts of *omote-ura* and *uchi-soto,* which are related to his theory of *amae.*[1] These concepts were originally formulated in his psychopathological analysis of Japanese behavior patterns. *Omote-ura* literally means "front-back" and *uchi-soto* means "in-out." The tentative working hypothesis is shown in Figure 1.

The two opposing views of Japanese society mentioned above can easily be explained by this diagram. The first view, which emphasizes harmony within Japanese society, deals simply with the *uchi-omote* relationship; the second, which focuses on the militancy of the opposition parties and labor unions, pays attention only to the *soto-omote* relationship. An accurate description of Japanese society requires us to examine the level of *ura* together with that of *omote* and to recognize the actual interrelationship between the two. Of course, in the former case—the view which considers Japanese society as a harmonious one—the nation as a whole is treated as the in-group unit, where-

	Omote (surface or formal arena)	*Ura* (backstage or informal arena)
Uchi (conflict among in-group members)	No conflict should exist.	Conflict does exist but is usually solved implicitly.
Soto (conflict with outsiders)	No concession should be made.	Negotiation is possible if neither party loses face and both can maintain integrity.

FIGURE 1

as in the latter case—the view which emphasizes the militancy of the opposition—the in-group unit is the opposition camp against the establishment.

Beyond this simple and fixed paradigm, it is my contention that the flexibility of the boundaries along these two dimensions of *uchi-soto* and *omote-ura* provides a valuable resource for conflict accommodation in Japan. Conflict accommodation includes three categories: conflict regulation, conflict resolution, and conflict avoidance. Conflict regulation means to manage conflicts in such a way that they do not create a violent clash, even though they cannot be resolved. The difference between conflict resolution and conflict avoidance lies in the fact that the former presupposes an awareness of the issue involved in the conflict whereas the latter tends to distract attention from the issue. Therefore, in the latter case conflict cannot be resolved, although it can temporarily be pacified. Conflict accommodation, as the broadest term to cover these three categories, becomes necessary when we try to deal with conflict avoidance in comparison with conflict resolution.

In applying this approach, one must be careful to avoid two difficulties. The first is that if we put too much emphasis on the uniqueness of political culture, we tend to fall into the trap of cultural determinism. If there is nothing in common between Japanese society and other societies, we cannot compare at all. The second is that by identifying a certain characteristic as a national trait, we tend to be ahistorical. The great change which took place after Japan's defeat in World War II cannot be ignored here.

To avoid the first difficulty, the trap of cultural determinism, we have to clarify to what extent the same scheme can be applied to other societies and to what extent there is a difference between Japanese society and others. This will be done in the course of explicating how the flexibility of these two dimensions is used for conflict accommodation in Japanese society. To avoid the second difficulty, the trap of ignoring historical change, we will trace the changing application of these two dimensions to conflict accommodation in both prewar and postwar Japan.

The *Uchi-Soto* Dimension

The distinction between in-group and out-group is not peculiar to Japan. As many sociologists have pointed out, behavior among in-group members tends to differ from behavior toward outsiders. Max Weber's famous distinction between *Binnenmoral* and *Aussenmoral* is one such example.[2] In the United States, the distinction has been widely accepted since W. G. Sumner published *Folkways* in 1907. In the case of Japan, however, the scope of the in-group depends on the situation; thus the area considered to be an in-group on different occasions tends to form concentric circles. In traditional Japanese society, the smallest in-group was the family; the next, the extended family. A hamlet, a village, a prefecture, and the nation could also successively be the in-group, depending on the situation. If two neighboring hamlets were in conflict with each other—say, on the issue of irrigation from the same river—each would form an in-group to fight the other. On the other hand, if their village was competing with other villages to obtain financial subsidies from the limited funds allocated to the prefecture—say, to construct a bridge or a school—the village became the in-group. In the same way, the prefecture could be a unit when it competed with other prefectures. In the end, if the necessity to compete with other nations was emphasized, the nation as a whole could form an in-group.

An attempt was made by the militarist leaders to expand the in-group beyond Japan's national boundary to absorb neighboring Asian countries as, for example, when they established Manchukuo and proposed the idea of the so-called Greater East Asia Co-prosperity Sphere. By Japan's Asian neighbors, however, this idea was simply considered to have been invented in order to justify invasion and to provide an ideological buttress for Japan's hegemony in Asia.

Although the distinction between in-group and out-group is commonly found in all societies, this pattern of concentric circles cannot be observed in diversified societies where many functional groups overlap with each other. This concentric relationship was typically found in traditional Japanese society, a predominantly agrarian society with little diversification, but a similar situation often exists even today. One faction against another in the same party is one in-group against another, for instance, but on other occasions one party against another forms the in-group.

The flexibility of the border between *uchi* and *soto* often plays an important role in maintaining social integrity and avoiding conflict. Let me illustrate by a concrete example. When a village head is drinking *sake* on the occasion of a festival, he is one of the in-group members of the village. When he orders the heads of the hamlets in his village to do something, however, he is an outsider vis-à-vis the in-group (the hamlet). His behavior as a fellow villager in the former case may make his job easier in the latter case. Even in present-day urban life, a section chief in a private firm or in the government bureaucracy will at least once or twice a year have a drinking party with the employees under his supervision. On such an occasion, he can be treated as a fellow member of the same group vis-à-vis the higher level—that is, the level of the bureau. He may gossip about their superior in order to strengthen the sense of solidarity. This sort of drinking party is useful and even necessary for a section chief or for any other boss in order to gain spontaneous support from subordinates during routine business operation.

The flexibility of the border between *uchi* and *soto* sometimes creates problems. An in-group is composed of those who can share the feeling of "we" among themselves and among whom the behavior associated with *amae* (emotional dependency) is allowed; but since it is nothing but a matter of feeling, not all the members involved necessarily feel the same way. The employer of a company may try to absorb all employees into an in-group in order to compete with other companies; in an industrial dispute, however, the employees may feel that the employer is not a part of "we" but rather of "they."

On the other hand, "dependent revolts" can often be found among employees in an enterprise union and also among students; the target of attack is, respectively, the company management and the university administration. By "dependent revolt" I mean a revolt motivated by the desire for *amae*—that is, a revolt to attract the attention of management or the administration in order to obtain more benevolent treatment.

A dependent revolt is an expression of ambivalent feelings: On the one hand, being rebellious, they consider management or the administration to be the target of attack and therefore exclude them from their in-group. On the other hand, in expecting better treatment by those attacked, they are by the same token dependent on the latter and therefore in a psychological sense trying to include them. The members of the enterprise union may say, "Our rival company increased wages by such-and-such. Why can't we have the same?" Or the students may say, "Why did the administration let the police come on campus? Don't we all belong to the same academic community with academic freedom?"

In general, despite this problem, the possibility of conflict can be avoided by enlarging the in-group or by absorbing the potentially opposing parties into the same in-group. Of course, the flexibility of the border between *uchi* and *soto* may also result in the entrenchment and shrinkage of the in-group. For instance, a serious factional conflict may appear within a political party. Depending on the situation, an organization may split into a number of factions. In this way factionalism, an important characteristic of Japanese society, is related to the flexibility of the border between in-groups and out-groups.

In order to absorb the potentially opposing parties into the same group, it is useful to have a common enemy against which the attention of the enlarged group can be directed. As Simmel put it, when the group as a whole enters into antagonistic relations with a power outside it, "the tightening of the relations among its members and the intensification of its unity, in consciousness and in action, occur."[3] Or to use Coser's expression: "Conflict with out-groups increases internal cohesion."[4]

The *Omote-Ura* Dimension

Just as the boundary between *uchi* and *soto* is flexible, so too is the border line between *omote* and *ura*. Before explaining this point further, however, we need to define the concepts of *omote* and *ura*. In the case of the distinction between *uchi* and *soto*, the difference approximates that between in-group and out-group. The concepts of *omote* and *ura*, however, have no equivalent expression in English. As an approximate expression, many may be reminded of the distinction between "front region" and "back region" proposed by Erving Goffman.[5] Indeed the distinction between *omote* and *ura* does involve something similar to that between "front region" and "back region," but there are some differences between the two.

In Goffman's usage, "front region," which is exemplified by a performance in front of an audience at the theater, means the presentation of self in a functionally specified field; *omote,* on the other hand, does not necessarily indicate the particular attitude to be adopted in such a functionally specified setting. Once a differentiation of function has taken place, the distinction between "front region" and "back region" becomes clear and no room remains for flexibility of the border between the two. *Omote-ura* can be defined only in relative terms; hence the border between the two remains flexible. Let me illustrate by giving a concrete example. When there is a gathering of the people in a hamlet, this means more *omote* compared with the personal discussions that take place between individual members of the hamlet, but more *ura* compared with the official discussions that take place in the village assembly.

Another difference between "front region–back region" and *omote-ura* is the latter's implication of legitimacy. Goffman's distinction between "front region" and "back region" does not indicate that the former has priority in terms of legitimacy. The two regions are functionally specified fields in each of which a particular form of appropriate behavior is required. But this is simply a matter of appropriateness and not of legitimacy. If I may be allowed to use an analogy, the distinction between "front region" and "back region" is similar to a horizontal relationship with an inflexible border whereas the concepts of *omote* and *ura* imply a vertical relationship with a flexible border.

Omote and *ura* also imply two distinctive elements somewhat similar to what Walter Bagehot called the "dignified part" and the "efficient part."[6] If we use these terms in a much broader sense than Bagehot did, a dramatizing element and a practical element are always necessary for all political activities in every country. But in the English constitution, as Bagehot correctly pointed out, there was a clear functional differentiation between the "dignified part," represented by the crown, and the "efficient part," represented by the parliament. In the case of prewar Japan, there was no such clear functional differentiation.

Keeping this explanation in mind, let me tentatively define *omote* and *ura* in the following way: *omote* means (1) publicly legitimate, (2) dramatized and dignified element, (3) with formality and rigidity; *ura* represents (1) privately allowed, (2) practical and efficient element, (3) with informality and flexibility. If we understand the terms *omote* and *ura* in this way, we can discover some unique characteristics of the relationship between the two in Japan.

First of all, *omote* and *ura* do not form a functionally differentiated dichotomy; rather, they represent two supplementary elements

which appear according to the situation. In this respect they are similar to the Chinese concepts of *yang* and *yin*.[7] Not only does the same
person behave on the *omote* level in one situation and on the *ura*
level in another situation, but sometimes even the same behavior
may be considered *ura* from one angle and *omote* from another, as
the example of the gathering of people in a hamlet indicates.

Secondly, in traditional Japanese society the publicly legitimate
element represented by *omote* could only be found in the relationship between superiors and inferiors in the hierarchical ordering of
the society, because legitimacy always came from above. It was ultimately the superior who decided how much *ura* could be permitted.
In the army, for instance, noncommissioned officers sometimes drank
with privates in the same barracks. One of them might say, "Let all
formality be laid aside!" But then all of a sudden one of the noncommissioned officers might scold or even hit a private, saying the latter
was too impolite.

Inferiors could not legitimately demand anything publicly; all they
could do was ask a superior to do them a favor, to relax a rule so their
wish could be realized. Sometimes their wish might simply be to be
free from intervention from above. In this case, *ura* connoted tacit
permission. During the war, for instance, almost all transactions of
important goods were strictly controlled by the government but,
depending on the occasion, free transactions were possible with a
yami (black market) price on the *ura* level. Whether this act on the
ura level was permitted or not depended entirely upon the will of the
authority. In other words, the amount of *ura* allowed was determined
soley by persons of superior authority.

The distinction between *omote* and *ura* and the proper use of these
levels of interaction could also be found among those who held the
same position in society. If two intellectuals who knew and trusted
each other talked privately near the end of the last war, for example,
they could express their pessimistic views about the future of the war.
Thus the conversation was on the *ura* level. If they were talking with a
few others, however, they had to modify their expression, and with
more than ten persons they had to say that Japan would never be
defeated.[8] In the last case, they were behaving on the *omote* level. In
this example, too, the *omote* phenomenon was indirectly related to a
vertical relationship. The reason they used an *omote* expression was
that they feared the conversation might become known to the police,
who might punish them for their anti-Japanese pronouncement.

How to use either *omote* or *ura* appropriately is a burden to everyone, because all must carefully judge exactly which level is to be used on a particular occasion. On the other hand, this distinction between *omote* and *ura* can also be useful in relaxing the formalism imposed by strict rules and avoiding conflict. Such and such is strictly prohibited, one may say. But this is a matter of *omote,* and in reality the rule can be relaxed depending on the situation so that there is flexibility in its interpretation and application. In this way, during the war, *ura* relationships could work as a safety valve to ease tension in the society. To put it another way, by using the *ura* level the society could be flexible in avoiding conflict while at the same time maintaining basic principles on the *omote* level.

To sum up, then, *uchi-soto* and *omote-ura* relationships, both of which can be seen in other societies, appeared in traditional Japanese society in a peculiar way. The flexibility of the border between *uchi* and *soto* was characterized by the enlargement of concentric circles; and the *omote-ura* relationship was closely related to the vertical relationship that existed in the hierarchically ordered society. In such a society, conflict could be avoided or accommodated either by enlarging the in-group so that the two opposing parties could be absorbed by the larger in-group or by introducing an *ura* relationship to ease the tension and work out practical solutions.

Changing Social Structure and Conflict: Prewar

Now let me deal with the historical development of modern Japan by using the ideas of *omote-ura* and *uchi-soto*. In referring to "traditional Japanese society," what I have in mind is the type of society established by the Meiji Constitution of 1889. The social structure under the Meiji Constitution can be described graphically with a picture of a cone topped by the emperor, as shown in Figure 2. Subcones were subordinated in this structure. The smallest cone was a hamlet, the continuation of the traditional rural community that developed in the premodern period. This hamlet was absorbed by another cone —the village, which was the smallest legal administrative unit. The village was a substructure of a prefecture headed by an appointed governor. The prefecture was a unit of national integration controlled by the national government or, more specifically, by the minister of home affairs. Thus a continuous line of delegation of power and authority existed: emperor → prime minister → minister of home affairs → appointed governor → village head → head of hamlet (although this was not a legally recognized position). The set of concen-

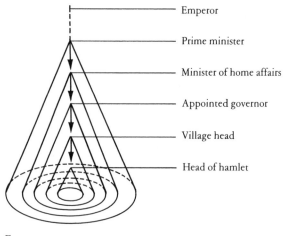

FIGURE 2

tric cones depicted in Figure 2 characterizes the emperor system established in the early Meiji period.

With modern development, however, social differentiation took place and, as a result, especially by the 1920s and 1930s, the modification of this prototype became necessary. Owing to the diversification of interests, the units of *uchi* were no longer necessarily concentric. Moreover, owing to the emergence of functionally differentiated agents for interest articulation, there was no longer a single line of authority running from the top of the political hierarchy to the bottom.

The emperor system responded to this changing situation by permitting relative differentiation on the intermediary level while strictly maintaining integration at top and bottom. In other words, relative differentiation was allowed only within the largest framework— that is, in the national cone headed by the emperor—whereas, at the bottom, the hamlet continued to form the basic unit for various functional organizations of farmers, veterans, youth, women, and the like. Of course, increasing urbanization created more problems. Even in urban areas, however, a basic unit similar to the hamlet was established. This was the workshop, in which workers could feel a sense of solidarity and in-group consciousness similar to that in a hamlet.[9]

This modified form of social integration, however, faced difficulty again in two ways. On the one hand, tenant disputes and labor disputes that occurred in the 1920s undermined conformity at the very bottom of society because these disputes split the basic units of hamlet and workshop. On the other hand, the communist movement which emerged in the 1920s explicitly challenged the emperor system for the first time in Japanese history. The establishment's response was drastic. The government severely suppressed communists and other Marxists by the application of the Peace Preservation Law promulgated together with the Universal (Manhood) Suffrage Law in 1925. There was no room for the defendants charged under the Peace Preservation Law to receive benevolent treatment even on the *ura* level, except for those who made *tenkō* (recantation), in which case they were treated with special consideration.

A more positive attempt to remedy the difficulties existing in the basic units of Japanese society is represented by the five-year plan for the regeneration of rural communities to restructure the hamlet and by the establishment of the Sampō organization (Association for Service to the Nation through Industry) to rehabilitate the workshop, both of which started in the 1930s. In the former case, large landowners (particularly absentee landowners) were deprived of their influence and cultivating farmers were encouraged to reorganize the hamlet in order to avoid tenant disputes. In the latter case, the government tried to replace labor unions with the government-established Sampō and to abolish labor disputes, paying token attention to working conditions. These attempts were partly successful, but new problems emerged in this reorganized system.

After the severe suppression of leftists, the greatest danger came, ironically, from the extreme rightists. The threat from the right was not simply a matter of violence by a handful of fanatic radicals; it was related to the basic structure of the political system. As we have seen, authority ran in a continuous line from the top to the bottom of traditional Japanese society. No one in an inferior position in the social hierarchy had the right to invoke a principle on the *omote* level. Rightists, however, dared to challenge this system by invoking the *omote*-level principle of *kokutai* (national polity). Again it was a historical irony that, because of their success in disseminating *kokutai* ideology, the government and ruling elites now had to face an attack from rightists who advocated the very same ideology.

Originally, the question of how much room to allow for *ura* was a matter which only the superior could decide. But now rightist radicals were trying to abolish *ura* among ruling elites by invoking the *kokutai* orthodoxy on the *omote* level. One typical example was the 1935 "Minobe Incident." Dr. Tatsukichi Minobe, a law professor at Tokyo Imperial University who advocated the legal theory which considered the emperor to be an organ of the state, was accused of being a heretic and forced to resign from all public positions. Despite the popular belief in the emperor's divinity, a belief taught through the national education system, it was taken for granted among the highly educated that Minobe's theory was a valid legal explanation of the emperor's actual position. As a result of the success of national education in propagating the exoteric view *(omote)* of the emperor's divinity, the esoteric legal interpretation *(ura)* of his position, which prevailed among the ruling elites, was attacked by the rightists.

This phenomenon of the lower dominating the upper was also related to the introduction of universal manhood suffrage. Because of the lack of mass-based organizations, the political parties had to appeal directly to voters. They found that the most effective emotional appeal was an attack on their rival party, accusing the latter of disloyalty to the emperor. As a result of this competition for loyalty between the political parties, an extremely patriotic mood was created. At this point the parties were attacked by the people, who criticized them for not being sufficiently loyal to the emperor and for working merely for their own vested interests.

The rightists' violent revolt ended in February 1936 when the attempted military coup was suppressed, but the nation's move toward the right continued in a more institutionalized way. The establishment of the Imperial Rule Assistance Association (IRAA) in 1940 was the final institutionalization of this tendency. Now a single cone, the IRAA, absorbed all subcones: political parties, labor organizations, agricultural organizations, business organizations, youth and women's organizations, and so forth.

In the context of this essay, the establishment of the IRAA has two important implications. First, in terms of the *uchi-soto* relationship, it meant the reestablishment of the concentric relationship between various in-groups, reconfirming the hamlet and workshop as the basic units. Second, it meant the introduction of the *Fuehrerprinzip* (principle of leadership), a term coined in Nazi Germany. This was an attempt to restructure the chain for the delegation of authority. In this restructured system, an inferior could ask something of a superior but could never demand. The decision was entirely in the hands of the superior, including the decision of how much *ura* inferiors could be allowed.

Once the IRAA was established, it began to suffer from various dysfunctions. First of all, the absorption of all functional groups into a completely monolithic organization meant that functional groups had lost their role. This was one reason for the establishment of the Imperial Rule Assistance Adult Group (Yokusō) as an auxiliary organization attached to the IRAA, the aim being to gain more spontaneous participation by encouraging people to participate in a voluntary movement. Once the institutionalization took place, however, it turned out to be the same as the IRAA. Secondly, the reestablishment of the unilineal chain by which the IRAA delegated authority resulted in bureaucratic formalism and inflexibility and thus created indifference or apathy among the masses. Even cases of unorganized sabotage emerged.

The IRAA was an organization based solely upon the *omote* principle of *kokutai* orthodoxy; there was little allowance for the *ura* relationship. Paradoxically, or perhaps naturally, the *ura* relationship spread widely without any tacit permission from superiors. By establishing the IRAA, which emphasized national cohesion as the in-group, the government tried to abolish all sorts of conflicts within the country and to mobilize a feeling of hatred against foreign enemies. To a limited extent, and temporarily, it seemed to be successful, but only at the cost of diminished integrative functioning in the long run.

The breakdown of the system was not directly due to the internal situation, but rather to the predominant military power of the Allied Forces. By the final stages of the war, however, because of the difficulties inherent in the system itself, as described above, together with the influence of American bombing, the Japanese political system had already lost much of its integrative function.

In sum, then, the traditional social organization of concentric cones established in early Meiji times permitted full use of the flexibility of the *uchi-soto* and *omote-ura* dimensions to manage conflict. The increasing diversification at the middlle level, however, produced less manageable forms of conflict. The government permitted some differentiation in the middle, but it severely repressed attacks on the top level of centralization and then took deliberate steps to strengthen the integrity of the lowest-level units of hamlet and workshop. But the inability to control new forms of conflict in the fractured cones, along with increasing right-wing demands for conformity to *omote*-level ideology without the counterbalancing flexibility of *ura* permissiveness, led the government to attempt to reimpose a monolithic cone structure through the Imperial Rule Assistance Association. This effort failed because of internal weaknesses and Japan's defeat in the war.

Why no internal forces existed to reform the political system from within is an interesting problem that needs careful analysis. At least in the context of this essay, we must note that the traditional method of avoiding conflict was not the same as resolving conflict. After the suppression of such rebellious elements as the communists, internal conflicts could be avoided temporarily by the traditional method mentioned above. But so long as the real reason for the conflict remained unsolved, there was still the potential for another conflict. If the conflict had become explicit, there would have been a movement for change in order to solve it. If a conflict is not fully recognized because of temporary avoidance, however, there is little awareness of the need for innovation or reform.

Social Structure and Conflict: Postwar Changes

As a result of Japan's defeat and the postwar reforms ordered by the Occupation Authority, drastic changes occurred in Japanese society. One of the most important changes in the context of this essay was the abolition of the national cone headed by the emperor. With the dissolution of the IRAA, the organizational basis for integral nationalism was lost. But this does not necessarily mean that individuals became independent as a result of their emancipation from the emperor system. What happened in fact was the emancipation of various organizations which used to be integrated under the one umbrella of IRAA. Two typical examples are the labor unions and the agricultural cooperatives.

The mushrooming of labor unions immediately after the defeat was of course due partly to the encouragement of occupation officials, but it was also due to the fact that the labor organizations which the IRAA established in every factory unintentionally prepared the way for the postwar emergence of labor unions. The particular pattern of Japanese labor unions, that is, the enterprise-based union, is also the legacy of the wartime situation in which branches of the IRAA were formed in every factory. Although the Labor Union Law of December 1945 stipulated that those who occupied supervisory positions were excluded from membership in labor unions, the majority of those who played an important role in the formation of labor unions were not rank-and-file workers; instead they were either white-collar workers or foremen.[10] Naturally, therefore, the organizational structure of labor unions even today tends to be similar to that of management.

The newly established agricultural organization (the Agricultural Cooperative Union) was forced by the Occupation Authority to follow three principles: It had to be voluntary, democratic, and independent of the government. In reality, however, the agricultural cooperatives were based on the hamlet unit and heavily dependent on the government, which controlled the rice and the chemical fertilizers necessary for agricultural production. Thus, despite the difference in basic principles, agricultural cooperatives turned out to be successors to the prewar agricultural organizations characterized by compulsory membership and government control.

In this way, the dissolution of the monolithic IRAA simply resulted in the fragmentation of the national cone. Each fragmented cone had the same structure as before, only the name was different. *Uchi-soto* and *omote-ura* relationships within each organization were not very different from before except that ascriptive status became less important as a result of the land reform and the dissolution of the *zaibatsu*.

Between the fragmented organizations, however, serious rivalries emerged unmediated by the superior agent which had previously guaranteed ultimate integration. Particularly noticeable in the period immediately after the defeat was the conflict between the government and labor unions. During the initial stage of the Occupation, authorities prohibited the formation of a national federation of employers' organizations for fear that it might discourage the labor union movement. Thus major conflicts were not between labor and management but between labor and government. This was true, too, because the labor movement at the time was not only interested in increasing wages but also in promoting socialist revolution. Despite the absence of a single national integrative organization like the IRAA, or perhaps because of its sudden disappearance, the Japanese people had not yet grown accustomed to living in a nascent pluralist society. It was partly for this reason that many union leaders wanted to foment revolution, hoping to seize power from the conservative politicians. The conflict between labor and government became so intense that it resulted in the intervention of the Occupation Authorities at the time of the attempted general strike on 1 February 1947.

Severe suppression of communists at the time of the Korean War destroyed the dream of revolution, but the ideological conflict between labor and government continued to be more important in Japan than in other countries—partly because, in Japan, government employees' unions were most active and played a major role in the labor movement. Beginning in 1955, the "spring offensive" became an annual event. Some may say that the spring offensive, which now includes several million workers and uses militant slogans, is an indication of ideologically radical and hence inflexible attitudes on the part of the labor unions. Empirical research demonstrates, however, that the beginning of the spring offensive signaled a shift in the labor unions' focus from ideological issues to the practical problem of wages.[11]

The spring offensive was first proposed by the Ohta faction in Sōhyō (General Federation of Labor Unions). This faction criticized the mainstream led by the Takano faction for being too interested in political ideology. The original idea of the spring offensive's planners was to focus the union's attention on the most important goal of the labor movement: to increase wages. For this reason they proposed that many unions join forces at a particular time of year in order to exert a stronger influence than was possible when each union fought individually against management.[12] Often the slogans of the spring offensive have included various political issues such as the problem of the U.S.–Japan security treaty, but this is a matter of *omote*. If we probe beneath the surface of the spring offensive, we find that labor leaders are less interested in political ideology than one may think from hearing their militant slogans.

When the spring offensive became an annual event and hence was ritualized, certain implicit rules were also established between the two parties concerned: the labor unions and the employers' organizations (not the government, as was the case immediately after the defeat). These rules of the game are not known to the public. In fact, many deny the existence of such ground rules because, every year, depending on differences in the economic and social situation, each party uses different strategies and the results are also different. But prior to the spring offensive, many can predict quite accurately how much of an average wage increase will result from the spring offensive. This means that there is an established format in the spring offensive. At least we can safely say that there is a tacit agreement between the two parties that the spring offensive has its own raison d'être.

Precisely because of this ritualization of the spring offensive, a certain amount of discontent has arisen among the rank-and-file union members. Some of them, in fact, have rebelled against their leaders and criticized them by invoking the *omote*-level leftist ideology they have been indoctrinated with by the leaders themselves. In the depressed economic conditions of today, however, many union members are well aware of their difficult position, particularly in regard to the problem of employment, and hence the influence of the small number of radicals, often called New Leftists, is still limited.

Parallel to the labor union, another important mass organization is the agricultural cooperative. These cooperatives organize virtually all households engaged in agriculture. Although their internal structure is not very different from that of the prewar agricultural organizations, one conspicuous change in the postwar period can be noticed in the militant struggle between farmers and government over increases in the price of rice. On the *omote* level this "struggle" is indeed militant, but on the *ura* level the leaders easily make concessions vis-à-vis the government, since they do not possess as much bargaining power as the labor unions. After all, it is the government which decides the amount of subsidies to be distributed in relation to the price of rice. The agricultural cooperatives' militancy is nothing but a strategy to attract the government's attention, although it also serves to impress their rank and file with the tough stand they have taken on the issue (and hence with the organization's reason for existence).

Lacking the right to strike, the only bargaining power they have is the block vote they can control in the rural constituencies where the government (conservative) party has firm support. In order to impress the politicians with the number of votes they can control, thousands of farmers come up to Tokyo to hold a mass meeting which Diet members from the rural constituencies are expected to attend. The recent overproduction of rice and the increased fiscal burden borne by the government, which must buy rice at artificially high prices, have made it more difficult for farmers to succeed in their demand for higher rice prices, as Michael Donnelly describes elsewhere in this volume.

Similar to the situation within the labor unions, there is discontent among the cooperative members, who consider their leaders to be too close to the government. But it is even more difficult than in the case of the labor unions for them to articulate their discontent, because of the conservative mood prevailing in rural areas.

Economically weaker organizations such as those of small and medium-sized enterprises have similar difficulties in the competition among interest groups.[13] In the late 1950s they were very active and vocal in supporting legislation favorable to them. During the period of rapid economic growth in the 1960s, however, the difference in economic power between large enterprises and small ones became more pronounced than before. Corporate mergers between huge enterprises also accelerated this tendency.[14] Moreover, the subcontractual relationship between large and small enterprises has made the latter subordinate to the former. Thus, under the present oligopolistic situation, a small number of huge enterprises actually control the market and also exert strong political influence even without engaging specifically in pressure tactics.

Various problems, such as pollution, have resulted from Japan's rapid economic growth. Labor unions, which strongly demand increases in wages within the framework of the enterprise-based union, are not in favor of solving such problems as pollution because they fear that the cost may adversely affect their wages. In the widely publicized case of Minamata disease caused by mercury produced by a chemical factory, the union members of the factory, at least at the first stage, actually suppressed the protest movement of the fishermen who were suffering from the disease.[15]

Those who suffer from pollution but do not belong to a large organization are not strong enough to compete with the industry creating the trouble. Even so, quite a few citizens' movements have emerged to tackle the problem of pollution. In fact, citizens' movements existed even before the issue of pollution attracted popular attention. The first embryo of a citizens' movement not under the leadership of the labor unions can be traced back to 1960, when massive demonstrations emerged against the Kishi Cabinet's undemocratic way of passing the revised U.S.–Japan security treaty in the Diet.[16] Such tiny organizations as the Koenaki Koe no Kai (Association of the Voiceless Voice) were organized among ordinary citizens to express their resentment at not being sufficiently represented by any of the huge established organizations.

With an increased distrust in all established organizations, which because of their vested interests are not seriously concerned with the unorganized citizen, many citizens started their own organizations to promote civic movements. One typical example is Beheiren ("Peace in Vietnam" Citizens' Committee), which protested the Vietnam War. Although Beheiren was dissolved when the war was over, its new type of organizational structure—a completely voluntary organization based upon individual commitment—is an important legacy for the citizens' movement. These examples are concerned with national or international issues, but with the increased interest in local autonomy, local issues have become more important, particularly those related to the problem of pollution.

The fact that there are now numerous citizens' movements, although small in size, indicates a new phase in the organizational situation. The conflict between large industries, which create pollution, on the one hand, and citizens' movements with a new pattern of organizational structure, on the other, is an unprecedented type of

conflict that cannot be solved by the traditional methods of manipulating the boundaries of *uchi-soto* and *omote-ura.*

Sometimes citizens' movements include individuals who belong to
a huge organization. This is one indication of the recent weakening
of group cohesion in big organizations. In the huge organizations of
today, even among those people who do not participate in a citizens'
movement, there are quite a few who do not want to make a total
commitment to their organization and try to preserve their freedom
outside it. This is particularly true among young employees. Some
may conclude from this fact that the *uchi* feeling in huge organizations will weaken in the future. At present, however, there is another element which is strengthening the *uchi* cohesion—that is, the
depressed economic conditions which oblige employees to depend on
the enterprise in order to maintain employment in rough times.

To sum up, then, in the historical development of social organizations after the defeat of Japan, the first phase was characterized by
the fragmentation of the national cone and by competition or rivalry
among the fragmented parts, which maintained almost the same internal structure as before. Then, in the second phase during the
1960s, oligopoly developed. The stronger organizations, small in
number and large in size, have been tightening their internal control
and increasing their influence vis-à-vis the outside world. The third
and present phase may be characterized by the emergence of citizens'
movements.

Current Applications of the Paradigm

Keeping this historical background in mind, how can we apply the
uchi-soto and *omote-ura* hypothesis to the present situation? The
applicability of the traditional method of accommodating conflict in
Japanese society, by the enlargement of the in-group in horizontal
relationships and the proper use of *omote* and *ura* in vertical relationships, should be examined in three different kinds of relationships:
within the established organizations, between large established organizations with equal power, and between large organizations and
outsiders.

WITHIN ESTABLISHED ORGANIZATIONS

Here the traditional method can still be applied with some modification, because there is continuity between the prewar and postwar

periods in terms of organizational structure. In the case of huge organizations, however, the use of the traditional method has become more difficult because of the contradictions inherent in this type of organizational structure. The difficulties within the big organizations of today may easily be compared with those of the IRAA described above. If the in-group becomes too large, the sense of natural solidarity diminishes and the sense of alienation among the rank and file tends to grow. Moreover, if monolithic integrity is overemphasized, it becomes more difficult for the organization to respond to the functional diversification occurring within it. On the other hand, if the organization relaxes its tight control by introducing the *ura* level, thereby tacitly permitting a certain flexibility, cohesion may be in danger.

We are not simply talking about huge commercial enterprises but also about big labor organizations. In fact, the militancy of the labor unions (or similarly of agricultural cooperatives) is related to the problem of their internal structure. As in the national situation in the 1930s, the lower-rank members, indoctrinated by the leadership, tend to invoke militant principles on the *omote* level. The leaders themselves are now bound by the *omote* principle, which was originally used by them to manipulate the members. Moreover, when the leaders try to negotiate with management on the *ura* level, and at the same time to pacify the possible discontent caused by their entering into negotiations, they have to pay lip service to militancy on the *omote* level again.

BETWEEN LARGE ESTABLISHED ORGANIZATIONS WITH
EQUAL POWER

The traditional method of conflict accommodation cannot be applied in this case because there is no superior organization which absorbs both of them. Nevertheless, certain ground rules can be established to avoid the destructive effects of conflict. A typical example can be found in the relationship between national federations of business organizations and those of labor unions. This relationship is not very different from that existing in other societies although, on the level of each enterprise, since unions are enterprise-based, in-group feeling can easily be established between the management and the union. Even in the relationship between such federated organizations, however, the particular internal structure of each organization has some influence. For instance, as mentioned above, they tend to be more militant on the *omote* level, as Thomas Rohlen describes in his study of teachers in this volume.

BETWEEN HUGE ORGANIZATIONS AND OUTSIDERS

In the case of the relationship between large organizations and outsiders, such as that between large enterprises and the citizens' movements, the traditional method of conflict accommodation cannot work because there are few ways to absorb the outsiders into the existing enterprise in-group. Only in exceptional cases, as when a large enterprise together with its related industries has predominant influence in the locality, can the enterprise try to absorb local people into its in-group by saying that the prosperity of the enterprise benefits the community as a whole.

In relationships with outsiders, it is also difficult to use the *omote-ura* strategy, which was originally useful in vertical relationships within a hierarchically structured organization. So far, no established method of conflict resolution has been found. Probably this is why many conflicts in this category continue for such a long time. In fact, even after many patients of Minamata disease were confirmed and the movement to tackle this problem emerged, it took almost twenty years before a judicial decision declared the manager of the factory responsible for the disease. Even today, many victims are still struggling to be registered as legally recognized Minamata patients.

While the outsiders mentioned above are making efforts to find a democratic way of conflict resolution, a few others are rejecting the democratic system as a whole. The Red Army and those who set bombs in a building belonging to the Mitsubishi Company are examples. Those who engage in such violent activities are nevertheless few. More important is the existence of a greater number of people who are not directly violent but believe that neither the traditional method of conflict accommodation nor the democratic way of conflict resolution can work in the present situation.

One special case should be added here. In the depressed economic conditions of the 1980s, huge enterprises are trying to adjust to the situation by reducing the production of their subcontractors (small and medium-sized enterprises). Thus the burden is shifted to these subordinate enterprises which thereby naturally face serious difficulty and are often forced to dismiss their employees as a result. In this case, those who are fired no longer belong to the factory in-group because the *uchi* feeling can be shared only among those who are working together with the expectation that they will continue to be coworkers until retirement. In fact, this custom of "lifetime employment" and the pattern of enterprise-based unions are the two major conditions allowing members of the enterprise to have the *uchi* feeling. Once an employee is fired, his expectation of lifetime employment is lost along with his union membership. Thus he becomes an outsider of both the enterprise and the union. It is usually very difficult for the labor union to fight against this sort of dismissal, partly because of the lack of in-group consciousness between those fired and those not fired and partly because of management's economic position.

As for the relationship between organizations with unequal power, one of the three basic categories can be applied. If the weaker organization is subordinate to the larger one by a subcontract, for instance, the relationship is close to the first category. If the difference is not very large between the two organizations, the relationship fits the second category. If the difference is extremely large and there is no common interest between the two, the relationship may belong in the third category.

EVALUATING THE RELATIONSHIPS

Now let us compare the three relationships. In the first type (within large organizations) we find the strongest continuity from the prewar days, and hence *uchi-soto* and *omote-ura* relationships are almost the same as before. As oligopoly emerged, the importance of this area became even greater; but at the same time inherent difficulties also increased. The second relationship (between large organizations) emerged in the postwar period but has almost become customary. The third relationship (between large organizations and outsiders) did not attract much attention until recently because the powerless outsiders who were the victims of large organizations used to bear their situation in silence. Since the conflict in this relationship is very new, no one can accurately forecast the future.

In terms of their relative importance in present-day Japanese society, the first relationship is still the most important. The second is supplementary to the first, but it is increasing in importance. The third relationship is not important at this moment, but it may increase in significance. If this evaluation is correct, then we can say that the traditional *uchi-soto* and *omote-ura* relationships have not lost their importance for avoiding conflict even today. At the same time, as this historical analysis of modern developments since Meiji times indicates, the traditional method of conflict accommodation has its own inherent difficulties. To the extent that an organization depends on the traditional method of conflict accommodation, the process of strengthening its integrity is inevitably accompanied by increased potential tensions, as exemplified by the case of the IRAA.

In this sense, it is too early to tell how long the traditional method of conflict accommodation can continue to work. As we have seen, the traditional method of conflict accommodation is not the same as conflict resolution. It simply means the temporary avoidance of conflict without solving the basic problem. As a result of this accommodation, tensions may accumulate. Consequently, the real conflict may emerge in the future. Even if there is no explicit conflict, the problem between huge organizations and outsiders, particularly underprivileged outsiders such as the victims of pollution, should be solved in a democratic way; otherwise, the democratic system itself cannot operate in the long run, because of the possibility of sporadic explosion of the accumulated resentment of the underprivileged.

What is of urgent need is creative political leadership that has the courage not to conceal or avoid conflict but to tackle and solve it, while remaining sensitive to discontent that may evolve into serious conflict. Such leadership may then help solve the problems of modern Japanese society.

NOTES

1. Takeo Doi, *"Omote* and *Ura*: Concepts Derived from the Japanese 2-fold Structure of Consciousness," *Journal of Nervous and Mental Disease* 157 (4)(1972): 258–261. For the concept of *amae,* see Doi, *"Amae*—A Key Concept for Understanding Japanese Personality Structure," in R. J. Smith and R. K. Beardsley, eds., *Japanese Culture: Its Development and Characteristics* (Chicago: Aldine, 1962).

2. Max Weber, *Wirtschaftsgeschichte* (Munich: Duncker and Humblot, 1924), p. 304.

3. Georg Simmel, *Conflict* and *The Web of Group-Affiliations,* trans. Kurt H. Wolff and Reinhard Bendix (New York: Free Press, 1955), p. 91.

4. Lewis Coser, *The Functions of Social Conflict* (New York: Free Press, 1956), p. 87.

5. Erving Goffman, *The Presentation of Self in Everyday Life* (New York: Doubleday Anchor, 1959), p. 106f.

6. Walter Bagehot, *The English Constitution, 1867,* 6th ed. (London: Paul, Trench, Trubner, 1891).

7. Derk Bodde, "Harmony and Conflict in Chinese Philosophy," in A. F. Wright, ed., *Studies in Chinese Thought* (Chicago: University of Chicago Press, 1953).

8. This example was taken from a story written in the diary of Morisada Hosokawa, the son of Marquis Moritatsu Hosokawa, who married the daughter of Prince Konoe. During the war he was working for Prince Takamatsu collecting information. See Morisada Hosokawa, *Jōhō Tennō ni Tassezu* [Information did not reach the emperor] (Tokyo: Isobe Shobō), vol. 1, p. 79.

9. Why the workers felt the workshop was a substitute for the primary group in rural communities can be explained by the pattern of urbanization in Japan. Rapid urbanization did not allow those who came to work in the cities to be psychologically ready for the new urban situation. They felt helpless and wanted a primary group on which they could depend. The employers tried to make the best of this situation by introducing into their organizations familistic principles, with an emphasis on group conformity similar to that in rural communities. For further details, see Takeshi Ishida, "Urbanization and Its Impact on Japanese Politics—A Case of a Late and Rapidly Developed Country," *Annals of the Institute of Social Science, University of Tokyo* 8 (1967): 1–11.

10. Kazuo Ōkōchi, ed., *Rōdōkumiai no Seisei to Soshiki* [Growth and organization of labor unions] (Tokyo: Daigaku Shuppankai, 1956), p. 79.

11. Kenji Kojima, *Shuntō no Rekishi* [A history of the spring offensive] (Tokyo: Aoki Shoten), 1975.

12. Ibid., p. 36f.

13. For detailed information concerning interest groups in Japan, see Takeshi Ishida, "Interest Groups Under a Semipermanent Government Party: The Case of Japan," *Annals of the American Academy of Political and Social Science,* (May 1974): 1–10.

14. For more information on corporate mergers, see Takeshi Ishida, *Japanese Society* (New York: Random House, 1971), p. 98.

15. Minamata disease is caused by mercury produced by the Chisso chemical factory. See Masuzumi Harada, "Minamata Disease as a Social and Medical Problem," *Japan Quarterly* 25 (1)(Jan.–Mar. 1978): 20–34.

16. For detailed information concerning the protest movements, see George R. Packard III, *Protest in Tokyo: The Security Treaty Crisis of 1960* (Princeton: Princeton University Press, 1966).

PART II

Conflict in Interpersonal Relations: Individuals, Families, and Villages

3
Nonconfrontational Strategies for Management of Interpersonal Conflicts

TAKIE SUGIYAMA LEBRA

Understood as a process, conflict refers either to the phase at which conflict is generated and intensifies or to the phase at which conflict is reacted to and managed. These two phases may be labeled "conflict genesis" and "conflict management" respectively. It is not that genesis and management are always distinguishable or that one is necessarily followed by the other; the same phenomenon may be placed in the context of either genesis or management. The distinction is only for analytical purposes. Overlapping with these phases are such pairs of conflict states as latent and manifest, hidden and exposed, uncommunicated and communicated. This essay focuses on the management phase.

Depending on the phases of conflict as well as on whether conflict is ego-directed or alter-directed, different emotions accompany conflict experiences: ambivalence, frustration, anxiety, commitment, guilt, shame, embarrassment, anger, grudge, hatred, contempt, and the like. Underlying the two-phase conflict process and these emotions is the human personality, which has been captured by a variety of psychological models: the familiar "frustration-aggression" model; the "consistency" model as in Festinger's "dissonance" and "dissonance reduction";[1] and the "relative deprivation" model in which the awareness of a gap between expectation and fulfillment is followed by an effort to fill the gap. Further, the conflict process, while it may be emotion-ridden as in these models, may be generated or managed strategically through a rational calculation of gains to be maximized and losses to be minimized. Thus the rational decision-making model is not precluded either.[2]

By conflict management I mean a reaction to a conflict situation without necessarily entailing a resolution. Management can involve procrastination, aggravation of conflict, or initiation of a new phase of conflict. The culturally available techniques for management at the interpersonal level (intergroup conflict is another matter) may be characterized as nonconfrontational. By confrontation I mean a direct challenge launched by A against B when A perceives B as the source of his conflict. It is not that Japanese never risk confrontations but that, as long as harmony, or the appearance of harmony, is to be maintained, nonconfrontational modes must be exhausted first. Probably this is a lesson which should have been kept in mind by the headman of Shinohata in Dore's account, when he learned that the village fire brigade had cut off the irrigation water in order to catch fish for a drinking party and had forgotten to readjust the dam to release the water. In response to the complaint made by the headman of the next village which was thus deprived of water for a short while, the Shinohata headman demanded a formal apology to be delivered by the fire brigade to the headman of the next village. This overreaction, or confrontational reproach, touched off a conflict escalation leading to the decision by the fire brigade, headed by the humiliated chief, to resign.[3] The modes of management discussed in the following sections are by no means unique to Japan only, but they may facilitate our understanding of the Japanese.

Anticipatory Management

Anticipatory management means that conflict is managed in a preventive manner before it is generated. Anticipating his inability to reciprocate, party A may refuse to accept a favor. A resident of Henna Buraku refused to take a *koden*-gift from Kida with the explanation that he could not make a return gift. Pressed to accept it since no return was expected, the funeral host was adamant: "But people around this area backbite against you if you don't make return gifts. I will accept your goodwill but please take the *koden* back. Accepting one, I would have to accept all others."[4] Help may be withheld to prevent a conflict between self-interest and altruistic obligation. This concern led one of Dore's informants to avoid benefiting from his own mechanical expertise: "Repair my own tractor? No. If you do that you end up 'clever poor.' All the neighbors start coming to ask you just to take a look at their machine. They think nothing of it. They're not particularly grateful. You lose a lot of time and you use up your spare parts."[5] Similar anticipation prevents one of my informants from traveling abroad: "Once my travel plan is found out by my neighbors, relatives, friends, they will all bring *senbetsu* [gifts for separation]. And, of course, they all will expect to receive souvenirs. I can't afford it. Isn't there any way of taking off without being noticed?"

Anticipatory management may require a painful, even masochistic, perseverance or effort, as when A anticipates an offer from B, his benefactor, that A wants to turn down. An informant, when he was a live-in apprentice with his uncle, knew he was going to receive a proposal from the aunt to settle down in the household as a *mukoyoshi* husband (one who adopts the wife's family name) to their only daughter. To avoid being trapped into this match, he tried to do everything that would alienate the aunt so she would give up the idea. His strategy was, as he put it, "to make myself hated as much as possible." He did so by working from dawn to midnight as hard as a man can work! Working hard is a good thing, but to do so beyond a point, my informant believes, brings hatred.

Negative Communication

Once conflict is generated, the victim A may express his frustration or anger to B, the source, but only in a negative manner—that is, by not communicating it. Instead of confronting B, victim A avoids seeing or contacting him, thereby letting B know how upset he is or how strongly he disagrees with him. In a face-to-face conversation, A may indicate no by refusing to respond to B. In Henna Buraku, "I did not answer" meant "I objected," and such a message of silence may be accompanied by feigned deafness.

As an expression of conflict emotions, silence may well be accompanied by some signaling behavior such as sulking. Even then silence could be an ineffective or even misleading means of communication: Japanese are so used to silence that they may see nothing wrong in it; silence could be taken as a sign of sincerity, *enryo* (social reserve), acquiescence, or even compliance, as when children are told not to talk back. Apparently the traumatic conflict that turned the whole community of Kurusu upside down, as observed by Smith, can be traced to this uncertainty inherent in communication through silence. It seems that at the meeting of the villagers the opposition to the project of allowing an outside company to build a chicken-processing factory was communicated by silence, which was in turn taken, deliberately or innocently, by supporters of the project as an expression of consent.[6] One of my informants, while abused by her mother-in-law and sister-in-law without being shielded by her husband, "did not say a word." This silence seems to have meant a curious mixture of "unequivocal" compliance, endurance, grudge, and grievance.

Situational Code Switching

Two parties in conflict may avoid each other but assume friendliness when certain situations call for it. In Takashima, Norbeck noted that persons in discord usually avoided one another but still exchanged greetings. Personal frictions were not permitted to interfere with *buraku* (hamlet) affairs. "Foresworn enemies discuss with no trace of rancor the issues at hand during a *buraku* meeting. . . ."[7]

Likewise an estranged husband and wife, or a daughter-in-law and mother-in-law, argue freely or refuse to talk to each other when left alone but pretend to be harmonious when guests are present. For this reason, the party anxious to restore harmony tries to set up formal occasions necessitating an invitation of outsiders. Any two persons, kin or nonkin, who have not been on speaking terms may thus be able to talk to each other behind a formal mask appropriate in a ceremonial interaction. Providing such opportunities may be taken as one of the functions of ceremonies like death anniversaries.

An emergency such as illness or death is another important occasion for code switching. A family member's terminal sickness or death may become a rallying point for reconsolidation of the broken family or for readmission of an expelled member. The sick or dying person may or may not be a party to the conflict but stimulates guilt in all concerned, which in turn provides a leverage for code switching. Several life histories told to me involve a young son who, after severing himself from his family either by running away or being expelled by his father, is called back home when his father or mother falls ill. Even a fake illness may be used to soften hostility, as happened to one informant.

Implicit in code switching for formal occasions is a reversal from formal restrained interaction to informal and intimate interaction. Frustrations and anxieties may be freely talked out when A faces B in intimate conversation, probably over a drink, especially set aside from the usual formal routine in which A is inhibited from self-disclosure. Routine code switching of this sort seems at least partly responsible for the ability of male Japanese workers to maintain emotional balance.

Triadic Management

To avoid confrontation between A and B, Japanese often create a triad to manage the situation. Conflict between A and B may be communicated indirectly through the third party X who, as a go-between, represents A or B or both. The practice of arranged marriage can thus be interpreted in light of conflict management in case A's proposal is rejected by B. Mediated communication like this presupposes a supply of volunteers to mediate as well as a willingness to rely upon mediators. Japanese society satisfies both these conditions.

The third party X may take a more positive role as an arbiter for A and B in conflict. When conflict is in stalemate, X, who commands respect from both parties, may provide a breakthrough by presenting himself as the person on whose behalf A and B are advised to forgive each other. "Save my face," the arbiter would say, urging the conflicting parties to relent, with a tacit threat that he will take offense if his intervention is not heeded. In response, the parties may comply, even though they would rather remain adamant against each other, in order to avoid humiliating the arbiter.

The arbiter's role is fused into a surrogate role that X can play for A or B. When B offends A, arbiter X may offer a vicarious apology to A. This form of vicarious responsibility is institutionalized in Japan, as recently demonstrated by the public apology and resignation of the Tokyo Metropolitan Police chief taking responsibility for a rape and murder committed by a patrol policeman—a surprising consequence by American standards of official responsibility.[8]

The third party X may not mediate communications, but by his presence he may dramatize conflict and put pressure on A or B. When X is perceived as A's ally, A's accessibility to X will threaten B and thereby embolden A. Conflict between mother-in-law and daughter-in-law is often intensified by the presence of a sister-in-law. Likewise, the daughter-in-law visits or invites her natal family over in order to display *her* side of the alliance. A son or daughter-in-law neglectful of the aged parent or parent-in-law may also be sanctioned against, overtly or covertly, by a group of aged neighbors who congregate regularly to exchange information on their children and in-laws.

Displacement

Displacement, a variant of triadic management, is manifested in diverse ways. In an attempt to convey his anger or disapproval to B, party A does so to X who is more vulnerable or whose retaliatory response A can better afford. A middle-aged contractor complains about his father-in-law, a retired contractor whose business he has inherited, for disagreeing with his modern way of living and doing business. "But he never tells me directly; he scolds my employees instead. My son, too, has been harassed." A mason recalls how his father, the master mason, rebuked him every time his apprentice employees went wrong with their jobs. The apprentices obviously understood this metacommunication and would console the son, saying, "When you get scoldings, we know they are directed at us." This informant believes one would be much better off if unrelated by kinship to a master.

Again, this kind of communication through displacement works only if the real receiver of the message is sensitive enough to catch it, as were the apprentice employees. Hypersensitivity, however, can be a cause of conflict. Many a grandmother complains of her daughter-in-law's harsh treatment of a grandchild, partly because, I found, she feels it was *atetsuke* or *tsuraate* (a covert slap in the face) against her, the grandmother and mother-in-law. The daughter-in-law, then, finds herself constrained from exercising her parental authority, while the mother-in-law indulges the grandchild even more, thus escalating the conflict.

The parent's overexpectation for a child's success, involving excessive investment in the child's education, may be understood as a form of displacement. The notorious *kyoiku-mama* (education mama) is more likely to be found among women who need compensations for unsatisfactory marriages and *kyoiku-papa* among men whose career ambitions have not been fruitful.

Displacement can be a rational strategy: "For instance, when asking a neighbor to stop playing the piano at night, the speaker may say *'shujin-ga-nemurenai-to yuu mono-desu-kara'* [since my husband says he can't sleep] rather than saying that she herself can't sleep."[9] The request or protest is made in the name of another, which is less offensive to a Japanese listener. This strategy corresponds with what I call playing a delegate's role.[10] The speaker may even present herself as in *itabasami* (caught in the middle) between her husband and the neighbor.

Further, A may release all his or her frustration with B upon X when confident that X will not relay them to B, the source of frustration. In this case X as a sympathetic listener offers a dumping ground for A's *guchi* (personal laments). Women in particular regard one or two close friends who would listen to their *guchi* any time as indispensable to their lives. Usually two friends exchange their *guchi* whether it is about their husbands, mothers-in-law, daughters-in-law, or children. *Guchi* release is meant not for counseling but for catharsis or emotional exorcism.

The supernatural may also play the role of X in a displacement drama. Party A's conflict emotions toward B may be expressed either *to* a deity or ancestor (as when A fervently prays at the household shrine or talks to it in B's presence) or *through* one supernatural entity or another (as when one allows oneself or a shaman to speak up in the voice of a spirit). The cult called Gedatsukai, as I observed in 1970–1971, provides its members with an ingenious method of getting possessed and acting out their conflict emotions. The possession ritual permits a volunteer member, in the name of a possessing spirit, to articulate his or her feelings toward self or others in front of the altar as witnessed by other members: The spirit host is free to praise, boast, support, thank, plead, assail, castigate, or forgive himself or others. Conflict management here is twofold. On the one hand, the spirit host can play the kind of role he has been deprived of in the secular world and thereby overcome dissonance between expectations and fulfillment; on the other hand, the host can release feelings which ought to be concealed in mundane life. Spirit possession, in short, allows one to fulfill cultural expectations while at the same time transcending cultural inhibitions.[11] Witchcraft beliefs involving two victims—the person possessed and the person accused of possessing—manifest another form of supernatural displacement, as reported by Teigo Yoshida in this volume.

It is only natural that the individual comes to identify himself with his ancestors as he gets older. But even in ancestor worship among the elderly one can detect a strategic management of conflict through displacement. My informants are hesitant to articulate their expectations for being looked after by their offspring in fear of self-imposition as *meiwaku* (burden), but they are explicit in expecting the duty of ancestor worship to be transmitted from generation to generation. This can be interpreted as a circumlocution for the elderly parents, who are themselves destined soon to become ancestors, to convey their own expectation for dependency.[12]

Self-Aggression

Direct confrontation is also avoided through self-confrontation or self-aggression. What might be called "remonstrative compliance" is an example. Party A expresses his grievance against B, his oppressor, by exaggerated compliance. A daughter protests the parental imposition of an arranged marriage by declaring that she will indeed marry the man, as did one informant. Party B's denigration of A with a derogatory label such as "Fool!" may be retaliated by A's acceptance of that label: "Yes, I really am a fool." What appears to be compliance is supposed to be understood as a remonstration. Apology by a victim may well be meant as remonstrative compliance. Party A's self-aggression is intended to arouse B's guilt. This is a form of masochism involving what Reik terms "rebellion through obedience."[13]

Self-aggression may even go so far as self-destruction. Japan has witnessed incidences of suicide in connection with the recent disclosure of major scandals involving bribery such as the cases of Lockheed, Nissho-Iwai, and KDD (International Telecommunication Co.). This phenomenon was captured in the media as "Suicide: The Japanese Way of Conducting a Scandal."[14] The most controversial of all was the case of Shigesada Yasuda, an advisory staff member of the KDD president's office, who jumped in front of an oncoming train (6 February 1980). He had been under police investigation as a key figure implicated in KDD's bribery of government officials with embezzled foreign gifts. His suicide note indicated that he was going to die as a "sacrifice" for his superiors. Self-destruction in this case is clearly a sign of resentment against the source of frustration.

This case was singled out as controversial because Japanese, in committing suicide, are expected to present themselves as conflict-torn, remorseful, or altruistic but not punitive of others. In fact all the other cases prior to that of Yasuda seem to have followed the expectation. Mitsuhiro Shimada, an executive of Nissho-Iwai, before leaping from a high-rise office building down to death (1 February 1979), wrote a suicide note addressing "everybody of Nissho-Iwai": "Men should maintain dignity. The company is eternal, and we should dedicate ourselves to its eternity. Each of us can work only for twenty to thirty years, but the company's life is everlasting. To protect the company's life we must be fearless like real men. For the suspected scandal which has denigrated the 'image' of the company, I feel remorseful. I am taking my responsibility."[15]

Yasuda and Shimada are thus studies in contrast as far as their suicide notes can reveal their motives. I speculate, however, that in a suicidal trauma an intropunitive or altruistic motive becomes confused with an extrapunitive or egoistic one. This confusion may be a clue to the confession of an informant that she had long vacillated between a wish to kill herself and a wish to kill her husband who had, she said, ruined her life. Similar confusion or ambivalence may underlie the suicide of the aged. Similarly, *shinju* (joint suicide) may involve a mixture of contradictory motives as it usually includes killing a death partner as well as killing oneself; even in love suicide the male partner may first kill the female and then kill himself, unless the two choose a method of dying together such as drowning. A reported case of school avoidance is suggestive of this point: The mother, after exhausting all available means in vain to persuade her daughter to resume school attendance, became so desperate that she embraced her child, cried, and proposed that mother and daughter drown together.[16] The proposal of dying together obviously indicates a mixture of the mother's self-punishment and punishment of the child or a combination of love and hate.

What deserves attention is that self-destruction for Japanese is a "tempting" answer to a wide range of conflicts whether intropunitive or extrapunitive, whether involving guilt, shame, or hostility, whether altruistic or egoistic. Death, or self-destruction in particular, was glorified in extreme terms by Yukio Mishima in his *On Hagakure: The Samurai Ethic and Modern Japan,* written three years before the author killed himself by disembowelment in front of stunned Self-Defense Force troops in 1970. Giving his interpretation of the text of *Hagakure,* Jocho Yamamoto's teaching for the samurai of Nabe-shima-Han, Mishima writes:

> When Jocho says, "I found that the way of the samurai is death," he is expressing his Utopianism, his principles of freedom and happiness. That is why we are able to read *Hagakure* today as the tale of an ideal country.[17]

> The occupation of the samurai is death. No matter how peaceful the age, death is the samurai's supreme motivation, and if a samurai should fear or shun death, in that instant he would cease to be a samurai.[18]

Mishima's own suicide is believed to have been meant to remonstrate with the Self-Defense Force for its lack of samurai spirit.

The general tolerance of suicide among Japanese is shown in a survey of high school students' attitudes: Only 30 percent disapproved of suicide, 28 percent did not think it bad, and 42 percent could not decide one way or the other.[19] Shimoyama, after proposing that a "cultural" attribute may be captured intuitively by examining the syndromes of rare mental cases, suggests with some cautions that the "death wish" *(kishi nenryo)* might be considered a Japanese characteristic.[20] He bases his argument on the case of a female patient under his psychotherapy who, deprived of close human relationships, had exhibited all signs of alienation, estrangement, hostility, and mistrust until a particular incident occurred. When she was hospitalized as a heavily bleeding victim of a traffic accident, the therapist (Shimo-yama himself) offered his blood. Later on, when she learned of this act and discovered that the therapist had insisted on having as much of his blood taken as needed "no matter what happened to himself," she was stunned, could not stop sobbing, and refused to eat. "That is how a death wish arose in her."[21] Shimoyama says that a death wish like this is certainly not unique to the Japanese. What does make a cultural difference in his view is that this feeling can be intuitively understood and shared by normal Japanese, but not by Westerners.

Indeed, the idea of death seems to play a significant role in conflict management for Japanese. The imagined death *(shinda tsumori)* often provides a breakthrough for a person in despair. "Imagine you are dead" is a common piece of advice for a victim of hopelessness to discover hope and gather the courage to make a fresh start.

The proclivities for self-aggression, including self-destruction, in-volve a tendency to react to certain conflict situations with self-accusa-tion. Some of the Thematic Apperception Test (TAT) responses sum-marized and interpreted by DeVos indicate self-blame as a Japanese reaction, particularly among women, to a stressful situation.[22] For example: "A husband comes home very late at night; the wife thinks it is for her lack of affection and tries hard; he finally reforms."[23] Another example: "An elderly brother did something wrong and is examined by the policeman; he will be taken to the police station, but will return home and reform. The younger sister also thinks that she was wrong herself."[24] A result of sentence-completion tests con-firms this assumption to an extent: In response to "I could not do it because . . . ," the Japanese displayed predominantly intropunitive feelings such as "because I am not yet competent enough," whereas the Italians tended to attribute the failure to other causes ("because I was too busy"; "because I did not like to do it"); the American respondents stood between the Italians and the Japanese.[25]

Self-accusation thus can be translated as interiorization employed for the purpose of conflict management. The relative importance of inner sanction showed up in responses to a sentence-completion test I designed and administered cross-culturally. In response to "After having done all sorts of bad things . . . ," the majority of every sam-pled cultural group—Japanese, Korean, and Chinese—projected an external or objective form of punishment such as "he was ruined" or "he was finished" or "I will be unable to be reincarnated." But the Japanese sample did so least (66 percent), the Chinese most (86 percent), the Koreans in the middle (79 percent). This order is reversed in the responses indicating subjective retribution, which ranges from guilt to repentance, to confession, to resolution to reform: "You feel uneasy at heart"; "he will feel regretful and guilty"; "he settled down to work seriously." The Japanese had 23 percent in this category, while 14 percent of the Koreans and 10 percent of the Chinese responded this way. This finding is consistent with my analysis of responses to other sentence fragments; in that case the Japanese sample stood out in focusing on inner rewards for certain good deeds.[26]

Guilt, as a form of self-aggression, is interlocked with an allocentric worry that one may have hurt another person; shame, in contrast, is more egocentric. In my study, the response to "If you do not know manners and etiquette . . ." suggests the Japanese sensitivity to the feelings of others. The majority in all cultural groups responded either egocentrically ("you will be ashamed" or "you will be called a barbarian") or with instructions that "you had better learn them" or "you should correct yourself to follow manners." But more Japanese (33 percent) than Koreans (8 percent) or Chinese (6 percent) showed allocentric concerns: "Your parents will be criticized" or "you will cause discomfort in the people around you."

Guilt is aroused especially when one feels that he has hurt his love object, hence the strong association discovered by DeVos in the TAT responses between the illness or death of parents, on the one hand, and the child's admission of guilt and repentance on the other.[27] This association provides, it seems, a psychological basis for the situational code switching discussed earlier; the death or serious illness of a family member enables people to restore family integration.

Guilt is a conflict emotion as well as a form of conflict management. To delineate the management phase of guilt more clearly we might well refer to instances of strategic "guilt-consciousness raising" to alleviate stress or transform self-identity. Gedatsukai is only one of many cults which people join to alleviate illness, interpersonal friction, and other predicaments. Along with supernatural displacement as described previously, this cult, like others, inculcates self-blame and self-denial in its followers as means of offering leverage for alleviation of suffering. The followers are told to reorient their aggression inwardly with the understanding that their troubles actually originated in themselves, that the wrong one sees in another is only a reflection of one's own wrongdoing, that one's suffering is nothing but a noxious element that has made a return trip to its origin. Followers are thus advised to eradicate all spiritual pollution from their inner systems in order to attain an "empty" selfhood.[28]

A study of the Reiyukai cult reveals a similar emphasis upon self-blame. A woman who was brought to a branch leader of this cult had made up her mind to divorce her delinquent husband, a man who had tormented her by his infidelity and gambling while depending on her supplementary income to support the family.[29] Instead of consoling the potential convert as expected, the leader blamed the whole trouble on her, the wife, rather than the husband because it was she who neglected the wifely duty of staying at home and, instead, managed a restaurant. "Even if the husband is injured or chronically ill and the wife is forced to become the major breadwinner, it is recommended that she apologize to her husband for having usurped his role."[30] Hardacre notes that there is sex asymmetry in that women, not men, are pressed to blame themselves. This is a crucial point in view of the fact that most of these cults appeal more to women than men. The seemingly absurd accusation encountered by this newcomer to Reiyukai apparently triggered her "salvation."

Naikan is a secular therapy which systematically builds up guilt in the client.[31] The client is supposed to reflect upon how much *on* (moral debt) he owes to some specific person, particularly his mother, how little he has returned to the benefactor, and above all how much worry and trouble he has caused her. He is guided to focus on *naibatsu* (inner punishment) and to discard *gaibatsu* (outer punishment). Egocentric indulgence and boasting are prohibited; sensitivity to the harm one has done to another is nurtured. By putting himself into another person's shoes *(aite no tachiba ni naru)*, the client is to recode his experience in reverse: His self-pity as a victim of the other's hate, contempt, or negligence is to be converted into a deep appreciation of having been in fact loved by the same person; his grudge against the other is to be thus recoded into apology and gratitude; his boastfulness as a benefactor for the other is to be transformed into a remorseful humility after realizing that even though he has actually hurt the other person, that person has continued to love him and sacrifice for him.

It should be noted that self-aggression involved in a therapy like Naikan or religious conversion is achieved through triadic communication—through a leader or therapist who may have charismatic power of persuasion. It should be noted too, that the guilt thus intensified is released through confession or self-disclosure, which revitalizes the client and helps him to make a new resolution. As Yoshimoto, the Naikan founder and counselor, says, "Before you jump, you must squat. As long as you remain standing, you cannot jump up." Squatting obviously refers to the guilt-ridden posture, and jumping to revitalization.[32]

Whether in a cult, in Naikan therapy, or in other forms of moral or religious persuasion, an extrapunitive emotion—grudge, hatred, anger—is to be converted into self-improving energy. It is noteworthy in this light that energy for achievement often turns out to have derived from a vindictive commitment. What occurs to my mind immediately is a scene from a drama, *Chichi Kaeru* [Father's return], written by Kan Kikuchi. The 28-year-old eldest son refuses to accept his delinquent father who, after deserting the family twenty years ago, has returned home now old and poverty-stricken. He says:

> I don't know how you feel, Mother, because you are a woman, but as far as I am concerned, my father, if there is one, is my enemy. When we were still small and complained to you, Mother, about hunger and some such hardships, you used to say, "All this is because of Father. Have a grudge against Father, if you wish." If I have a father at all, it is he who has tormented us throughout since my childhood. I started to work as a waiter at the prefectural government when I was ten, and Mother earned money by pasting paper on match boxes. When Mother had no pasting job for a month, the whole family, four of us, skipped lunch. Have we forgotten all that? *I studied hard simply in order to avenge myself upon him, in order to look down upon the man who abandoned us.* I wanted to let him know you can attain manhood even if your father deserts you.[33]

In this drama the vindictive son has passed the difficult civil service examination and entered a respectable and secure career.

Another illustration of vindictive achievement in a real (as opposed to fictitious) world is a letter to a newspaper editor from a high school student with regard to the class discussion on why college entrance is desirable:

> My class consists entirely of those who did not make the prefectural high school. So they don't want to be defeated again by their former junior high school classmates who successfully entered the prefectural school. Also, because they failed in the entrance examination, their parents have been targets of malicious gossip among the neighbors, they said. They want to enter college, they argued, in order to triumph over the neighbors."[34]

Acceptance

As a final strategy for nonconfrontational management one should mention the acceptance of a conflict situation in equanimity. Instead of rejecting or correcting an undesirable state of affairs, the individual persuades himself or is advised by someone to accept it. The idea of acceptance joins hands with fatalism or the belief in the karmic chain of predestination as phrased in such terms as *unmei, shukumei, sadame,* and *innen.* As pointed out by Minami, the common people of Japan have been socialized through "popular culture," represented by popular songs and Naniwabushi tales, to accept whatever hardships, tragedies, or absurdities they encounter as their *sadame* (destiny).[35] Once such fatalism is instilled in the masses, Minami continues, songs and tales with fatalistic themes are demanded and thus further reinforce fatalism. The fatalistic acceptance of misfortune leads to *akirame:* resignation. The person who is not ready for *akirame* is disapproved as *akirame ga warui:* resistant to *akirame.*[36]

The acceptance of *innen* should be added to supernatural displacement and guilt consciousness raising as conflict-management strategies shared by many religious cults in Japan. It is not that one's *innen* cannot be altered. Cults, in fact, offer ways of cutting one's *innen* bondage. The new freedom, however, cannot be obtained unless the *innen* is first recognized and accepted as such. *Innen* applies indiscriminately to every person, every occurrence, every experience. The cult of Gedatsukai, for example, applies the concept of *shikijo no innen* (*innen* of sexual emotion) to the victim of spouse abuse, divorce, premature widowhood, husband's promiscuity, prostitution, love suicide, rape, gynecological disorder, breast cancer, miscarriage, impotence, and many other misfortunes.

Fatalism facilitates the impersonalization of a highly emotional experience, which further reduces to an acceptance of "nature" or the "law of nature" as conceptualized in the symbols drawn from the Chinese cosmology: The inevitability of an event, for example, is judged in terms of the Chinese calendrical cycles, its spatial location or direction, and so forth. The subjective will, emotion, or reasoning, which accounts for conflicts, is to dissolve into nature. Hand in hand with such "naturalism" is a reliance upon diviners *(uranai)* as revealed in the life histories I collected, for a resolution to a crisis.

Equanimity, associated with acceptance, is equated with a "thought-less" or "empty" state of mind. Traditional arts such as tea ceremony, calligraphy, and *shakyo* (brush-copying of sutras) are supposed to lead one to such a state. Some of my middle-aged and older informants are learning or practicing these arts to "calm down" their upset hearts. In a way these activities offer occasions for escaping from a stressful life. Kabuki, Noh, and Bunraku seem to perform the same function for frustrated housewives, a Tokyo University-educated housewife admitted, because these traditional stage shows present a world which is totally separated from the real world.

Acceptance of things *arugamama* (as they are) is the main tenet of Morita therapy.[37] This makes sense, considering that it is a psychotherapy primarily for *shinkeishitsu* patients who are obsessed with normality and thus tend to find themselves in acute dissonance between what they perceive of themselves and what they "ought" to be. Patients are urged to accept whatever bothers them, including their physical or mental problems, *arugamama* instead of trying to control or correct them. A Morita therapist would tell a client to accept the hopelessness of his case, to "obey" his symptom, to "unite" with it, even to enact it. ("Try to blush" might be the advice for an erythrophobic patient who is morbidly afraid of blushing.) Rejection or repulsion is viewed as merely intensifying the symptom in a vicious circle. The principle of *arugamama* thus involves the liberation of mind from intellectual thinking, emotions, and volitions and its confrontation with "facts." In this sense, it is at the opposite pole from the escapism as mentioned above.

Acceptance of one's stress or conflict is facilitated by the realization that similar problems are shared by others. This feeling of "cosuffering" or "equality" is utilized by Morita therapists treating hospital patients. The patient with *taijin kyofusho* (anthropophobia: the fear of offending others by one's imagined bodily symptoms or abnormalities) is convinced that he is being eccentric, but he finds in the hospital what might be taken as a mirror reflecting himself—that is, other patients like himself. The feeling of equality thus acquired is an important step toward destroying the troublesome conviction. Moreover, by watching fellow patients he comes to realize that their symptoms are not as striking or unpleasant as they claim they are and that therefore his affliction, too, is a product of his subjective distortion of reality.[38]

Conclusion

Conflict management at the interpersonal level in Japan has been characterized here as nonconfrontational. We have analyzed several strategies in the preceding pages: anticipatory management, negative communication, situational code switching, triadic management, displacement, self-aggression, and conflict acceptance. Conflict management does not necessarily mean a resolution of conflict, though, but rather may intensify or systematically mobilize conflict emotions. The most salient strategy in this respect is guilt-consciousness raising for therapeutic—religious or secular—purposes. Thus the very same cultural values may both intensify conflict and be used for its management. The ultimate goal of self-transformation cuts across different strategies. Whether through religious conversion or secular therapies, whether through self-aggression or conflict acceptance, what is ultimately aimed at is an empty, egoless, joyful, and thus conflict-free self.

In conclusion I want to refer to a theoretical issue concerning contrastive models for studying Japan. When we focus on conflict, we seem to accept the conflict model and reject the harmony model as if the two were mutually exclusive. This is an oversimplified dichotomy that fails to capture reality. In fact, the logic of bipolarization may well be reversed: the more harmony-oriented, the more conflict-sensitive. If the Japanese place more value, as I believe they do, upon social interdependence, cooperation, solidarity, or harmony than, say, the Americans, they are more likely to interfere with one another's actions. The norm of harmony may be precisely what makes people more aware of conflicts with others, conflicts between their self-interest and obligations, and so forth. The unrestrained pursuit of one's own interest at the expense of another's goes against the norm of sociability. Concerned with his own interest, the individual will find the imperative of sociability and harmony oppressive. In other words, the cultural value of harmony may intensify, instead of mitigate, conflict. This effect is observed in a rural community—*mura* or *buraku*—where interdependence is an inescapable norm. In describing Shinohata, Dore observes: "The 'harmony of the village' has its cost. Underneath the placid landscape there are geological faults—a personal incompatibility, a clash of economic interest, a belief that one has been cheated—along with tensions built up which require occasional release."[39]

That the maintenance of harmony itself can be responsible for intensifying conflict is further suggested by the following passage: "Competition within a group which is in theory harmoniously united tends to become fiercer and more emotionally involved than in one where competition is accepted as normal. As such it leaves scars after the event in the resentful humiliation of the defeated."[40] This passage was quoted by Smith in connection with a major conflict that occurred in Kurusu.[41] Elsewhere, in Niiike, researchers witnessed tensions and disputes over water control—the very basis for village solidarity.[42] All these observations seem to point out that conflict is inherent in harmony or at least interlocks with it.[43] Benedict viewed the Japanese in terms of such bipolar adjectives as polite but insolent, rigid but innovative, submissive but not amenable to control, loyal but treacherous, disciplined but insubordinate, and so forth.[44] These bipolarities may make more sense if the "buts" are replaced by "therefores."

In a social unit, like a *buraku,* characterized by its closure and tight network of cooperation, intense competitiveness, jealousy, and hatred may indeed predominate, though such conflict emotions usually may not surface. A resident of Henna Buraku, as reported by Kida, a participant observer, described the fellow villagers as always having their eyes wide open for every chance to "tear up *(himmuki)* and win over one another. . . . Others' misfortunes are celebrated by cooking red-bean rice, and their good fortunes are cursed."[45] That one should distrust insiders, contrary to general expectations, more than outsiders, was revealed by another resident: "There is nothing to be feared about graveyards or the dead. They are dead and can do nothing. What is more frightening, you see, is a human being, alive and kicking. But mind you, it's not someone remote and unknown, but people who are around you and close to you."[46] Kida was warned by another informant not to be put off his guard with the villagers however friendly they became because "the mouth and belly are two different things."[47] Obviously this kind of mistrust and hostility does not repudiate but rather validates Kida's claim that the *buraku* has its unity.[48]

What appears as a proof of unity may turn out to underscore the prevalence of disunity. In reference to the *tonarigumi* (an organized neighborhood unit), an informant, who had just moved into that area as a bride, says she was surprised to find that every *tonarigumi* meeting was religiously attended by all the ten women representing their respective households. The reason, she realized, was that one member's absence would encourage all the other members present to gossip about the absentee and her family. "You show up just to avoid being spoken ill about."

Implicit in this paradox is the fact that harmony is necessitated by the kind of interdependence that runs all the way from the positive extreme to the negative extreme. Positive interdependence or what

Deutsch calls "promotive interdependence" refers to the situation in which A can attain his goal only if B can.[49] Negative interdependence or Deutsch's "contrient interdependence" refers to the opposite: A can attain his goal only if B cannot. In a *buraku* the former may be exemplified by its members' participation in collective enterprises—emergency aid, labor exchange, rituals, mutual entertainment, and the like—which benefit all the participants sooner or later if not all at once. What demands our attention is the fact that the same members of the community tied together in promotive interdependence are also constrained by contrient interdependence (A's win entails B's loss). Harmony in this circumstance requires one to refrain from outdoing others and to remain unobtrusive because "a protruding stake will be pounded down." The result is a reservoir of frustration and repressed hostility.

In short, I am suggesting that the two contrastive models—conflict and harmony—might be more profitably used in conjunction with one another than disjointly. This essay was written with the goal of discovering where and how conflict and harmony are dovetailed.

NOTES

This research was aided by the National Science Foundation (Grant BNS76-11301), the Japan Society for Promotion of Science, and the University of Hawaii Japan Studies Endowment, which is funded by a grant from the Japanese government. Research assistance and typing service by Linda Kumura were indispensable to the completion of this study. I wish to express my gratitude to all.

1. Leon Festinger, *A Theory of Cognitive Dissonance* (Stanford: Stanford University Press, 1957).

2. Markus and Tanter attempt to synthesize different models into a "conflict model." See Gregory B. Markus and Raymond Tanter, "A Conflict Model for Strategists and Managers," *American Behavioral Scientist* 15 (6)(1972): 809–836.

3. Ronald P. Dore, *Shinohata: A Portrait of a Japanese Village*, (New York: Pantheon Books, 1978), pp. 272–277.

4. Minoru Kida, *Nippon Buraku* [Japanese hamlet] (Tokyo: Iwanami, 1967), p. 5.

5. Dore, *Shinohata*, p. 268.

6. Robert J. Smith, *Kurusu: The Price of Progress in a Japanese Village*, 1951–1975 (Stanford: Stanford University Press, 1978), p. 232.

7. Edward Norbeck, *Takashima: A Japanese Fishing Community* (Salt Lake City: University of Utah Press, 1954), pp. 116–117.

8. *Japan Times,* reprinted in *Hawaii Hochi.* 16 January 1978.

9. Osamu Mizutani and Nobuko Mizutani, "Nihongo Notes," *Japan Times,* reprinted in *Hawaii Hochi,* 20 June 1979.

10. Takie Sugiyama Lebra, *Japanese Patterns of Behavior* (Honolulu: University of Hawaii Press, 1976), p. 123.

11. Takie Sugiyama Lebra, "Taking the Role of the Supernatural 'Other': Spirit Possession in a Japanese Healing Cult," in W. P. Lebra, ed., *Culture-Bound Syndromes, Ethnopsychiatry, and Alternate Therapies* (Honolulu: University of Hawaii Press, 1976); Takie Sugiyama Lebra, "Ancestral Influence on the Suffering of the Descendants in a Japanese Cult," in W. H. Newell, ed., *Ancestors* (The Hague: Mouton, 1976).

12. Takie Sugiyama Lebra, "The Dilemma and Strategies of Aging Among Contemporary Japanese Women," *Ethnology*, 18 (1979): 337–353.

13. Cited in G. Piers and M. B. Singer, *Shame and Guilt* (Springfield, Ill.: Charles C. Thomas, 1953), p. 26.

14. *Japan Times,* reprinted in *Hawaii Hochi,* 3 March 1980.

15. *Hawaii Hochi,* 3 February 1979.

16. Shusaku Sato, *Toko Kyohiji* [Children in school refusal] (Tokyo: Kokudosha, 1968), p. 52.

17. Yukio Mishima, *On Hagakure: The Samurai Ethic and Modern Japan,* trans. Kathryn Sparling (Tokyo: Charles E. Tuttle, 1978), p. 8.

18. Mishima, *On Hagakure,* p. 27.

19. Eishi Katsumata, "Jisatsusha no Shinrigakuteki Tokucho" [Psychological characteristics of the suicidal person] "Jisatsugaku" [Science of suicide], in K. Ohara, ed., *Gendai no Esupuri Bessatsu* [Esprit of today: special issue] (1970).

20. Tokuji Shimoyama, "Ningen Gaku Teki Shinri Ryoho ni Okeru Nihonteki Tokusei" [The Japanese characteristics of psychotherapy viewed from the standpoint of humanistic science], *Seishin Igaku* [Clinical psychiatry] 17 (13)(1975): 28–34.

21. Shimoyama, "Japanese Characteristics of Psychotherapy," p. 33.

22. George DeVos, "The Relation of Guilt Toward Parents to Achievement and Arranged Marriage Among Japanese," in T. S. Lebra and W. F. Lebra, eds., *Japanese Culture and Behavior: Selected Readings* (Honolulu: University of Hawaii Press, 1974).

23. Ibid., p. 128.

24. Ibid., p. 129.

25. Takao Sofue, "Aspects of the Personality of Japanese, Americans, Italians and Eskimos: Comparisons Using the Sentence Completion Test," *Journal of Psychological Anthropology* 2 (1)(1979): 11–52.

26. Takie Sugiyama Lebra, "Compensative Justice and Moral Investment Among Japanese, Chinese and Koreans," *Journal of Nervous and Mental Disease* 157 (1973): 278–291.

27. DeVos, "The Relation of Guilt."

28. Takie Sugiyama Lebra, "The Interactional Perspective of Suffering and Curing in a Japanese Cult," *International Journal of Social Psychiatry,* 20 (1974): 281–286.

29. Helen Hardacre, "Sex-Role Norms and Values in Reiyukai," *Japanese Journal of Religious Studies* 6 (3)(1979): 445–460.

30. Ibid., p. 454.

31. Inobu Yoshimoto, *Naikan Yonjūnen* [Forty years of Naikan] (Tokyo: Shunjusha, 1965); Nikichi Okumura, Koji Sato, and Haruo Yamamoto, eds., *Naikan Ryoho* [Naikan therapy] (Tokyo: Igaku Shoin, 1972); Takao Murase, "Naikan Therapy," in W. P. Lebra, ed., *Culture-Bound Syndromes, Ethnopsychiatry, and Alter-*

nate Therapies (Honolulu: University of Hawaii Press, 1976); Lebra, *Japanese Patterns of Behavior,* pp. 201–214.

32. Inobu Yoshimoto, "Naikan no Hōhō to Jissen" [The method and practice of Naikan], in N. Okumura, K. Sato, and H. Yamamoto, eds., *Naikan Ryoho* [Naikan therapy] (Tokyo: Igaku Shoin, 1972), p. 30.

33. Kan Kikuchi, *Chichi Kaeru; Tojuro no Koi* [Father's return; Tojuro's love] (Tokyo: Kadokawa Bunko, 1971), p. 16. (My emphasis and my translation.)

34. *Asahi* (Osaka edition), 9 October 1978.

35. Hiroshi Minami, *Nihonjin no Shinri* [Psychology of the Japanese] (Tokyo: Iwanami Shoten, 1953), p. 127.

36. Ibid., p. 138.

37. Akihisa Kondo, "Morita Ryoho" [Morita therapy], *Seishin Igaku* [Clinical psychiatry] 8 (9)(1966): 707–715; Takehisa Kora, "Morita Therapy," *International Journal of Psychiatry* 1 (1965): 611–645; Shomo Morita, *Shinkeishitsu no Hontai to Ryoho* [The essential characteristics and therapy of Shinkeishitsu] (Tokyo: Hakuyosha, 1960); Takehisa Kora and Koji Sato, "Morita Therapy—A Psychotherapy in the Way of Zen," *Psychologia* 1 (1958): 219–225; Lebra, *Japanese Patterns of Behavior,* pp. 215–231.

38. Hiroshi Iwai and Toru Abe, *Morita Ryoho no Riron to Jissai* [The theory and practice of Morita therapy] (Tokyo: Kongo Shuppan, 1975), pp. 121–122.

39. Dore, *Shinohata,* p. 266.

40. Ronald P. Dore, *Land Reform in Japan* (London: Oxford University Press, 1959), p. 343.

41. Robert J. Smith, *Kurusu: The Price of Progress in a Japanese Village, 1951–1975,* p. 237.

42. Richard K. Beardsley, John W. Hall, and Robert E. Ward, *Village Japan* (Chicago: University of Chicago Press, 1959), pp. 126, 136–138.

43. This view is in line with certain sociological theories of conflict. Simmel begins his analysis of conflict with the assumption that antagonism, aversion, repulsion, hostility, and dissociation are inherent in social order. The functionalist view of conflict, conveyed by Simmel, is seconded by Coser, who thinks violence contributes to a new social equilibrium. Similarly, Gluckman argues that the African "rituals of rebellion" are to dramatize the existence of social order by displaying its opposite. See Georg Simmel, *Conflict* and *The Web of Group-Affiliations,* trans. Kurt H. Wolff and Reinhard Bendix (New York: Free Press, 1955); Lewis A. Coser, *Continuities in the Study of Social Conflict* (New York: Free Press, 1970), pp. 53–110; M. Gluckman, *Rituals of Rebellion in South-east Africa* (Manchester: Manchester University Press, 1954).

44. Ruth Benedict, *The Chrysanthemum and the Sword: Patterns of Japanese Culture* (Boston: Houghton Mifflin, 1946), pp. 1–3.

45. Kida, *Nippon Buraku,* p. 98.

46. Ibid., p. 99.

47. Ibid., p. 102.

48. Ibid., pp. 36–42.

49. Morton Deutsch, *The Resolution of Conflict* (New Haven: Yale University Press, 1973), p. 20.

4
Analysis of Conflict in a Television Home Drama

AGNES M. NIYEKAWA

How do average Japanese handle conflict in their daily lives as they interact with people at work, at home, in their social circle, and among strangers they encounter? A culture is usually described in the abstract, and so is cultural behavior. If one were to describe a social interaction in which a *meshita* or *kōhai* (junior) disagreed with or shouted at his *meue* or *sempai* (senior), a Japanese is likely to say, "That cannot happen in Japan. It must have been at a party where he was drunk." We are led to believe that such behavior is unthinkable in Japan and can happen only in unusual circumstances, but is it truly so? Are the Japanese constantly "behaving" according to social expectations? While the norms of social behavior may be quite different from those of the United States, Japan seems no exception in having its range of personalities: from the subservient to the domineering, from the shy to the overbearing, from the selfless to the self-centered. These different personalities could not possibly follow the code of behavior in exactly the same way. Brown and Levinson, in their theory of politeness phenomena as universals in language usage, have this to say in one of their footnotes:

> It is reasonable to assume that in every society, in at least some social arenas, there is room for the creation of social relations by the choice of behavioural strategies. . . . Social relations thus created are no less social relations than those ascribed. It is an empirical question to what extent and in what domains in any particular society an individual's social relations are an outcome of behavioural choice as opposed to jural prescription.[1]

To what extent the Japanese may behave according to "behavioral choice" rather than "jural prescription'" however, is not known.

There obviously must be room for behavioral choice even for the seemingly code-abiding Japanese. Using a television home drama as the source of data, this study analyzes the ways in which conflicts in daily life are handled and resolved by the Japanese.

The Television Home Drama

The use of a television home drama appears to be an excellent way to overcome the difficulties of assessing behavior in natural settings. The observational method, by the very presence of an observer, affects the behavior of those observed. The interview approach, like any other method relying on self-report, has built into it the perennial problem of the difference between what people say they do and what they actually do. The unobtrusive method is the best approach if one is interested in behavior in a specific situation only.[2] However, considering all the legislation regarding individual rights to privacy on the one hand, and standards for professional ethics when human subjects are involved on the other, television dramas are the best way to obtain data on the behavior of the same individuals in different situations and to assess how conflicts in daily life are handled as they arise. The television home drama enables an outsider to have a close look, so to speak, into personal and private aspects of life in Japan, particularly since these home dramas are characterized as down to earth. During a recent interview, Takashi Hoga of the New York Office of Fuji Telecasting Co. discussed Japanese television programs and commented as follows:

> The Japanese do not enjoy situation comedies. The most popular TV fare is "home drama," a form of soap opera without the "sexploitative aspects" of its American counterpart. . . . The Japanese serials are "rooted in the Japanese character." The constant is less comedy than a home setting. There are hilarious moments but it is mostly serious. They are family-oriented and watched by everyone from grandmother to little children. They present stories of actual family life and allow parents to use some of the materials as examples to children. They give a sense that what is on TV is acceptable. The programs try to help audiences exorcise their daily frustrations. It is entertainment but with situations that give practical guidance, an example to emulate. The programs are not culturally bankrupt.[3]

For this study on conflict at the interpersonal level, a television home drama series entitled *Daikon no Hana III* or "Radish Blossoms

III" was selected. The serial, broadcast in Japan in the mid-seventies, is set in present-day Japan. The drama centers around a widower, Tadaomi Nagayama, who is a retired captain of a navy cruiser, his family members, and close associates. The hero Kanchō (Commander), as he is called by his two loyal former subordinates, is an old-fashioned man in his late sixties who frequently creates problems for others because of his fussy and eccentric ways. He objects to his son's interest in Mariko, a bar hostess, enlists his former subordinates' cooperation in trying to break up his son's relationship with her, but eventually gives in to their marriage. His former subordinates, Lt. Sōma and Sailor First Class Ishikawa, are also his closest friends and live not far from him. Their association has extended over three decades, and their relationships are definitely stable, solidary, and intimate. Their status difference from the navy days has been maintained. This accentuates their status relationship based on age, education, and social class. The hero lives with his second son Makoto, rather than his first son Isamu, whose wife, a professor's daughter, refuses to live with her fussy father-in-law. Makoto constantly berates his father and criticizes him to his face while showing a great deal of concern by his actions. These characters with different personalities, values, and social backgrounds find themselves in many conflict situations.

The series was extremely popular in Japan to the extent that five versions of *Daikon no Hana* appeared. (The actors playing the ex-navy men remained constant, but their spouses and children varied from one version to another.) The popularity of the series in Japan as well as in Japanese communities abroad seems to be due in large part to the actor Hisaya Morishige, who plays the role of Kanchō, and to the realistic way the problem of aging is depicted in the story. It is the third version that was used for analysis in this study.

The series, consisting of thirty fifty-minute installments shown on television over a thirty-week period, was audiotaped and videotaped for analysis. The thirty installments in the series may be roughly divided into three equal parts: the first ten deal with Mariko's acceptance as a possible daughter-in-law by Kanchō from the time of Makoto's encounter with her; the second ten deal mostly with the efforts of Mariko and her family members to become acceptable to Kanchō's family up to the wedding; and the last ten deal with the problems of how the three adjust to living together. Throughout these parts, the major theme of conflict is the difference in values between the tradition-bound Kanchō and his sons who represent the younger, but not so young, generation. Numerous minor conflicts are intertwined with major conflicts, and the viewer is presented with typical Japanese scenes as well as some shockingly atypical episodes.

Major Conflicts

For the purpose of this study, a major conflict is defined as one that takes at least a full installment (fifty minutes) to get resolved. Here I want to describe some major conflict situations along with details that become relevant to discussions under separate headings later.

As an ex-navy officer, Kanchō holds onto traditional values, particularly when it comes to status and family background. When he realizes that Makoto is getting deeply involved with a bar hostess, he resorts to all kinds of schemes to break the two apart. In one episode he invites Mariko, her boss the proprietress of the bar, and Makoto's boss Kume and coworker Tsuchioka to his house to show them the Nagayama family background in the hope that if Mariko herself does not get discouraged, at least her associates will realize the great status difference between Mariko and Makoto and talk her out of marriage.

During the course of the evening, he discovers that the proprietress of Mariko's bar is in fact the daughter of a former navy admiral who ranked far above him and that she became a bar owner in order to support her father and family after the war. Kanchō falls sick from embarrassment for not having shown her due respect. Even this incident, however, does not soften his stand on Mariko. The solution comes when Kanchō, who likes to be hyperbolic, pretends to be on his deathbed and gives his last will and testament to the Sōmas and Ishikawas who gather round. He says he is sorry to have to go without having settled Makoto's marriage, and he asks them as his guardians to make sure that Makoto's wife comes from a solid background, not someone of *mizushōbai* background. (*Mizushōbai* refers to occupations that involve serving drinks and entertaining men, such as geisha, bar hostess, and the like.) Just at that point Makoto, called back from work, dashes in accompanied by Mariko. When Kanchō stops her at the threshold, Mrs. Ishikawa steps out of the room, sits next to Mariko on the wooden floor of the corridor, and makes a dramatic announcement that she too worked at *mizushōbai* before her marriage to Ishikawa. She says that she had no choice but to work at a *koryōriya* (eating place where sake is served) after her father's bankruptcy to support the family with a sister who had tuberculosis. She makes her husband testify to the fact that she was a virgin at the time of their wedding.

While Kanchō considers Mrs. Ishikawa to be uncouth and has never gotten along with her, he is moved by this awkward revelation and politely asks both Mrs. Ishikawa and Mariko to enter the room. With Makoto announcing that Mariko quit the bar that very day, the stiff atmosphere suddenly relaxes. The Sōmas and Ishikawas excitedly discuss where Mariko might find a job, and eventually the Sōmas offer Mariko work at their restaurant. Mrs. Sōma, however, does ask Kanchō whether he regards *their* restaurant as a *mizushōbai* place. Without giving a yes or no response, he says he cannot refuse a request coming from someone he has appointed guardian. The matter is settled when Kanchō formally requests the Sōmas to look after Mariko as a *yome* (daughter-in-law) candidate of the Nagayama family.

This example of the way in which a major conflict is resolved can be considered typical of the series. Seldom is a major conflict resolved by individual effort. Relatives and friends get involved in trying to solve the problem. Earlier in the installment described here, Mariko is advised by her brother to quit the bar, but she says she cannot leave until she pays back all her father's debts and puts her brother through college. Later her father's girlfriend drops by and advises her to quit her job if she ever wants to marry Makoto. In another scene, Kentarō, Mrs. Sōma's adult son, visits Makoto at his office and suggests during lunch that if Makoto himself asked Mariko to quit her job, she would do it. Makoto's image as a kind person is reinforced by his response that he cannot do so because of her father and brother. Even Kentarō's prediction that Mariko's father will remain a derelict as long as she supports him meets Makoto's resistance. He says when he thinks what his own father would do if he were suddenly told to support himself, he could not possibly ask Mariko to do such a thing. Although Makoto does not get to follow Kentarō's advice because Mariko has quit her job by the time he sees her that afternoon, these scenes show that many people close to Mariko and Makoto contribute to solving the problem in a harmonious way and even go out of their way to do so.

This installment concludes with three separate family scenes. At the Sōmas, Mrs. Sōma is congratulated by her son for helping to solve Mariko's problem. The whole family then celebrates with drinks, relieved that they can make up to Mariko after having inadvertently insulted her the day before. At the Ishikawas, Mrs. Ishikawa expresses cathartic relief for having let out her long-held secret about her background and is praised by her husband for having guts *(dokyō)*. She expects her teenage daughter to be shocked about her *mizushōbai* background, but her daughter Hanako tells her that she knew all along. When Mrs. Ishikawa asks Hanako the source of the information, her husband tries to divert her attention by asking for a snack. (A sudden change of topic to avoid response in an uncomfortable situation is one of the sixteen ways to say no in Japanese).[4] At the Nagayamas, Makoto is humming while doing his chores. Kanchō teases him and says that Makoto must have aged because in his younger days he used to stand on his head whenever he was happy. Makoto takes it as a challenge. The last scene shows both of them struggling to stand upside-down against the wall. This ending is typical of practically all the installments in the series except one that ends in suspense. The final scene is usually a warm family gathering of eating and drinking around the table at home or at a small restaurant or bar. There is much joking and teasing of one another, and down-to-earth squabbles over food or personal habits, but in general it is a peaceful and lighthearted scene.

As in the preceding example, the most frequent cause of major conflicts is the difference in values held by Kanchō and the younger generation represented by Makoto, Isamu, and his wife. Mrs. Sōma's son Kentarō, a younger person but slightly distant from all of them, serves as an effective intermediary when he does appear on the scene. Kanchō with his traditional value system gets support from the Sōmas and Ishikawas, but their backing is due more to loyalty than to conviction, since they do not come from a samurai background. They often support Makoto and Mariko and try to smooth the relationship between Kanchō and the younger couple. When Mariko loses 50,000 yen with which she was entrusted by Kanchō to buy special food for the New Year, for example, they all advise her not to tell Kanchō. They predict he will criticize her and say a woman with a *mizushōbai* background does not know the value of money. Mr. Sōma and Mr. Ishikawa, who took her shopping, loan her some money so that she can at least get the essential items. Mrs. Sōma suggests that Mariko ask for her father's help. By this time Mariko's father has gone straight, has married his girlfriend, and is holding a job as a guard, which he got through the help of Makoto's boss. As Mrs. Sōma suggests, he is proud of being asked for financial help by his daughter for the first time in his life and does everything he can to produce the 50,000 yen.

Many of the major conflicts, such as arguments over the wedding ceremony, are similarly solved by advice from people around the young couple: Makoto's boss, the Sōmas, the Ishikawas. It is not a group effort, but each individual's personal contribution, that leads the stubborn party to make a compromise. Seldom does a major conflict get resolved by the individual concerned.

Minor Conflicts

Because most of the major conflicts are resolved harmoniously in this fashion with other people pitching in, so to speak, one gets the impression that the series emphasizes traditional values. When one looks at minor conflicts that are momentary incidents, not running through the whole fifty-minute installment, one gets quite a different impression. In an earlier study of intrapersonal conflict in this drama—situations in which two opposing forces work on the same individual as he interacts with another person—I examined the outcome of conflicts in terms of which force won.[5] The major forces creating intrapersonal conflict in the thirty-six cases I examined can be reduced to three elements: *giri*, ego orientation, and politeness.

Giri

It is not surprising that *giri*, the feeling of obligation, should be a major source of conflict for characters in this drama, since the interpersonal relationships depicted are essentially intimate and of long duration. But when one examines how conflicts are resolved only in a minority of cases (five out of thirty-six) does *giri* prevail over other factors. An example will illustrate the case.

Mr. Ishikawa, who now operates a liquor store with his rough and domineering wife, is working in the kitchen of Kanchō's house. When he is criticized by Kanchō for his clumsiness in handling food, he mumbles to himself and retorts to the effect, "What a way to get treated for working like a slave for someone else when I have my own work to do!" Just then the telephone rings, and his wife asks Kanchō whether her husband is there. Kanchō tells her that he left some time ago, and Mr. Ishikawa gets ready to rush home. When Kanchō disappointedly asks, "You're going home?" he responds, "Yes. . . . It's going to be hell when I get home." Kanchō's expression of dejection, however, results in Ishikawa's bringing out prepared food from the kitchen to serve Kanchō in the next scene and Kanchō's offering him sake. Other examples of *giri* involve mainly the feeling of obligation, coupled with *ninjō* (personal affection), to the retired navy captain by his former subordinates despite their feeling of guilt to their wives. (Repetitive cases, such as Ishikawa's sneaking out bottles of sake from his store to give Kanchō, were counted only once in this sample.)

EGO ORIENTATION

Ego orientation, whether it is the modus operandi of the person or his preference, constitutes the major force in about two-thirds of the cases examined. While the stereotyped image of the Japanese would have him observe *giri* at all cost, be polite to others, and suppress his individuality in the process, ego orientation comes out rather strongly in this contemporary home drama. There are three bold characters: the fussy Kanchō; Mariko's father, who knows no restraint or *enryo* and is little more than a bum until he reforms in order to make Mariko acceptable to the Nagayama family; and the assertive Mrs. Ishikawa of lower-class *shitamachi* background. They account for less than 40 percent of the cases in this category, however. Ego orientation is expected to play more of a role within the family, where politeness and *enryo* can be discarded to a large extent under the strong bond of blood relationship, and where one can show one's dependency need *(amae)*. Indeed, almost all the conflict situations in relation to a blood kin (nine out of ten) show ego orientation determining the immediate outcome, often leading to greater interpersonal conflict.

An example of such a case is Mariko's objecting to her father's plan to give an authentic performance of *yasukibushi* dancing at her wedding. Mariko has essentially supported her father with her income as a bar hostess and lets him continue his gambling and drinking until she quits her job. She tells her father that his dancing will only embarrass her at the wedding. Her plea develops into an argument and he sulks, saying he simply will not attend the wedding if she is ashamed of him. Her identification with the family she is marrying into and her wish to be proper in the eyes of other guests, the reasons for her objection, result in even greater conflict. She eventually makes up with her father by buying him a *tenugui* (towel) for use as a headband for his performance at the wedding.

POLITENESS

The third major force contributing to intrapersonal conflict is politeness. It is the social expectation of politeness that prevents one from behaving as one might prefer to behave. As might be expected, this force was not found to predominate in an *uchi* (in-group) situation among blood kin, nor among the three characters with strong individuality mentioned above. Reluctant politeness, or the inability to say no was found only among certain individuals. In other words, some people find it easier than others to say no. Despite my expectations, not many cases fell in this category, although this outcome is due partly to the classification scheme used in the study. Where *giri* dictates that one behave in a certain way to another, politeness works in the same direction. Consequently all such cases were classified as *giri*. Cases classified as politeness are limited to conflict where being polite to the person results in going against the *giri* one owes to a closer person or against personal preference. Less than one-fourth of the cases fell in this category.

An example is the hospitality extended to Mariko when Makoto unexpectedly walks in with her. The Sōmas and Ishikawas had been gossiping about Kanchō and Makoto, sympathizing with Kanchō's position that women of *mizushōbai* background are undesirable as marriage partners and preparing to give Makoto a lecture about her. Faced with the presence of Mariko and Makoto, the Sōmas politely entertain her, only to find themselves in greater conflict later. In general, cases falling in this category lead either to greater conflict or to masochistic resignation. On their honeymoon, for instance, Makoto and Mariko meet an older couple on a belated honeymoon. The old man takes a liking to Makoto, and the honeymoon couple not only ends up spending all their time with the older couple but Makoto is asked to give the old man a massage in the evening. The insensitive old man misinterprets Makoto and Mariko's sulking expression during dinner; he thinks they are not in love but have been forced to marry due to unwanted pregnancy, adding insult to injury. Even while denying it to the old man, Makoto finds it impossible to ask the old couple to leave them alone. Thus Makoto and Mariko decide to cut short their honeymoon and return home a day early. While this is an extreme example, whenever politeness is the major determinant of behavior the conflict is resolved only temporarily, resulting in greater inner tension.

To summarize this analysis of a sample of minor intrapersonal conflicts, neither *giri* nor politeness played as strong a role in determining the outcome of conflicts as did ego orientation. This tendency may make the drama appear more realistic; it may also very well reflect the behavior of Japanese in everyday life today.

Analysis of Utterances

Various attempts were made to analyze the verbal interactions systematically by existing methods, but they all proved to be futile. A television home drama, unlike a stage play or a sociopsychological experiment on group interaction, consists of many short scenes, not all of which are sit-down discussions. In many scenes, characters talk while performing their daily chores. For instance, there were nine scenes in the first twenty-five minutes of the twelfth installment. More than half, or 55 percent to be exact, of the 527 utterances in this twenty-five minute period consisted of fewer than five words; only 5 percent consisted of more than twenty-five words. Less than one-third of the utterances were complete sentences. Many characteristics of Japanese verbal interactions were evident. The speaker is constantly interrupted—that is, from an American point of view—by grunts and short phrases *("Mm, so, so")* or repetition of what was said *("A, Mariko-san ga ne")* or *("Ippan mo")* to indicate that the person is listening to what the speaker is saying. In such interactions, the great problem in systematic analysis is determining the unit of analysis.

BROWN AND LEVINSON'S FRAMEWORK

One approach that appeared to be particularly suitable for this study was Brown and Levinson's framework. In their lengthy paper "Universals in Language Usage: Politeness Phenomena" (1978), they observe:

> Indeed, we proffer this paper in part simply as a piece of descriptive apparatus for the recording of interactional quality in some more sophisticated way than the use of gross labels like "respect" and "familiarity," with which anthropologists have hitherto seemed content. In elaborating the apparatus, and in claiming crosscultural validity, we do however go further: we see the endeavour as performing an explanatory role in the linking of social structure to behavioral patterns in a way that participants themselves do. And such efforts to link observables to underlying abstract social dimensions, which requires an understanding of the systematics of those observables themselves, cannot but be part of an empirically based social theory that has a concern with social relationships.[6]

They analyze politeness in terms of the notion of "face" derived from the English folk term and Erving Goffman's analysis.[7] Face is something an individual has an emotional investment in; it can be lost, maintained, or enhanced. Politeness is directed at preserving the addressee's positive face and not impinging on his negative face. Positive face is defined as the desire to be ratified, understood, liked, admired; negative face is the desire not to have one's action impeded and to be free from imposition. Acts that intrinsically threaten face are referred to as "face-threatening acts." Brown and Levinson then describe strategies to reduce face-threatening acts, among which are positive politeness directed to the addressee's positive face and negative politeness directed to the negative face. Within each category, there are more than ten specific strategies. One positive politeness strategy is to claim in-group membership with the addressee by using in-group markers; another is to claim a common point of view by seeking agreement or avoiding disagreement; still another is joking. Negative politeness strategies include not coercing the addressee and giving him the option not to act by being indirect or by hedging. They give numerous examples from English, Tzeltal, and Tamil.

Brown and Levinson claim that the seriousness of a face-threatening act is a complex function of three variables: distance, power, and rating of imposition. Cross-cultural variations are attributed to differences in these universal social dimensions. It is therefore possible to distinguish between positive-politeness cultures and negative-politeness cultures. Positive-politeness cultures can be characterized as having few serious face-threatening acts; impositions are regarded as small; social distance permits easygoing interactions; relative power is never very great. Examples given by Brown and Levinson are the "friendly backslapping" cultures, as in the western United States, certain New Guinea cultures, and among the Mbuti pygmies. In contrast, they say, the "negative-politeness cultures are those lands of standoffish creatures like the British (in the eyes of the Americans), the Japanese (in the eyes of the British), the Malagasy, and the Brahmans of India."[8] Why the Japanese are qualified as "in the eyes of the British" is a little puzzling except that the authors themselves are British.

Since Brown and Levinson's classification of Japan as a negative-politeness culture seemed appropriate, we attempted to code the verbal interactions among various characters in the television drama. It was soon discovered, however, that their framework was strictly theoretical, and not conducive to coding. It also became evident that detailed coding loses sight of the forest for the trees. The application of Bales' and Borgatta's interactional analysis system in addition to Brown and Levinson's politeness coding failed to provide a better picture of the interpersonal interaction during a conflict.[9]

The problem with Brown and Levinson's framework is that their classification, according to the examples they gave, emphasized the *form* of the utterance. If one were to code by form, ignoring the content of what was said, the heavy emphasis on negative politeness in Japanese would have been supported. There were an overwhelming number of cases, however, where one would code an utterance as a case of negative politeness on the basis of form, while in terms of meaning one would code it differently. For instance, a statement starting with a remark designed to reduce the threat to face—*"Okotoba o kaesu yō desu ga . . . "* (I don't mean to challenge what you say, but . . .) or *"Kono sai iinikui koto mōshiagemasu kedo ne . . ."* (I'm going to say something that's not easy to say, but . . .)—would be classified as negative politeness. What followed such a remark was frequently rather bold, however, considering that it was usually addressed to a person of higher status, as from Mr. Sōma to Kanchō or from Makoto's coworker Tsuchioka to his boss. Thus the content of the following remark often suggested that the statement be classified as a case of *positive* politeness, emphasizing in-group membership or indicating the speaker's concern for the addressee, or as a case of a "baldly on record" statement threatening the addressee's face. This was one reason why we had to abandon the coding of utterances by this method. During the course of trial coding, though, one could not help but be impressed by all the open disagreements and accusatory remarks that could be made in polite speech. Although the coding was expected to substantiate Brown and Levinson's claim that Japan is a negative-politeness culture, coding the speech addressed to Kanchō by his former subordinates and their wives in fifteen installments, or half of the entire series, showed that less than one-sixth of all their utterances could be classified as cases of negative politeness in form and content.

Goldstein and Tamura, in comparing Japanese and American speech, point out that in American English respect goes with formality whereas in Japanese respect can be expressed in formal as well as informal speech.[10] One might add a corollary that in Japanese it is also possible to be intimate in formal speech.

THE WHOLE VS. THE DETAILS

Close scrutiny of transcribed speech reveals that Mr. Sōma and Mr. Ishikawa, even though they are extremely loyal, considerate, and cooperative to Kanchō, are fairly free to express disagreement and dissatisfaction and even to make accusatory remarks to Kanchō. Because these remarks usually occur in the larger context of assisting Kanchō, they do not seem to stand out in the memory of the viewer. The overall impression one gets from the series, or even each installment, is that Kanchō is lucky to have these two faithful subordinate friends who are so willing to make sacrifices for him. They quarrel with their wives about taking Kanchō out fishing on Sunday when he is depressed. They volunteer to share the cost of reimbursing a bar hostess when Kanchō spills food all over her kimono. The screening out of "noisy" or inconsistent details in grasping the whole gestalt may very well be a phenomenon in human perception, which is oriented toward making a meaningful whole out of all the stimuli received by the sense organs. Certainly there is evidence of that process in the perception of speech in these dramas.

Jorden in her paper on female speech severely criticizes the use of radio and television drama and movies as the source of speech data.[11] She argues that the overlays, repetitions, interruptions, hesitations, self-corrections, and amplifications which characterize natural speech are seldom found in these dramas. If one were to compare the television script with transcribed natural speech, one would indeed find this to be the case. But the actual utterances made by actors and actresses deviate considerably from the script. There is a great deal of ad libbing by the players; the script serves mainly as a detailed guide to the sequence of interactions, the points to be made, and the settings and formats to be used in the fifty-minute segment.

A comparison of the script with transcribed actual utterances indicates that the utterances are less consistent, less smooth, and, because of the many hesitations, repetitions, interruptions, self-corrections, and amplifications, about 70 percent *longer* than the script in word count. While spending hours transcribing the tapes, I discovered that on the first hearing of a passage, the hesitation sounds such as *ya, ma,* and *sono,* adverbials such as *chotto, ittai,* and *nan te,* and repetitions were often missed. On the second hearing, I managed to catch some of these phrases but often misplaced them; only on listening to the same segment for the third time would I get the passage correct. For instance, *"Sore kara asoko no jōshi de ne"* gets corrected to *"Sore kara, a hora, asoko no jōshi de ne"* on second hearing and finally to *"Sore kara, a, asoko no, hora, jōshi de ne"* on third hearing. It appears that in our selective perception, we screen out the meaningless "noise" in the utterances and perceive them as well-formed sentences. In other words, what we perceive is much closer to the smooth, consistent text of the script than the faithful transcription of actual utterances. Is it not likely that a similar condensation to a more consistent, sensible story is taking place in our interpretation of what we *see* on the television screen?

SAYING NO OR GETTING OUT OF UNCOMFORTABLE SITUATIONS

At one point in the study, after the series had been viewed a number of times, we decided to look for examples of saying no or getting out

of an uncomfortable situation. Contrary to expectations, the search
turned out to be unproductive, for the participants expressed disagreement fairly frequently and bluntly. There were a few instances
of what one expects of Japanese interactions, such as Makoto's encounter with the older couple on his honeymoon, but such cases were
rare. In one scene in the first installment, Makoto's boss asks him to
meet an expected visitor in the evening. Makoto is planning to propose marriage that night to Hiroko, a girl his father approves, so he
responds with an unenthusiastic *"Ya"* ("Yes, I'm listening"). When
he is given further details on how to handle the visitor, however, he
hesitatingly starts *"Ha, anō, Henshūchō . . ."* ("Yes, editor-in-chief,
but . . ."') and his boss completes his sentence for him: "I'm sorry
but I want to leave early tonight." To Makoto's surprised expression,
his boss responds by saying that unless one can read something as
obvious as *that,* one cannot become head of a section. Thus, in the
one instance an employee was going to say no to his boss, it was not
even necessary. All he had to do was to indicate his reluctance by the
intonation in addressing his boss, and the boss read his mind.

Other examples appeared more than once: suddenly changing the
topic to avoid answering a question, repeating part of the utterance as
a question with a certain intonation, and mumbling to oneself. We
have already seen how the topic can be shifted abruptly. The second
case, repetition in question form with an intonation indicating reluctance, is exemplified in interactions between Mariko and Kanchō.
After Kanchō accepts her as a potential daughter-in-law, he gives her
training in etiquette *(gyōgi minarai)* at his home. To his *"Soo, ojigi
desu yo. . . . Ichido yatte gorannasai, soko de"* ("Yes, bowing. Try
it, right there"), she responds enthusiastically, *"Ojigi o surun desu
kā?"* ("I have to bow?"). She immediately gets corrected on the way
she phrased this question and does not get excused from bowing.

The third case, mumbling to oneself, is seen fairly frequently in
the series. Mr. Sōma, Mr. Ishikawa, Mariko, and Mariko's stepmother
do it at least once in relation to Kanchō. Mumbling usually comes
after a reluctant yes, and in a low voice, but sufficiently loud to be
barely audible. It can be distinguished from what preceded in two
ways, the lower voice and the shift in level of politeness. The speaker
up to this point has been using the polite *desu-masu* style of speech,
but he switches to the plain style in grumbling to himself. The
addressee often hears the mumbling, but when he asks to have it
repeated the speaker responds "I was just talking to myself" and gets
out of the embarrassing situation. An example was presented in the

discussion of *giri,* where Ishikawa is preparing food for Kanchō. Earlier in the scene, Kanchō gives instructions on how to cut the tofu in a loud voice from the living room and then asks Ishikawa whether he can hear. Ishikawa responds, *"Kikoemasu yo! Sore dake ōkina koe dashite kikoenakya, mō tsunbo da yo, jōdan ja nai!"* ("I can hear you! Don't be silly! I'd be deaf if I couldn't hear something so loud!") The second sentence is in the plain style, expressing the speaker's resentment privately. While questioning or mumbling may help to communicate to the addressee the speaker's unwillingness to respond to the order, these two examples show that if the addressee is not sensitive, or chooses not to be, they will not help the person get out of the unpleasant situation.

Speech Level, Status, and Conflict

A review of what was found and what was not found suggests that a reexamination of the correspondence between level of speech and personal relationship is in order. Level of speech is accepted as a universal feature of language, and its relationship to solidarity (distance, or degree of intimacy) and power (status) has been discussed extensively by Brown and Gilman in relation to the second-person pronouns T/V (*tu* and *vous* in French; *tu* and *usted* in Spanish; *du* and *Sie* in German): "*T* derives its common definition as the pronoun of either condescension or intimacy and *V* its definition as the pronoun of reverence or formality."[12] Status differences result in nonreciprocal usage of T and V: the higher-status person is addressed by V and addresses the lower-status person by T. The distance or intimacy dimension, on the other hand, leads to reciprocal usage: mutual T if the relationship is intimate, mutual V if it is not. There are, however, social class differences; among equals, upper-class people tend to use V whereas lower-class people tend to use T. The Japanese *keigo* system, although it has another dimension of *uchi-soto* in addition to the two dimensions of power and distance and is thus more complex, has much in common with the T/V system.

The use of T, or the plain style in the case of Japanese, generally means that formality can be done away with in the relationship, for the addressee is either someone of intimate relationship or someone of lower status who can in effect be ordered around. The use of V, or the polite *desu-masu* style in Japanese, on the other hand, means that the relationship is distant and respect must be shown. In this case the speaker is not in a position to express his true feelings as freely as when he is using T, for the addressee is either a person of higher status or not an intimate. It is therefore expected that the speaker's inner conflict is greater when he is using the polite style than the plain style of speech. If he wants to express his displeasure while using the polite style of speech, he will have to do it in a round-about way.

These general rules can be observed in Kanchō's speech. Since he is the person of highest status most of the time—being the oldest, having held a fairly high status before, and coming from a samurai background—he is addressed in the polite *desu-masu* style, the equivalent of V, by everybody but his sons. He in turn addresses most of the people surrounding him in the plain *da* style (the equivalent of T). The exceptions are Mrs. Sōma, who was formerly married to a banker and who resembles Kanchō's late wife, and Makoto's boss Mr. Kume. An interesting shift in Kanchō's level of speech is observed in relation to Tatsuko Endō, whom he falls in love with. When he is introduced to her in a *miai* (initial meeting in an arranged marriage) which Mariko's father set up without anyone's knowledge, Kanchō looks down on her, using the plain T because she appears to have no manners and works as a cleaning lady. He comes to respect her when he gets to know her better, though, and shifts his speech to the polite V in courting her; she herself continues to use the plain T indiscriminately to everybody including Kanchō, reflecting her open and unassuming personality. Aside from these examples, many temporal shifts for effect are observed in Kanchō's speech.[13] The latter shift (metaphorical code switching) is usually done automatically and unconsciously while its effect is communicated, as in the use of the Japanese passive,[14] and hence is not noticed by either the speaker or listener unless transcriptions are examined.[15]

Makoto similarly observes the general rules in his choice of speech level. Except to his father, his brother, and occasionally his coworker Tsuchioka, he uses the polite V to almost everybody appearing in the drama. In speaking to Mariko, his level changes twice, reflecting his relationship to her. The first time he speaks to her while sober, he sees her as the daughter of a blackmailer and speaks despicably in T. During their courtship, his speech is V mixed with occasional T; and by the time of their honeymoon, he is using T again.

The Sōmas and Ishikawas consistently use the polite V to Kanchō, Makoto, and Mariko. Between husband and wife, however, the Ishikawas use reciprocal T whereas Mr. Sōma uses T to his wife and she uses V to her husband. Mariko, almost always the lowest-status person in all the scenes of the drama, uses V to everybody but her father and brother. She comes to mix T occasionally in speaking to Makoto as they become closer, especially after her marriage.

These findings are consistent with the universal rules of sociolinguistics. The speech levels generally reflect the relationships among the interacting individuals. What does not follow the universal rules, however, is the extent to which the content of speech can be at the T level while the style is at the V level. Mrs. Sōma shouting at Kanchō *"Nagayama-san. Mariko-san (wa) Makoto-san no oyome-san nan desu yo. Nagayama-san no oyome-san ja nain desu yo!"* is not much different in intensity and directness from *"Nagayama-san, Mariko-san (wa) Makoto-san no oyome-san yo. Nagayama-san no oyome-san ja nai no yo."* ("Mariko is Makoto's wife, not yours") except in the level of politeness—the former is V, the latter T. Given the ideal model of Japanese social structure and behavioral code, as well as the universal rule on the setting in which V is to be used, this example comes as a surprise. Yet it is in no sense an isolated case.

Perhaps the general rule that greater intimacy leads to ignoring status differences and hence to the mutual use of T does not apply to the Japanese. In European languages, when two people different in status become very close the person of lower status is permitted to use intimate T-level address forms.[16] In Japan, however, once a status hierarchy is established it holds for the lifetime of the individuals concerned. Your grade school teachers remain of higher status than you even if you become prime minister. Your teachers may adjust their speech level in speaking to you, now a prime minister, but you continue to speak to them as your *sensei*. Similarly, in the relationships between Kanchō and his former subordinates, the intimacy may grow over the years but the status hierarchy once established will never change. Thus the Sōmas and Ishikawas continue to speak at the polite V level, while the content of speech reflects the intimacy achieved over the years. This is also likely to be the case with Japanese wives who use V level speech to their husbands.

Thus it appears that in Japan only between people of equal status is it possible to shift from V to T as they become more intimate, as in the case of Makoto and Mariko. Mariko's speech to Kanchō, her father-in-law, however, remains at the polite V level, even though she spends more time with him than with Makoto after her marriage. This pattern is to be expected on the basis of the preceding discussion. In other words, status supersedes intimacy in determining the level of speech in Japan except among blood kin in the immediate family. When the relationship is intimate, however, it is possible to express feelings more directly than expected in polite speech.

Value Messages

The preceding generalization might possibly be rejected as being based on a drama with too many eccentric characters who are atypical of Japanese. Such comments, or remarks to the effect that the speech and behavior in this drama are not natural, have not been heard so far. The characters and events seem to be in the realm of likely possibility.

The unexpected findings, not only the outcomes of intrapersonal conflict but also the discordance in the content and level of speech, may be traced to the fact that the drama showed much of the *ura* side of life in Japan. Non-Japanese seldom get a close look at the everyday happenings in Japanese family life that are considered private and personal; the characterization of Japanese is usually made in terms of their *omote* behavior. (See Takeshi Ishida's essay in this volume for a discussion of the concept *ura-omote*). When atypical behavior is pointed out to a Japanese, it is treated as an exception caused by unusual circumstances. Behavior deviating from the culturally prescribed code has not been studied because it is supposed to be rare or because it appears only in an *ura* setting and hence is not accessible for observation.

Yet it is the realistic depiction of the characters through their down-to-earth *ura* behavior that enables the viewer to identify with them. Hoga, cited earlier, says that these home dramas give practical guidance to viewers and offer them examples to emulate.[17] Certainly an objective viewer will notice that there are value messages embedded in this entertaining program. Considering the impact of television, it is well worth examining the values communicated by this serial *Daikon no Hana III*. The educational messages carried in this conflict-ridden serial can be grouped into three major categories: the psychology of the aged, traditional values worth preserving, and new values that older people should understand.

Aging

The main theme of this serial is coping with and by the aged. This theme essentially supports Palmore's findings that in Japan, due to traditional values, the aged can maintain their relatively high status and integration despite industrialization.[18] Theories on aging would predict a decline in the status of the aged with modernization, for the factors that gave the aged status in preindustrial or predominantly agrarian societies—namely their accumulated wisdom through years of experience as well as their power over land, extended family, government, and religious and other institutions—do not hold in a rapidly changing, technologically oriented society with high mobility. That is exactly the case with our hero Kanchō, who finds himself considered old-fashioned and his opinions not only rejected by his sons but seen as interfering. His past position as commander of the navy cruiser *Hidaka* carries no weight among his sons' generation. The only way he is making himself needed is as house husband, handling all the domestic chores since he became a widower. Yet even these services become superfluous when Makoto gets married and Mariko takes over the household chores. In the last installment of the series, Kanchō, feeling unwanted despite Mariko's devotion to him, decides to leave them without any destination. The series ends happily when Mariko persuades him to stay because he is needed as the grandfather of the child to be born.

The psychology of the aged is not made very explicit; rather it is communicated by repeated incidents in which Kanchō interprets actions by the young as signs of rejection and behaves like a thwarted child as well as other occasions when Kanchō is delighted to be the focus of attention. In other words, the subtle message is there: that the aged Kanchō wants desperately to be part of everything that is going on.

TRADITIONAL VALUES

Among the traditional values reinforced in the serial are *oyakōkō* (filial piety) and the close relationship among relatives, friends, and associates. Filial piety may best be exemplified by the events of the first installment.

Although Makoto is characterized as an *oya-omoi* son (considerate to his parents), he is so direct most of the time as to be rude. On two occasions, he even hits his father in anger. Yet when Hiroko asks him to choose between her and Kanchō because she could not possibly live with his fussy father, he chooses his father. That night he gets drunk at the bar and repeatedly says that a man can choose a wife from among countless women, but he has only one father. Kanchō, who approves of Hiroko, anxiously asks Makoto on his return home how Hiroko took the proposal. Makoto simply says that he was rejected. Kanchō later finds out directly from Hiroko what transpired on their last date and is deeply moved. That evening, he calls Makoto a liar for not telling him the truth. He then says that while a child cannot kick out his parent, a parent is entitled to kick out his child, so he is kicking Makoto out of the house; he should find a place to live with the woman he likes. All this is said by Kanchō in a harsh way with a great deal of effort while he is trying not to cry. Makoto takes the whole thing lightly, jokes, and says he would never move out of this house because he loves his father's cooking.

This touching scene, which comes at the end of the first installment, communicates three messages at the same time: the value of filial piety, a father's love for his son, and the Japanese macho image. Rather than saying so directly, Kanchō expresses his love and appreciation by scolding his son. Expression of tender feelings is considered unmasculine, and this norm is reinforced here. Although it may not have been the program's intent to preserve such an image of masculinity, it can nevertheless have such an effect on the audience. Makoto later becomes more ego-oriented when it comes to Mariko, and he frequently argues with his father on this issue. Yet his concern for his father is shown again when he goes through a great deal of trouble to arrange a trip to Hong Kong for his father after seeing his disappointment when Mr. Sōma wins a round-trip ticket to Hong Kong.

The positive aspects of having close associates who offer help, advice, and support were mentioned earlier. From the American point of view, their involvement in other people's lives would be regarded as meddling. Some of the younger people in Japan today prefer the American way of less intimate association with others that frees them from *giri* and the accompanying ritual of gift giving. Yet even these viewers are likely to have been impressed by the warmth and strength of the moral support friends provide and how much they genuinely share in the joys and sorrows of others. It is hard for viewers to dislike the Sōmas, the Ishikawas, Makoto's boss, and even Mariko's reformed father. As I pointed out earlier, most of the major conflicts could not have been resolved harmoniously without their personal contributions. The program delivers the message that the traditonal value of *giri* is well worth maintaining.

The series depicts minor traditional customs as well, not necessarily with an objective to reinforce them. One such custom is the formal apology: A character gets off the cushion, sits straight on the *tatami* or wooden floor, and bows deeply to apologize for grave mistakes.

Kanchō behaves in this way to the Ishikawas, Mrs. Sōma to a customer, Mariko's father to Mariko and Kanchō, and Mrs. Ishikawa to Kanchō. Speaking to the deceased at the Buddhist altar as if the person were still alive is another custom that is reinforced. While in this drama only Kanchō does so, this custom was observed in a few other television home dramas during the same period as *Daikon no Hana III*. Kanchō not only burns incense regularly but reports the domestic news to his dead wife. He also goes to the altar to speak to her when he feels sad or depressed. This custom, like keeping a diary, may very well serve as a means of private catharsis for the Japanese.

A tradition shown for no obvious educational value except to prepare the uninformed novice is the teasing of the newlyweds. Marriage changes the status of the wife from a *soto* (out-group) person to an *uchi* (in-group) person. The Japanese language therefore requires that the reference term for a person be changed after marriage. When Makoto refers to his wife as "Mariko-san" right after his honeymoon in speaking to the people at his office, Tsuchioka teasingly says *"Mariko-san datte!"* ("Look at him referring to her as Mariko-san!"). Makoto hurriedly corrects himself and says first "Mariko" but settles for *"kanojo"* (she). Mariko, on the other hand, gets teased when she refers to Makoto as *shujin* (my husband) on her first visit to Makoto's office after the honeymoon. In other words, whether one's usage is correct or not, the newlywed gets teased. While this teasing may appear as tasteless to some Americans, both Makoto and Mariko take it as good sports. In fact, Mariko seems pleased by it. Perhaps the teasing is done in the spirit of prolonging the marriage congratulation while at the same time it is meant to correct the individual's habit if the appropriate usage has not been fully adopted.

NEW VALUES

The new values emphasized in this series are equality of people and tolerance for the life-style of the young. Makoto is the exponent of equality, particularly since he falls in love with a girl who is unacceptable to his status-conscious father. Makoto also lectures his father frequently not to take advantage of Mr. Sōma and Mr. Ishikawa because times have changed and people are equal today. In one scene Makoto comes home drunk and behaves rather like Mariko's father after the two of them have spent a night out at some cheap eating place and a burlesque show. Kanchō and Makoto's brother Isamu are disgusted by Makoto's lower-class behavior, but Makoto's lecture on the positive side of Mariko's father's life-style has an effect on Isamu. Isamu admits that there is some truth to what Makoto says, that they have been brought up properly and told to look only upward, and how much more relaxed life would be if they stopped being so vain. Later, however, when Kanchō gets involved with Tatsuko the cleaning lady, there is a reversal of positions. Now Kanchō says that there are no high or low jobs, that all work is respectable, while Makoto and Isamu try to persuade him that Tatsuko is no match for a former navy captain. The Sōmas and Ishikawas tend to think the same way as Makoto, but Mrs. Sōma's son Kentaro points out that Kanchō is just a retired man without a job, while Tatsuko is a working woman, and therefore there is no great status difference after all. These discussions are expected to have an impact on viewers. The frequency with which the topic of status appears suggests that discussion of this theme was one of the program's educational goals.

The other new value stressed is the younger people's life-style. The preference of young couples to live by themselves, as in the case of Isamu and his wife, is accepted by Kanchō. In fact, he makes a number of attempts to find a new place so Makoto can marry Hiroko or, later, to let Makoto and Mariko be by themselves. His well-motivated efforts, however, invariably create more problems (and provide some of the most hilarious scenes in the drama). In daily life Kanchō does not show as much understanding and tolerance toward the young couple. He often mentions his late wife, who was supposedly shy and reserved to the last day of her life. The Sōmas, including Kentaro, and the Ishikawas, try to teach Kanchō to become more tolerant of the young couple's ways and leave them alone. For instance, disturbed by the mushy way Makoto and Mariko interact with each other, and the attention Makoto gets from Mariko, Kanchō feigns a heart attack. Mariko handles the situation excellently and is praised by Kanchō as well as by the doctor, but all the people who gather in this emergency get furious at Kanchō's ruse. Mariko, however, defends him, saying it was good to have this emergency drill as she would be better prepared should a real attack come.

Mariko, as in the instance described above, takes sides with her father-in-law so often that it leads to quarrels with Makoto. Mariko thus does not always represent the ego-oriented young in this drama. In fact, in her eagerness to please her father-in-law to make up for her poor family background, she behaves like the traditional daughter-in-law. Yet because of her cheerful personality and genuine concern for her father-in-law, it cannot be said that she portrays the stereotyped suffering daughter-in-law. She is the one who enables the three of them to live more or less peacefully together. There may be a lesson intended here in the way Mariko copes with the old man.

The value messages, then, whether old or new, appear to have a single goal: to guide viewers of various ages to learn and accept the values of others in order to reduce conflict in everyday family life.

Summary

This analysis of conflict in the television home drama *Daikon no Hana III* has shown that major conflicts tend to be solved not single-handedly by the people directly involved but with contributions from their intimate friends. Intrapersonal, minor conflicts, however, were found to be resolved, often only temporarily, by ego-oriented decisions most frequently and only secondarily by such forces as *giri* and politeness. Characters were often able to say no to requests, for in a large number of cases the person of lower status expressed disagreement freely to the one of higher status. This unexpected finding was examined and related to level of speech. In Japan it seems that only between people of relatively equal status does polite speech shift to plain, informal speech with an increase in intimacy; among people of different statuses, the speech level determined by the initial status relationship holds no matter how intimate they become. Intimacy is often expressed by the content of speech—by disagreement, for example—while the polite level of speech is maintained. Finally, the home drama was examined as a carrier of value messages: the need of the elder to be included in every activity, the importance of the traditional value of *giri*, and the introduction of new values of greater tolerance for different life-styles and respect for people in all walks of life. Whether the viewers grasped these value messages in the abstract or not, they were presented with plenty of evidence that they contribute to conflict resolution.

NOTES

Thanks to KIKU TV of Honolulu for making available the written script of *Daikon no Hana III*.

1. P. Brown and S. Levinson, "Universals in Language Usage: Politeness Phenomena," in E. N. Goody, ed., *Questions and Politeness* (Cambridge: Cambridge University Press, 1978), p. 307.

2. E. J. Webb, D. T. Campbell, R. D. Schwartz, and L. Sechrest, *Unobtrusive Measures: Non-reactive Research in the Social Sciences* (Chicago: Rand McNally, 1966).

3. O. Dekom, "Bringing Japanese TV Shows to America," *Sunday Honolulu Star-Bulletin and Advertiser (TV Week)*, 30 November 1980.

4. See M. Imai, "To Avoid Rudeness, Japan has 16 Ways of Saying 'No,' " *Japan Economic Journal*, 25 December 1979, p. 12; and K. Ueda, "Sixteen Ways to Avoid Saying 'No' in Japan," in J. C. Condon and M. Saito, eds., *Inter-Cultural Encounters with Japan* (Tokyo: Simul Press, 1974), pp. 185–192.

5. A. M. Niyekawa, "Expressions of Conflicts in the Mass Media," paper presented at the Association for Asian Studies meetings, Chicago, April 1978.

6. Brown and Levinson, "Universals," p. 247.

7. Erving Goffman, *Interaction Ritual: Essays on Face-to-Face Behavior* (Chicago: Aldine Press, 1967).

8. Brown and Levinson, "Universals," p. 250.

9. See R. F. Bales, *Interaction Process Analysis* (Cambridge, Mass.: Addison-Wesley, (1950), and E. F. Borgatta, "A New Systematic Interaction Observation System: Behavior Scores System (BSs System)," *Journal of Psychological Studies* 14 (1963):24–44.

10. B. Z. Goldstein and K. Tamura, *Japan and America: A Comparative Study in Language and Culture* (Rutland and Tokyo: Charles E. Tuttle, 1975).

11. E. H. Jorden, "Female Speech: Persisting Myth and Persisting Reality," in *Report of the Second U.S.-Japan Joint Sociolinguistics Conference* (Tokyo: Japan Society for the Promotion of Science, 1974), pp. 103–117.

12. R. W. Brown and A. Gilman, "The Pronouns of Power and Solidarity," in T. Sebeok, ed., *Style in Language* (Cambridge, Mass.: M.I.T. Press, 1960), p. 258.

13. A. M. Niyekawa, "Code Switching in a Stable Relationship: An Analysis of a Japanese TV Drama," in *Proceedings of the Symposium on Japanese Sociolinguistics* (San Antonio: Trinity University, 1978), pp. 151–180.

14. A. M. Niyekawa, *A Study of Second Language Learning—The Influence of First Language on Perception, Cognition and Second Language Learning: A Test of the Whorfian Hypothesis* (OE-6-10-308) (Honolulu: University of Hawaii, 1968).

15. J. Blom and J. J. Gumperz, "Social Meaning in Linguistic Structures: Code Switching in Norway," in J. J. Gumperz and D. Hymes, eds., *Directions in Sociolinguistics* (New York: Holt, Rinehart and Winston, 1972), pp. 407–434.

16. See Brown and Gilman, "Pronouns"; and R. Brown and M. Ford, "Address in American English," in D. Hymes, ed., *Language in Culture and Society* (New York: Harper & Row, 1964), pp. 234–244.

17. Dekom, "Bringing Japanese TV."

18. E. Palmore, *The Honorable Elders: A Cross-Cultural Analysis of Aging in Japan* (Durham, N.C.: Duke University Press, 1975).

5
Spirit Possession and Village Conflict
TEIGO YOSHIDA

Foreign scholars have generally regarded Japanese villages as harmonious communities where serious conflict is rare and exceptional, yet every one of the more than a dozen villages my colleagues and I have investigated have evidenced regular social tensions and serious conflicts. The question to ask, however, is not whether conflict exists in Japanese villages. It certainly does. Rather we need to look more closely at *how* conflict is caused, and among *whom,* and to ask what regular patterns can be seen. We need, in other words, explanations for how conflict is expressed, controlled, and resolved in Japanese villages—the elemental face-to-face communities of the nation.

My interest for two decades has focused on spirit possession in village communities, and this essay delineates the processes of social conflict that surround the subject. The analysis is based on my fieldwork over twenty years in many regions of Japan except Hokkaido. After describing the nature of Japanese spirit possession, I wish to examine the kinds of social conflict that are associated with it. Since the forms of conflict are quite diverse and much work has already been done on some forms (overt sanctions, uprising against authorities, intervillage hostility), I will limit myself to the analysis of this largely ignored aspect of village conflict, particularly because an analysis of spirit possession reveals certain dynamics of conflict within village social relationships.

The Belief in Spirit Possession

According to traditional beliefs widely found in Japan, the spirits of foxes, weasels, badgers, snakes, and other animals, the spirits of living people, and the spirits of deceased persons may possess people and cause them to fall ill, suffer accidents, or become mentally deranged. In this context the meaning of *tsuku* (to possess) is similar to that given to the word "possess" in the Shorter Oxford Dictionary, which is "of a demon or (usually evil) spirit: to occupy and dominate, control or actuate"; in the same dictionary the word "possession" means "the fact of possessing a person or the fact of being possessed by a demon or spirit." According to Raymond Firth, "spirit possession is a form of trance in which behaviour actions of a person are interpreted as evidence of a control of his behaviour by a spirit normally external to him."[1] I will follow this definition, with the reservation that in the Japanese context illness, accidents, and other forms of misfortune are in some cases the most pervasive evidence of spirit possession. Trance is not unknown, but neither is it a necessary or central aspect of the syndrome.

Apart from the belief in possession by animal and human spirits, some families in certain villages are believed to "hold" fox or other animal spirits. Spirit possession can be found throughout Japan. The phenomenon of spirit "holding," however, is weak or nonexistent in much of northeastern Japan, whereas it is common (but not universal) over most of southwestern Japan: the Chūgoku (the San'in region in particular), Shikoku, Kyūshū, Chūbu, and Kanto regions. The ratio of animal-spirit-holding families within the village also varies regionally. Among our sample, for instance, spirit-holding households numbered 43 of 99 households in Kōchi prefecture, 13 of 43 households in Shimane prefecture, 46 of 49 households in another Shimane village, and 33 of 181 households in Gunma prefecture. Kōchi and Shimane have the highest ratio of animal-spirit holders (50 to 100 percent), while the ratio is relatively low (less than 20 percent) in the Chūbu and Kanto regions. Animal-spirit-holding cleavages in village society are generally traditional and well defined because the holders inherit their status lineally within households.

If one or both parents are holders, their offspring, irrespective of sex, are considered to be holders also. In some areas holders are referred to as belonging to the "black side" or simply called "black." While the holding of animal spirits can be transmitted either paternally or maternally, in some villages transmission through the female line is emphasized. In patrilineal Japan, the holding of animal spirits is believed to be transmitted most strongly from mother to daughter. In the San'in region, for example, when a girl from a fox-spirit-holding family marries, it is said she takes seventy-five foxes along with her to her husband's house. More fundamental, however, is the belief that birth or marriage to a holder of an animal spirit automatically makes one a holder also, regardless of the holder's or recipient's sex. In villages in Kōchi and Shimane prefectures when a girl from an animal-spirit-holding family marries a man who is not a holder, it is not only her husband who becomes a holder—even his parents and brothers and sisters are usually considered to have become animal-spirit holders.[2]

The belief in spirit possession can also be understood as an attempt to explain the inexplicable: undeserved misfortune, illness, death, success, happiness. It is believed, for example, that a fox brings money to his master's house or digs trenches in others' paddies and draws water into his master's land and that spirits bring silk cocoons and other things from neighboring houses into their master's house to make him rich. Explanations of this sort abound on the subject of why some animal-spirit holders are wealthy. The sudden bankruptcy as well as the rapid accumulation of wealth of spirit holders can also be attributed to the power of their spirits. Spirits may also abandon their holders or turn against them when their masters' fortunes begin to fail. This behavior is seen as causing a sharp decline in a holder's economic situation.

Spirit holders are believed to have a mystical power to possess others and cause them to become ill or to experience misfortune. Naturally, they are much feared. In former times discrimination against spirit holders was often severe. There are instances where fox-spirit holders accused of having made people sick by sending their foxes to possess them were totally ostracized by other villagers. Petitions to the feudal authorities in 1828 and in 1825 from spirit holders in Okino-shima asking for relief remain as documents of such discrimination.[3] In Kōchi in 1472 the Lord of Tosa, Chōsokabe, tried to exterminate dog holders by burning down a whole village inhabited by them. Unlike the *burakumin* who were also discriminated against in rural Japan at the time, spirit-holding households did not live in separate villages or hamlets but resided squarely within most village societies.

At present serious discrimination against spirit holders rarely surfaces in village life. Yet those who are not animal-spirit holders remain strongly opposed to marriage with holders. This marriage taboo is strictly kept even today in villages where the notion of animal-spirit holding remains strong. After gaining the confidence of villagers one hears a flow of private conversations detailing much interest and concern in the subject. *Kitsunemochi* (fox-spirit holders), *inugami-mochi* (dog-spirit holders), *osaki-mochi* (weasel or fox-spirit holders), and other animal-spirit holders are referred to as *suji* (vein), *tsuru* (vine), *warui-hō* (bad side), *yotsu* (four-legged), *ashimochi* (legged), or *kuro* (black). Those who are not holders are known as *ii-hō* (good side) or *shiro* (white).

Theoretically, all spirit holders are believed to have mystical powers to possess people, but in practice only certain spirit holders are thought to have actually possessed others. Here it should be recalled that villagers clearly distinguish between spirit holding and spirit possession itself. I want to underline the fact that spirit possession of others usually occurs in the context of "realistic" conflicts among villagers.[4] The primary cause for spirit possession of another is recognized by villagers to be hatred, jealousy, envy, and other emotional antipathies. Prior social conditions, namely intravillage conflict, set the stage for possession. My analysis of spirit possession in many varied villages confirms a basic pattern in which spirit holders are thought to send out their animal spirits to possess others with whom they are known to be in conflict.

Consider several cases of spirit possession we have investigated. Our first case is of *ikiryo* possession in Kōchi prefecture.[5] The *ikiryo* is a spirit of a living human which may possess another. *Ikiryo,* unlike animal spirits, are not held by certain families but by everyone. The village in question is socially divided into two groups: those who are dog-spirit holders or "bad side" and those who are not dog-spirit holders or "good side." Actual cases of possession by dog spirits (that is, accusations) ceased some time back. In this village resentment, envy, and jealousy are richly associated with *ikiryo* possession as the following case illustrates.

A farmer and his wife were possessed by the same *ikiryo,* but at different times. His headaches and his wife's gynecological disease were both attributed to possession by the same woman, according to the explanation they received from a faith healer *(kitōshi)* in their village. The farmer firmly believed what he had been told. He told us that he and his wife had been possessed because he had aroused her resentment by winning a dispute with her family over the boundary of some arable lands. He also believed that the woman whose spirit possessed him and his wife had been envious of his family's being well-off and happy while she had been suffering from poverty and many misfortunes including the deaths of her husband and blind daughter. According to neighbors this landowning farmer had become wealthy through socially disapproved activities during World War II. Before the war, he bad been merely a tenant. The woman accused of possessing him and his wife was born in the same neighborhood. As his fortunes rose, she had become poorer, especially when her husband died leaving her to care for their small children. Both parties, the possessing widow and her "victims," belonged to households known traditionally as dog-spirit holders, but they shared no ties of kinship.[6]

In a village in Gunma prefecture in 1953, a three-year-old boy was taken seriously ill and fell into a near-coma for a week, neither crying nor talking. Since it is said that a child seriously possessed by an animal spirit does not cry or talk when sick, his parents thought that he might be possessed by an *osaki* (weasel) held by some family and asked a faith healer to diagnose the boy. He concluded that the boy's illness was due to the bite of an *osaki* owned by another villager named Saito. The faith healer attributed the possession to Saito's grudge against the boy's father. The two men had been on bad terms for a long time. The boy's family had been tenants on the land of a third family for many generations. When this patron family decided to sell part of their land, Saito had hoped to buy it but was outbid by the former tenant, the boy's father. Saito's grudge stemmed from this episode.

Another informant mentioned that long before this episode the two men had jointly established a factory for the manufacture of starch. Apparently Saito's monopolization of the profits had caused the boy's father to become so angry that he made a public complaint. An influential man in the village mediated this conflict.

The hostilities continued. A few years later Saito removed part of the stone wall of a reservoir that was common property of the neighborhood association. He needed to widen a passageway for his truck, but he should first have received permission from the neighborhood association. When members of the association made a strong protest, its representative was again the boy's father, who accused Saito and brought the matter to trial. The conflict was apparently resolved after Saito paid a fine,[7] but clearly this result left him very angry. The faith healer later involved in this case was a member of the same village and of course knew this series of events and the villagers' feelings about them. In this case, it seems that the faith healer, in my interpretation, simply supported the general opinion of the villagers in attributing the child's illness to possession by Saito.

In order to cure the illness the faith healer had to perform ceremonies of exorcism on three separate occasions. (He noted that ordinary cases require only one ceremony; the deeper the grudge or the more serious the illness, the more exorcism is required.) The idea that Saito's *osaki* was the possessing spirit became public knowledge and generated further tension and conflict between the two families, but some twenty years later when we visited the village they did not openly show animosity. As in this case, the legacy of conflict in Japanese villages often lies below the daily surface of propriety—out of view, so to speak, to the eyes of neighboring villages and casual visitors.

When the boy was said to be possessed by Saito's *osaki,* Saito's widowed mother was still alive and active. According to some informants, this rather passionate woman was responsible for the possession of not only this child but others. She and the possessing *osaki* were identified because her personality was seen as aggressive and emotional. After she died her household was no longer accused of spirit possession.

In our third case, also in Gunma, a man named Yonesaki became very weak due to influenza. The interpretation was that he was possessed by a spirit *(osaki)* held by a neighbor, one Nishimura. The Yonesaki family is not an animal-spirit-holding family. In a mentally deranged state the possessed man announced, "I came from a neighboring house." Since spirits are known to speak through those possessed, the victim's elder brother Yasuo, head of the Yonesaki family at the time, fired his gun under his neighbor's house in an effort to kill the *osaki.* The possessed man shouted aloud at that time, "Yasuo is going to kill me." Since local faith healers did not succeed in driving out the *osaki* from the victim's body, his elder brother went to a famous Inari shrine in Oji to take a magical tablet to exorcise the spirit from his younger brother. The victim had said, "I will leave when the tablet arrives." When his brother came home with the tablet, the man died. Descendants say the victim's corpse had a hole in its abdomen caused by the *osaki*'s bite.

According to contemporary informants, the direct reason for this possession, which occurred in 1910 or so, is that the victim's family had won disputes with the Nishimura family over the boundary of farmlands. Nishimura's father was engaged in various businesses, one after another, raising carp, dairy cattle, and so forth, but he did not succeed in any of these ventures. Informants also mention that the father, Nishimura, and his son (the present head of the family) were both known as stingy and greedy. Furthermore, they have been contentious, taking unsuccessful legal action against several persons over land boundaries. Though the Nishimura house has been relatively wealthy, the socioeconomic status of the Yonesaki house was higher at the time of the event. In this case again, the accusation of possession stems from interhousehold conflicts outside the kinship domain.

The next case is also an old one from Gunma. An old Buddhist priest was possessed by a spirit *(osaki)* held by the Kato family. The priest spoke in a mentally deranged state saying the *osaki* had come there to possess him because he had failed to put on the proper robe for a Buddhist ceremony at the Kato house. The Kato family was one of the poorest in the community, and the priest's failure to put on a formal robe indicated that he looked down on their house. Another reason given by villagers for the possession was that the Kato household was too poor to feed their *osaki* well, so the spirit went to the priest to be fed better. This was revealed in what the possessed priest said in his delirium. A faith healer tried to drive out the *osaki* from the priest but did not succeed.

A member of the same neighborhood tried to take the priest to Kato's house to exorcise the *osaki,* carrying him on his back and taking along the *osaki*'s favorite food. He addressed the spirit: "This is your house. Here is your food. Please return to your house." This did not work either. Soon after the priest died. Again it is said that the belly of the priest had been badly bitten by the *osaki*.[8] This event occurred between persons living in the same neighborhood; no kinship relation existed between the priest and the Kato household.

In a village in Shimane prefecture, a 51-year-old widow is thought to have possessed a man, Mr. Shinagawa, forty-nine years old. The year of this case is 1966. When Mr. Shinagawa built a work shed, he wanted to serve dinner to the neighbors who had helped with the construction. All dishes were prepared in the main house, but when the guests came in most of the food had been eaten. Only fish bones were left. They found the mark of a beast's claw imprinted in the rice cakes. Villagers labeled this event *sawari,* a word that denotes illness, accidents, and other misfortunes caused by something mysterious. *Sawari* includes spirit possession. Some quickly decided that Mrs. Yamashita (or more precisely her fox spirit), notorious for possessing her fellow villagers, was responsible for this act, but other villagers argued that cats must have eaten the food. Mrs. Yamashita belongs to the fox-spirit-holding families of the village, and because she has been a widow since the age of thirty-six, her personality is considered unusual. Widows not only live in near isolation, but are often thought to have sexual liaisons with married males. The victim in this case is not an animal-spirit holder. He and Mrs. Yamashita have been on bad terms since World War II, however.

According to Mrs. Yamashita, she had suffered great hardship. During the war she had to pay her government share of the harvest despite her poverty. She had no husband, moreover, and had to raise her seven children by herself. It is noteworthy that one of the men in charge of collecting the rice tax for the authorities was her victim. She stated, "Whenever I meet him, my feeling of resentment comes up, recalling bitterly what he did to me during the war. At that time I had to give away all the rice I grew, so that I was left with none to feed my family. I had to buy rice though I had little money."9 Both Mrs. Yamashita and the victim in this case belonged to the same social stratum of *kokata* (client-tenants).

In a separate case, the same Mrs. Yamashita is thought to have possessed Mrs. Kubo in 1967. Mrs. Kubo's pains in her loins and legs were attributed to possession by Mrs. Yamashita's spirits. The reason given was that the victim had won a land boundary dispute from Mrs. Yamashita. Hearing of the gossip accusing her, Mrs. Yamashita announced to her neighbors, "They say I possessed Mrs. Kubo, but I had nothing to do with it." The tensions and sense of conflict between the two houses were only aggravated by this denial. In this example, too, the victim belongs to the *kokata* class. Here again we encounter the opinion that Mrs. Yamashita's personality is emotional, aggressive, and envious.

Another man, Yoshino, age thirty-seven, a janitor in the high school, is thought to have been a victim of Mrs. Yamashita's spirit. He and his wife attributed his headaches and neurosis to possession by her fox spirit. A faith healer diagnosed him and confirmed this. While the victim had less land than Mrs. Yamashita, his family has more money because five of the members earn salaries. It is said that Mrs. Yamashita's envy of his higher income explains the possession. The victim's household also belongs to the *kokata* class.

In a final case a woman, age thirty-seven, in Gunma prefecture fell from the eaves of her house and, unable to walk, was bedridden. Her family thought she had been pushed off by a spirit, because she said she had seen a big *osaki* on the eaves. They also found some animal hair on the ground under the eaves. While in bed, the victim began talking in a delirious way and in answer to her family's questions declared, "I came from a house with no children." At that time, among the village's spirit-holding houses that of Nakano was notorious for possessing villagers. Mrs. Nakano, a barren woman, was further suspect because she was regarded as aggressive and unyielding.

Listening to what the victim was saying in her delirium, her family soon concluded that it was Mrs. Nakano's spirit. According to the victim's daughter, Mrs. Nakano was envious of her mother's many children as well as her outstanding skill in sewing. The two women had been in the same sewing class when they were girls.

The Social Patterning of Possession

As these cases clearly illustrate, spirit possession is viewed by villagers as the result of preexisting tensions and conflicts among people and households of the same community. Based on our detailed analysis of some eighty-five cases of spirit possession collected during fieldwork, we have drawn up a list of common social-structural features. Now let us look at these characteristics in detail.

AN INTERHOUSEHOLD PHENOMENON

Possession by spirits tends to be an interhousehold phenomenon. If one person is envious or resentful of another, the possessor or possessed may be a different member of the household involved in the antagonism. A husband, parent, or child may substitute as victim or even holder for the central antagonists. The victim is not necessarily the household head but may be his wife, mother, or child. This appears to be an expression of the traditional Japanese tendency to merge the identity of the individual in the household to which he or she belongs.[10] When compared to beliefs regarding mystical attack in Indonesia, for instance, the Japanese characteristic is striking. According to my research in both Java and Bali, sorcery is quite conspicuously an interindividual phenomenon that frequently occurs between relatives and family members.

SOCIAL RELATIONSHIPS

Spirit possession is much more likely to occur in certain social relationships than in others in Japanese villages. In all the villages we investigated, spirit possession was said not to occur within a family or among kin. We did find a few exceptional cases of spirit possession among kin, but statistically the indigenous notion was supported as these cases were rare and never occurred between patrilineally related households.[11] Three of eighteen instances of possession in a village in Gunma prefecture occurred between kin and in each, social conflict between kin was the basis for possession.

In one of the exceptional cases, a man was possessed on his way home accompanying his younger brother's bride (from a different village) on their wedding day. He fell unconscious and was taken to his parent's house where the wedding was about to be held. He was in bed on the second floor of the house. There was much confusion in this house, because the possessed person was in bed upstairs and the wedding was going on below. Villagers assumed that the *osaki* possessing him had come from the bride's house. The victim stayed in bed and ate very little for several days but recovered later. He became possessed again from time to time, however, and committed suicide a few years later. Before this event he had had continuous conflicts with his parents for years. His deaf younger brother was favored by his parents. Because the parents thought the victim's wife did not pay enough attention to the deaf brother, they were angry and decided to leave the house. After building a separate house and moving there, the parents continued to have arguments with the victim, especially about the younger brother's future. The younger brother's wedding was being held in the parents' house, not as it should have been in the victim's or main *(honke)* house, and this undoubtedly contributed to the victim's tension. Past family conflicts that had not been resolved had prevented the wedding from occurring in the socially proper location. The point is that family problems among patrilineally related persons created the tension, but it was the new bride's family that was blamed for the possession.

It seems that only among nonpatrilineal kin who fail to follow the norms of proper kin relations will spirit possession be perceived. In view of the fact that when possession occurs, it is not only the victims, their families, and other relatives who may suffer but also the "assailants," possession appears to serve as a form of mystical punishment of nonconformists in the realm of kinship. It is a very serious thing to be named an assailant by one's fellow villagers, and a calamity for both victim and assailant to be kin.

SOCIOECONOMIC STATUS

In one Shimane village four of the five patron-landlords are fox-spirit holders, including the wealthiest and most powerful patron-landlord in the village. In this village patron-client relationships are socioeconomically the most important. All five patron-client pairs were between fox-spirit holders and those who are not fox-spirit holders, yet spirit possession does not occur within the patron-client relationship and clients are not possessed by patrons. Possession does occur, however, between client-tenants belonging to different patron-land-lords. This pattern can be related to the fact that the vertical patron-client relationship is traditionally well controlled, while the relationship between client-tenants belonging to different patron-landlords is likely to create envy, jealousy, and social conflict. This pattern appears to parallel those in societies where witchcraft accusations are most likely to involve the same social stratum rather than different strata. Relations between strata can be controlled by regulative social institutions (the hereditary master-client relationship is one),[12] but some status relations are both competitive and less institutionally regulated.

CONFLICT IN PATRON-CLIENT RELATIONSHIPS

The absence of possession does not mean that conflicts do not occur within patron-client relationships. Rather, conflicts are not uncommon and can develop to the point that the vertical economic structure they represent breaks down. In one village on Sado Island (Niigata prefecture) we have studied, subordinate clients and tenants initiated rural class conflict in 1943 and succeeded in the same year in terminating their subordination to their masters.[13] In a fishing village on Iki Island (Nagasaki prefecture), the relationship between the fish wholesaler and boatowner patrons and their client fishermen, which had epitomized the traditional patron-client relationship, was overturned in the 1920s, primarily because of the disputes raised by the fishermen with the wholesalers. In order to increase marine production the local government had helped the fishermen gradually shift the sales of their catch to other wholesalers outside the old patron-client system. The old wholesalers lost their power, and the boat-owning fishermen gained economic independence.[14] These conflicts between economic strata brought about striking changes in the internal structure of both villages, but the disputes surfaced and were resolved in a relatively short period of time. The social cohesion of the village was subsequently restored. In this connection it seems significant to note that in villages where strong vertical social relationships have broken down we have not found beliefs in spirit possession or spirit holding.

STEM-BRANCH RELATIONS

In villages where stem-branch *(honke-bunke)* relations among households and cognatic kin are functionally the most important (in mutual aid of all kinds and in ritual activities), spirit possession occurs most frequently among unrelated neighbors and among families whose farmlands are in close proximity. In such communities, unrelated neighbors are under the least social control in their relations with one another and proximity is a predictor of conflict. Hierarchy does not operate to any significant degree (in the absence of patron-client relations), and the general authority of kinship is weak as it cannot be extended beyond kin relations. Just as in the previously noted higher incidence of possession among tenant-clients belonging to different patron-landlords, nonkin neighbors interact within a social context that does not provide strong institutional control over their relations. Structural equality means that their interests tend to clash.

It is here, within the least ordered of village relationships, that spirit possession is most common. Conflict leading to the accusation of possession occurs most frequently where villagers rub elbows regularly but without the regulation of highly specific social prescriptions and restraints. In this regard, it is interesting to note Mary Douglas's argument that witchcraft is associated with the inarticulate, unstructured, and ambiguous areas of society. She sees it as serving to clarify social definition.[15] Furthermore, among the Azande in Africa witchcraft does not occur between the noble and commoner classes nor among kin, but it is likely to occur among the commoners and between unrelated neighbors.[16] In a Mysore village, witchcraft is unlikely to occur among the vertical intercaste and patron-client relationships, but it is apt to occur among members of the same caste.[17]

CONFLICT WITHIN THE VILLAGE

It is also significant that possession by *ikiryo* and animal spirits occurs primarily within, not between, villages. During times of drought, intervillage conflicts concerning water rights have been frequent in the Japanese countryside and persons of different villages often have quarrels. But they pursue these conflicts openly and with little restraint. Members of the same village, on the other hand, are under heavy constraint because of their common membership in the village. They have few and very limited ways to express their antipathy. Inside a village, unity is always stressed, and the weight of the complex interweaving of social relationships reinforces this ideal. The combination serves to suppress the open expression of conflict. Tensions lie below the surface, feelings run deep, grudges persist, but the surface of relations is managed to exhibit harmony. The opposite is true in intervillage conflict. In fact, the open expression of conflict between villages tends to reinforce the internal solidarity of each village.

THE COMPLEX OF TRAITS

In summary, then, spirit possession is not likely to occur within a family context, nor among kin, nor among households ordered by vertical ties, nor between people who can hate and quarrel openly. It is most likely to occur between families and individuals who interact often, have interests that compete, and thus accumulate reasons to hate and envy each other, yet must outwardly act as cooperative neighbors. This segment of village society is one of proximity filled with friction, a state common to villages the world over. That possession occurs here should be no surprise. What distinguishes Japanese villages appears to be the power of internal institutional controls limiting the generation of conflict in certain relationships and the power of the ideology of village solidarity to suppress the expression of hostility between the rest. Social conflict, tension, and all sorts of antipathies when suppressed by social norms create the conditions for an active pattern of spirit possession, a classic example of emotional projection. The only other necessary condition is an active belief in possession and in many instances an identifiable group of spirit holders. Many areas of Japan lack this most basic precondition for some unknown historical reason and, of course, the entire complex cannot develop in the modern urban context except under unusual circumstances.

The Social Functions of Spirit Possession

As we saw in one of our illustrative cases, accusations of spirit possession can create further tension and conflict in a village. Relations between holders and nonholders are often marked by avoidance and strain. Traditionally, nonholders avoided buying houses or arable lands owned by holders, because they were afraid of becoming holders by association. In this and many other ways the beliefs in spirit possession constituted barriers to a smoothly operating society and from an early date authorities tried to abolish these folk beliefs. Historical records indicate that a lord of Matsue-Han announced publicly in 1791, "Belief in *hito-gitsune* (man-fox) is a fallacy, and the notion that 'foxes' come along with the transmission of the house and lands from fox holders to people is wrong." In 1907 the Committee of Education in Shimane prefecture stated that "beliefs in spirit possession should be abandoned in order to abolish the taboo against marriage with spirit holders." In 1947, in order to erase the same marriage taboo, all members of a certain village got together in the shrine of their *ujigami* (tutelary god) and swore not to discriminate against spirit holders concerning marriage. Those who assembled in the shrine included both spirit holders and others. After the meeting in the shrine they all drank sake together to cement the pact. But the expenses for the feast were voluntarily paid by the fox holders alone.

All such efforts over two hundred years have been unsuccessful in abolishing the marriage taboo.[18] According to Ishizuka, the ratio of intermarriages between animal-spirit holders ("black") and others ("white") in four selected villages in Kōchi and Shimane prefectures was only 5 to 7 percent.[19] Animal-spirit holders often told me of their feeling of resentment against nonholders with respect to the marriage taboo. They said, "We always have trouble finding spouses for our children." When they cannot find spouses for their children within the group of animal-spirit holders in their own village, they search among spirit holders in neighboring areas. This problem, which occurs regularly, is itself a source of division, tension, and subsurface hostility within the community. Victor Turner says that witchcraft beliefs "feed back into the social process, generating tensions as often as 'reflecting' them."[20] They also affect the way social tensions are repressed and give added dynamic to the times when they surface.

In instances of intermarriage the nonholder's parents and relatives usually terminate kin relations in order to defend themselves against the contamination. In villages where mutual aid and cooperation in subsistence and other activities are carried out between kin, this act constitutes a significant disruption of the basic patterns of social support and interdependence. It is difficult for people to make a living without the help of kin. This termination of kin relations, called *en-giri,* is found in all the villages under consideration. Thus the marriage prohibition and the practice of *en-giri* create further conflict and antipathy between the two sides.

The division between animal-spirit holders and others can also become the basis for political divisions, both in elections and in other political activities. In 1976 in one village in Shimane prefecture, for example, a proposal to sell communal lands to a developer hoping to make a golf course was led by a prominent patron-landlord, a fox-spirit holder. The group opposed to selling the land was led by the village's other leading patron-landlord, a man who is not a fox-spirit holder. The groups divided rather clearly between holders and non-holders, and the event seems to have reinforced the cleavage between the two groups. The schism centering on spirit possession can readily be mobilized to reinforce other social divisions and exacerbate other kinds of conflict.

Spirit possession and animal-spirit holding have, it is clear, many dysfunctional aspects as far as individuals, households, and entire villages are concerned. The divisiveness it contributes to overall village relations undermines certain forms of cooperation and adds to the general level of interpersonal tension.

Yet spirit possession and spirit holding may also serve positive functions. As we have observed, spirit possession is most likely to occur either between unrelated neighbors or between villagers of the same social stratum, since serious conflicts are most likely to arise from the tensions and frictions within these relationships lying in the "soft" or least structured part of the community. Clearly, since it is believed that arousing the envy or resentment of animal-spirit holders can lead to being possessed by their spirits, most people try to conduct themselves in ways that do not provoke the envy, resentment, or anger of holders. Belief in spirit possession constrains social conflict, we must presume. To villagers it is wise to live in an inconspicuous manner, since the undue display of wealth or success is taken as a sign of greediness and punished by the spirits of envious spirit holders. Openly stepping above one's peers is a dangerous move. Generally speaking, those most likely to be possessed are nonconformists to the village norms.

Furthermore, the fear of accusation is a form of constraint on spirit holders. Women are believed to be more likely to possess people than men, and the kind of woman who is judged most likely to do so is viewed as envious, obstinate, unyielding, and aggressive. Such personality traits all deviate from the village standard. Women fear being suspected of having an active possessing spirit and though open accusations are rare and narrow in focus, the general constraint on female behavior is real. In a village in Kōchi prefecture, to go further, it is believed that an exorcism ritual can cause the death of the person whose *ikiryo* has possessed someone.[21] Such beliefs certainly oblige women holders to behave in a proper and friendly manner with their fellow villagers, especially those who are otherwise unrelated in a significant way.

Spirit possession can thus be interpreted as a mechanism for the reaffirmation of traditional norms and roles. Here we find much that parallels the functional analysis of witchcraft in Africa. Mary Douglas argues, for example, that "witchcraft beliefs are essentially a means of clarifying and affirming social definition."[22] Certainly Japanese spirit possession buttresses conventional social definitions, particularly in the less clearly defined part of village social structure.[23]

Nor can the continuity of belief in spirit possession in Japanese villages be fully understood without considering how they contribute to the social cohesion of the community. At times, such beliefs do generate further conflict, but on the whole they constitute a threat that inhibits conflict and thus contributes to the maintenance of order in villages, at least on the surface of their daily affairs. The threat is part of a cosmological order that envisions retribution for acts contrary to village solidarity and conformity but does not assume the source of retribution to be a distant omnipotent force. Nor is a clearly targeted evil agent the cause of damage and fear.

It is fascinating to compare Japanese spirit beliefs with Western notions of evil in this regard. Unlike the Western concept of a fallen god or spirit like Satan, Japanese conceive the source of evil to be located in the human social world. The ultimate source of evil is, of course, the animal spirits, but they become active only when their masters feel envy, resentment, and other strongly negative emotions aimed at others. Neither human nature nor nature itself is immutably good or bad or caught in a struggle between such forces. Rather, for Japanese living in their tight communities, hell is oneself and one's fellow villagers.

It is especially notable here that possession is not a willed product of human creation. It results from relationships and emotions inconsistent with the ideal of village harmony. Evil is *potential* in feelings and relationships, and it is located in relations *between* holders and nonholders. Animal-spirit holders are not evil per se. "Hell is our animals," they complain, and there are many instances where holders have built *inari* (fox) shrines in their yards or made other devices in order to tame, satisfy, and thus control their animals, rendering them unable to work evil. Where beliefs in *ikiryo* possession prevail, it seems "hell is ourselves" to villagers because the *ikiryo* spirits of all community members (excepting children) are believed to have the potential to possess people. The social and cosmological arrangements of spirit holding and possession center on the village community, reflecting its tensions and structure and causing its members to wish for and strive for better relations. The portrait I have drawn, however, is one far from the picture of solidarity and harmony that emerges from a comparison of surface behavior between Japanese villages and those of other countries.

It should be clear, however, that spirit possession itself is not what Coser has in mind by the term social conflict. As he states, "Social conflict always denotes social interaction."[24] For the same reason spirit possession does not fit Coser's category of "nonrealistic conflict" either, since it is a mystical attack on another operating strictly on the belief level. It does not involve tangible social interaction between the parties, although it does retroactively refer to past conflict. The animal-spirit holder is believed to possess others without even knowing it. Spirit aggression is not consciously initiated. The animal spirits are thought to work in sympathy with the feeling of their master, but human direction is not assumed. In all of this, the character of the Japanese psychology of conflict in face-to-face groups can perhaps be perceived as it vents hostilities in ways that are vague, indirect, and even convoluted to the point of being self-directed.

The Question of Origins

The earliest record of dog-spirit holders *(inugami-mochi)* appears in 1666, and documents in the San'in region indicate that the notion of fox-spirit holders *(kitsune-mochi)* dates back to around 1786. Although there is no clear historical evidence to explain the origins of animal-spirit holding in villages, several theories have been advanced. The first argues that faith healers of one kind or another who used mystical powers including fox spirits for divination and the curing of illness eventually became taken locally as fox-spirit holders. They were increasingly feared for their use of magic for evil purposes. A second theory holds that newcomers to villages in the middle of the Edo era who became economically powerful in the locality were accused of being fox-spirit holders by the village's earlier inhabitants because the prosperous newcomers were both a serious threat to them and a target of envy.

These two theories are not necessarily exclusive. My own findings indicate that both can be at least partially substantiated. While the founder of fox-spirit holding in one village was a wealthy newcomer in the early seventeenth century, for example, in another the founder of a fox-spirit-holding household was a medium who came from outside and settled there after marrying a woman in the village.[25] In both theories, it is outsiders in one sense or another who are made into spirit holders when they are successful in the village context. In Japanese folk belief, both faith healers and strangers are seen as having magical powers—witness the Ebisu cult focused on strange visitors—and these powers may be benevolent as well as malevolent, depending on the specific context.

Whatever the ultimate origins of beliefs in animal-spirit holding in rural Japan, there is a marked pattern: Villages with this belief have a different social structure than do villages without it. Villages dominated by hierarchical *dozoku* organization rarely have animal-spirit-holding beliefs.[26] *Dozoku*-dominated villages have tightly arranged relationships and less shifting of relative status among households. Villages where animal-spirit holding exists, however, have a great variety of significant social relationships and groups that crosscut and pull against each other. No single relationship or structure dominates the village or all its relationships. Branch households are not established as the tenants of the main house, for example, and stem-branch relationships seldom coincide with landlord-tenant relationships. A certain degree of cohesiveness between stem and branch houses may exist, but stem-branch relationships and groups are not organized into an overarching hierarchy and the genealogical recognition of patrilineal relationships seldom reaches more than three or four generations. In addition, one finds various social functions apportionately among kin, patron-client relations, fictive kinship ties, neighborhoods, religious associations, and age groups as well as endogamous groups, animal-spirit holders, and nonholders. Membership in these groups, and thus loyalties and obligations, are inherently crosscutting. The complexity and fluidity of this type of village seems to explain why it has greater structural tension and is more susceptible to interpersonal and intergroup friction and conflict. We have documented the fact of more frequent friction and conflict between factions in these villages compared to the standard *dozoku* village,[27] and it should be no surprise that spirit possession is also common in them.

Moreover, in villages where spirit holding is said to exist (primarily in the Kanto and southwestern regions) we find more mobility in both residence (horizontal) and status (vertical) terms. The rise and fall of socioeconomic status has been relatively frequent over the last hundred or more years. Ecological conditions—steep mountains, rocks, bad soil—have enhanced social mobility because villagers are unable to practice the stable cultivation of wet rice. Farmers in these areas have had to depend on wheat, beans, and root crops, and they have engaged in the manufacturing of mulberry tree paper and in sericulture. Sericulture, the production of raw silk by raising silkworms, is a notably unstable economic activity. During the last years of the Edo era, sericulture became popular in Shimane, for example, and, supported by the policy of the Meiji government, it flourished in one closely studied village until the 1950s. Villagers themselves recognize that the rise and fall of socioeconomic status among households was due largely to the economically unstable nature of sericulture. Such vertical mobility and shifting economic fortunes undoubtedly was a major source of social conflict, envy, jealousy, and hatred among villagers.[28] My hypothesis is that spirit possession beliefs, social structure, economic instability, and various kinds of mobility are all closely interrelated in the history of rural Japan. Social conflict and its reception or regression in the village context is at the center of this complex.

As Kunio Yanagida remarked some twenty years ago,[29] belief in spirit possession and animal-spirit holding in Japan is not only a local and regional phenomenon of interest to folklorists and scholars of folk religion; it is a topic important to the study of Japanese society and culture in general. Its relationship with social conflict in tightly arranged communities is particularly revealing in this respect.

NOTES

I wish to thank Thomas P. Rohlen, Pat Steinhoff, and Ellis Krauss for providing me with the opportunity to participate in the workshop "Conflict and Conflict Resolution in Japan" and to present this paper to the meetings. I am particularly grateful to Thomas P. Rohlen for revising the English and supplying valuable comments. I also wish to thank Hitoshi Ueda, Koichi Maruyama, Fujiko Ueda, Emiko Namihira, and Sakumi Itabashi, who participated in my fieldwork in Japanese villages and helped me collect other data. The material used in this study is based on fieldwork begun in 1960 and financially supported by grants from the Scientific Research Fund of the Japanese Ministry of Education, the Wenner-Gren Foundation, and the Research Institute of Comparative Education and Culture, Kyushu University, to which grateful acknowledgment is made.

1. R. Firth, "Problems and Assumptions in an Anthropological Study of Religion," *Journal of the Royal Anthropological Institute* 89 (1959): 129–148.

2. Teigo Yoshida, "Spirit Possession and Kinship," *East Asian Cultural Studies* 11 (1972): 45–46.

3. Y. Hayami, *Tsukimono-mochi Meishin* (Tokyo: Hakurin Shobo, 1957).

4. L. Coser, *The Functions of Social Conflict* (New York: Free Press, 1964), p. 49.

5. Teigo Yoshida, "Seinan Nihon Sonraku ni okeru Chitsujo to Henbo," *Research Bulletin of the Faculty of Education, Kyushu University* 18 (1967).

6. Ibid., p. 251.

7. S. Itabashi, "Gunma Ken no Ichi Sonraku ni okeru Tsukimono to Shakai Kozo," master's thesis, Department of Cultural Anthropology, University of Tokyo, 1975.

8. Ibid.

9. Teigo Yoshida and H. Ueda, "Tsukimono Gensho to Shakai Kozo," *Research Bulletin of the Faculty of Education, Kyushu University* 14 (1969): 0–0.

10. Ronald P. Dore, *City Life in Japan* (Berkeley and Los Angeles: University of California Press, 1958), p. 155.

11. Yoshida, "Seinan Nihon Sonraku."

12. S. Epstein, "A Sociological Analysis of Witch Beliefs in a Mysore Village," in J. Middleton, ed., *Magic, Witchcraft and Curing* (Garden City: Natural History Press, 1967); see also E. E. Evans-Pritchard, *Witchcraft, Oracles and Magic Among the Azande* (Oxford: Clarendon Press, 1937), pp. 104–105.

13. Teigo Yoshida, "Social Conflict and Cohesion in a Japanese Rural Community," *Ethnology* 3 (1964): 219–231.

14. Teigo Yoshida, K. Karuyama, and E. Namihira, "Technological and Social Changes in a Japanese Fishing Village," *Journal of Asian and African Studies* 9 (1974): 1–16.

15. M. Douglas, *Purity and Danger* (Harmondsworth: Penguin Books, 1970), p. 124.

16. Evans-Pritchard, *Witchcraft, Oracles and Magic.*

17. Epstein, "Sociological Analysis."

18. Hayami, *Tsukimono-mochi Meishin.*

19. T. Ishizuka, *Nihon no Tsukimono* (Tokyo: Miraisha, 1959), p. 134.

20. V. Turner, *The Forest of Symbols* (Ithaca and London: Cornell University Press, 1967), p. 144.

21. Yoshida, "Seinan Nihon Sonraku."

22. M. Douglas, ed., *Witchcraft, Confessions and Accusations* (London: Tavistock, 1970), p. xxx.

23. J. Beattie, *Other Cultures* (London: Cohen and West, 1964), pp. 208–209.

24. Coser, *The Functions of Social Conflict,* p. 38.

25. Teigo Yoshida, *Nihon no Tsukimono* (Tokyo: Chuokoron-sha, 1970); Teigo Yoshida, "The Stranger as God: The Place of the Outsider in Japanese Folk Religion," *Ethnology* 20 (1981): 87–99.

26. Keith Brown, "The Content of Dozoku Relationships in Japan," *Ethnology* 7 (1968): 113–138.

27. Teigo Yoshida and H. Ueda, "Spirit Possession and Social Structure in Southwestern Japan," *Proceedings, VIIIth International Congress of Anthropological and Ethnological Sciences* (Tokyo, 1968).

28. Itabashi, "Gunma Ken no Ichi Sonraku."

29. Kunio Yanagita, "Jobun," in Y. Hayami, *Tsukimono-mochi Meishin* (Tokyo: Hakurin Shobo, 1957).

PART III:

Conflict in Movements
and Organizations:
Labor, Education,
and Women

6
Conflict and Its Resolution in Industrial Relations and Labor Law

TADASHI HANAMI

The world of Japanese industrial relations has two faces. One is its highly developed capacity for cooperation between labor and management; the other is its character when disputes arise and cannot be settled by the conventional means.

Much emphasis has been given to the harmonious face of Japanese industrial relations in English literature, and Westerners, including specialists in Japanese society, generally hold the image of Japanese employees as loyal and obedient to their employers and see Japanese enterprise unions as cooperative with management. Both images are, of course, encouraged by Western managers, government officials, and even trade unionists who admire the tremendous success of the Japanese economy in recent years and attribute part of that success to harmonious industrial relations. We can also say that the image of harmonious industrial relations is a product of the comparison with the more adversarial activities of the Western labor arena. Finally, nostalgic appreciation of traditional Japanese culture and customs and the incorrect impression that traditional Japanese society was inherently consensual has been coupled with an ideological alienation from troubled industrialized society in the Western world to produce an excessively rosy picture of the situation in Japan.

Japanese society too is now highly industrialized. It has problems common to such societies: pollution, overpopulated cities, mass culture, and so forth. Labor disputes do indeed exist in Japanese industrial relations, and Westerners who look closely will find many cases of serious troubles and disputes in which company facilities are pasted with union posters, the red flags of unions are hoisted on top of company buildings, and company premises are occupied by union members. Crippling strikes in public transportation (including the National Railways, in which strikes are prohibited by law) occur like clockwork every spring when waves of strikes in many industries are staged as part of a campaign called *shuntō* ("spring wage offensive"). Postal workers and teachers in public schools, who are also prohibited from striking, regularly engage in a variety of actions including slow-downs and large-scale leave-taking.

Yet statistics reveal that the number of working days lost due to labor disputes per number of employed workers is smaller in Japan than in the major industrialized countries of the West. The mere international comparison of statistical figures concerning labor disputes, however, can be a cause of serious misunderstanding. Recent work in this field indicates that certain reservations and modifications are needed before meaningful conclusions can be drawn from international statistics.[1] Countries use different ways of measuring labor conflict, and even the ILO's data concern only some parts of the many forms of worker protest. In this essay, I seek to set out the salient characteristics of industrial conflict in Japan in order to frame the reality of Japanese industrial relations. My goal is to help Western readers see both faces and appreciate that they actually are part of a single pattern.

Characteristics of Labor Disputes in Japan

In 1960 Ross and Hartman published their international comparisons of strike participation rates and lengths of strike duration.[2] According to them, participation rates are low and strike duration is long in certain Scandinavian countries, Canada, and the United States; the participation rate is low and strike duration is short in West Germany, Holland, the United Kingdom, and Denmark; and the participation rate is high and strike duration is short in France, Italy, and certain Asian countries, including Japan. In recent years strike duration in European countries has tended to become shorter; today the levels in France, West Germany, and Italy are almost the same as in Japan. One can no longer contend, therefore, that strikes in Japan are shorter in duration than in Western countries in general. The trend toward shorter strikes in Europe may be partly attributable to the growing number of wildcat strikes and to the shift of disputes from the industrial to the enterprise level.[3] But the important point is that in Japan the short average duration of strikes has been a persistent pattern. Why? Because the classic notion found throughout Western industrial relations that the strike is the crucial and ultimate weapon of labor negotiations never developed in Japan. Especially in Britain, Germany, and the United States, the strike has been regarded traditionally as the weapon to be invoked after the possibilities of bargaining have been exhausted.

Recently there has been a change in the meaning of strikes in the West. K. G. J. C. Knowles writes: "Yesterday they were battles; today few of them are more than protest demonstrations."[4] Although the present-day strike may have become essentially a demonstration, it also means, as Abraham Siegel points out, that " 'sporadic' . . . and spontaneous strikes give way to the new-fashioned strike which has become 'enlightened, orderly, bureaucratic' . . . almost chivalrous in its tactics and cold-blooded in its calculatedness."[5] If it results from unemotional and cool calculation, a strike tends to be deferred as long as a possibility of peaceful negotiation exists. Thus in Western countries a strike can be considered an ultimate weapon in the sense that workers do not go on strike and companies do not declare a lockout until several bargaining sessions have been held and both parties realize that further conciliation is impossible.[6] English-speaking nations commonly refer to a strike as a "walkout," reflecting the fact that workers usually leave the job site and do not return until the dispute is settled.

In Japan strikes rarely continue more than a few days. One-hour or two-hour strikes are not unusual. Even in the case of a long dispute, the union may repeat many waves of short strikes. That is, workers may go on strike and return to work without any settlement of an issue. A strike, then, does not mark the final stage of negotiations; rather it is often a starting point. Unions in Japan go on strike even before negotiations begin as a means of initiating serious talks. It is not unusual, especially in small enterprises, for the employers not to know why the union is striking. In extreme cases, unions even go on strike to celebrate the establishment of their organization. A Japanese strike is also different from the West in that the strike is rarely a walkout. It is usually a "walkin." During strikes, union members usually stay in the working place and hold meetings or engage in various union activities.

Strikes are regarded as demonstrations of the workers' will or readiness to fight. They are designed to attract the employer's attention. It is not necessary for strikes to continue until the employer is forced to agree to the union's demands. Strikes as walkouts would not fit this goal of initiating and encouraging negotiations. Rather union members need to be present at the workplace and engaged in various activities.

This point leads to another characteristic of industrial relations in Japan. In Western countries a strike is the most typical form of industrial action. Other kinds of action, except picketing and perhaps boycotting, are rather exceptional. Sit-down strikes do occur occasionally in Western countries, but they remain little more than symbols of the world unrest in the 1930s. In most countries they are illegal,[7] although in the 1960s the "sit-in" or "*gherao* tactics" (nonviolence as practiced by Gandhi in India) emerged in Britain, France, and Italy.[8] Except in France and Italy, the strike is so central that the term "acts of dispute" is used infrequently in industrial relations. This right to perform acts of dispute is always referred to as "the right to strike." In Japan the terms "acts of dispute" and "right to perform acts of dispute" are used more frequently. The strike is neither the most typical nor the most important act of Japanese labor dispute. In fact, Japan is most remarkable in the variety of acts of dispute that occur there daily. If we look at the history of the European labor movement, we can, of course, find a variety of acts of dispute in Germany and in English-speaking countries. But, at present, disputes for the most part are limited to strikes, picketing, boycotts, and lockouts. Slowdowns and work-to-rule actions are the rare exceptions.[9] In Japan, many acts of dispute, besides the strike, are used frequently. Any act that might effectively shock employers and arouse their attention as well as that of the public will accomplish the purpose. The strike is only one such tool.

Slowdowns and work-to-rule actions are not only common but legal according to most court decisions. The same is true of partial strikes. Refusal to perform part of a job or refusal to follow certain orders are two tactics frequently used in disputes. Disobedience is both a common act of dispute and one regarded as legal. Pasting up posters inside the workplace, taking vacations for the purpose of disruption, refusing to turn over money collected from customers to the company, seizing car keys or tires in trucking and taxi industries, and so forth are examples of actions frequently used in disputes. Unions may commit more malicious acts when their relations with management became hostile. They often paste posters all over the walls and windows of the company, attacking management and reviling executives personally. Picketing may be carried out in such a way as to block traffic near the company with union members standing arm in arm shouting insults in almost deafening tones at those passing by.

Violence and threats of violence occur not only on the picket lines but also at bargaining sessions. Union members will sometimes force management personnel to stay in the bargaining room against their will, surrounding them with a crowd of hostile workers. Through loud threats and incessant noise, management is often forced to accept union's demands against its will. In recent years such extreme cases have become infrequent, especially in large enterprises, but they still happen in small enterprises and are a potential threat in large enterprises if a serious conflict arises. Most frequently conflicts of this magnitude occur in cases of collective dismissal caused by a business crisis.[10]

Reasons for Violence and Recklessness Among Unions

The labor movement, even in Western countries, has a legacy of violence. Nevertheless, violence is hardly considered intrinsic and essential to contemporary industrial relations. This is certainly the case in collective bargaining. As a general rule, a union's bargaining power depends on (1) how many workers are organized in a particular labor market or in a particular enterprise; (2) the extent to which the union can hurt the employer's business when it goes on strike; (3) how long the union can support its members during a walkout; and (4) how well the union can control its members during a strike so that they will not break rank under pressure. If a union has great resources or power in these terms, it need send only a single representative to meet with management to submit its demands and communicate its readiness to strike if not satisfied with management's response. If a union is weak in resources, it is necessary to send many workers who threaten, shout, and upbraid management in an effort to force capitulation. Arm's-length methods will not work. Clearly it is a sign of union weakness in Japan that the strike so often takes the latter form. If unions could organize a majority of the workers in an enterprise and control them to avoid strikebreaking, they would not have to picket en masse, occupy plants, and apply other pressure tactics and harassment.

By international standards, Japanese unions are rather weak. As has been noted, that they are enterprise-based rather than industrywide in nature explains much of their weakness. Enterprise-based unions are especially sensitive to the business fortunes of the company in which they exist. The union's leadership is often white-collar and many are ultimately promoted to management, a prospect that causes many leaders to be very cautious. It is also true that Japanese unions generally have weak financial positions.

Sit-downs and the occupation of company premises during a strike are also at least partly explained by the particular character of enterprise unionism. The company is the union's only real domain. Its activities are conducted on company premises. Even the typical location of the union office is within the company's office building. This seems symbolically proper to many unionists. Enterprise unions want to have their members within the company's facilities, and the frequency of slowdowns, partial strikes, refusal to do certain jobs, work-to-rule actions, and the like reflect the same basic attitude. All these actions are taken within the workplace and without totally abandoning work itself. Such acts also fit the typically poor state of union finance, since members can claim at least part of their wages. If the purpose of dispute actions is to shock and annoy management, not to press management economically, why should unions risk losing all wages? It is natural that they prefer acts they can carry out while members still receive some wages.

More basic reasons for the miscellany of dispute actions lie in the characteristics of the Japanese employee/employer relationship. Because of the lifetime employment system, Japanese employees have a comparatively strong enterprise consciousness and loyalty toward the firm. Employees are usually given powerful incentives to identify with their firm, and, in fact, most firms resemble closed social groups analogous to households. Company members are destined to experience if not "total emotional participation in the group" then at least a quite powerful personal identification with it.[11] Conflict is not expected in such groups; it is expected that a group member's dissatisfaction should be understood by others without having to be expressed explicitly. In such a personal relationship a person who expresses dissatisfaction openly and raises demands explicitly will be disapproved of as a poor group member. In Japanese society ordinary people feel "awkward" and hesitant in asking for things even when they are fully entitled to them.[12] Ideally, a subtle process of adjustment initiated by the superior party should resolve problems. Obviously this is just an ideal. In such a situation within the enterprise "family," one in which employees hesitate to ask even for what they are entitled to, it takes great courage to ask for a wage increase or better working conditions that are not contractually promised. Just to raise demands and gain attention in some firms, workers need to destroy the daily personal relationship and normal atmosphere within their company. The employers, especially small enterprises, often complain that the employees who enter union activities used to be very polite "nice guys" but suddenly changed in character and became rude after they started participating in union activities. In order to destroy the day-by-day harmonious relationship of the enterprise family, union leaders assume a rude, inhuman, and even violent attitude and go on to stage unnecessarily reckless actions. Wearing armbands and headbands, hoisting flags, pasting up posters, attacking management people personally—all these rather childish actions make sense if viewed as a means to change the atmosphere of the enterprise "family."

Such a sudden change is found not only in the attitudes of individuals who become union activists but also among cooperative, enterprise-conscious unions that adopt a militant radical posture. Most enterprise unions enjoy a relationship of mutual understanding and harmony with management in companies with a stable union-management relationship marked by a well-organized and established union that has been fully accepted by management. Once such a steady and harmonious relationship between union and management is undermined, however, by accident, by the intent of either side, or by a crisis in the business, a real confrontation emerges and the union starts to behave recklessly and sometimes violently. Even in the case of large enterprises with good union-management relations there is always the possibility of a sudden emergence of real confrontation. As the individual employee's attitude toward an employer can shift from polite and respectful intimacy to vile rudeness, so the union's attitude to management can also change from amicable partnership to intense hostility. As Simmel has pointed out, the greater the degree of normal intimacy the greater the potential for fierce conflict.

Rights, Obligations, and Contracts

The ideal relationship between employees and employers in Japan is akin to the traditional one among family members. No notion of rights and obligations in the Western sense has developed. The employee/employer relationship, as well as all contractual relationships in the labor field, lack clearly defined obligations and rights. In Japan economic arrangements are often conducted without the aid of a written contract, and when contracts are written they are simple and their provisions are abstract, general, and vague.

The abstractness and vagueness of Japanese contracts is based on the presumption that the parties to the contract have, or will have, a close personal relationship and can rely on mutual understanding and trust. Westerners consider it important to describe in precise and detailed terms the standards to be applied in every possible disagreement. They feel it is best to prepare the ground to settle conflicts before they occur by presenting a complete description of the rights and obligations of both parties. Japanese, on the other hand, think it is both impossible and unnecessary to provide such an extensive written description. They believe that despite very detailed clauses in a contract, unanticipated developments are bound to occur and that it is more important to establish mutual understanding and trust. Only on the basis of such understanding, Japanese believe, can disagreements successfully be resolved. Since economic deals in Japan are affected by emotion and sentiment, parties to a contract always expect some flexibility in its implementation. The detailed enumeration of specific provisions, from their perspective, is fatal to the important quality of flexibility.[13]

Instead of enumerating detailed and precise provisions, most Japanese contracts call for "consultation in good faith" or for "amicable consideration" with typical phrasing like "should disagreement arise, both parties will consult each other in good faith." Japanese contracts do not specify resolution processes applicable to all possible disagreements. The reluctance to have rights and obligations clearly defined is found not only in the individual relationship between employee and employer but also between unions and management. In this sense the latter relationship does not differ markedly from business contracts in general.

There have been cases, however, of unions going on strike when consultations failed and labor and management could not agree on the interpretation of a contractual clause that, despite its vagueness, had been accepted by both parties when the contract was drawn up. These cases resulted in the dismissal of the union leaders on the grounds they broke the contract. Subsequently, however, the courts rejected the employers' claims on the grounds that the ambiguity of the contract's wording made it technically impossible to break the contract.[14]

In most Western countries, an implicit or explicit "no strike" clause guarantees that both parties will respect the content of the agreement and will not go on strike or stage lockouts during the term of the contract,[15] but in Japan the signing of a collective agreement does not necessarily result in peaceful relations. Even in industries in which strong, mature unions regularly sign collective agreements with management, the rights and obligations of both parties remain so vague and uncertain as to make "consultation in good faith" and "settling things amicably" a critical implicit provision of the contract. If such consultations fail, and under various conditions this is possible, unions will go on strike, and mutual trust and understanding falter. When that happens, the contract's intent is void and negotiations become difficult. From this point on unions become reckless, and violent acts of dispute may occur. Employers often then dismiss the union's leaders for being responsible for such activities or for breach of contract.

The overall processes by which conflicts arise and are resolved in Japanese labor relations are themselves rather different from those of the West. The differences fit together in a distinct pattern. If we envision the variety within labor-management relations arranged along a continuum beginning with the normative state of full cooperation and ending with a state of total abrogation, then we have established a yardstick along which the processes of conflict and its resolution move relationships. I will outline the crucial stages and turning points that typify the Japanese situation.

In enterprises in which unions are recognized and agreements are concluded between union and employers, labor-management relations are fairly smooth. This is our starting point in examining the processes by which other states are generated. A climate of collusion *(nareai)* between the employers and the union representing the majority of employees is the essential quality. *Nareai* is a feeling of emotional intimacy between persons outside the kinship group. Basically the relationship is one of patronage and dependence, though the unions frequently put on an outward show of radical militancy in their utterances and behavior. This state is idealized both in Japanese culture and in the public pronouncements of company managers.

Because the unions are enterprise-based and represent the employees of a particular firm, their activities are conducted principally within the confines of that enterprise. The unions are, therefore, dependent on the privileges granted them by management, in the form of office space in company buildings, meeting rooms, telephones, furniture, stationery, and photocopy services. These facilities, provided free of charge by the companies, symbolize the intimacy of their relationship with the unions. It is not unusual to find full-time union officials being paid by the company management, and the practice of granting employees leaves of absence for union activities is common. Such extensive privileges are found more frequently in the larger enterprises, where it may be said without exaggeration that the unions function at the company's expense. This will undoubtedly sound strange to anyone familiar with trade unions in the West and their fierce independence from management.

Japanese consciousness produces a tendency to settle conflicts by mutual understanding and to regard all disputes as problems to be resolved within a restricted circle. Disagreements and grievances are supposed to be solved amicably *(nashi-kuzushi)*. Patience and forbearance are at a premium. Solving problems by *nashi-kuzushi* is often little more than softening their impact and postponing substantive deliberations since subordinates are not supposed to express disagreement or state grievances openly. They are expected to endure hardship in anticipation of the benevolent consideration by a superior. Should disagreements and grievances eventually be made public, the parties defer to each other and settle matters through "emotional understanding" or by "letting the dispute flow to the water." This uniquely Japanese attitude allows disputes to be settled in a natural way with the passage of time, without introducing positive artificial action by a human agency.

An important drawback to this amicable method of settling disputes is that no rules exist to regulate the conduct of both parties except the concept of amicable mutual understanding. Thus when the mutual trust inherent in this emotional relationship is lost, disputes erupt and become difficult to manage. The relationship moves to another state as trust declines.

At this early point, various kinds of conciliation are possible, including the rise of mutually trusted third parties. The third party is usually someone who is respected by both parties or can be said to "have face" *(kao ga kiku)* with both. In most cases, this person will be someone who is influential in the small circle to which both parties belong. Conciliation or arbitration usually takes the form of an attempt to "save the face" *(kao o tateru)* of this influential person and to entrust *(azukeru)* the dispute to him. He is not expected to settle the matter in accordance with reason or a universal standard. He does not necessarily make clear-cut decisions about who is wrong or right, nor does he inquire into the respective rights and obligations of the parties. The objective is to settle the dispute in such a way as to restore and maintain the friendly personal relations within the small society involved. Dispute settlement of this kind is certainly not unique to Japanese society but is also found in other non-Western societies that attach great value to kinship and community relations and where harmony, or the absence of conflict, is highly prized.[16] It is also the major form of conciliation in marriage counseling and the like in Western societies.

The effectiveness of this method of dispute settlement depends on the third party's prestige and on the degree of trust that both disputants are willing to place in him. Nothing better illustrates this than the fact that both parties often say that although they are not satisfied with the go-between's solution, they will abide by it in order to save the face of the third party. The social relational context again provides the critical ingredients: trust, obligation, and face.

Government agencies often serve as this third party intermediary in labor disputes. There are two reasons for this. It is very difficult to find a private person who can command enough power and prestige to be respected by both parties in industrial relations, especially when they have a strong antagonism for each other. They will respect the government, however, because of the strong tradition of government authority among Japanese. The second reason is related to the problem of accessibility and availability of dispute-settlement institutions. In civil cases the courts play an important role in solving cases by means of reconciliation,[17] but this is possible only after one of the parties has brought the case to litigation. Ordinary Japanese, however, are more reluctant than Westerners to go to court for civil disputes since litigation is regarded as a challenge to the assumption of an amicable personal friendship. In cases of industrial dispute, another governmental dispute-settlement institution is available, namely the labor relations commission (LRC) system. The remarkable feature of this institution is that it is a tripartite body. Each commission consists of an equal number of commissioners representing the public, labor, and employers. Thus disputing parties feel that access to the commission is easier than to the courts. Almost all severe labor disputes are handled by the labor relations commission; the private arbitration system, which plays an important role in American industrial relations, is negligible in Japan.

The LRC provides a type of conciliation: mediation and arbitration based on the Western model. Since the principles on which this system is based are Western, the parties are reluctant to seek settlement by this body, which is unfamiliar and not consistent with traditional Japanese dispute settlement. They seek settlement by the LRC only after their relationship and mutual trust have been so damaged that amicable settlement following traditional processes has become impossible. If they use the LRC they prefer conciliation rather than mediation or arbitration. In 1976, out of 1,270 cases of dispute settlement handled by the LRC, 1,241 were conciliation cases, while 26 were mediation and only 3 involved arbitration.[18] Note that conciliation is the most informal method, the one closest to the traditional approach, and arbitration is the furthest removed. In the case of mediation, it is the usual practice for the LRC to submit its proposal only after both parties have reached an understanding. Kaoru Ōta, the former president of Sōhyō (General Council of Labor Unions), described one dispute settlement at the Central LRC involving Hajime Maeda, then chairman of Nikkeiren (Japanese Employers' Association). Both were members of the Central LRC.

> My talk with Mr. Maeda was carried out completely without data. . . . On the day before the scheduled strike, at the final stage I gave him a figure which I had arrived at only by intuition. Mr. Maeda also quoted a figure which was based on his intuition, in the way horse traders bargain by touching fingers under their sleeves. The Public Member's role was only to present this result wrapped up in a neat package.[19]

Although public members are appointed from among so-called men of knowledge and experience, when it comes to actual conciliation their understanding of the theory of wages or industrial relations does not count. More important is whether both parties can trust them as individual persons, and this depends less on their ability than on their personality. A sarcastic and commonly expressed view of conciliation by the LRC is that "they add both sides and divide by two." That is, the LRC decides the amount of a wage increase by dividing by two the sum of the amount demanded and the amount offered. This view implies a rather casual approach to dispute settlement and one which is similar to the traditional principle of *kenka ryō-seibai* (both disputants are penalized equally). Since settlement by the LRC is not based on theory, however, this approach is as valid as any.

The LRC also has a semijudicial function in unfair labor practice cases, although courts have jurisdiction over legal disputes in industrial relations. The machinery is there, but the number of the adjudication cases handled by the courts and the commissions is surprisingly small in comparison with Western countries. As Table 1 indicates, the ratio of legal cases to the total labor force is much higher in the

TABLE 1   *Labor Adjudication Cases*

Country	Number of Cases		Employed in the Civilian Labor Force (1975)[a] (thousands)	Number of Cases per Thousand Employed
United States				
NLRB	34,569	(1976)[b]	84,783	0.407
Japan				
Commissions			52,230	
Labor Relations	1,417	(1976)[c]		0.027
Legal Courts	2,719	(1976)[d]		0.052
West Germany				
Labor Courts	376,186	(1974)[e]	24,828	1.515

[a] ILO, *Yearbook of Labor Statistics*, 1967.
[b] NLRB, *Annual Report of the NLRB*, 1976.
[c] *Rōdō linkai Nenpō*, 1977.
[d] *Hōsō Jihō* (journal of the Lawyers' Association), vol. 29, no. 7, 1977.
[e] Bundes Ministerium für Arbeit und Sozial Ordnung, *Arbeits- und Sozialstatistik*, 1975.

United States and Germany. In the United States it is about fifteen times higher and in West Germany thirty times higher.

In Japan, precisely because the labor-management relationship depends on trust and goodwill rather than contractual rigor, there is great sensitivity at this stage. The tendency of modern lawyers, particularly in the United Kingdom and the United States, has been to neglect the dynamics of early conciliation in favor of a highly developed system of adjudication.[20] Yet even those who accept the validity of conciliation as a method for settling disputes still look at labor relations and international relations as being exceptions. According to them, disputes in these two areas can be solved neither by legal arguments nor by formal adjudication as fully accepted substitutes for force, strikes, or war.[21]

The guidelines on which the conciliation procedure is based—that is, (1) the reestablishment of a normal relationship rather than the reasonableness of respective claims, (2) the preservation of cooperation and harmony, and (3) the avoidance of an immediate settlement —could usefully be introduced into dispute settlement procedures in Western societies. The traditional methods of conciliation are not always effective in Japan, especially when business conditions are forcing a serious cutback on management.

Insofar as the function of enterprise unions is to maintain and improve the working conditions of employees in a particular enterprise, the unions try not to break down the emotional interpersonal relations within the enterprise but, instead, try to use them to foster industrial relations within the enterprise based on collusion. Should the confrontation between labor and management develop to the point that an amicable settlement based on mutual trust is no longer possible, however, the dispute will continue for a long time and will often deteriorate to the point of violence and brutality.

Most protracted labor disputes in Japan, such as those at the Mitsui Mining Company in 1959 and 1960 and at the Nihon Steel Company's Muroran Plant in 1953, began when the company tried to dismiss large numbers of employees. According to Kaoru Ōta: "A labor dispute over dismissals inevitably develops into a large-scale conflict, since dismissal threatens the union members' very livelihood. It would not be an exaggeration to say that the only serious labor troubles in Japan have occurred in cases involving fights against dismissals."[22]

Large-scale dismissals not only shatter the mutual trust that exists between labor and management but also threaten the very foundation of the enterprise union's existence. This threat arises because unions recruit their members exclusively from among employees of a particular enterprise. The unions, therefore, have no other way of fighting mass dismissals except by total opposition. They often resort to desperate means, which they label "honorable defeat," that are reminiscent of the kamikaze tactics used by the Japanese army during World War II. Despite the high degree of organization in a union and the success of its bargaining, a sudden brutal fight is likely.

The "permanence with possible sudden upheavals" and "patience with internal turmoil," which, according to the psychiatrist Bin Kimura, characterize Japanese personal relations, also explain why labor disputes develop into full-blown upheavals when the limits of endurance are reached. I found this poem in a union report on the dispute at the Kishima Coal Mining Company of 1957:

> Having a common enemy to hate,
> I found it easy
> To talk of money.[23]

This poem clearly illustrates that under normal circumstances, union members find it awkward and difficult to talk of money. Only when employees look upon the company as an enemy can they talk freely about economic demands. Japanese labor relations being what they are, one needs to hate the company in order to confront it in a dispute. Without hate, employees can muster only halfhearted opposition and are soon ready to compromise.

Once the lines are drawn, through a breakdown of trust and communication, the conditions are set for a pattern of dispute evaluation that is typical. First the union strikes and resorts to picketing or occupying the plant to halt production. The company then summons police to disperse the strikers. This move usually fails because in recent years police have been reluctant to get involved in labor disputes. Next the company seeks a court injunction against the workers. The injunctions are often denied because the courts too are reluctant to intervene when the unions are not engaged in violent or destructive actions but are merely occupying a plant peacefully. Finally, a breakaway union is organized. When enough workers secede to join the breakaway organization, the dispute ends with the defeat of the union that started the strike.

Mutual harassment escalates and violence becomes a real possibility. Lacking fixed procedures for coping with hostility, and increasingly angered and frustrated by the sudden shift in the other party's attitude, both sides strike out to injure the other's leadership. The *Asahi Shimbun*, one of the leading newspapers in Japan, reported the following story on 7 February 1972. A union had pasted about four hundred posters on the wall of a company building, protesting the dismissal of several members. The company hired workers to tear off the posters and clean the building and then asked the union to pay the cost of the cleaning work, which amounted to 5,415 yen (about $18.00 at that time). Upon the union's refusal, the company deducted the money from union dues that were collected automatically from the members' wages under a checkoff arrangement. The company gave further notice to the union that they would deduct another 836 yen (about $4.40) for the cost of cleaning another plant that had also been defaced by union posters.

Pasting posters on the walls and windows of company buildings is a common practice of Japanese unions, whenever they wish to attack the "reckless" policies of management or advertise their "modest" demands. The content of the posters often refers, in scurrilous language, to the personal affairs of the company president or other management personnel. These attacks are scrawled on paper of poor quality; and when the company tears the posters down, new ones are pasted up immediately. As a result the buildings become completely defaced by the starch paste. Even though such practices are certainly a nuisance and cause trouble between labor and management, they are so commonplace that they have little news value. Why, therefore, should the newspaper report the incident cited above?

In this instance the management, angered by the union's mischief, demanded reparation for the damage. Generally Japanese employers, unlike their Western counterparts, do not require unions to pay for damages caused by its members. Instead they prefer to dismiss the union leaders (who, in most cases, are employees of the company) who have led unlawful activities. This contrast in the employers' response is found because Western union leaders are usually professionals rather than company employees; rendering dismissal as a means of punishment would be impossible. Japanese employers generally seem to be more interested in maintaining relations with cooperative and loyal employees than in recovering economic losses resulting from union activities. They consider it more beneficial to expel militant union leaders from the enterprise and to encourage obedient union activities than to make an issue of a small amount of money for damages.

In this context, the reaction of management in the aforementioned case appears businesslike and rational. Considering the small amount of damage, however, the steps management took bordered on the malicious; the main intent was to embarrass the union. The aftermath of this incident is striking. The 6 June edition of the *Asahi* related that the union had brought a charge against the director of the company alleging that he had embezzled the union's money. The police reported the case to the prosecutor, but whether or not it was brought to trial was not reported.

It is not at all exceptional in Japanese labor relations for unions to level charges against management. Companies also punish labor leaders by disciplinary measures or charge them with violence and other crimes. In fact, both parties often indulge in emotional confrontations. In small, medium, and large companies, the union's red flags can be seen flying on the top of company buildings. In one instance, a company removed a union flag from the top of a building and threw it into a nearby river. The union took a photograph of the flag drifting in the water and submitted it in court as evidence that management unlawfully interfered with the administration and activities of the union. When management removes posters or flags put up by a union, they are often accused of seizure of property. In innumerable cases, especially in disputes of small and medium industries, collective bargaining takes the form of a mass meeting in which both sides harangue each other and often clash violently.

Although the unions act recklessly, employers too can behave strangely. While engaged in bargaining with a union, one company president suddenly started performing a traditional Japanese dance. Later on, he poured gasoline and paint thinner on his own building, then occupied by union members, in an attempt to set it on fire. The emotional element cannot be underestimated.

That unions and management in firms once harmonious come to indulge in mutual harassment illustrates the need to see Japanese labor relations in terms of processional changes and a deep reservoir of potential conflict. In order to paint an accurate picture of Japanese industrial relations, we have to examine how discord exists alongside harmony. It is this very coexistence that is one of the decisive factors essential for an understanding of Japanese industrial relations.

Under the stress of prolonged conflict, the weaknesses of unions become apparent. In Japan this weakness is epitomized by the emergence of second unions. Several important points concerning the general characteristics of conflict in Japan are raised here. First, the outcome is often decided by betrayal. Second, betrayal is a normal practice since conflict is not based on a definite cause. Third, the outcome is determined behind the scenes and the battle in the field is more akin to posturing.

These three points are applicable to labor disputes in Japan. In the first place, the outcome of labor disputes is often determined by a split in the union organization. Second, the confrontation between labor and management is not defined because the relationship between labor and management is ambiguous and the personal relations between employers and employees are influenced by the process of assimilation. Third, the outcome of a labor dispute is often decided by dealings behind the scenes. It is quite common for union leaders to utter militant slogans at the bargaining table while making back-door deals with the company.

In a typical case of a trade union split, the moderate union members withdraw because of their dissatisfaction with "militant" union executives. Usually these antiexecutive groups start out as minorities, but within a short period they emerge as majorities, leaving the original union in a minority position. Breakaways often occur in the course of labor disputes and play a decisive role in their outcome. Recognizing this, the companies naturally try to instigate such breakaways. The second union is often organized with the support, if not the active initiative, of the company itself. The rapid growth of the second union is certainly due to company inducements and to the promise of favorable treatment, but there must always be a number of members who are willing to accept the inducements.

It may be said without exaggeration that most unions, no matter how strong their organizing capacity, carry within them the seeds of a split. There are several good reasons for this. As new employees start working in enterprises, they consider joining the union as a matter of course. In extreme cases newcomers are treated as union members even before they know it. Newcomers join a union for no particular reason, except perhaps that everyone else does. They feel that if they refuse to join they might be regarded as strange. Those who do not join are often labeled reactionaries; clearly it takes some courage to withstand this kind of pressure. Here we find a reversal of the original spirit of trade unionism, when it took enormous courage for workers to organize and join a union.

Even in the industrialized countries of the West, the voluntarism of traditional trade unionism has long since faded and apathy among union members has grown.[24] The peculiar situation of Japanese unions is that workers interact with their own union exclusively at the workplace and their identification with the enterprise union is often based on, and does not contradict, their identification with the company. Union leaders often complain of "union organization without spirit."

An examination of union splits indicates that most of the anti-executive groups tend to break away rather hastily and easily. They do not discuss the matter patiently with other members. The postwar union movement adopted democracy as the ruling principle in union administration, but, acccording to Matsuta Hosoya, "the situation merely goes to show what democracy is like without individual independence, that is, it leads to unbridled rivalries and organization."[25] Democracy is a principle for regulating the administration of groups, whereby decisions in the group are made in accordance with majority rule—presuming that there is a difference of opinion among individual members. Majority rule does not exclude the recognition of minority opinions and respect for them. Compared with these generally held premises, we can easily see that there can be no democracy in a union movement that does not admit the possibility of different opinions within its organization and in which opposition all too easily develops into a split.

In my view, however, there are more fundamental reasons, connected with the Japanese mentality, for the unstable nature of the union movement. The question is why democracy has not matured into a working principle. In traditional Japanese society, in which great importance was attached to harmony as a social value, it was extremely difficult for internal criticism to find expression within the group. In postwar Japanese society the situation is even more complex. People still retain the traditional values but, at the same time, democratic values (especially freedom of speech) are strongly emphasized. Internal criticism is therefore quite common; in the case of labor unions, perhaps this criticism is too common. This rather popular practice of internal criticism does not contradict the aforementioned traditional negative attitude toward directly confronting fellow group members, since the members who wish to criticize the group's majority do so only when they are in contact with outsiders.

Violence in pursuing the conflict between management and labor often precipitates the development of a second union. The Kongō Seisakujo Company dispute began in March 1965 when management announced its plan to cut 219 employees. After several short strikes and other preliminary actions, union members pasted the walls and windows of the company with posters threatening bodily harm to various managers. The participation of outside union activists encouraged a growing sense of crisis.

As often happens, the union was racked by internal dissension. Those union members who disagreed with the union executives' policy had, as early as 14 May, initiated a signature campaign against them and had collected 207 names. After such a large number of members had expressed dissatisfaction with their leadership, the union's executives became uneasy. Relations between the company and the union had degenerated following an unsuccessful attempt to negotiate the dispute on 17 and 19 May. On 20 May, the two groups of union members confronted one another within the company facilities, shouting and jostling each other. This series of setbacks led the union leaders to desperate activities. The confrontation between the union and the company got progressively more serious when a rumor spread that the union might occupy the plant. The rumor was given credence by the union's preparations to stay overnight at its offices and the prospective stay of the managerial staff at the technical center of the company. Groups supporting the union leaders entered the plant and pushed past the plant guards. These protesters, including quite a few outsiders, gathered around the technical center and created a disturbance from midnight on 20 May to 24 May. The commotion was greatest on 20 May when the union learned which section of the plant was scheduled to be cut back and the names of those who were to be laid off. They held mass meetings and demanded a meeting with management and an explanation of the layoff plans. During that time, they pounded violently on drums, broke windows, and shouted through loudspeakers held to the ears of the managerial staff. One of the directors of the company and the chief of personnel suffered ear trauma because of the noise and the latter received blows that left bruises on his back.[26]

Before the end of May 1965 a group of 324 workers had withdrawn from the main union and started their own organization. Thereafter the parent union got smaller and smaller until it comprised only 70 workers, at which time the dispute was finally settled. In most cases in which unions resort to violence, a situation similar to that seen in the cases involving mass picketing and plant occupation exists. The common characteristics are that unions do not control a majority of the employees in the enterprise or that secondary unions are involved, putting the strikers in a desperate position. Furthermore, even unions that organize a majority of workers sometimes lose the support of their members and fall into a minority position because of the excessively militant attitudes of the union executives during disputes.

The attitudes and behavior of students during the campus turmoil in the 1960s had features in common with unions in serious labor disputes. Students went on strike and demanded collective bargaining. They forced school presidents, deans, and professors to attend their mass meetings and accept their demands. If the professors did not comply, the meetings continued until they were completely exhausted and finally surrendered. Such collective bargaining, often called mass bargaining, occurred quite often during the period of disorder following World War II and occasionally still arises in industrial relations in Japan. Closing classrooms by constructing barricades is similar in nature to mass picketing and sit-down strikes. Independent lectures and seminars organized by students also strongly resemble union takeovers.

When the closing of a campus continues for a long time, students of antistrike factions often try to remove the barricades, which results in collisions with the student groups who insist that the closing should continue. This is almost the same situation one encounters when prolonged labor disputes bring about the creation of second unions or when workers forcibly try to cross picket lines. Tragedy often results. During campus unrest the university administration often employs guards and fierce dogs and summons mobile campus police, much as the employers use *bōryokudan* or call the police to expel workers engaged in a sit-down strike. University authorities frequently resort to lockouts in order to keep out troublesome students.

This similarity raises a fundamental problem—namely, whether the violence found in industrial relations and in the student movement may not be deeply rooted in the Japanese mentality. Yōnosuke Nagai, a political scientist, comments on this point:

> Groups of students stage so-called mass bargaining sessions not unlike mass trials during which they unilaterally criticize university authorities. In this type of bargaining, they take advantage of the anonymity of people in a group, a psychological phenomenon that allows free rein to savage and sadistic impulses which otherwise remain suppressed at the level of the subconscious. Emotional judgments are foisted on others in the form of one-sided, ready-made conclusions, a process which is almost unthinkable in Western society and is very oriental by nature.[27]

The use of physical power instead of dialogue is regarded as a pathological symptom of immature labor relations, however. Indeed, cases of mass bargaining or violence, which used to be quite common during the postwar period, today tend to be thought of as oddities happening only in less-developed areas of labor-management relations such as small enterprises. Even in larger enterprises, however, once the relationship between a union and the employer deteriorates, similar violence occurs. Whether violent incidents are destined to continue to decline is not certain; so much depends on the economic and political context of the time.

When we state that the organizational weakness of Japanese unions is the fundamental reason for their unreasonable behavior, we must keep in mind that this weakness resides in their inability to bargain collectively in the Western sense of the term. Perhaps the real problem is that Japanese unions are not only incapable of bargaining but, like the student movement, they are not very interested in bargaining. Radical organizations, including unions and student groups, often do not really intend to bargain and settle disputes. Rather, they wish to carry on a dispute for the dispute's own sake, to continue fighting to keep their organization alive. In such cases, the rational way to reach a settlement based on the calculation of economic gains and losses does not work. It becomes imperative at this point to see how the dispute settlement machinery is working in Japanese industrial relations.

Conflicts of Rights vs. Interests

In Western industrial relations the difference between a conflict of vested rights *(Rechtstreit)* and a conflict of interest *(Interessenstreit)* is generally recognized.[28] The former is defined as a legal dispute concerning existing vested rights and obligations and is usually handled by the courts; the latter is a dispute to establish new rights and obligations and is not regarded as a legal dispute but one to be settled by negotiation between the parties. In Western society, when a conflict of interest is not settled by negotiations—whether or not acts of dispute have taken place—they are supposed to be settled by conciliation, mediation, or arbitration by a private or public agency, rather than by the courts. This distinction is based on the premise that a conflict of interest is by its nature impossible to settle by applying legal norms.

Suppose, for example, that a dispute arises over the interpretation of a wage agreement that is still in force. This is a conflict concerning the vested rights of workers to wages and the employer's obligation to pay. On the other hand, suppose that the workers demand wage increases and a conflict arises because the employer refuses. This is not a conflict concerning existing vested rights and obligations and is not a matter of legal opinion. This kind of conflict must be settled by a third party, involving existing machinery for settling public disputes. The labor disputes that we have been discussing have been conflicts of interests.

In Japanese industrial relations, the distinction between conflicts of vested rights and conflicts of interests has not been clearly made, except perhaps on a purely academic basis. This is simply because Japanese industrial relations depend on vaguely written contracts that cannot be concerned primarily with the exact definition of the rights and obligations of the parties to a potential dispute. In one not exceptional case, the court ruled that "the provision in question is so obscure, it is almost impossible . . . to ascertain what kind of practices existed in fact and which working conditions were agreed upon by the parties and were to be included in the contract when it was concluded."

Since the provisions of the agreements between the parties in Japanese industrial relations are so obscure, the courts and the LRC find it difficult to carry out their function as judicial institutions—namely, to ascertain the facts and find solutions based on legal norms. Japanese courts are thus called upon to perform the task of rendering a legal judgment on issues in which the rights and obligations of both parties are obscure and uncertain.

For instance, Japanese courts often have to decide on the reasonableness of a staffing level of retirement age in a particular enterprise in order to decide whether a dismissal is valid. It is extremely doubtful whether such a judgment on the fairness of certain management decisions is legally possible for the courts and, even if it were possible, whether it is appropriate. Management representatives complain with some justification that although the judges might be well trained for legal judgments, labor-management issues are outside their competence and, in any case, they (not the judges) are responsible for the conduct of the enterprise.

When the judges decide the reasonableness of certain management actions on the basis of "abuse of right," it certainly is a valid legal judgment. However, judgments on the basis of abuse of right rest in the final analysis on one's concept of social justice. In connection with the problem of the "appropriateness" of an act of dispute, for example, social justice is hard to determine in the field of labor law, where the views of both parties are so divided. A brilliant labor law scholar, who has scrutinized the supporting arguments in labor cases in postwar Japan, commented on this point:

> There are two important standards resorted to and cited in past legal cases in the field of labor, that is, "reason" and "abuse of right," both of which are rather flexible "blank" norms. . . . Since the standards cited do not necessarily mean standards of judgment, this does not necessarily mean that the judgment is subjective. However, judging from the statements of the legal decisions, Japanese court decisions in labor law cases tend to allow some kind of "qualitative" judgment, sometimes more or less subjective, depending on its legal construction. As a result, the substance of such judgments has the following characteristics: (a) a soft-focused grasp of the issue; (b) obscure legal construction; and (c) ineffective judgment, especially in case of provisional injunctions. Thus the legal decisions in labor cases incline strongly toward arbitration or reconciliation.[29]

The tendency of judges to settle cases by reconciliation rather than by ordinary trial is natural, if one takes into account the characteristics of Japanese industrial relations and the need to settle the dispute adequately. This tendency is strong among judges who have more or less specialized in labor cases, and some judges make no secret of their conviction in this matter.[30]

As we have seen, in Japanese society a dispute is generally regarded as a threat to the norm of harmonious personal relationships. Bringing a lawsuit against someone is equivalent to a direct attack. And after a trial has started, if the plaintiff persists in his suit and rejects suggestions for compromise, he is likely to be abhorred for his coldness and stubbornness. The cultural norms translate into social pressures that make both parties more or less ready to accept compromise. According to Kawashima, from 50 to 56 percent of civil cases at the court of first instance usually finish in judicial compromise or withdrawal—with withdrawal meaning that accommodation took place ouside court procedure.[31] It is shown that between 1972 and 1976 more than half the labor cases were resolved either by compromise or withdrawal. This pattern is even more evident in the unfair labor practice cases submitted to the LRCs. For most of the same years, more than 70 percent of the cases were resolved by compromise or withdrawal.

Conclusion: Different Conceptual Bases for Settling Labor Disputes

In the Western system of labor relations, strikes and conflict itself are viewed as a last resort in the dispute process, a poor substitute for more civilized and less destructive modes of determining social policy.[32] Although no one has questioned the presence of serious conflicts of interests in industrial relations, most observers are convinced that, at least in the majority of industrial societies, the mode of this conflict has been institutionalized through collective bargaining.[33] The present industrial relations system is the outcome of efforts to institutionalize conflict. Disputes are turned over to union and management specialists who have established procedures for resolving conflicts. The spontaneous qualities of industrial conflict are quickly repressed and regulated in this system. Indicative of this approach is the theory of the "withering away of strikes" that was current in the 1950s. Ross and Hartman observed a dramatic decline of strikes in the 1950s in comparison with the 1940s and the 1930s, and they did not see "any substantial evidence of any impending revival of strike activity in Northern European countries."[34] This prediction was proved false, however, by the occurrence of strikes, especially wildcat strikes, in Scandinavia and West Germany in the late 1960s and early 1970s, not to mention the earlier strike explosion in Great Britain.[35] The institutionalization of resolution processes may delay or preclude strikes in many cases, but it also attempts to depersonalize and make abstract many disputes that are anchored in the concrete reality of work relations. Let us call this reality "group conflict."

In industrial relations, disputes tend to become institutionalized by the emergence and acceptance of trade unions and their involvement in dispute settlement, especially through the collective bargaining process. Group conflicts in labor relations, however, are not necessarily organized. In fact, labor disputes are often started by unorganized groups, as with the wildcat strikes that have been common in the early stages of the union movements in all industrialized countries. Generally the development of such institutions as collective bargaining, works councils, and grievance procedures, as well as private arbitration, has come only after prolonged efforts to replace spontaneous group conflicts at the workshop level with organized resolution processes at higher levels removed from the scene of the conflict. Although groups of workers today are organized and integrated into bargaining and other negotiation processes, the fact remains that labor disputes are originally and fundamentally group conflicts. Spontaneous strikes, often led by natural work-floor leaders, are more akin to group conflict than to organized conflict; their strike actions are sometimes not endorsed by the unions and may be considered illegal by the state. Even in the highly industrialized countries where worker organizations play a major part in dispute settlement, unresolved disputes result in wildcat strikes.[36] Existing Western labor institutions find hard-core conflicts very hard to cope with no matter how well organized the institutions are. This aspect of labor relations does not wither away.

In Japan, as we have seen, the concrete management/union and employer/employee relationship is the all-consuming reality, and no resolution is possible that does not address this fact directly. Legal remedies, abstract rulings, or compromises that are not going to mend the actual breach and restore mutual trust have little effect. In other words, institutionalization has not meant removal of disputes from the fundamental group-conflict situation. The reasons lie in the qualities of Japanese industrial relations already discussed— namely, the mutuality assumed in the employer/employee relationship, enterprise-based unions, Japanese norms about conflict resolution, and, finally, because most serious disputes (involving dismissals) occur in small and medium-size firms.

In Japanese industrial relations there is little inclination to deflect conflicts away from their source, since mending the relationship is only going to occur when its true character remains at the center of the resolution process. Shifting disputes to impersonal arbitration or redefining and abstracting them into legal terms will not restore trust and mutuality. Rather, such steps become weapons in the struggle. For similar reasons, complex machinery for settling disputes has not been set up between unions and management to govern the process of problem solving within companies. Mutual trust cannot rest on settlement processes dependent on abstraction or deflection. Conflicts in Japanese industrial relations must remain "real" to the very, often bitter, end. All industrial relationships are in fact continuous and grounded in both parties' perceptions, emotions, and willingness to cooperate. But they differ in the degree of mutual involvement. Resolution processes in any society must be appropriate to the degree of mutuality necessary for the relationship to continue.

In the West, where mutuality is not expected to be as deep as in Japan, deflection and abstraction are effective under most circumstances, but the results do nothing to deepen the basic relationship. By contrast, in Japan, where mutuality is expected to run deep, the failure of highly sensitive but informal early warning systems, employee forbearance, and conciliatory steps typically leads to a sudden cloudburst of hostility that is most difficult to contain and reverse.

Thus, although comparative statistics on industrial disputes in various countries show strikes in Japan to be short and work hours lost to strikes to be relatively low, they certainly do not establish that there is minimal conflict in Japanese industrial relations. The very measures used have different meaning in the national context.

NOTES

1. See, for instance, Malcolm Fisher, *Measurement of Labour Disputes and Their Economic Effects* (Paris: OECD, 1973).

2. Arthur M. Ross and Paul T. Hartman, *Changing Pattern of Industrial Conflict* (New York: Wiley, 1960).

3. See Norman F. Dufty, *Changes in Labour Management Relations in Enterprises* (Paris: OECD, 1975), p. 12ff.

4. K. G. J .C. Knowles, *Strikes—A Study in Industrial Conflict* (Oxford: Basil Blackwell, 1952), p. 4.

5. Abraham Siegel, "Method and Substance in Theorizing About Worker Protest," in *Aspects of Labor Economics: A Report of the National Bureau of Economic Research* (Princeton: Princeton University Press. 1962), p. 44.

6. France may be the most significant exception to this pattern among Western countries. French strikes are considered actions by individual employees who are then joined by other workers. The situation has been changing in recent years, however,

and today's strikes are being called by unions and have become part of the strategy and tactics of collective bargaining. See Folke Schmidt, "Industrial Action: The Role of Trade Unions and Employers' Associations," in Benjamin Aaron and K. W. Wedderburn, eds., *Industrial Conflict—A Comparative Legal Survey* (New York: Crane, Russak & Co., 1972), p. 48.

7. See Benjamin Aaron, "Methods of Industrial Action: Courts, Administrative Agencies and Legislatures," in Aaron and Wedderburn, *Industrial Conflict*, pp. 95–97.

8. B. C. Roberts, "Die Zunahme in der Entwicklung Industrieller Unruhen seit 1945 and ihre Tendenzen," in *Arbeitskonflikte und Arbeitskampf,* (Cologne: Peter Hanstein Verlag, 1973).

9. Slowdowns and the practice of working to rule are widespread and effectively used in the United States and, to a lesser degree, in some other Western countries too; however, they often are illegal. See Aaron, "Methods of Industrial Action," pp. 81–83.

10. A detailed description of labor disputes in Japan is found in Tadashi Hanami, *Labor Relations in Japan Today* (Tokyo: Kōdansha International, 1979).

11. Chie Nakane, *Japanese Society* (Berkeley and Los Angeles: University of California Press, 1979), p. 19.

12. Takeyoshi Kawashima, *Nihonjin no Hō Ishiki* [Legal rights consciousness of the Japanese] (Tokyo: Iwanami Shoten, 1967), p. 119.

13. Ibid., pp. 116ff.

14. Nenoki et al. *v.* Sanseki Taika Renga Co. Ltd., Ōita District Court, 20 October 1954, 5 RKMS 628; Mieno et al. *v.* Iwataya Department Co., Fukuoka District Court, 19 May 1961, 12 RKMS 247; Koyori *v.* Japan Air Lines, Tokyo District Court, 26 February 1966, 17 RKMS 102.

15. Gino Guigni, "The Peace Obligation," in Aaron and Wedderburn, *Industrial Conflict*, pp. 128ff.

16. Readers will find several striking similarities between the Japanese style of settling disputes and that of tribes in the developing countries; see P. H. Gulliver, "Dispute Settlement Without Court," and Laura Nader, "Styles of Court Procedure," in Laura Nader, ed., *Law in Culture and Society* (Chicago: Aldine, 1969).

17. For the role of the law courts in effecting reconciliation in civil cases rather than handling legal decisions, see Takeyoshi Kawashima, "Dispute Settlement in Contemporary Japan," in A. T. von Mehren, ed., *Law in Japan* (Cambridge, Mass.: Harvard University Press, 1964), p. 48.

18. Central Labor Relations Commission, *Rōdō Iinkai Nenpō* [Annual Report of the Labor Relations Commission], 1977.

19. Kaoru Ōta, *Tatakai no Nakade* [In the midst of struggle] (Tokyo: Aoki Shoten, 1971), p. 301.

20. Dan F. Henderson, *Conciliation and Japanese Law—Tokugawa and Modern* (Tokyo: University of Tokyo Press, 1965), vol. 1, p. 3.

21. Ibid., pp. 6–7.

22. Ōta, *Watashi no Keisei-ron to Keieisha-ron,* p. 105.

23. Kishima Tankō Rōdō Kumiai [Kishima Coal Mining Employees Union], *Teki yori-mo Ichinichi Nagaku* [One day longer than the enemy] (Tokyo: Kishima Tankō Rōdō Kumiai, 1958), p. 120.

24. A major contribution to the literature on trade union apathy is Joseph Gold-

stein's *Government of British Trade Unions* (London: Allen & Unwin, 1952). See also G. W. Brooks, *Sources of Vitality in the American Labor Movement* (Ithaca: Cornell University Press, 1960).

25. Matsuta Hosoya, *Nihon no Rōdō Kumiai Undō* [Labor union movement in Japan] (Tokyo: Shakai Shisō Kenkyūkai, 1958), p. 267.

26. Kongō Seisakujo Company Case, Central Labor Relations Commission, 1 July 1970, 43 FRKM 607.

27. Yōnosuke Nagai, *Jūkōzō Shakai to Bōryoku* [Soft-structured society and violence] (Tokyo: Chūōkōronsha, 1971), p. 77.

28. The distinction between conflicts of "rights" and of "interests" is admitted in theory in most Western industrialized countries, such as Germany, the United States, Sweden, Austria, Britain, Italy, and France—although in the latter three countries the distinction is less important in practice. For details, see K. W. Wedderburn, "Conflicts of 'Rights' and Conflicts of 'Interests' in Labor Disputes," in B. Aaron, ed., *Dispute Settlement Procedures in Five Western European Countries* (Los Angeles: Institute of Industrial Relations, University of California, 1969), pp. 65–66. In Germany this distinction is admitted to be essential and fundamental in the ordering of labor relations. It was introduced during the Weimar Republic, when special conciliation boards *(Schlichtungen)* were established and it was necessary to distinguish between their jurisdiction and that of labor courts. The classic concepts were established by Erwin Jacobi, one of the leading labor lawyers at that time. He characterized disputes over rights as those to be decided by "legal judgments" according to the legal order, while disputes over interests were to be settled by an adjustment or voluntary agreement corresponding to the interests of both parties. In case of failure, a legal decision was not possible. For details, see Thilo Ramm, "Labor Courts and Grievance Settlement in West Germany," in B. Aaron, ed., *Labor Courts and Grievance Settlement in Western Europe* (Berkeley and Los Angeles: University of California Press, 1971), pp. 93–94.

29. Kōichirō Yamaguchi, "Rōdō Saiban no Kyakkan Sei" [The objectiveness of legal judgment on labor cases], *Jurist* 487 (1971): 29.

30. As an example among a number of such opinions, see *Rōdō Hanrei* [Labor cases], nos. 151 and 164.

31. Kawashima, *Nihonjin no Hō Ishiki*, p. 150.

32. R. Dubin, "Industrial Conflicts and Social Welfare," *Journal of Conflict Resolution* 2 (1957): 179–185.

33. R. Dubin, "Constructive Aspects of Industrial Conflict," in A. Kornhauser, R. Dubin, and A. M. Ross, eds., *Industrial Conflict* (New York: McGraw-Hill, 1954), p. 47.

34. A. M. Ross and P. T. Hartman, *Changing Patterns of Industrial Conflict* (New York: Wiley, 1960), p. 176.

35. R. Hyman, *Strikes* (London: Fontana, 1972), pp. 83ff.

36. The resurgence of wildcat strikes in most industrialized countries is diverse and depends on the nature of industrial relations in each country: wage drift in England, for example, and dissatisfaction of white-collar workers in Scandinavian countries and minority groups in the United States. A more fundamental and universal cause is the failure of the established industrial relations systems to solve the problems and remove the dissatisfactions caused by the very nature of the technological setting of today's work processes. In the United States, for instance, several studies indicate

that the main cause of wildcat strikes is the inability of centralized bargaining and contract administration and the established grievance procedures to solve the frustration and dissatisfaction of individual workers. See Leonard R. Sayles, "Wildcat Strikes," *Harvard Business Review* 32 (6)(1954): 42–52; J. B. Atleson, "Work Group Behavior and Wildcat Strikes: The Causes and Functions of Industrial Civil Disobedience," *Ohio State Law Journal* 34 (1973): 751–816.

7
Conflict in Institutional Environments: Politics in Education

THOMAS P. ROHLEN

Basic divisions that arise within institutions can have one of three basic outcomes. They may lead to the destruction of the encompassing social fabric of the institution itself (as in religious schisms, social revolutions, party splits, and marital divorces); they may be resolved and the basic institutional fabric restored; or they may reach a plateau state of indecisive permanence with each side sufficiently strong to defend its position and the institution adjusting to a situation of predictable conflict. In the first instance, the conflicting sides within the institution emerge as independent institutions themselves, each side developing increased strength until something like mitosis occurs. In the second, the incipient strength of the one opposing side fades and the conflict subsides. The last possibility is one of continuous, but limited, conflict between well-organized parties within an institution that retains much of its own organizational integrity. Partisan conflict and institutional order accommodate to one another. The case to be considered here is of the third kind. It is about intense political partisanship within a national school system.

The all-or-nothing alternatives cited above are exceptional.[1] Public institutional environments, because they are complex and dense with varied relationships, seem capable of housing considerable conflict without loss of functional identity.[2] It happens that the major political cleavage in postwar Japanese society has run through a number of public bureaucratic institutions. Education is a prime example and one which offers wider lessons.

The type of conflict to be considered here is fragmented by institutional structure and the necessities of cooperation in schools. Contra-

dictions among simultaneous developments, the compartmentaliza-
tion of tensions, and disjunctures among partisans of the same side
prevent momentum from gathering. A state of "animated suspension" ensues and conflict is increasingly "institutionalized." Neither
winning, losing, nor giving up, both sides go on playing what
appears more and more like a game.

Conflict in Japanese Education

No Japanese institution in the postwar period has experienced more
conflict than public education.[3] Schools,[4] universities,[5] whole school
systems,[6] and the machinery of national educational policy[7] have all
witnessed intense and persistent conflict between politicized teachers' unions and equally politicized administrative authorities. Fist-
fights in the Diet, teachers' strikes, sit-ins, mass arrests, and legal
suits have regularly marked the relationship. The resulting hostility,
distrust, and acrimony have often divided faculties and paralyzed
schools.

At first glance, there seems to have been little variation in the pattern of confrontation. Each side has remained tied intimately to one
of Japan's two opposing political camps. On the face of it, an analogy
between political conflict in Japanese education and the kind of warfare waged between the entrenched German and Allied forces in
World War I is suggested, since many years of heated but indecisive
battles have led to a stalemate but no general truce. Ad hoc ceasefires
in some localities, intense skirmishing in others, and the ever present
possibility of general hostilities characterize the present situation. A
closer examination reveals the struggle within education to be very
different at each administrative level within the national school
system.

The American Occupation opened a seeming Pandora's box of
political and administrative changes in the realm of public education.[8] It permitted the unionization of teachers, and this resulted in
the creation of a powerful counterforce to the official administration.[9] It stripped the Ministry of Education of some of its former
powers and distributed them to prefectural, city, and local school
boards, thus dismantling in part the former highly centralized character of authority. It introduced new and quite different educational
goals and pedagogical theories aimed at reinforcing a democratic
political system. Prewar education had been a powerful instrument of
political legitimation for the regime in power. The occupation sought

to remove that possibility by creating an educational outlook that was adamantly independent yet strictly neutral in terms of political party support.

These changes, quickly and often naively introduced by the Americans following their own ideals, created a greatly altered field of authority and power within education, but they failed to separate education from politics. Quite the contrary—since 1945, Japanese education has been as involved with politics as ever before. But rather than a pliant institution readily utilized by the government, education has been a battleground between the conservative and leftist camps. Both sides have attempted persistently to use public education to legitimize their interpretations of social reality and each has attempted time and again to wrest greater control of education from the other.[10] Because they are sharply divided by ideological differences, both left and right give high priority to educational issues. Yet, despite three decades of persistent and intense conflict, neither side has much reason to claim victory.

Japanese politics has been described as a system of "hegemonic bipolarity."[11] The hegemonic quality derives from (1) the Liberal Democratic Party (LDP) control of majorities in both houses of the Diet and (2) the resulting hold by the conservative camp of other decision-making apparatus including the national bureaucracy and its affiliated advisory and consultative bodies. The bipolar quality stems from the fact that the opposition, while removed from direct control, possesses the means of obstructing, delaying, and altering decisions because of its resources for preventing the implementation of decisions within public institutions where the opposition has a strong union power base. Precisely in such areas are conservative efforts to weaken the leftist opposition most intense. Education, because of the entrenched position of the teachers' union, is a prime example of this kind of situation. The conservatives control national decision-making processes for education, but the arena of policy implementation lower down in the system is strongly influenced by the union. The most significant conflict occurs in local school systems where the political contest is rather evenly matched.

A Theoretical Framework

The diffuse nature of conflict in Japanese education calls for a comprehensive approach that pays attention to the character of events at the grass roots where implementation of national policy must actually occur. I will attempt this by using an approach that centers on context, process, and compliance.[12]

Schools and prefectural offices of education constitute distinct *levels* of the institution, and each has its own manner of absorbing and participating in national political struggles. The *context* or institutional environment of conflict at each level possesses distinct qualities which influence conflict processes. Like three-dimensional tic-tac-toe, we are dealing with an interplay between levels as well as between partisan camps. Political maneuver is the name of the game at the national level, for example, since political parties dominate; but at the school level face-to-face interaction and the need for daily cooperation greatly influence the outcome.

I treat each bureaucratic level as a distinct social-cultural subsystem shaping the development, containment, and resolution of conflict. The accumulation of conflict episodes from one level to another is often inhibited by the many differences involved. In rare historical moments of crisis and fluidity (such as revolutions and wars), conflicts readily transcend bureaucratic levels to become "universal," but the more usual state of institutional affairs is one in which bureaucratic separation is not readily overcome. Local habits prevail over transcendental politics.

In this case, conflict involves the participation of thousands of low-level constituent groups, school faculties, and two separate organizations that both aim to mobilize or control the same groups. Arbitrary distinctions between *institution* and *organization* will be used here. By institution, I mean the entire framework of public education including the teachers, the schools, the prefectural and national bureaucracies, and the Japanese Teachers Union (JTU). By organization, I refer to the partisan elements that seek power over the institution—namely the administration and the union. Before the war, there was no easy distinction to be made between administration and school system, since authority was singular. The occupation's insistence on a separation of powers and the rise of an adversarial union within the institutional framework forced administrative authority to assume the posture of a partisan organization similar in its power-seeking intent to the union. Only in the postwar era have officials had to fight for authority. Only in the postwar period has the institution, in effect, had two heads.[13]

Vertical lines of command and communication connect the levels in both organizations. As in all organizations, the downward *command* direction is the more active and articulate. Initiative and information flow down in much greater quantity than they flow up. What normally moves upward are statistics and other information for decision makers. Important messages from below are irregular, hesitant, and unusual. But the relative silence of lower levels masks a critical power: the capacity to alter, disregard, and even subvert higher authority. Power in organizations is potentially quite illusory as it depends on the *compliance* of semiautonomous lower levels. When higher levels lead organizations into conflict, they call upon and thus test the compliance of lower-level units. Each lower unit's response, we may assume, depends on a fairly careful evaluation of what will be gained and lost as calculated from its own perspective. Far from being automatic, the degree of compliance reflects the fit between the contextual factors at different levels.

The framework just set forth cannot explain why conflict arises, but it can account for much of the pattern of its expression through an analysis of the way lower levels respond to higher-level directives and the way higher levels anticipate the response of lower levels in their initiatives. This is the pattern in which institutionalization is revealed.

Observers of the Japan Teachers Union have noted a gap between its leadership and the rank and file of teachers.[14] This gap reflects the historical fact that the national organization was formed by political activists before most teachers were unionized. The process of extending the union to the grass roots was in general one of drawing less politicized teachers into a highly political organization. Today the political interests and ideological commitments of the leadership remain distinctly to the left of the average teacher. As time passed, the immediate postwar sense of political confrontation ebbed considerably among average Japanese. If a majority of teachers were as radical as the leadership, the JTU would be powerful indeed. Such teachers, however, would hardly be equipped to work at the routines of teaching. Schools could not fulfill their role staffed by committed ideologues and radicals. The gap between leadership and rank and file within the union more and more reflected not only the union's history of top-down development but also the inherent differences of character between levels in the institution. Teachers experience a very different milieu from union leaders, especially those at the politicized national level. As a result, they view conflict from separate perspectives.

Political scientists have seen the JTU as primarily a mass organization composed of individual teachers making individual decisions to follow or not to follow union leadership.[15] This has led them to see the problem of union power as a product of the degree of agreement between the leadership and the rank and file. I find problems with this approach because it misses the school context and the dynamics of union affairs at the local level. Individual attitudes, in other words, are only part of a far more complex political game played out within a national institution. Schools and prefectures differ enormously as far as educational politics is concerned. These variations, as I see it, are more powerful in shaping the pattern of conflict and the power of the union than any attitudinal gap within the union. A "mass movement" approach overestimates the independence of individual actors and underestimates the constraints imposed by social structure.

Elements and Structures

Diagrams are the most economical way to introduce the framework of these relationships. Figure 1 lists the key players and the three crucial levels. A more interesting way of diagramming the same situation borrowed partially from Thurston (1973) portrays the overall structure in terms of the typical degree of interactional distance between the opposing sides (Figure 2). Such distance is in inverse proportion to the shared involvement between them in maintenance of institutional routines.

What is not evident in either diagram is the existence of important divisions within each partisan organization at the national level. Disagreement often exists between the Ministry of Education and influential LDP politicians. Initiatives come from both sources, but as a rule the party politicians are more aggressive in challenging the union. Both the ministry and the party influence the advisory bodies appointed to give "nonpartisan" guidance to national policy.

On the union side, a key division exists between supporters of the Japan Socialist Party (JSP) mainstream and supporters of the Japan Communist Party (JCP). The socialists have had a majority of the votes (about two-thirds) at national conventions for almost the entire postwar period. The mainstream controls the national headquarters and national policymaking, but it does not control all prefectural unions or national staff positions. Approximately one-third of all member unions are antimainstream and affiliated to the Communist Party. In the same prefecture, it is not uncommon to find both mainstream and antimainstream JTU unions representing different sets of

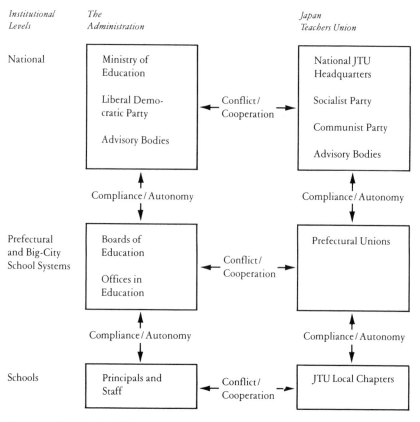

FIGURE 1   *Institutional Structure*

teachers (public high schools, private schools, elementary and middle schools, nursery schools). As a rule the Socialist and Communist parties have made uneasy coalitions in local elections where neither could succeed alone, but they have maintained a rigorous competition within the union movement as this is a major base of strength, especially for the Socialist Party. A key point about structure in our analysis is that with each step lower in the structure the distinction between institutional and political affairs is less clear cut. Matters of power and ideology progressively merge with matters of maintaining the daily efficiency of education.

The physical separation between the two sides is also greatest at the top. In fact, in physical terms the JTU headquarters and the Ministry of Education are housed separately and formal representatives of the two sides at the national level rarely meet. The personnel at this level also have less in common than at lower levels. Ministry officials are

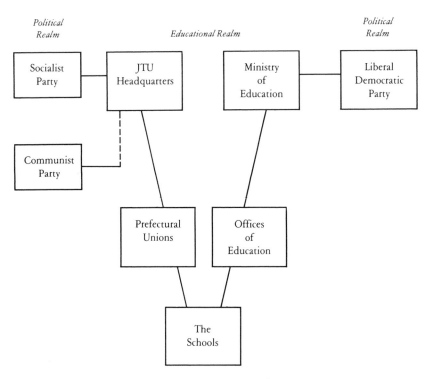

FIGURE 2   *Overall Structure in Terms of Interactional Distance*

career bureaucrats, recruited from elite universities, while union leaders, after some years as local teachers, have worked their way up to positions in the union's headquarters. At the prefectural level, on the other hand, JTU offices are typically in prefectural and city government buildings facilitating regular communication and frequent meetings between the parties. They share the experience of teaching in the same school system, and some of those facing each other at the bargaining table have taught together. Finally, proximity and mutual acquaintance are, of course, greatest at the school level where interaction is nearly constant. An examination of conflict at each level will illustrate how the institutional environment affects national efforts to mobilize support or create administrative discipline.

The School Level

Schools and, more specifically, their faculties are small groups ordered around a set of coordinated daily activities that bring most teachers into face-to-face contact. As such, they constitute a particular form of social environment for conflict.

Public schools always have many goals (indeed they almost inevitably seem to have too many), and setting priorities among them is never easy. When political and ideological differences are strongly represented, the potential for conflict is great. Faculties also have their share of personal and incidental frictions. These can become greatly intensified when they coincide with political divisions.

A principal and vice-principal, the appointed agents of the board of education, are legally responsible for the conduct of each school. High school faculties generally meet weekly with the principal to discuss school policy. Teachers also elect from their ranks a set of faculty leaders who assume the key posts of intermediate authority and responsibility such as directors of each academic grade and supervisors of student discipline. These teachers work both with the principal and with the faculty as a group. The JTU has organized nearly all high school teachers in most parts of Japan. Principals and vice-principals are excluded from union membership. Each school JTU local elects its leadership and discusses union policy separately from the weekly faculty meeting.

As a rule, the ultimate locus of power is the weekly teachers' meeting.[16] If it supports the principal, then he runs the school. If the union controls the meeting because it is consistently supported by the majority of teachers, then it can virtually run the school. If neither the union nor the principal dominates, but both are aggressive in seeking power, then faculty meetings become arenas of considerable struggle and hostility. Both sides must submit proposals and maneuver to gain support. Behind-the-scenes scheming and lobbying then become very active. Japanese do not savor open confrontation and animosity, especially in groups of colleagues who must continue to work together, but such inclinations have not precluded the occurrence of much public conflict within school faculties during the postwar period.[17] I was permitted to sit in on but one actual teachers' meeting during a year spent in five Kobe high schools, but I heard repeatedly of troubled meetings and I personally observed one red-faced shouting match between a number of teachers during a hastily called lunch hour meeting I witnessed by accident. The fact that I was excluded from faculty meetings is clear testimony to their sensitivity. Japanese may take internal conflict for granted in cases like this, but they want it to remain private.

Victory or defeat in these meetings is often determined by simple majority vote, yet neither side can sustain significant power if their margin of victory is persistently small. The alienation of the losers leads to problems of compliance and morale among coworkers. Schools need an atmosphere of goodwill and cooperation. Simple majority rule is not sufficient to keep schools functioning well in the long run. It is rather unusual in Japan to have a persistent recourse to voting to solve problems in polarized circumstances, and even hard-nosed Japanese teachers do not take well to the repeated application of a majority rule principle. Votes are regularly followed by efforts at compromise and fence mending.

More to the point, however, is the fact that in most high schools neither the union nor the administration commands extensive faculty loyalty. Some are firmly in the hands of the principal and some are "union castles," more or less controlled by the union leadership, but in most schools the majority of teachers are independent. Conflict occurs between small sets of committed teachers that attempt to influence the majority as issues arise. In these schools, the faculty response to particular issues is uncertain and compromise is the pattern. The partisan camps face basic limits on what they can achieve; they can lose influence by being too aggressive or extreme in their positions.

Centrist leadership generally emerges within these schools. It focuses less on political issues and more on the unity and integrity of the school itself. The school, rather than the administration or the union, becomes the main focus of loyalty. The school-centered system of norms puts education and students above politics; it decries divisiveness among teachers and seeks a comfortable faculty atmosphere; it protests the interference of outsiders, both the union and the administration alike; and it claims the uniqueness of local (school) problems and solutions. Centrist leadership may come from individuals ostensibly part of one or the other side. Some principals subvert the Office of Education's authority, and some union leaders temper directives from union headquarters. The majority of high schools in Kobe retain considerable autonomy as a result, but it is a capacity to resist change, not to initiate new directions. Thus, while teachers remain members of the union and are still partially committed to it and while principals generally carry out administrative orders, there are very real and usually well-understood limits to what a faculty will agree to do in the event of political pressures initiated above the school level. In the majority of schools, the ingredients for serious political conflict are in place, but the presence of a strong center serves as a buffer.

What links grass-roots independence and political centrism in public institutions? This is a crucial question in the analysis of postwar Japan. First, party membership is not extensive even among teachers. Most are made politically conscious by virtue of their jobs in a politicized institution. Their reaction is generally to resist partisanship. Second, the work routines upon which order and efficiency depend require cooperative face-to-face interaction. This demand supersedes ideology as the critical source of "reality" for most schools. Third, the value of community solidarity remains notably strong and emotionally real at the lower levels of Japanese institutions, such as schools. Fourth, grass-roots coworkers share a sense of what is practical that derives from immediate experience and this is very different from policy or ideology as understood at the national level. These matters combine to make higher-level commands and directives seem intrusive and often misguided, especially as they come down through politicized organizations involved with ideological matters and bent on what appears to be divisive conflict. Centrist instincts and independence from higher authority are mutually reinforcing at the lowest levels of politicized institution.

The local JTU chapter in each high school is the basis of the entire union organization. Not only is it crucial to the retention of a broad membership and therefore the assurance of a sound financial and negotiating base, the local is the crucial connection between an organization led by union professionals who are committed leftists and the great mass of teachers. JTU chapter leaders are elected by school faculties. Teachers with all sorts of divergent interests and philosophies are chosen.[18] With the exception of a minority who hope to rise in the union, their careers are tied to teaching and to the schools where they work rather than to the union.

In centrist schools the chapter leader's task is to be a sensitive broker between the teachers, the principal, and the union's prefectural leadership. He must arbitrate between the ambitious programs and demands of the JTU prefectural and national headquarters and the far less committed, school-centered and reluctant membership of his local. As viewed from union headquarters, the successful chapter leader is one who mobilizes support for union campaigns. There are many of these, too many in fact, and they invariably rely on the voluntary participation of JTU members. Chapter leaders must recruit for these campaigns as well as mobilize teachers for the more serious sit-ins, work stoppages, and strikes that accompany bargaining and national JTU campaigns. Viewed from the school perspective, however, the successful chapter leader is one who does not demand too much of members but uses union power to keep the principal's authority in check.

The latitude for choice and the variety of responses to the job of chapter leader is significant, for the response of chapters to wider JTU efforts ranges across a spectrum from very high commitment and compliance to shallow and empty gestures of support. At the extremes are chapters entirely for or against union activism, but the majority occupy a middle ground characterized by a constant game of balancing pressures and making compromises. Most chapters neither flatly deny nor fully submit to higher union authority.

The election of chapter leaders is obviously of great interest. It sets the tone. The slate of official candidates is rarely contested, but considerable deliberation is involved in their selection. The existing leadership is in a position to nominate its own replacements. Who they consult in this selection process is of crucial importance. In centrist schools the broad spectrum of teachers is involved. The nominations are made in a spirit that is bipartisan. In fact, outgoing leaders work hard to preserve the character of their chapters in the succession process. This holds for cases of activist JTU chapters too. In such schools, however, consultations are among union loyalists, just as leftists may be excluded from the deliberations in schools with an antiunion orientation. Traditions in local union leadership are very resilient.

It remains to be explained why, in such a highly politicized context, nominations should regularly go unopposed. Most teachers find the prospect of working as a JTU chapter leader quite unappealing. Only some leftists are keen. In centrist schools, however, they are not appropriate. Rather the job is treated as one of the various responsibilities seasoned teachers share. It is parceled out like other administrative jobs through consultation. In centrist schools teachers, as a rule, do not seek the job but assume it out of duty.

Union activists may be frustrated by assignments to schools where they are prevented from fully expressing their commitment. They often ask for transfer to schools with active JTU chapters. As such requests are granted, certain schools become magnets for activists. These are the "union castles."

Yama Commercial High School is regarded as one of the union castles in Kobe. About one-third of the faculty are union activists and the chapter has produced many leaders for the citywide union organization. One Yama teacher, long a union leader, had become a Communist Party candidate for the prefectural assembly. The local is strongly tied to both the national union movement and the Communist Party, and personal advancement upward in the movement is relatively common from Yama. The work of the chapter in such matters as gaining greater rights for teachers, advancing the cause of minority groups, and introducing the study of social injustice into the classroom is widely acclaimed in union circles. It is a model chapter.

At Yama the union is so strong that it encounters little resistance in using faculty room wall space for election posters supporting the Communist Party. Frequent union announcements urging teachers to attend political meetings, contribute to party campaign funds, and volunteer for its activities punctuate the quiet of the faculty room. Yet it was made quite clear to me by a number of Yama teachers that they do not support the Communist Party and strongly resented this invasion of the school's faculty room by political activists. The union's supporters succeeded in opposing past unsympathetic principals, causing the school board to begin selecting principals who would avoid confrontations. The union thus gained ascendancy within Yama. Newly assigned teachers quickly learned not to oppose the union openly, but during my study some veteran teachers on the faculty were still willing to stand up to it.

Nothing better illustrates this chapter's power than an incident that occurred in the late sixties. The principal had ruled against several resident Koreans in favor of Japanese applicants who had the same entrance exam scores at the cut-off point among candidates. The union investigated, proved discrimination, published the evidence, and, after much acrimony, forced the principal to resign. Today at Yama such decisions are made publicly and by the faculty not the principal. Ethically the union's activist leaders were perfectly correct, but many teachers in Kobe were shocked. The union had transgressed a crucial unstated principle of Japanese organization: Keep school problems within the school. Many teachers who do not like the union's politics point to this incident to illustrate how activism disrupts school unity. Yama was in fact severely divided for the next decade. Raising a public protest had meant rejection of the convention of exhibiting mutual trust and respect within the group. The Japanese inclination would be to quietly resolve or even ignore such problems. Leftist politics asserts ethical principles of a universal sort that can be very contradictory at times to the norms of group process. Where the union is quite strong, universal norms dominate faculty dialogue. The popular leftist word *shutaisei* (vaguely "independence") is best understood as the will to overcome group-oriented sensibilities for the sake of larger principles. We are entering the world of *uchi/soto* and *tatemae/honne* here. For many teachers the union's insistence on ignoring these distinctions makes it a disruptive force in schools. The truly independent and principled are hard to live with in any society. When they are in political alliance in Japanese schools they are very hard to deal with indeed. The majority of teachers prefer the fellowship, security, and order of a well-knit group, but at Yama where the union is the majority a different kind of group has evolved.

The Yama local, for all its power and accomplishments, is not operating without serious resistance from certain teachers. In the absence of a strong principal, some teachers have learned to argue with the union in a manner reminiscent of the union's actions where it is out of power, as the following episode illustrates. A thief had somehow entered during the night and a number of teacher's desks were rifled. A few teachers had lost some money and articles of minor value. The police were called in to investigate by the principal. When a search of the premises and interviews turned up no leads, they asked to check the teachers' room for fingerprints. To isolate the thief's prints they would have to fingerprint the teachers.

This seemingly innocent proposal was met with immediate opposition from the union. It is against the law in Japan for public school teachers to engage in political activities; and while this law is not regularly enforced, the Yama union leaders regarded fingerprinting as a serious threat. The police could then easily document their participation on behalf of the Communist Party in elections and so forth. In a political showdown the police would find it easier to arrest them. Thus, although it would prevent the police from possibly solving the crime and restoring the money lost by the teachers, the union leaders argued that the police should not be allowed in the teachers' room. It would be an invasion of academic freedom, they said, by a known instrument of political oppression.

A meeting of the teachers was hastily called for the lunch hour for, as is typical of Yama, the principal said the decision had to be made by the faculty. While some sat at their desks correcting papers and others nibbled at their lunches, the union's leaders, speaking over a portable PA system, presented their case in a forceful manner. I had not been informed of the issue beforehand and, hearing the tone, had taken the statements to be another in a long series of political announcements and campaign pep talks stemming from the union. In Yama, such things are virtually part of the day's routine. But I was awakened with a start when one of the gym teachers stepped to the microphone to argue against the union's position. He said that the money the teachers had lost should be recovered and that the fear of being fingerprinted was the union leaders' problem. He and many of the other teachers had nothing to fear from the police, he said, because they are not "lawbreakers." Collecting fingerprints in an investigation is a normal practice, and the union's suspicions are part of their paranoia about the police. Let the police in, he concluded.

As he spoke, there were angry calls of protest from union activists and he, too, progressively raised his voice as he went along. Faces turned red. The shouting did not stop when he finished. A union spokesman took the microphone to counter his arguments. Many teachers appeared quite bothered by the show of temper and, after turning around to look briefly, bent their heads to concentrate on their lunches or the papers at their desks. Only two other speakers seconded the arguments of the gym teacher, however, and when a vote was called by the union, the police were kept out by a small margin. A larger number of teachers abstained.

The union's supremacy in this school has not inhibited the forceful expression of conflicting opinions—quite the reverse—but it has made it an unpopular place to work for nonpartisan teachers. Requests for transfers out are unusually high, and the only teachers who seek transfer in are ardent union and party sympathizers. In terms of my overall scheme for analyzing conflict and power, union castles like Yama give high compliance to JTU directives but are largely unresponsive to administrative efforts. Compliance in Yama's case, furthermore, is limited to JTU directives unopposed by the Communist Party.

The union situation at Otani High School is quite a different matter. About eight teachers are regarded as "union people," and year after year they rotate among themselves the key union positions in the school. Elections are regularly held but no other candidates are brought forward. Occasionally the chapter's leaders gather a majority of the faculty to their position, but just as often their voices fall on deaf ears. A majority of teachers hope to stay neutral, simply out of disinterest. All the younger teachers, the four gym teachers, and perhaps ten of the older teachers are "opposed to the union teachers but not necessarily to the union itself." One had been a union leader in his previous high school.

The Otani principal, on the other hand, is a senior educational statesman of outstanding character and respected for his dedicated service to education. His presence partially isolates the union loyalists, since they cannot move strongly against him. The principal, too, plays a cautious game. The union officers, for example, meet clandestinely every Wednesday afternoon after lunch to plan their position for the faculty meeting later in the day. Since union meetings during school time are illegal, the principal could order them to stop, but he says nothing.

There are no political posters in the faculty room, and requests for volunteers for outside union campaigns generally fall on deaf ears. The chapter's leadership remains firmly committed to their cause, but their influence over the faculty is not strong. They rarely can muster the supporting votes for an aggressive position and have had little success recruiting the younger teachers. Adept at public argument and convinced that open conflict is healthy, these leaders persist in the assertion of ideological positions despite evidence that they are slowly losing ground. Labeled behind their backs as "troublemakers," "too argumentative," or "disinterested in faculty unity" by their opponents, their political commitment makes retreat to a low profile difficult. We can sense the dynamics of conflict in Otani in the following case, one that illustrates the complexity and explosiveness of even apparently simple issues.

The junior class trip is an ancient and venerable custom in Japanese high schools. Once an opportunity for students to see something of the larger society, the class trip is appreciated today primarily as a source of postgraduation nostalgia. Otani's junior class goes skiing. Our interest in these trips arises because of a more implicit but equally vital role they play in the life of Japanese schools. They are part of a set of events in which school unity is symbolized. Although the trip is voluntary, great efforts are made to encourage full participation of both students and teachers. Scholarships are even provided students who cannot afford the personal costs involved. Often the principal himself goes along. Chaperoning some four hundred students is no easy task in itself, and having to learn to ski, no doubt, compounds the burden of this "voluntary" work for some teachers. But it is also a fact (but not one publicly mentioned) that the trip interferes with teacher moonlighting. Furthermore, the JTU objects that no special pay is given for participation in this and other extracurricular activities. The union raises this point to the level of high political significance by talking about voluntary tasks as "exploitation" by the "reactionary" school authorities.

A few weeks before the 1975 annual trip, the volleyball coach confronted the teachers with the unusual request that the juniors on his team be excused from participating. As he explained, the volleyball team had a chance to win the prefectural championships, but if his players went skiing they could lose condition, miss critical training sessions, and expose themselves to the risk of accidents. The team members wanted to stay home and practice. The coach reminded his colleagues that the school rarely enjoyed athletic success. A victory would boost school morale, especially since his players, due to their lack of height, were considered a Cinderella team.

Initially most teachers felt no strong objections. The idea was unusual, but so were the circumstances behind it. But then a member of the union's steering committee rose and expressed strenuous opposition. A very bad precedent would be established, he argued, and the principle of full participation in school events would be undermined. The team, he thought, would simply have to do its best in the circumstances.

Many of the forty-odd teachers at the meeting were greatly surprised at this response. The propriety of the coach's plan, once questioned, did seem debatable, but among fellow teachers many such debates are avoided in the name of good relations. If the issue of right and wrong was cloudy, what was clear to all was the politics of the parties to the emerging dispute.

Strange as it may seem, political conflict in Japanese high schools centers less on what teachers do in class than on what they do when classes are finished. According to official policy, teachers are expected to stay until 5:00 P.M. serving as advisers and supervising extracurricular activities. No salary supplements encourage this behavior, however, and in fact a majority of teachers leave shortly after classes are over. Administrative efforts to enforce official policy and thereby encourage after-school programs and closer faculty-student relations run head on into the competing ambitions of the union for teacher time and energy, since its campaigns, joint union actions, seminars, and so forth occur in the afternoons. It is the union's interpretation that a teacher's duties end when classes end; extracurricular activities, therefore, deserve salary supplements. Moonlighting complicates the matter further. Neither the union nor the administration approves, but union policy provides, inadvertently, a protective umbrella for teachers with side jobs.

Where does the volleyball coach fit into all of this? Among the teachers who regularly stay after school, gym teachers are the most notable. Their jobs require and encourage close contact with students in extracurricular activities. Even most of their weekends are tied up in school sports activities. They tend to be among the keenest on school spirit, teamwork, and the idea of sharing more than just academic subject matter with students. At Otani, the handful of other teachers who normally join them in staying after school are their friends, and they too stress close contact with students and dedication to the school. This group, furthermore, is close to the principal, old fashioned in educational philosophy and opposed to many union policies. Here was the true rub.

The volleyball teacher as part of this group (and an avid ski enthusiast to boot) is normally a keen supporter of the junior class trip. The members of the union steering committee, on the other hand, are normally its loudest critics. The antagonisms felt between the two sides over the years, however, apparently caused the union leadership to forget their usual stance on the issue of "voluntary" teacher participation in extracurricular affairs. The irony was compounded by the fact that it was the union leaders who were making a strong plea for the school's traditional ideal of full participation—an ideal at the very heart of Japan's well-known proclivity to group solidarity, which, under many circumstances, leftists vehemently criticize as a buttress for conservatism. Almost everyone was momentarily confused.

Considered in the context of faculty relations, the union's opposition was clearly a partisan act rationalized in the name of group unity. The volleyball coach, on his part, acknowledged the contradiction in his request by asking that it be treated as exceptional. He urged a pragmatic approach (what might be labeled situational ethics). If there was a principle involved, he said, it was the good of school and team, no more and no less. What was known of his daily commitment to students and extracurricular activities lent his request power, just as the tendency of the union's leaders to pursue partisan politics weakened their assertion of the principles of full participation and unity.

Political allies of both parties were quick to see a fight, and among them the argument became heated. The meeting was adjourned and over the next week people could speak of little else. The principal astutely offered to mediate the impasse. He proposed a private meeting in his office between the coach and a representative of the union. No other solution seemed feasible since a vote would be close and too divisive to hazard, given the Japanese preference for consensus. In making his proposal, the principal acknowledged the good intentions of both sides (a mild piece of managerial hypocrisy), and having thus allowed the union to save face he proceeded to resolve the immediate issue in favor of the coach, as was generally expected. But he accompanied his action with a strong pronouncement supporting the union's point about the value of full participation in school activities. It was this aspect of the total embroglio that he was particularly interested in from the start. The principle of participation, he knew, was crucial to the maintenance of administrative authority.

Important ideological qualities of school-level conflict can be perceived in this event. First, several sets of norms are discernible in this conflict. One centers on the school and its recognized patterns of cooperation, customary practices, and group relations. Participation in voluntary activities symbolizes acceptance of the notion of school unity. It is not an abstraction but an implicit value found in cooperative activity.[19]

The official administrative rules and guidelines set forth by the Ministry of Education provide another set of norms, a list of dos and don'ts, based on an employee/employer notion of contractual duties that is rationalized by ministry and LDP moralizing about the duties and responsibilities of teachers. Staying until 5:00 P.M. is an abstract duty that is easily interpreted as serving the goal of administrative control.

A third set of norms comes from the leftist ideology of the JTU. Its basis is an interpretation of Japanese society and politics that assumes the conservative government to be illegitimate. Opposition is morally correct and the true expression of democratic principles. By this perspective, teacher participation in any event (union or school) is correct or incorrect depending on the political character of the activity. And since this is often a complex problem, union leadership even at the school level must constantly interpret right from wrong. The "leftist" perspective is based neither on school relations nor a legal formulation. It starts in an interpretation of social history and comes quickly to focus on questions of legitimacy in the conduct of institutional authority. Like the "administrative" perspective, the JTU approach is abstract in origin, but it lives only when the actions of teachers in schools do not comply with administrative expectations. The sincerity and dedication of the leftist teachers themselves become a central part of the message.

Behind these three rather clear-cut perspectives lies the shadow of educational history as conventionally interpreted. In a nutshell, prewar education is viewed as nationalistic and militaristic and therefore bad. In its negative character, it was accountable for contributing to Japanese militarism and imperialism. But teachers then were vital, dedicated, and unified around certain moral and social goals. Education was bad, but schools were good. Then, as now, intrusive politics polluted the local atmosphere. The assumption is that good relations and high morale develop best in an apolitical arena. By this perspective both the ministry and the union, despite their claims to be representative of postwar democracy, appear to most teachers in schools as essentially political and bureaucratic organizations seeking the same kind of authority wielded before the war by the Ministry of Education.

The school that "elects" neutral leaders is not interested in supporting or opposing high union policies so much as in staying a safe distance from all political activities and tendencies. Sakura High School has such a "centrist" union. The few activists in the school are carefully kept from control of the chapter. They must focus their union participation outside. Union activities are formalities largely and kept to a minimum. The head of the chapter, however, is busy attending prefectural and citywide union meetings, both to keep in touch and to lobby for his school's interests in policy formulations. He often asks for faculty support for some JTU activity primarily to maintain the credibility of his chapter.

Sakura is a night school. Its teachers are campaigning through the good offices of the union to kill an Office of Education proposal that would consolidate all the city's night schools into one as a solution to declining enrollments. The school's principal quietly encourages this lobbying. The faculty's reluctance to take stands on political issues is something very different from its keen interest in this matter. Independence from JTU politics is regularly tempered by the realization that the union has valuable leverage in the policymaking process. One evening, the students were being taken to see the movie *Mary Poppins*. Why? Because the teachers were going to City Hall to join a sit-in. They explained, "We do not want to appear to be an unsupportive chapter." It is worth noting in this regard that schools with more difficult educational tasks such as night schools and vocational schools are also ranked lower as workplaces by teachers. Locals in such schools more regularly have gripes with the administration and more use of union leverage.

In terms of numbers across the landscape of Kobe's twenty-eight public high schools, there are three or four union castles, a few totally dormant union chapters, and about eight similar to my second example (Otani). The majority resemble the Sakura case: independence mixed with appreciation of union usefulness.

Conflicts arise at particular times for a remarkable variety of reasons. In polarized schools, they are especially unpredictable and beyond the ability of teachers to control. The same miniscule matter that suddenly animates one faculty with tension and anger may in another school cause only the slightest ripple of concern. The difference lies of course in the fundamental relationship between the union and the administration. If it is one of assumed hostility, every suggestion and move by either side is suspect. Lacking a basis of trust, the grounds for solving problems other than by confrontation—and here I include forcing a victory through votes in faculty meetings—are missing. Persistent confrontation is rare, however, as it carries high costs for the union. If schools are seriously disrupted, parents and local politicians become angered. Most typically, the injured party in their eyes is the administration. The principal is "just doing his duty," while the union is "obstructing normal routines" for political purposes. The PTA can be a powerful force aligned against the union.

Conflict also creates powerful interpersonal tensions that show physically on the teachers. Physiological suffering is enough to make most of them anxious for a return to normal "harmonious" routines.

The numerous lines of relationship among a faculty also inhibit conflict. On the formal side, teachers are part of groups with responsibility for the instruction and supervision of particular grade levels. Cooperation here is very important. They also belong to subgroups centered on common academic subjects. These ties crosscut union loyalties and ideological commitments and serve to dampen faculty ardor. Most informal relations, on the other hand, reinforce political faction lines. Teachers who drink together, for example, tend to share common political viewpoints.

It is essential to realize that the management of many students and activities requires a high level of cooperation among virtually all teachers. A noisy classroom affects neighboring classes; an ill-prepared class is a burden to the next teachers; a delinquent student who goes unattended by a homeroom teacher sets a bad example; and so forth. Hostility, distrust, and power seeking in this environment are especially disruptive. Again, since the union must take the initiative to resist administrative incursions, the onus of being the troublemaker most often falls on its shoulders. But principals too are quite limited in power.

Many school histories are indeed marked by well-remembered moments or even months of political conflict, but even in the most conflictual situations daily routines are not regularly suspended and following high points of antagonism both sides seek accommodation. Pressure to follow politically inspired policies, left or right, typically alienates teacher sympathies. This explains much of the general caution exercised by both the JTU and the Ministry of Education in launching national campaigns that require broad teacher compliance. The union gambles when it decides to call for extensive local resistance; the ministry likewise takes a chance when it attempts to enforce its more disagreeable policies. Many campaigns, they realize, have served only to reveal their weakness. In sum, at the school level, despite considerable political conflict of a sporadic kind and much subtle maneuvering, a situation exists in which most high-level initiatives are not likely to meet with widespread success. As we have seen in these examples, the very nature of most school-level conflict is so local and particular in origin that it cannot be generalized. Rarely does it spread to other schools. Only at higher levels, where the origins of conflict are most calculated, does the organizational machinery exist to orchestrate broad conflict-producing campaigns.

The Prefectural Level

The picture at the prefectural and big-city level is also one of remarkable variation. Prefectural school boards are legally the employers with whom the teachers' unions must negotiate. The strength of the JTU in the prefecture, the politics of the school board, and the history of interaction between these two are the leading forces shaping the character of conflict in each of Japan's forty-seven prefectures and seven autonomous big-city school systems. A national JTU decision to strike or a ministry order to punish strikers, the two conventional heavy weapons employed by each side, produce a wide range of responses. One needs a prefecture-by-prefecture scorecard to track the outcomes, and both the ministry and the JTU headquarters do, in fact, follow developments in this fashion much as military commands would track complex engagements involving many units.[20]

Prefectural school boards are comprised of citizens distinguished for social service or cultural accomplishments appointed by the governor. Their influence is exercised through offices of education, where administrative power actually rests. Personnel matters, policy proposals, and the supervision of schools are all responsibilities of this office. Its head is a political appointee of the governor.

Offices of education are best understood as semiautonomous entities operating within a framework established by the various national laws regulating education. They are open to certain pressures or "guidance" from the Ministry of Education since that office finances parts of public education, enforces the nation's education laws, establishes national standards, sets school curricula, and approves textbooks. Matters left to the prefectural level for decision include partial budgeting, districting, entrance examinations, school expansion, the quality of instruction, personnel administration, special education, discipline, and curriculum improvement. Offices of education are not likely to produce significant innovations in areas where the Ministry of Education has primary authority and where national coordination is essential for reform. Yet, particularly if they belong to "progressive" administrations, they need not toe the ministry line closely. If the governor or mayor will support noncompliance and the legal precedents are not clear, offices of education can show independence and ministry efforts to discipline prefectural school systems have not been notably successful.[21] Kobe's office of education, for example, remains cautiously independent. It limits the flow of information that reaches the ministry whenever it is convenient and legal. It takes warnings and scoldings from the ministry stoically and actively argues its case at the national level when necessary.

How responsive are offices of education to ministry directives to punish union leaders and striking teachers? This is a particularly sensitive matter. Public employee strikes are illegal, but only prefectural offices of education can punish striking teachers. Borderline unions trying to build their strength and strong prefectural unions in the mainstream (Socialist Party) vanguard are more regularly and severely punished, except in the jurisdictions of "progressive" coalition governors and mayors. During the *shuntō* strike of 1975, for example, nearly every teacher who went on strike belonging to Shiga prefecture's very weak union received some kind of punishment; whereas only nineteen union leaders out of more than ten thousand strikers were punished in Tokyo where the school board is appointed by a governor backed by the Socialist and Communist parties. Shiga had a conservative governor who sought to blunt an effort at reviving JTU strength. "Progressive" administrations do not embrace the JTU. They have many contrary interests, but they avoid confrontations and this means not complying with Ministry of Education directives aimed at weakening the JTU.

Prefectural-level conflict also reflects recent history. Are the two sides on a collision course or disengaging from a previous higher level of conflict? To what degree each side complies with national-level directives is framed by the direction of their local relationship. At any point in time, some prefectures are entering periods of escalating hostility while others are moving toward greater compromise and rapprochement. Local political elections often set the direction.

Offices of education are staffed by people who come from the ranks of teachers. After serving in the administration, they return to positions in the schools. The responsibility to implement policy and almost all of the contact with schools is thus in the hands of teachers temporarily detailed to administrative jobs. All are seasoned teachers, but few are at the edge of retirement. They earn appointments by excellence as teachers and loyal service. They are neither strong supporters nor adamant opponents of the union. Respected, hardworking, and aligned with the administrative goal of maintaining efficient schooling, these staffers are also politically savvy. They tend to be firm pragmatists who can navigate the tricky waters of education politics.

No one is hired from outside the teacher corps and there is no regular track into school administration. After working from five to ten years at the office of education many are assigned to positions as vice-principals and ultimately as principals. The most promising are promoted to leadership within the administration. In effect, the office of education is the center for recruitment and training of an elite cadre of educational administrators. The group created in this manner deals with the union leadership.

Of approximately the same age and experience, the prefectural unions' leaders are former teachers recruited up through union channels during the same general time span. The two groups are very different in their politics, their personalities, and even in their styles of dress, but they are destined to face one another regularly.

In prefectures with strong unions and conservative governors, clashes are predictable. In several documented instances, following a gradual escalation of hostilities, the governor appointed an official of the Ministry of Education to head his office of education.[22] Using the legal and police power already in place, the new chief administrator declared open war on the union. In time, the union increased its strike and protest actions and, for a while, conflict engulfed the prefectural school system. Arrests of teachers, police searches of union offices, and the administrative punishment of union leaders in schools was accompanied by repeated union sit-ins, demonstrations, complaints in the legislature, and intensification of union activities in individual schools.[23] Not only were ministry experts brought in but the Tokyo JTU, we can be sure, was well represented on the union side too.

No such heavy hand of authority is visible in Kobe, a city with a "progressive" mayor. Supervisors from the office of education circulate almost daily among the schools, listening, observing, and consulting. They concentrate on learning about the conditions and they know a remarkable amount about the political situation of each school. But they are careful to wait for the appropriate time and place to take corrective action. Their major concern is that things run smoothly. A low profile, but persistent management, is characteristic.

Even though they seek to avoid union opposition to their plans, suspicion on both sides is strong and dislike of the other's leadership stemming from past confrontations can also be a factor. The union's power is threatened in a very real manner by the very fact of good administration. And the office of education has a real interest in weakening the union. Personnel management is often the critical means to this end.

In hiring new teachers, there is a concern to avoid potential union activists. Transfers and promotions are more critical. Through judicious use of transfers, the offices of education work to gain ground in establishing their control over school faculties. They can weaken union leadership in one school by removing or adding teachers according to their politics. The tactic of "writing off" a union castle allows them to reduce union influence in other schools. What can be accomplished quickly is limited, however, and the union stands ready to fight political transfers.

Offices of education vary according to local politics, but on the union side the degree of variation is even greater.[24] In six prefectures the JTU represents but a very small fraction of all teachers; in another eleven, its membership hovers below the 50 percent level. A few of these weaker prefectural unions have a feisty leadership,[25] but as a rule aggressive moves by such weak unions lead to further declines in teacher enrollment rates. All these prefectures are rural in character and their politics are notably conservative.

The capacity of a prefectural union to call out its forces successfully depends on the compliance of hundreds of separate school chapters and, as we have seen, the dynamics of conflict at that level are notably complex. Even among the prefectural unions that have the highest rates of enrollment, the degree of actual participation by members in strikes and other actions varies considerably. The Fukuoka and

Osaka unions, for example, both have the same enrollment rates, yet they averaged 85 and 35 percent respectively in the level of membership participation in recent strike actions.[26] The reliability of school-level support is a product of union discipline, the political consciousness of teachers, and school-level leadership.

Furthermore, the mainstream or antimainstream character of local leadership is a good predictor of how much energy prefectural unions will put into campaigns initiated by Tokyo JTU headquarters. Mainstream unions are typically more aggressive; antimainstreamers hold back in some national campaigns. Mainstream leaders are working their way up in the national union hierarchy and often owe personal loyalty to leaders at national headquarters. It is in their personal interest to mobilize with dedication. The interests of prefectural antimainstream leaders are different, since their basic concern is to maintain and strengthen their own local base of support. Chapters with centrist leadership are also, of course, problematic. Their mobilization in serious disputes is far from certain and the degree of their participation in all kinds of campaigns is hard to predict. Prefectural JTU politics must be made with these limitations in mind. Estimating the proper degree of opposition and managing to draw out maximum support from the various chapters is the heart of JTU leadership at this level.

Other important limitations are also at work. JTU policies cannot lead to the loss of respect for teachers on the part of parents and students who are politically naive and ideologically disinterested. The legitimacy of union authority fluctuates in the locality according to public perceptions of which side is acting correctly. At the beginning of issue-oriented conflict, however, it is often difficult to predict even how teachers will view each side's actions. This also makes for caution except in the case of JTU mainstream, strongly entrenched, prefectural unions. Otherwise the quasi-independence of a majority of chapters is a basic source of organizational uncertainty. Many prefectural unions compromise ahead of the national headquarters or enter campaigns halfheartedly for this reason.

An internal threat must also be considered in the equation. Prefectural JTU officers must be confirmed annually by an election involving all union members. Normally these elections rubber stamp an uncontested, official slate of candidates, but if a group of teachers keen on the Socialist Party, for example, wish to oust a Communist Party oriented leadership (or vice versa) and are willing to organize and await the right opportunity, takeovers are possible. As a rule there is remarkable continuity of factional control at this level, testifying to how difficult it is to manage a prefectural union takeover, but the possibility alone introduces a further reason for caution. Where the leadership (Socialist or Communist) is more radical than the membership, highly politicized policies have the greatest likelihood of alienating the membership and preparing the way for a takeover by the other faction.

In 1976, for example, the JTU decided on a major campaign to oppose the ministry's directive to all school boards that they establish an intermediate supervisory level in every school. What happened prefecture by prefecture was most revealing. The pattern of resulting conflict was quite varied. Known as the *shūnin* system, the administrative change converted the set of senior faculty positions to paid jobs in the administration. No new responsibilities were created, but the union saw the *shūnin* system as an attempt to extend administration power and authority deeper into the fabric of school organization. The extension of salary benefits to the senior teachers made them subject to administrative influence and challenged the notion that middle-level offices belong to the faculty. Administrative appointment would replace collegial election. Furthermore, despite the ministry's refusal to offer supplemental pay for extracurricular work, in creating the *shūnin* system it established a selective plan of extra pay benefiting only the older teachers.

Yet the ministry's justifications for this innovation were not unreasonable. The number of middle-aged teachers had increased considerably in the seventies, but the number of openings for promotion to principal and vice-principal had expanded very little. The traditional capstone of a male teaching career, a principalship, was a receding possibility for many deserving teachers. Their morale was down. The *shūnin* job was presented almost as a consolation to those unable to achieve the dignity and status of a principal's position. It was also argued, again with justification, that the middle management level was weak, unpopular, and increasingly the source of inefficiency and friction in school organization. Teachers I spoke with in Kobe confirmed both the union's fears and the ministry's rationale and some added further observations. The real meaning of the change would depend primarily on the administration-union situation in each school. A de facto *shūnin* system was already in place in schools with strong principals; in schools where the union was strong, this innovation would not shift the balance of power. They also doubted that the high costs involved in political strife would justify the benefits of winning or losing to either side. Notice their school-centered perspective on the national issue.

The origins of the conflict may even have been accidental. Michio Nagai, the first minister of education in a long time to be interested in opening and maintaining a dialogue with the national JTU, reportedly did not like the *shūnin* idea but found himself committed to it through LDP pressures and previous ministry commitments.[27] For a number of weeks before the JTU's decision to totally oppose it was taken, there was considerable negotiation of the issue between his office and JTU headquarters in Tokyo.[28] Relations between the union and the ministry had been improving up to that point, but conflict over the *shūnin* plan returned them to one of uncompromising confrontation.

The ministry ordered all school boards to comply; union national headquarters ordered all prefectural and big-city teachers' unions to resist. Within days, the *shūnin* system was confirmed and established in a few prefectures. In others, even three years later, no progress had been made toward its institution. Where school administrations sought relatively harmonious relations with strong unions (this was especially true in cities like Kobe), the administrations themselves avoided compliance with the ministry's directive. Tokyo, for example, announced it would establish the system only with the agreement of the union, which was, of course, not forthcoming. Hyōgo opted to leave the choice up to individual schools, saying, in effect, that no change was necessary. Where strong mainstream unions and determined offices of education confronted one another, as in Hokkaido, Fukuoka, and Kagoshima, a drawn-out period of protests, strikes, punishments of strikers, and police raids on union headquarters punctuated the gradual institution, school by school, of the *shūnin* system. Three years later a handful of schools, the union castles, were still holding out in each of these prefectures.

The dates and styles of school board decisions varied.[29] Most prepared the way with much private consultation with their local unions. Those that quickly followed the ministry's lead were, in effect, challenging weak unions to resist. The amount of time that elapsed between school board decision and actual implementation at the school level also varied presumably in relation to the degree of behind-the-scenes union resistance and the complexity of the compromise process. Strikes also differed in intensity, number, duration, and degree of teacher participation. In many cases, they seem to have been staged more for the benefit of national JTU headquarters than to stem the tide of change. Punishments also varied greatly. Prolonged conflict was limited to a small number of prefectures. Careful compromise, partially disguised by more aggressive public postures, was the outcome in other places like Tokyo, Osaka, and Kobe. Only where the union was weakest did the new system go into place almost overnight. If we remind ourselves that the majority of teachers and students belong to urban areas where local autonomous compromises were worked out, then we can conclude that the *shūnin* battle had no real winner or loser. The *shūnin* crisis, the greatest conflict in education in a decade, revealed how the institutional context served to differentiate the process and produce results that were themselves ambiguous. Lower-level compliance with national initiatives varied greatly for reasons that were institutional and local, not just because of an attitudinal gap between teachers and JTU leaders.

To summarize, then, the prefectural level of conflict is generally characterized by three traits: considerable independence from national authority; a distinct set of institutional and organizational interests separate from those of the school and the national levels; and limited authority over, but great reliance on, school-level responses. Both sides conduct themselves in a complex manner that involves considered orchestration of antagonistic and compromising stances, public and private contacts, ideological and practical considerations. Both sides are involved with local elections and aware of the power of voter reaction to conflict in education. Both sides also seek to satisfy higher organizational authorities without alienating their constituencies at the school level.

In order to innovate as well as to maintain order and efficiency in the daily conduct of a whole school system, cooperation and consultation between the office of education and the prefectural JTU are usually necessary. Because they are responsible for the actual administration of school routines, personnel systems, and enormous bureaucratic detail, administrations can tolerate only limited amounts of opposition from a union before the system breaks down. The unions, for their part, have reason to cooperate in order to gain a voice in these smaller matters and thus represent local teachers' interests more effectively. Neither side normally wants prolonged conflict, for it undermines their essential capacities as organizations, tied as they are to the regular functioning of the school system.

In contrast to the schools, however, union-administration relations are not conducted in a small-group atmosphere. Face-to-face consultations and negotiations occur to a larger extent than at the national level, yet the separate organizations and organizational interests of both sides are strictly preserved. One measure of this separation is the bifurcation of career paths.

If, however, one or both sides do decide to intensify their antagonism and push for more power, bitter, intense, and costly conflict can result. The reasons why such conflict can become so intense are the same as those explaining why compromise is normally so necessary: More is at stake when cooperation is necessary to run the system. Simmel's point about the potential for destructive intensity being proportional to the degree of intimacy fits here, but most notably as an aspect of school-level conflict. The potential for damage is a great encouragement for moderation.

The National Level

Throughout the postwar years, it is at the national level that the sides have been drawn the most clearly, where disagreements and antagonisms have received the greatest public exposure, where policy has been most politicized, and where education has been tied most explicitly to the general struggle between the two political camps. The means for pressing conflict have also been different.

The Ministry of Education and the conservative party have attempted to weaken union influence by changing education laws.[30] The national legislature was at times embroiled in conflict over education. The JTU national headquarters, for its part, has waged a persistent campaign of criticism of ministry policies. Its well-developed system of research, investigation, and committee deliberation amount to nearly a shadow ministry.

In the Diet, where the LDP has had a permanent majority, education bills of a highly political nature have been forced through preceded by tumultuous clashes, sometimes including violence, but the government has on other occasions withdrawn bills in the face of fierce minority opposition. The intensity of the conflict waxes and wanes but remains essentially political. There is less reason to compromise at the national level, since responsibility for the normal functioning of school systems lies elsewhere.

The ministry and LDP are in control of policymaking. The JTU's role is one of fixed opposition. Both sides are geared for conflict and their normal public postures are hostile.[31] In the union personnel system, individuals competent in one or more aspects of mobilizing for conflict rise to leadership positions. Tokyo headquarters has an abundance of people from the most activist mainstream prefectural unions. Promotions in key areas of the ministry also go often to bureaucrats with the necessary mettle and skills to pursue conflict with the union.

The top level of any institution is characterized by a density of information and a premium on effective communication. Control depends on establishing a "world view" for the institution and promulgating guidelines for conduct. At the national level in education, however, ideology is inordinately important in Japan. The political allies of each side see education in ideological terms. Intellectuals and extremists are attracted to the politics of education. Removed from the concrete administration of school systems, both sides spend much time and resources in direct symbolic controls: rules, rationales, policy arguments, research, propaganda.

Officials from the national JTU headquarters and the ministry have little, often no, public contact and their back-door associations have been quite limited. In the fifties and sixties they purposely chose to isolate themselves as part of their strategy for conflict, a recourse much less common at the prefectural level and impossible in schools. Removed from the daily affairs of schooling, preoccupied with politics and ideology, confronting an imposing array of local variation, both sides at the national level naturally deal in grand generalizations and abstractions.

Only when one side has actively sought to change the power balance by a bold move has national conflict passed down through the entire institution. The union at lower levels can take certain initiatives, but only the government side has the power to change the law. The great political clashes of the postwar period have been ignited by government moves. Many of these were justified as efforts to counter union challenges compounding at lower levels, but the fact remains that broad confrontations have begun with the ministry.

Several close examinations of conservative decision making in education reveal that LDP dietmen with a special interest in education (the *bunkyōzoku*) have been the mainspring of most aggressive moves against the union.[32] The question of initiative is complicated by several facts: Not only does the ministry contain bureaus and factions with different persuasions and degrees of party affiliation but ministers of education bring with them different attitudes toward conflict with the union. What is clear is that fighting the union is seen by many LDP politicians as an aspect of dealing with the political opposition. Within the Ministry of Education, there are many officials who would prefer to avoid conflict because improved education rather than defeat of a political enemy is their major goal.

Furthermore, the ministry "doves," we may presume, focus their attentions on urban situations where indeed the LDP intentions of weakening union power have not succeeded, whereas the largely rural-based Diet members of the *bunkyōzoku* are interested primarily in prefectures where the efficacy of aggressive moves is much higher. Lower-level variations even help explain differences within the conservative camp. The case of the decision to institute the *shūnin* system illustrates this point, as it was a small group of largely rural Diet members (along with certain more politically oriented bureaus within the ministry) that led the way. The year and a half of conflict that followed led to such checkered results that both factions could claim justification for their position. As already noted, the national JTU has its own internal factional problems that limit its capacity to take initiative at the national level.

In sum, then, the national level is politically the most polarized of the three and, due to the low degree of mutual involvement in maintaining the institution, the least limited in the pursuit of conflict. National campaigns to shift the power balance are infrequent, because they are largely ineffective. Hostile posturing in legal, symbolic, and ideological terms is not proof of power; perhaps just the reverse. As we would expect given the overall high quality of Japanese public education and the continuing power stalemate, there is always a lot of smoke but only periodically very much fire. Following each outbreak matters return to a rather noisy, but nonetheless tame, stalemate.

Conclusion

It remains to summarize the lessons of this case of conflict within a large institution as they apply to conflict theory in general. Institutional environments differ widely according to many factors: the way formal authority is distributed, the number of relevant levels within the hierarchy, the degree of functional diversity among vertically aligned divisions (education has little because schools are functionally so similar), the degree of outside pressure for normal functioning, the degree of relevance of ideological concerns, the institution's world view, the relevance of outside political forces, and the nature of the partisan organizations within the institution. All of these matters, for example, distinguish one system of education from another and distinguish education from other types of large institutions.

The invariable qualities are those between conflict processes and those *dimensions* of any environment (institutional or otherwise) that govern the manner in which conflict is pursued. Stating these dimensions involves rather awkward language, but in this case they have been:

1. The "tangibility" of interaction (from daily face-to-face to impersonal and abstract)
2. The price of no cooperation (from intolerable chaos to no effect)
3. The "connectedness" of institutional elements (from greatly dispersed independence to immediate and highly integrated authority)
4. The nature of power and authority (from compliance to physical force)

Because institutional environments are differentiated and complex, the conflict processes differ from level to level within the system. The pattern of connections among the many conflict processes within one institution assumes a distinct character that is not just additive, because conflict in each part of the whole has the potential to inspire or inhibit conflict in other parts. The anticipation of such intrainstitutional influences becomes a major factor itself.

As each element comes to appreciate the costs of conflict (including those initiated elsewhere in the institution) and as noncompliance increases when costs are high or when the expectation of noncompliance from subordinate elements is high, the partisan inclination to initiate and escalate conflict is inhibited. Experience with such limitations grows over time in institutional environments. Partisan organizations may remain, but they do so by maintaining a public posture of hostility while adjusting their actions to fit a more informed sense of the real costs, benefits, and possibilities of pursuing conflict in such an environment. The gap between *tatemae* and *honne, omote* and *ura*, grows.

The result is a greater institutionalization of conflict. Not only are the processes of conflict instituted in the sense of regularized, but conflict is adjusted to the nature of the institution. And neutral means of coping with political polarization arise within the institution. "Institutionalization" means all three tendencies. Much of the accommodation in this case occurred at a level so low in the overall structure as to be generally imperceptible to nonparticipants.

Institutionalization implies lack of change. But if we consider the lowest level we see very real change in such things as patterns of school control. Such changes are notable if the relationships affected are ubiquitous to the institution. In the case of Japanese education, the democratization of many schools' faculties and the notable degree of independence of some schools from high authority can both be attributed to the opening wedge of administration-union conflict. Much the same kind of change occurred in relations between students and faculty during the student protests of the 1960s despite the failure of most confrontations with university officials at higher levels.[33] Such change of a micropolitical sort is largely ad hoc, varied, and lacking in institutional legitimacy.[34] Its permanency is not assured except by the persistence of the initial pressures behind it. When microlevel change accumulates, however, it presents higher-level authorities with clear evidence of the limitations constraining their power and causes them to act with greater caution and indirectness, playing for time.

Normally we assume that the higher the level of organization, the more we will find symbolic emphasis on unity and powerful mechanisms for conflict resolution. Pomp and circumstance, high courts, and other aspects of a singular higher authority typify our normal assumption that conflicts arising at lower levels of an institution are solved at higher levels to which they are taken. Institutional civil war seems unnatural, a point made by the many Japanese teachers who found politics alien to education. In this case, however, pressures for conflict resolution lie largely at lower levels. Ad hoc solutions are found there because the option of taking problems to higher authority is largely missing. The failure to compromise in the policymaking process at the top means they are sought in the implementation stage at lower levels. Micropolitical change thus appears dynamic because of macropolitical deadlock. The majority of Japanese schools are more independent and less political than anyone would predict from events at the national level.

Institutional levels greatly affect the character of conflict processes. At the national level, they remain largely symbolic, predictable, and at arm's length. Hostility is deliberate and seldom marked by the intensity of emotion that accompanies conflict in schools. The notable exception has been Diet debates of education bills which themselves have had a face-to-face component. Conflict in schools, on the other hand, quickly permeates all activities and relationships. It is not easily forgotten nor easily objectified. It becomes personal and destructive of the fabric of trust and mutuality. Faculty unity at the school level, furthermore, is largely an assumed goal, the key to cooperation and goodwill. As Simmel so astutely noted long ago, "When unity is the point of departure and the basis of the relationship, and conflict arises over this unity, the synthesis between monism and antagonism of the relation can have the opposite result. A conflict of this sort is usually more passionate and radical than when it does not meet with a prior or simultaneous mutual belongingness."[35]

History contains many documented cases of well-organized conflicts within institutions, but all of these are of short duration and involve swift revolutionary change or powerful repression of dissent. In postwar Japan, neither of these conclusive results has occurred in education. It is likely that other public institutions would tell the same story as the school system if examined closely at all levels.[36] It has been the institutional context that has forced the "institutionalization" of left-right conflict.

We have, I think, found in this story the answers to two fundamental questions: How could postwar education remain so effective despite intense internal political turmoil? And what has happened to the deep political schism which divided the public bureaucracies that were unionized during the American Occupation? Considered in this manner, postwar Japan can be seen to be working through some of its basic conflicts at a level of society that is rarely considered in detail and by processes that are widely misunderstood.

NOTES

Support from the Japan Foundation for a year of fieldwork in Japanese high schools (1974–1975) is gratefully acknowledged.

1. Anthropological studies of conflict processes have led to a questioning of notions (labeled functionalist) about conflict necessarily moving toward a point of resolution. The analytic assumption of an integrated, well-functioning society as a starting point is rejected as inappropriate. Conflict is seen not as aberrant but as inherent to the social and cultural character of social systems large and small. Equilibrium is not inherent either, since there is no reason to assume a priori that power is balanced. See Lloyd Fallers, *Bantu Bureaucracy* (Cambridge: Cambridge University Press, 1956); Victor W. Turner, *Schism and Continuity in an African Society: A Study of Ndembu Village Life* (New York: Humanities Press, 1957); and Alan R. Beals and Bernard J. Siegal, *Divisiveness and Social Conflict: An Anthropological Approach* (Stanford: Stanford University Press, 1966). We will return to the questions of inevitability and equilibrium at the conclusion of this essay.

2. Beginning with Simmel, theories of conflict have long recognized the distinction between intimate and impersonal relations, but the influence of institutional structure on conflict within large organizational entities has not received theoretical

attention as far as I can tell. There are, on the other hand, numerous case studies of the politics of organizations and bureaucracies and an equally sizable literature on union-management conflicts. These works tend, however, to focus on other factors and limit their attention to specific events or levels of organization rather than considering the overall pattern—battles rather than wars are described. Historians who look at institutions over the course of time, by contrast, rarely have access to the kinds of details necessary to reveal the complexities of the general pattern, especially if the overall outcome is near stalemate.

3. This statement is confirmed by Yoshio Sugimoto, "Quantitative Characteristics of Popular Disturbances in Post-Occupation Japan (1952–1960)," *Journal of Asian Studies* 37 (2)(1978): 273–291, who through a review of newspapers from 1952 to 1960 found that public employee unionists, especially railroad workers and teachers, were the most active in public disturbances and that educational issues had greater penetration throughout all prefectures as sources of disturbances than issues such as the U.S.–Japan Security Treaty Revision of 1960.

4. John Singleton, *Nichu: A Japanese School* (New York: Holt, Rinehart and Winston, 1967); Kenjiro Inazumi, *Hikisakareta Kyōiku* (Tokyo: Kyōiku Kaihatsu Kenkyūsho, 1974); Thomas P. Rohlen, "Violence at Yoka High School: The Implications for Japanese Coalition Politics of the Confrontation Between the Communist Party and the Buraku Liberation League," *Asian Survey* 16 (7)(1976): 682–699.

5. See Byron K. Marshall, "The Tradition of Conflict in the Governance of Japan's Imperial Universities," *History of Education Quarterly* (Winter 1977): 385–406, for a historical view of conflict in the public university system. The conflicts he describes do not involve a powerful union but, rather, opposition between two institutions—the Ministry of Education and the university.

6. See Inazumi *Hikisakareta Kyōiku,* and many accounts in the Japanese press.

7. Benjamin Duke, *Japan's Militant Teachers: A History of the Left-Wing Teachers' Movement* (Honolulu: University of Hawaii Press, 1973); Donald R. Thurston, *Teachers and Politics in Japan* (Princeton: Princeton University Press, 1973); T. J. Pempel, "The Bureaucratization of Policymaking in Postwar Japan," *American Journal of Political Science* 18 (4)(1974): 647–664; and Yung H. Park, "Education Policy-Making in Contemporary Japan: A Study of the Liberal Democratic Party and the Ministry of Education," unpublished manuscript, 1978.

8. There are many accounts of the changes in policy during the American Occupation. The most succinct is contained in Tetsuya Kobayashi, *Society, Schools and Progress in Japan* (Oxford: Pergamon Press, 1976). See also Mark Gayn, *Japan Diary* (New York: William Sloane Associates, 1948); Robert King Hall, *Education for a New Japan* (New Haven: Yale University Press, 1949).

9. Duke, *Japan's Militant Teachers;* Thurston, *Teachers and Politics in Japan.*

10. Duke, *Japan's Militant Teachers;* Thurston, *Teachers and Politics in Japan;* Park, "Education Policy-Making in Contemporary Japan."

11. Pempel, "The Bureaucratization of Policymaking in Postwar Japan."

12. See Terence K. Hopkins, *Bureaucratic Authority: Convergence of Weber and Barnard,* in A. Etzioni, ed., *Complex Organization: A Sociological Reader* (New York: Holt, Rinehart and Winston, 1961), for a discussion of compliance as used here.

13. Compare Duke, *Japan's Militant Teachers,* and Thurston, *Teachers and Politics in Japan,* both of whom have viewed this situation in terms of the JTU experience,

with T. J. Pempel, "The Politics of Higher Education in Postwar Japan," Ph.D. dissertation, Columbia University, 1975, and Park, "Education Policy-Making in Contemporary Japan," both of whom have considered authority and decision making from the ministry perspective.

14. Duke, *Japan's Militant Teachers;* Thurston, *Teachers and Politics in Japan.*

15. Both Thurston and Duke treat the subject largely in this manner.

16. Thurston's discussion of the school-level character of union chapters is a solid beginning, but it oversimplifies matters in the direction of giving the union leader and principal more authority and initiative than they typically possess. Their knowledge of teacher sentiment, whether expressed openly in meetings and votes or implied in more subtle circumstances, deeply influences their conduct with one another and with higher authorities. Silent teachers are telling their leaders a great deal, and unenthusiastic compliance is usually of very limited duration.

17. Roger W. Benjamin, "Images of Conflict Resolution and Social Control: American and Japanese Attitudes Toward the Adversary System," *Journal of Conflict Resolution* 19 (1)(1975): 123–131, presents research evidence to the effect that Japanese are more inclined than Americans to view adversary processes with distaste. This theme has been a major one in cultural portraits of Japan from a comparative perspective.

18. Singleton, *Nichu: A Japanese School,* writes of a teacher who though personally opposed to union policies and goals dutifully carried out his responsibilities on the union's behalf once elected to the position of leader of his school's local. Did he do this out of loyalty to the school's faculty or out of a peculiar notion of duty (strong in Japan) that sees suppression of self in fulfilling social roles as virtuous? Probably some of both. This is an extreme case, yet it illustrates the complexities of the union's organization at ground level.

19. The emphasis here on the influence of face-to-face relations in small groups as a key factor inhibiting conflict can be distinguished analytically from the emphasis on Japanese norms per se as they inhibit conflict. The power of cultural norms for inhibiting conflict is, however, significant in groups like faculties that are neither very intimate nor very small. But I would add that the norms actually contribute to the escalation of conflict when events in such groups go so far as to symbolize the collapse of mutuality. By not acknowledging conflict openly, Japanese norms set the stage for a radical breach, even violence, if conflict is not carefully managed. See T. Hanami's essay in this volume for further discussion of this point.

20. In order to follow the course of various prefectural-level developments across the country, I relied on two sources: a news clipping service that publishes monthly virtually all the education-related newspaper articles from all the nation's local newspapers and Ministry of Education statistical computations on prefecture-by-prefecture strikes, punishments, and strike participation rates. See Ministry of Education, "Kyōikuin no soshiki suru shokuin dantai no gaikyō: 1976," unpublished report, 1977; and other unpublished compilations regarding the *shūninsei* issue.

21. I have not found any published material on ministry efforts to control independent offices of education; my generalization here stems from what I was told by Kobe administrators. Interviews at the ministry might produce a different picture, as undoubtedly its officials have a higher estimate of their power.

22. See Inazumi, *Hikisakareta Kyōiku,* on Fukuoka prefecture; see newspaper articles from Kagoshima prefecture contained in the education clipping service Kirinuki Sokuho from 1976.

23. Union legal suits to contest punishments are costly and time-consuming. (They last for many years.) Moderate offices of education and school boards are thus reluctant to follow ministry directives to punish striking teachers simply to symbolize their illegality. Only the most conflict-oriented prefectural administrations consistently and on a large scale punish teachers for striking.

24. Ministry of Education unpublished report entitled "Kyōshokuin no soshiki suru shokuin dantai no genjo," undated.

25. Some unions in the just under 50 percent category (Kagoshima, Miyazaki, Kumamoto, Nagasaki, Fukuoka, and Aomori) have very high enrollment rates of new teachers. They are aggressive, mainstream unions; disciplinary action against them by prefectural administrations is common.

26. Inazumi, *Hikisakareta Kyōiku.*

27. A story I have heard from several Japanese professors of education close to Tokyo authorities.

28. Interview with Michio Nagai in 1981.

29. Based on the informal tabulations of the Ministry of Education and local newspaper reports supplied by the education clipping service Kirinuki Sokuho.

30. Pempel, "The Politics of Higher Education," and Park, "Education Policy-Making in Contemporary Japan," are the two examinations of the ministry I am depending upon primarily. Yawao Wada, *Mombushō* (Tokyo: Kyoikusha Shinsho, 1974), provides general information on the ministry.

31. On the JTU see Thurston, *Teachers and Politics in Japan,* and Duke, *Japan's Militant Teachers.*

32. Park, "Education Policy-Making in Contemporary Japan," and Pempel, "The Politics of Higher Education."

33. James G. March and Johan P. Olsen, *Ambiguity and Choice in Organizations* (Bergen: Universitatsforlaget, 1976).

34. See Tom Burns, "Micropolitics: Mechanisms of Institutional Change," *Administrative Science Quarterly* 6 (1961): 257–281, for a discussion of the micropolitics of organizations.

35. Georg Simmel, *Conflict* and *The Web of Group-Affiliations,* trans. Kurt H. Wolff and Reinhard Bendix (New York: Free Press, 1955), 42.

36. Labor campaigns that do not center on a single institutional context have proved to be very different in Japan. See Sepp Linhart, "Shuntō: On the Institutionalization of Social Conflicts in Present-Day Japan," *Proceedings of the Fourth Kyushu International Cultural Conference, 1977* (Fukuoku UNESCO Association, 1978) for an excellent analysis of the dynamics of nationwide joint-wage campaigns. Contrast this account with labor disputes within companies such as those described by Tadashi Hanami in this volume and by R. C. Clark, "Union-Management Conflict in a Japanese Company," in W. Beasley, ed., *Modern Japan: Aspects of History, Literature and Society* (London: Allen & Unwin, 1975).

8

Student Conflict

Patricia G. Steinhoff

College students have been at the center of many of postwar Japan's most visible conflicts. While training to become the country's economic, political, and technical leaders, they have also been its most virulent critics. Students have provided both workers and organizational expertise for a variety of social protest movements in Japan, and they have protested conditions within universities as well. Throughout its postwar history, the Japanese student movement has been engaged simultaneously in external conflict with representatives of the state and universities and internal conflict among factions of participating students.

Since student conflict is open and acknowledged in Japan, the purpose of applying conflict theory in this study is not so much to find conflict beneath a veneer of harmony as it is an attempt to discover a coherent pattern in a complex tangle of conflicts occurring on many levels simultaneously.

Perhaps the most visible pattern in postwar Japanese student conflict has been its progression from a massive, relatively unified movement with widespread popular support in the late 1950s to a much smaller, badly divided movement which had lost most public support for its increasingly violent tactics by the 1970s. A second pattern has been the movement's strong attraction for the "best and the brightest" of the student population. Elite universities have been major centers of violent student protest, and the central ranks of the more radical student organizations have been filled with highly intelligent, competent, emotionally healthy students from stable homes. The movement was led, and followed, into violence by normal young people who had been marked for success in the mainstream of Japanese society.

A variant of conflict theory called labeling theory can be used to explicate these two patterns and trace their connections to various levels of conflict in the student movement. The thesis of labeling theory is that when a large, well-organized group comes to feel threatened by a far smaller, less powerful group, the dominant group will try to manage the conflict by discrediting its small enemy. It accomplishes this by identifying, or "labeling," the smaller group's members as deviant in some way that requires removal of their full social rights and the imposition of official supervision over them. Often a new category of deviance has to be invented to match the situation or an old category must be newly tailored to fit. This process requires an elaborate campaign to convince the public that the behavior is both illegitimate and dangerous. Usually a corps of specialists is created who can help identify and supervise the "deviants." An important corollary of the argument is that such a strategy can only be fully effective if the targets of the campaign cooperate by accepting the label and incorporating it into their personal identity. The theory has been applied to the Prohibition movement in the United States as well as to such phenomena as juvenile delinquency and mental illness.

This essay argues that such a labeling process occurred in the conflict between the Japanese student movement and civil and university authorities. It was not necessarily deliberate policy; nor was it inevitable. Rather, certain conditions facilitated its emergence, and others supported it once it began. The result was that the authorities succeeded in shrinking and containing the student movement, but at the same time they helped radicalize a segment of the movement into guerrilla and terrorist activity that perpetuated the conflict on new terms.

By the late 1960s, a 29,000-man elite police force, the Kidō-tai, devoted its time to controlling student riots and gathering intelligence on specific student organizations; plainclothes police conducted round-the-clock surveillance of more than a hundred student activists. The national government, by the passage of special legislation, had obtained the right to intervene in university conflicts involving students. Several thousand college students acquired arrest records during the late 1960s and early 1970s, and hundreds have served time for a variety of offenses related to participation in the student movement. Arrests and trials stemming from student protest activities continue to the present time, and a handful of Japanese student activists have been on international wanted lists for terrorist activities since the early 1970s. Beginning in 1969, Japanese corporate employers systematically excluded ex-student activists in their recruitment, a practice upheld by a 1973 Supreme Court ruling. Student activism of a certain type had clearly become a category of deviance against which the forces of the state were deployed. Substantial numbers of individuals were losing social rights and privileges because of their participation in such activities. Moreover, the very people affected had previously been certified as the legitimate heirs of the society by virtue of having surmounted the major qualifying hurdles of the college entrance exam system.

Whether this set of circumstances can be considered an example of labeling depends on how well the evidence fits the theory. Whether the appellation is useful depends on what other aspects of student conflict are illuminated thereby. In this essay I aim to demonstrate both the appropriateness and the utility of a labeling theory interpretation of student conflict by tracing the causes and consequences of the labeling process through various levels of conflict.

The Postwar Student Movement

The postwar student movement emerged shortly after the war ended, when students returning to the universities banded together in self-help groups for economic support and then began to criticize university policies. From its inception, the movement defined itself as a conflict group representing the interests of students. Many of the most active students were sympathetic to the Japan Communist Party (JCP), which was then enjoying its moment of glory as the only group in Japan that could claim to have been right about the war. A similarly ideological student movement had flourished briefly during the 1920s, only to be thoroughly suppressed in the next decade.[1] The postwar movement thus began with some lessons learned but no institutionalized arrangements for representing student interests in the new Japan. Conflict began, and it evoked responses.

Neither side was without models. The student movement drew on the theory and experience of the international communist movement; the universities and government drew on their prewar experiences in controlling political dissent. Both sides drew on Western democratic models deliberately and on traditional Japanese culture unconsciously. Out of the initial conflict there quickly developed the one institutional arrangement that has been the foundation of the postwar student movement, providing simultaneously its legitimacy and its economic base: the *jichikai*.

Each college (or, in large, differentiated universities, each faculty) has an officially recognized student self-government association to which every enrolled student automatically belongs. The university acknowledges the *jichikai* by incorporating its dues into the tuition payment system, thus ensuring a stable economic base for the organization. All students are entitled to vote for delegates to the self-government association, who in turn elect a smaller committee to run it. Simultaneously with the establishment of *jichikai* throughout Japan, an organization with close ties to the Japan Communist Party united all the *jichikai* into an All-Japan Federation of Student Self-Governing Associations (Zen Nihon Gakusei Jichikai Sōrengō, abbreviated to Zengakuren).

Zengakuren followed the Communist Party's sharp change of direction in the early 1950s, from promoting peaceful democracy to seeking immediate revolution, despite some internal controversy. When the JCP line abruptly shifted back in 1956, certain segments of the student movement became disillusioned with the party. As the internal split grew wider, some student leaders were purged from JCP membership, which further widened the breach. By 1960 there were clear JCP and anti-JCP factions within Zengakuren, and within a few years there were separate Zengakuren organizations reflecting JCP and anti-JCP positions. The JCP no longer in any sense controls the student movement, although it still has some influence over the relatively moderate faction that is allied with it.

The break with the JCP freed the student movement of conflict generated by the pressure to follow a party line that did not always appear rational. At the same time, it created a new source of internal conflict. Without any external standard by which to judge the correctness of a policy, the movement was left to its own ideological devices. The students soon proved to be extremely creative in devising new ideological justifications for different courses of action. The only standards by which these new alternatives could be evaluated was the willingness of members to follow them, a willingness based primarily on personal power. The problem of ideology and policy was critical, because the students were more or less continuously involved in external conflict.

Two aspects of this external conflict have contributed particularly to internal conflict. First, the movement has been engaged almost continuously in making decisions about whom to conflict with, what the issues of conflict would be, and how to carry on the conflict. Second, since much of the external conflict has been unsuccessful in achieving its aims, the movement has been continuously involved in reevaluating its failures and seeking new directions.

Coser has pointed out that organizations engaged in continuous external conflict have greater need than other groups for internal unity and are more likely to try to suppress internal dissent.[2] As the student movement has splintered, each faction has carried over much of the internal organization of the original unified Zengakuren. The procedures for arriving at decisions and ensuring compliance are very similar in all the organizations, though of course there are individual variations in style or emphasis. Consequently, it is still possible to talk about mechanisms of conflict management in the student movement, even though the movement is now composed of a number of distinct groups which harbor varying degrees of hostility toward one another. Clearly the development of antagonistic relations between groups within the student movement creates more external conflict for each separate group, which in turn further increases the pressure for internal unity and suppression of dissent.

Four basic decision and compliance procedures are used in the Japanese student movement. The first establishes who can make decisions and who should comply with them; the second specifies further how decisions will be reached and compliance ensured; the third handles instances of individual or group noncompliance and provides further means of obtaining ultimate compliance; the fourth specifies what will happen when all the others fail. A clear measure of the seriousness of conflict within the Japanese student movement is the frequency with which the fourth procedure is invoked.

DEMOCRATIC CENTRALISM

Democratic centralism is the term used within the international communist movement for an arrangement whereby each level of an organization elects representatives or delegates to the decision-making body at the next higher level. In Japan the system was first established by having the student body elect *jichikai* representatives, who in turn elect a working leadership group. Zengakuren further elaborated the principle by having each university or faculty *jichikai's* ruling group elect delegates to one of several regional district federations of student self-governing associations. They in turn elected a central committee and chairman. The regional committees elected delegates to the national-level federation, which elected a national central committee and chairman.

The ideologically distinct student political organizations that emerged out of the original Zengakuren compete for control of the economic and organizational bases of campus-level *jichikai,* but they maintain their own hierarchical national organizations that parallel the original Zengakuren pattern. Thus the system of campus or faculty-level associations layered upward to national organizations along democratic centralist principles remains the standard organizational arrangement of the Japanese student movement up to the present.

In the late 1960s, *zenkyōtō,* or all-campus joint struggle committees, emerged as an alternative organizational form that was deliberately horizontal, spontaneous, and participatory, in contrast to the vertically controlled "sects" into which Zengakuren had disintegrated. Even these groups, however, soon developed both internal organization and intercampus alliances along democratic centralist lines.

In communist-run countries, democratic centralism offers a means of recruiting cadre and permitting token representation, while heavily concentrating decision-making authority at higher levels of state-run organizations with obligatory membership. These conditions are not found in the Japanese student movement. Although all students are automatically enrolled in a *jichikai* and have their dues paid for them, they have no further obligation to the organization.

The fusion of relative independence of the grass-roots participants, plus democratic centralist organization, has two contradictory implications for conflict. On the one hand, within either a Zengakuren federation or an independent ideological organization that works in and through the *jichikai*-Zengakuren structure, the arena of potential policy conflicts is severely limited by democratic centralism to relatively small groups of elected delegates and officials. On the other hand, within this limited decision-making arena the potential for severe conflict is great. Delegates and officials at each level are chosen on the basis of their support at the next lower level; hence they have a certain constituency and power base behind them. Conflicts over policy positions taken by individuals easily harden into divisions between factions with independent bases of support in particular regions or universities. Because of democratic centralist principles of decision making, those at the bottom are not free to take sides in such debates as they choose; their position is committed in advance by the actions of their delegates. Individual members can go along or with-draw relatively easily, but generally they would have difficulty es-pousing the other position in a dispute. Every specific dispute carries the potential of dividing the entire organization along predeter-mined lines. The accumulation of several disputes along the same fault line increases the danger, even when the issues are not major. Furthermore, this conflict potential can be activated by personality differences as well as ideological differences.

SŌKATSU

Within the contemporary Japanese student movement, particularly its New Left, *sōkatsu* refers to a routine process of evaluation of the group's political acts, and determination of future policy as a result of this evaluation. The process has four critical elements.

First, the *sōkatsu* begins with a thorough criticism of past acts and interpretations. Conflict and opposition are encouraged as a means to discovery of the correct new direction. Yet it is clearly understood that conflict is appropriate only for a particular phase of the process and that the phase will end when the *sōkatsu*'s conclusion is accepted.

Second, the visible product of *sōkatsu* is ideology, which must be created anew to interpret changing circumstances and justify new tac-tics and strategy. Whatever the practical merits of a proposed new direction, it cannot be accepted until it has been properly clothed in ideological garb. *Sōkatsu* is, therefore, essentially a process of legiti-mation. Not personal authority, but specific courses of action, are legitimized through a *sōkatsu*, and the source of legitimacy is the par-ent ideology. A line of argument that stretches from the original ideological basis of the organization to the specific new course of action legitimizes it, while at the same time the *sōkatsu* procedure itself legitimizes the argument.

Third, *sōkatsu* encompasses not only the emergence of a new ideo-logical statement of direction but also its acceptance by all partici-pants. Within the body making the decision, relations are often suffi-ciently horizontal that no individual has the legitimate authority to announce his or her decision and have it accepted by the group. Members of the group must formally accept the *sōkatsu*. This approv-al carries the authority to suppress opposition and terminate conflict. There are, however, no clear norms guiding the use of such authority.

Fourth, since Marxism assumes progress toward an end state of rev-olution, the process of *sōkatsu* contains a built-in bias toward radical or active solutions. These solutions may not necessarily be acceptable to the majority, and may not appear wise or feasible, but the ideological assumptions underlying the decision-making process give them a certain undeniable legitimacy. The result is that if a moderate direction is accepted, advocates of the more radical alternative may break ranks to pursue their vision of the correct course. If the more radical direction is accepted, some of the moderate forces may break away in a bloc or withdraw individually, but others will be carried along reluctantly into actions that they approach with strong reservations.

SELF-CRITICISM

Self-criticism is another widely used means of conflict management which has deep roots in the international communist movement. As a social process, self-criticism involves a formal denunciation of one's past actions as being the product of an incorrect ideological perspective (often attributed to some personal weakness or failure such as being bourgeois), followed by a statement of acceptance of the correct view and submission to the authority representing it. It may be undertaken voluntarily, or it may be coerced by some authority.

Self-criticism is a common practice, but not one that is taken lightly. It implies deep soul-searching and intellectual effort. Although regarded as a healthy practice for both the organization and the individual, it is understood to be a demeaning and personally painful act. The process of self-criticism is private and psychological, yet self-criticism is a social form which channels thought into a particular kind of public product. Self-criticism must be couched in ideological terms, it must contain certain elements, and it must ultimately express a relationship of individual submission to authority. It is a ritual of compliance evoked by prior noncompliance or conflict.

FACTIONAL DIVISION

When democratic centralism has not contained conflict within a designated arena, when a complete *sōkatsu* cannot be achieved, or when individuals refuse to submit to self-criticism, the only remaining procedure for resolving conflict is to split the organizaton into independent factions. Factional disputes in the student movement are invariably couched in ideological terms, even though they may reflect individual followings or structural cleavages in the organization.

By definition, the division of an organization into factions represents a breakdown of common norms for conflict resolution. Factional disputes have been marked by violence at least since 1964, when the Chūkaku and Kakumaru factions of Kakkyōdō (one of the national student groups that split off in the early 1960s) fought their first known battle with helmets and poles. That factional dispute has continued unabated for nearly two decades.

The degree of violence involved in factional disputes is apparent from official statistics on student movement incidents. Between 1968 and 1975 there were 1,776 internal factional disputes which came to police attention because of their violence. They involved 4,848 injuries, 44 deaths, and 3,438 arrests.[3] Even during the peak years of violence in student confrontations with university and civil authorities, more students were injured in internal disputes than in clashes with external enemies. Not all factional divisions involve violence, of course. Some are simply bitter verbal disputes which cannot be resolved. Others involve walkouts from meetings, followed by the establishment of a separate factional identity.

The sheer volume of factional splits in the student movement since the early 1950s is quite staggering. The original Zengakuren has produced at least thirty-two separately named factions—and just one of these factions, the New Left Kyōsandō, has spawned fifty-four distinct factions of its own.[4]

Truly remarkable in light of the violent, normless antagonism between factions is the degree to which factional opponents retain their identity as subunits of the same parent organization. Despite its total inability to constrain or direct the activities of its warring factions, the parent organization often continues to exist and to perform some functions on behalf of all the factions. Even when the parent organization is dormant, the ancestry of its factions is publicly acknowledged. It is not unusual for student movement publications to identify themselves with triple-decked organizational affiliations. The Red Army Faction's newspaper *Sekigun,* for example, is currently published by a group identifying itself as the Proletarian Revolutionary Faction of the Red Army Faction of the Communist League. And the rival factions Kakumaru and Chūkaku are both directed by the parent organization Kakkyōdō, which maintains separate departments to handle the affairs of each group.[5]

Given the short generational turnover of students, usually four years, the continuity of the movement over thirty years is probably just as remarkable as its penchant for factional division. It can also be argued that without the mechanism of factional division to terminate insoluble conflict, the movement itself could not have survived so long.

As has already been suggested, the mechanisms for managing conflict within the student movement are closely connected to the progression of the movement's external conflicts with civil and university authorities. In particular, the propensity for internal disputes to be managed by factional division along ideological and tactical lines made the movement vulnerable to the kind of response the government was constrained by its own circumstances to make toward student conflict.

Student Conflict

Because its original organizers were allied with the Japan Communist Party, the postwar Japanese student movement developed three key features which have long outlived the affiliation: first, student interests were defined very broadly and student involvement in national and international issues was expressly encouraged; second, the student movement was tied both to Marxism as an ideology and, initially, to the JCP as a source of policy, both of which affected the movement's tactics and ideological interpretations of events; and third, certain organizational features were brought into the movement from the international communist movement which affected its responses to external pressure and internal conflict, as described above.

The first two features contributed substantially to the authorities' perception of the student movement as a threat. Because of its broad definition of interest and its ideological base, the movement organized people to express political opinions. Many of those opinions were widely shared by the public but opposed by the government in power. The student movement posed a potential threat because it raised issues and expressed opinions which were shared by a much broader public that, if fully mobilized, would have posed a serious threat to the government's power. Moreover, the student movement espoused a revolutionary ideology that was basically incompatible with existing bases of power, and it was allied with an opposition political party that was already regarded as dangerous.

Despite this perceived threat the student movement was in fact an interest group with little economic power and few resources to promote its interests. Student conflict must be understood from the outset as a contest between groups with very unequal power. Students have no natural standing as an important interest group in Japanese society. Though they may be designated for future economic and political power, they do not possess these resources as students, and their numbers are relatively small compared to other interest groups. Hence their first and most frustrating task has been to force their opposite numbers to pay attention so that the student message could be conveyed. Within the universities, student interests do have some credibility. They may still have to force officials to pay attention, but they have considerably more leverage with which to do so. In either setting, the movement's major resource is the time and energy of its members. Because of the structure of Japanese higher education, students who have succeeded in entering a university are pretty well assured of leaving with a degree, even if they do minimal academic work. They can therefore safely be full-time activists.

TACTICS AND DEMANDS

The tactics used by the student movement, both inside and outside the university, may be seen as an escalating series of attempts to force attention so that certain demands may be made. The tactics rely on the students' major resources: numbers and time. Two escalating sequences of conflict tactics have been used. Taken as a whole, one sequence may be seen as more expressive, the other as more instrumental.

The *expressive* sequence focuses on ways to deliver a general message about a student position on an issue. The first step in conveying student messages is usually the distribution of handbills or the presentation to officials of petitions carrying large numbers of signatures. The next step is the nonviolent mass demonstration or rally. Slightly more aggressive as an expression of conflict is the snake-dancing demonstration, and a small but critical step beyond that is breaking through police lines to storm some symbolic territory near the parade route or rallying point.

Storming a barricade remains an essentially expressive form of conflict because there is no intention of retaining control of the territory or using control of it to bargain. Gradually, however, storming of a barricade began in the 1960s to shade into a more explicitly violent confrontation-demonstration in which similarly armed forces of students and police fought pitched battles over access to some specific territory. The confrontation-demonstration represents the peak of massed combat force that students have been able to conduct, given their limited numbers and resources. The next stage of escalation in expressive conflict has been a shift to guerrilla tactics by small groups. In the late 1960s and early 1970s, many small-scale guerrilla attacks were carried out by the most radical segments of the student movement. From 1969 to 1975 there were 192 incidents involving explosives, including 102 actual explosions.[6]

By contrast, the *instrumental* sequence of conflict tactics focuses on exacting some concession as a result of the conflict. The guiding model for this type of conflict is labor negotiations, so it was natural that the first tactic would be the student strike. The next step is some form of temporary territorial occupation, such as the sit-in *(suwari-komi)*. This, too, tends to be largely a means of conveying a demand. It bears some relation to storming the barricades in the expressive sequence of tactics, but it is generally a more orderly, deliberate action in which the emphasis is on presence in a place and refusal to leave it, rather than on the effort of getting into the place.

Temporary occupation of territory shades into a tactic which has proved to be moderately successful as a device for initiating negotiations: prolonged, forceful occupation of territory. A further step in this instrumental conflict sequence is the taking of hostages, usually in connection with a territorial occupation.

Although the two sequences of tactics, expressive and instrumental, seem logically distinct, in fact certain student groups have moved from one series to the other or have used both series for different purposes. It is a long step indeed from peaceful demonstrations to guerrilla attacks, but the actual progression consists of small, gradual increments in the level of violence. Each increment has been deliberately planned as a course of action in response to the failure of the previous level of conflict. While few students march along in a peaceful demonstration one day and throw Molotov cocktails the next, some have moved through sequences of conflict tactics within a matter of weeks or months. Since shifts in the level of conflict are also deliberate policy decisions by organizations, various degrees of violence also coexist in the student movement at the same time, as tactics espoused by different groups. Because different groups with different orientations are acting simultaneously, from the outside it may appear that the mildest demonstration can suddenly burst into flames.

Conflict tactics are a means to convey a demand for change to an audience that is perceived as inattentive or resistant. Although many tactics may be used to convey the same message, a change in tactic often leads to a change in the nature of the demand. In general, the expressive sequence of conflict tactics has been used by the student movement primarily to express very general demands for structural change which are unlikely to be met (terminate the security treaty, stop aiding the Vietnam War, oppose nuclear weapons, end capitalist oppression). As the series escalates, the ideological justification for the conflict shifts from action as a demonstration of concern about the message to be conveyed. Now it becomes action *as* the message conveyed.

By contrast, the escalation from strike to occupation or taking hostages temporarily alters the power balance between the students and their opponents. Even though they are ultimately surrounded by vastly superior force, the students who have occupied space or taken hostages have some bargaining power, and they may succeed in getting the attention of their opponents. Their situation then becomes a curious mixture of strength and weakness, typically reflected in the presentation of a motley collection of more specific demands. Some demands may still appear to be nonnegotiable, but more concrete items also appear. They are usually accompanied by a symbolic demand for an apology or an official's participation in mass-bargaining *(taishū dankō)*. The ultimate weakness of the student position is usually reflected also in a demand for amnesty or safe conduct.

While the instrumental sequence offers some possibility of success, this is only possible by a change in the nature of the demands which, when met, will constitute success. Thus it is not surprising that some groups still find expressive conflict tactics more ideologically appropriate than instrumental tactics.

THE RESPONSE OF AUTHORITY

The starting point of student conflict is a perception of the opposition as inattentive to the message. Lacking any more direct means of conveying a concern so that it will be acted upon favorably, students press their claims by means of conflict. The civil and university authorities may respond to the students' demands, their tactics, or both.

Responses to the conflict's message vary along a continuum that reflects the relative power imbalance of the parties to the conflict. Inattention even to a message conveyed by means of conflict implies that the respondent has sufficient power that he is free to ignore the demand. The mildest forms of conflict, such as petitions, rallies, and peaceful demonstrations, are of course the easiest to ignore. Just a step beyond inattention is the peremptory rejection of demands as being unworthy of serious consideration. Since basic conflicts of interest are involved, this too may be regarded as a matter of power. If the Diet has sufficient votes to renew the security treaty or to pass the Subversive Activities Law or the University Control Law despite massive, violent public protest, this is as much a raw demonstration of power imbalance as it is a statement about the merits of the alternatives. On the other hand, some demands made in the course of student conflict are nonnegotiable for the parties to whom they are directed, either because they lack the power to meet them or because it is a matter of basic survival for them not to do so.

A substantial step beyond peremptory rejection is the willingness to negotiate over student demands. Sometimes the very willingness to negotiate prompts a change in the nature of demands, if students had not really anticipated the possibility of such a response. In other instances, particularly events such as hijackings and hostage taking, the capturing of sufficient temporary power to force negotiations is the explicit aim of the conflict tactic.

Negotiation as a response to a continuing student conflict violates many of the normal Japanese cultural assumptions about a negotiating or bargaining situation. Negotiations take place most effectively when there are opportunities to meet informally in order to achieve full nonverbal communication and build mutual trust. These circumstances do not obtain when students with temporary control over places or people negotiate with authorities over the return of such control. Even in the Japanese labor relations model, which is the closest comparison, the parties already know one another and have some avenues of *"ura"* communication to counteract the *"omote"* expressions of militant conflict.[7] These channels frequently develop in on-campus disputes, but they are quite unlikely in guerrilla actions involving strangers as targets. Above all, negotiations precipitated by student conflict are always understood as a response coerced by a very temporary shift in the normal balance of power, which would otherwise permit a response of inattention or peremptory rejection. Negotiations are entered into reluctantly and often resentfully, because they symbolize loss of power on the part of the authorities. If students' right to negotiate over the issues were regarded as legitimate, such conflict tactics would not be necessary; the situation is by definition regarded as an illegitimate encroachment by the authorities who are coerced into responding.

The results of such negotiations extend the continuum of possible responses. The mildest step is a response which acquiesces to a symbolic demand. The most typical forms of this acquiescence are participation in a mass-bargaining session or a formal apology. Mass bargaining *(taishū dankō)* is found as an expressive tactic in Japanese labor relations, but its practice in the student movement has taken on a rather different aura. In the student version, responsible officials agree to meet with the students at an open meeting and discuss the issues before them. What ensues is an extended public degradation ceremony in which the official, no matter how arrogant or apologetic his initial stance, is challenged and confronted until his defenses have been broken.[8]

Closely akin to mass bargaining is the demand for some form of apology for a previous action or attitude. Sometimes a mass bargaining meeting itself is the occasion of an apology, while at other times the apology may be delivered more formally and impersonally. Both responses represent a symbolic acquiescence to student demands and student power. The students may derive considerable temporary satisfaction from having exacted the demand, but they have not permanently altered the conditions of their relationship by this process.

The next small step in the sequence of responses is agreement to demands which themselves arise out of the temporary quality of the students' bargaining position. In order to get themselves into a position of sufficient power to coerce a response from authorities, the students have had to place themselves at considerable physical risk. They gain bargaining rights by holding territory or persons, but they do not have the power to maintain their position indefinitely. They also hold sway within a very limited environment, surrounded by the greater opposing power which their action has provoked into attention.

Whatever the original demand may have been, in such circumstances it almost inevitably becomes coupled with a demand for amnesty or safe conduct so that the students may extricate themselves from the situation without having to suffer its natural consequences. In many such situations, the students lose ground as the conflict progresses; ultimately, therefore, they win only the amnesty or safe conduct and nothing else of substance. Even this represents a substantive point on which the opposition acquiesces only because it is forced to, however. It is a more serious demand to acquiesce to than a *taishū dankō* or apology, because it requires suspending the law. Yet it is a relatively weak demand in that it simply restores to the participants what they had before the conflict began and does not give them any new rights.

The next level of response is acquiescence to a genuine, substantive demand. In campus disputes officials can sometimes be brought to this point as a way of permitting students to save enough face to terminate a protracted standoff. Some minimal demands can be agreed to, both sides can claim victory, and the incident ends. The degree to which small bands of activists have been able to maneuver the whole Japanese government into making substantial concessions, however, is quite amazing.

On the one hand, it can be argued that terrorist or guerrilla actions are the one and only way that very small groups can temporarily alter the balance of power in order to get their message across to an extremely powerful opposition. On the other hand, there is always the possibility that even such extreme acts will meet with inattention or peremptory rejection. When the power imbalance is great, in fact, the response to student conflict need not even address the demand; it may simply focus on the tactic. This response of course reinforces the students' sense that no one is listening.

The range of responses to student conflict tactics constitutes a finely graded sequence. Beginning with simple toleration of the conflict activity, the sequence then moves from regulating the activity by permits, rules, and police presence, through various degrees of forceful resistance, up to terminating the conflict activity by force. The sequence then shifts focus to control of the participants. The next step is arrest and prosecution of the actual participants in conflicts, followed by arrests and prosecution of persons believed to have planned or organized the activity, even if they were not present when it occurred. The logical culmination of this sequence of responses is an effort to transform the consciousness of those who committed the acts of conflict, so that the actors reject their own participation and thereby discredit the actions. Parallel to this effort are attempts to eliminate the organizations through which individuals have acted.

Although these responses form a natural series, there is no requirement that responses begin with the mildest possibility or move progressively through the sequence. In fact, that is considerably less likely than the probability that students will begin with the mildest level of conflict and move progressively to more aggressive acts. The response to conflict depends more on the political environment than it does on the inherent nature of the provocation.

Japanese civil authorities in the postwar era have dealt with student conflict under the shadow of their prewar and wartime reputation for repression and brutality. The prewar bases for control of ideological and interest group conflict, the Peace Police Law of 1900 and the Peace Preservation Law of 1925, were rescinded by the occupation, and any new substitutes had to be consistent with the postwar constitution's much stronger protection of civil liberties.

During the summer of 1952, when students were violently protesting the proposed Antisubversive Activities Law and under JCP sponsorship were also engaged in violence on behalf of other causes, the attorney general denied a request by the police to have Zengakuren outlawed. Both the police and the Ministry of Education would have liked to control student political activity by outlawing the organization that sponsored it, but the legal climate of the immediate postwar era would not permit such an easy form of labeling.

The main instrument developed to control the postwar student movement is the Antisubversive Activities Law *(Hakai katsudō bōshi hō,* abbreviated to *Habōhō),* which passed in September 1952. Intended quite explicitly to suppress subversive acts by communists, the law was prompted by the extremely militant and revolutionary line which the JCP took in the early 1950s as a result of criticism from Moscow. Since at the time the student movement was closely allied with the JCP, the law from its inception was intended partly to control student conflict. Like its prewar predecessors, the *Habōhō* is directed against groups. In this new version, however, the basic crime is not defined in terms of the group's beliefs, but rather in terms of its *bōryokushugi-teki* subversive activities.[9] The actual subversive activities proscribed by the law, however, are all drawn directly from the existing criminal code.

The Antisubversive Activities Law stipulates three different types of penalties for commission of these various crimes. First, there are criminal penalties for individuals who commit the acts proscribed by the criminal code, but the penalties are often stiffer in the *Habōhō.* Second, organizations which have committed the proscribed acts (or show strong evidence that they are likely to do so) may have certain activities suspended. Third, organizations which have actually committed the specific criminal code violations, or have aided an organization that has, or have repeated violations after an initial suspension of activity, may be disbanded officially.[10]

Imposing the second and third penalties on an organization, however, requires an elaborate hearing procedure with various due process and public notice guarantees. The effect of this intricate piece of legislation has been to strengthen the government's hand against individual students who commit criminal acts for political purposes and to legitimize official investigation of student political organizations; at the same time, however, it deters official efforts to prohibit student political activity by organizations. Consequently, officials have expended enormous amounts of time and energy regulating student conflict which they could not legally prevent.

The Kidōtai, or riot police, were established at about the same time as the Antisubversive Activities Law in order to control riots and violent demonstrations. Since the student movement had been in the forefront of previous riots and violent demonstrations, this unit provided an enforcement arm oriented quite explicitly toward control of the student movement's actions. During the late 1960s, the Japanese police devoted considerable attention to investigating student organizations and keeping individual student activists under close surveillance. Police activity was not limited to the elite force trained to respond to violent civil conflicts; specially designated investigative units were finely attuned to organizational and ideological developments within the student movement.

Government attempts to regulate specific acts of student conflict have also been severely restricted by court interpretations of the right of assembly, thought, and expression. Not until the late 1960s would public opinion or the courts tolerate aggressive use of state force to control student conflict. Consequently, as demonstrations escalated in violence, the police carefully calibrated their responses. With the exception of the Bloody May Day of 1952, when police fired upon a rock-throwing crowd attempting to storm the Imperial Palace grounds, the use of force has been studiously limited to nonlethal means.

The official response to student conflict on university campuses has been considerably more uneven, but not any more violent. Students have greater legitimacy on campus, and school officials have few resources with which to respond, short of calling in the civil authorities. During the early 1950s, police did enter the campuses regularly to deal with both on and off-campus violations. Their incursions caused so much tension that finally the police agreed not to enter campuses unless requested to do so by university officials. The result was a situation in which both students and university officials came to regard calling police on campus as an extreme last resort signifying the complete breakdown of normal relationships within the university.

As a consequence of this understanding, universities tolerated a great deal of conflict which in any other location would have been terminated by force. Even when the government became determined to intervene, the understanding between school officials and the police was regarded as so firm that new national legislation was required to alter its terms. The University Control Law, passed after bitter student opposition in 1969, provided that the minister of education could close departments or whole universities if a campus conflict was not settled within nine months (or six months after the conclusion of an earlier conflict).

The Antisubversive Activities Law and the Riot Law in the regular criminal code have remained the basic instruments for direct control of student conflict. The 1969 University Control Law did not broaden the range of actions that could be prosecuted; rather, it extended the reach of the existing provisions by increasing the probability that the existing sanctions would be applied when the offending activity occurred on university campuses, which police previously had not been able to enter without an invitation.[11]

Given these limits on authority, the legal sanctions available could not be brought to bear on the student movement with any great force until the movement itself began systematically to test the limits of the law. Despite scattered incidents, this did not occur with any regularity until the mid-1960s. It began first on the campuses, which were in practice outside the reach of the laws. Only in 1967 did student protests of national and international policy begin routinely to include some violation of law which would permit the police to arrest students. Since the context of such events usually involved the breakaway actions of a splinter student group violating limits agreed upon by a larger coalition, the application of the law tended both to label splinter groups and to create more factional division within the student movement.

Less formal means of sanctioning students have also been utilized, but they seem to have followed, rather than preceded, the application of the law. Students enjoyed a certain modicum of public support up until the very late 1960s, in part because of public sympathy for some of the causes they espoused. Only when student activism came to be associated with such disruptions of normal life as violent demonstrations in public areas and prolonged interruptions of academic activity did public opinion and the mass media begin to reject the legitimacy of student protest.

Similarly, it was not until 1969 that private corporate employers regarded student activism as sufficiently deviant to preclude an offer of lifetime employment security. This move was not for want of precedent, since corporate employers conduct detailed investigations of prospective employees in order to detect such undesirable characteristics as family instability or *burakumin* minority background.[12] Until the late 1960s, in fact, ex-student activists were sometimes actively sought as aggressive management material. Though the exclusion of student activists from the very positions for which they had been educated was accomplished by private action, it was not fully legitimate until the Supreme Court upheld the practice in 1973.

The Application of Labeling Theory

Labeling theory argues that deviance is not a fixed category of either persons or acts; rather, it is the result of a certain kind of social conflict. As Lofland puts it: "Deviance is the name of the conflict game in which individuals or loosely organized small groups with little power are strongly feared by a well-organized, sizable minority or majority, who have a large amount of power."[13] The relationship between the student movement and civil and university authorities in postwar Japan appears to fit these conditions. Although the actual power imbalance between the two sides was great, the authorities were very concerned about the symbolic threat posed by the movement's ideology, goals, and tactics.

Japanese governments have a long history of sensitivity to symbolic threats posed by small, ideologically committed groups. In the postwar era the Japanese government could no longer deal with such threats as the Tokugawa shogunate had dealt with Christians or even as Taishō and Shōwa governments had dealt with communists. Yet it did acquire the means to begin labeling persons in the student movement as deviant and thereby eligible for certain restrictions. As Lofland points out:

A primary indicator of . . . the type of conflict called deviance in a total society is, then, the existence of state rulings and corresponding enforcement mechanisms that provide for the possibility of forcibly removing actors from civil society, either by banishment, annihilation, or incarceration. Again, it is precisely those actors who have little power and who are not organized toward whom such actions can most successfully be undertaken.[14]

The Japanese government did not have a completely free hand, but it was able to achieve these basic instruments of control.

Initially the student movement employed a number of conflict tactics which aimed to draw attention to student demands—demands which authorities perceived as a symbolic threat. The civil and university authorities who were the target of these tactics and demands had far greater power and resources than the students, but they were severely constrained in their responses by both law and public opinion. Their ultimate power enabled them to respond to student demands by inattention or refusal to give serious consideration, while the constraints on their use of power led to a measured and relatively tolerant response to the actual tactics used.

The failure of their initial tactics, plus the generally tolerant atmosphere, led the students to explore more aggressive tactics to convey their demands more forcefully. The gradual escalation of tactics and responses, plus continued resistance to the major student demands, produced conflict within the movement over tactics and goals. Then the third feature of the movement's early Marxist affiliations, its internal mechanisms for conflict management, constrained its responses to this set of circumstances. The movement's organizational arrangements simultaneously encouraged the acceptance of more radical tactics and produced factional division within the movement, thus creating a range of independent groups which espoused different tactics.

This condition, in turn, permitted the civil authorities to concentrate their response on the more radical segments of the movement, setting in motion the process of labeling that became overt in the late 1960s. To the extent that the student movement was an extreme expression of general public concerns, the movement as a whole might be regarded as the object of the labeling effort. But the movement had splintered and produced a range of groups espousing different ideologies and tactics. Thus the most extreme elements inside the student movement became especially appropriate targets for labeling.

Although some in the government would have liked very much to label all student political activity as deviant and illegitimate, that authority was not granted. The combination of legal restrictions and sympathetic public opinion permitted only a much narrower line to be drawn. Only the more radical subgroups in the movement that engaged in violent confrontational tactics could be labeled deviant. That label could be imposed on the basis of existing criminal law, including the 1952 Antisubversive Activities Law and the Riot Law. The existence of a large, special police force provided an enforcement arm combining the expertise to determine who fit the label and the authority to apply the legal sanctions that confirmed it. And although the law could not as readily be applied against organizations, the function of determining where the label applied could be extended to whole groups rather than individuals.

During the 1970s, the Antisubversive Activities Law was also applied to the nonparticipating leaders of groups that engaged in illegal activities—yet another means of labeling the group as a whole. This effort was reinforced by the actions of corporate employers, who could not have supported the labeling of a major segment of their recruitment pool for managerial positions but could participate when the designation of deviants was more narrowly restricted to certain groups and certain degrees of participation. Public opinion also came to support this narrow deviant label.

The usefulness of this labeling theory interpretation of student conflict in Japan lies in its ability to relate the visible external conflict between the student movement and authorities to the less visible processes of conflict which went on simultaneously inside the student movement and inside the heads of individual students. Although the analysis thus far has emphasized the imposition of a label by those with power and motivation to do so, a critical element in the process is *acceptance* of the label by participants in the movement. How deeply such labels permeate the individual's identity greatly affects the ultimate outcome of the conflict. At its broadest, then, a labeling theory explanation of conflict involves two converging processes: creating and imposing the label of "deviant" on certain acts and persons and the individuals' acceptance of the label as a central feature of their identity.

Labeling theory distinguishes sharply between the occasional performance of an action that might be called deviant and an individual's identification of himself as a person who is defined by such deviance. As a strategy of conflict, the effort to label a threatening group as deviant cannot succeed completely unless the targets of the campaign begin to accept the label as a source of personal identity. Such acceptance cuts off the self-proclaimed deviant from the rest of society and changes his behavior further. This makes it easier for others to restrict his right to participate in normal society, and correspondingly harder for him to return to the mainstream.

One escalates into deviant identity as a result of a long series of circumstances, choices, and events. Each step funnels the individual into a higher probability of eventual acceptance of an identity cen-

tered on a deviant role, but no single step is definitive. Each step .
involves a choice, but the alternatives are increasingly limited.

In this political application of labeling theory, deviant acts occur as
a result of deliberate group decisions. The steps of performing a
deviant act and accepting a deviant identity merge together, since a
person is first committed to the group and then participates in activities as a group member. The individual has accepted a certain identity as a student activist voluntarily, but the nature of that identity
becomes transformed by a combination of the direction the group
takes and the label the authorities impose on the group and its
actions.

Thus there are several problematic issues for the acceptance of
deviant identity in this political context: How are individuals drawn
into the groups? What is their psychological state as they make decisions about group actions? And what alternatives to participating in
these acts do they think are open to them? Although these appear to
be consecutive phases of an individual's experience, they are better
understood as a set of simultaneous possibilities that are present continuously during the person's involvement. At each moment a person
experiences certain entry possibilities, certain exit possibilities, and a
certain quality of participation, all of which are interrelated. Escalation into a deviant identity occurs when the sequence of small choices
one makes systematically narrows the options for future choices.

ENTRY

To the extent that the student movement is an interest group, it
attracts students who want to improve some aspect of their condition.
The drawing power of purely student issues waxes and wanes. Some
aspects of the student condition are well-nigh universal and thus
perennially available to anyone who wants to raise them as issues.
Other problems arise in a more specific time context and for that reason alone may attract more attention. Such temporal issues may also
appear to be more soluble than perennial ones.

Much of the activity of the postwar Japanese student movement
has been directed toward social and political problems off the campus. While the Marxist framework of the movement provides a general motivation for participation, the movement's attractiveness has
clearly been related to the availability of immediate causes which
could be interpreted as contributing to the main process of revolutionary change. Some causes, such as the campaigns opposing the

Antisubversive Activities Law and the Security Treaty, have been national issues in which students have joined. In other cases, students alone have pressed the issue or, by supporting some small and powerless group, have thereby created a public issue.

There are also social reasons for entering the student movement, and conviction may follow entry as well as precede it. The more viable the activities of the student movement, the more attractive it becomes—not only because of the educational effect of the visibility but also because that is where the action is. And the more visible and exciting the movement appears to be, the more it will attract the average student with only an average degree of political interest or ideological commitment.

The likelihood that students would enter the student movement has varied with time as issues peaked and waned. During some periods, and on certain campuses, the movement was quite dormant. At other times and places, the issues were so salient and the movement so vibrant that the majority of students entered at least temporarily. The peak level of participation is estimated to have been about two-thirds of the student body, so entry has always been a matter of individual choice.

The opportunities for entry into the student movement have also changed dramatically over the three decades of the movement's existence. During its first postwar decade, there was only one, unified student movement: Zengakuren. Beyond one's nominal and obligatory affiliation with a college or faculty *jichikai*, one could either choose to participate or choose not to participate in *jichikai*-sponsored activities. Heavy *jichikai* participation might lead to entry into a higher level of Zengakuren, which in turn might lead to certain partisan commitments in internal Zengakuren disputes.

During the second decade of the movement, while the number of different groups proliferated rapidly, the range of entry options for an individual did not keep pace. Every student belonged then, as now, to one faculty of one university. Transfers between universities are relatively rare, and even transfers between faculties are not routine, so students are effectively limited to the range of organizations present in their immediate institutional environment.

The interplay of democratic centralism with factional division made it unnecessary for a high-level factional split to be reproduced at the local level. Far more common was the result that one *jichikai* was controlled by one faction and the *jichikai* at another school by the opposing faction. As rival organizations developed completely independent national identities, they did a fair amount of campus organizing of new chapters that could compete for control of a *jichikai*. Still, schools tended to be dominated by one group because the sharing of power within the *jichikai* has never been institutionalized.

In the third decade of the movement, beginning in the late 1960s, some student political groups were able to maintain an organizational presence independent of the *jichikai* system, thus opening up additional avenues of entry. At one extreme was the Red Army Faction, which did not aim for *jichikai* control and raised its funds by other means. At the other extreme were the *zenkyōtō* or joint struggle committees which sprang up on some campuses as a means of uniting students for a particular issue, regardless of whether they belonged to a particular "sect" or were unaffiliated.

To the extent that more than one organization was available for initial entry at a particular school, students could do a certain amount of shopping among groups before committing themselves. Once they had actually joined a sect or participated heavily, however, their subsequent avenues of entry into other groups were constrained by a new set of rules. Aside from the *zenkyōtō,* there was little horizontal movement between independent organizations, a pattern found throughout Japanese society. The main routes of entry into other organizations came about when the organizations themselves either divided or united in a coalition, carrying along the individual members. Since these maneuvers went on constantly, it was relatively easy for students to find themselves participating in activities of an organization they had never consciously entered.

Within these structural constraints, the likelihood of a student's entry into the movement was determined by the usual social and psychological elements of personality, personal interest, background, and social ties. These factors affected not only whether someone would enter but what one would enter. A few student movement subgroups are considered to have developed a specific member "type," but the importance of personality in student movement recruitment should not be overestimated. The time and place of a student's career have been vastly more important determinants of whether he or she would enter a particular organization. Choice and chance are so intricately intertwined in the entry and recruitment process that personality trait explanations of even the most extreme forms of student movement participation are questionable. This understanding of recruitment is essential to a labeling theory interpretation of participation.

Still, the ordinary Japanese student did not simply walk down the street and join a guerrilla or terrorist group. Entry into the most extreme groups in the student movement involved prior socialization, which was usually obtained through a series of entries into progressively more militant environments. Some entries were deliberate acts of individuals seeking a purer expression of their beliefs; others occurred because of a configuration of circumstances which the individual did not control.

PARTICIPATION

Participation in the student movement means, first and foremost, participation in the external conflicts that are the movement's raison d'être. Participating in any of the movement's external conflict tactics was an exciting, intense, solidary experience which could be intrinsically satisfying regardless of its outcome. Yet by and large the actions of the student movement failed to produce the desired changes. Thus despite the immediate sense of accomplishment, the long-term experience of participation was one of repeated failure. Some either did not care sufficiently or were more tolerant of short-term failure and sanguine about long-term success. Others, frustrated by their inability to produce change immediately, pushed for new tactics that might be more effective in at least arousing the attention of their intended audience.

The conflict tactics used by the movement required numbers of people in roughly inverse proportion to the amount of personal commitment needed to carry out the act. Demonstrations required a large headcount for any effect, but the degree of individual commitment demanded of participants was minimal. Guerrilla attacks could be carried out by small numbers of people, but their commitment had to be intense. During the late 1960s, conflict tactics ranging from peaceful demonstrations to guerrilla attacks were utilized simultaneously by different elements in the student movement. Hence the differences in tactics reflected variations in degree of commitment, rather than in the absolute numbers that could be mobilized for a particular issue or at a particular time.

Within the student movement, commitment is closely related to the intensity of small-group interaction. Coser has described the two poles of this continuum with his distinction between churchlike and sectlike organizations.[15] Churchlike organizations require only a partial commitment of their members, who are presumed to have other affiliations as well. Such organizations can tolerate more internal conflict because they expect differences among their members, who may be unified only in the one area of the group's purpose. Because the organizations can tolerate internal conflict and are only intermittently engaged in external conflict, they are able to attain larger size. This in turn reduces the intensity of interaction among members.

Sectlike organizations, by contrast, base their unity on the presumed likeness of their members, from whom they demand total commitment. Such organizations are usually engaged continuously in external conflict, are less able to tolerate internal disagreement, and feel the strongest enmity toward ex-members who share the same goals but differ on means. The great demands of membership keep such organizations small. Although these descriptions match the range of settings for interaction found in the Japanese student movement, Coser's theory does not even hint at the complex relations between these polar types that the Japanese situation has displayed.

The vast majority of students entered the student movement through a churchlike organization, usually during one of its intermittent external conflicts. If they moved from the fringe of such an organization toward its core, however, they found the environment increasingly sectlike. Democratic centralism facilitated the maintenance of a large, churchlike mass organization with a sectlike leadership. The internal conflict management mechanisms of *sōkatsu* and self-criticism were quite clearly designed to protect the fundamental unity of opinion required by a sect. Use of such techniques requires intense small-group interaction. The ultimate conflict management technique is factional division, which is patently sectlike.

As organizations within the student movement divided and subdivided, many of the new, smaller units applied sectlike criteria to their entire membership. In fact, such groups are even called "sects" *(sekuto)* within the student movement. Sectlike demands became more appropriate because the organizations were operating in an environment of more and more continuous conflict. In addition to the increasingly acute state of external conflict with university and civil authorities, groups born out of factional splits were also engaged in a new external conflict with their erstwhile comrades. Just as students could find themselves belonging to a group they had not deliberately entered, so they could find themselves enmeshed in a "sect" although they had joined a "church."

Yet if some slid into intense, small-group participation, others actively sought such an environment or created it by their own actions. Viewed over a thirty-year time span, the Japanese student movement has certainly experienced a great deal of conflict and internal division. But the length of time a student spends in the movement is comparatively brief, and most of the organizations have outlived a student generation. So long as the organization is not on the verge of splitting into independent factions, the internal atmosphere of a sect is warm, supportive, purposeful, and solidary. The aim of its conflict management techniques is, after all, to shift conflict outside the group by enforcing consensus inside. Even the ultimate solution of factional division manages neatly to preserve the sense of unity and active solidarity for the participants inside each faction.

Yet the conflict is only pushed outside (along with the people who embody it) when the basic conflict management strategy has failed. The primary way that conflict is moved out of the arena of group interaction is by pushing it back into the individual. One has to decide on his own when to accept the *sōkatsu* and when to submit to self-criticism, but there is no structural support for failing to do so. Consequently, an individual can successfully withhold his agreement only when he has some other source of support, either from other group members or from his own personality and his external environment. Lacking this, he either submits or finds some way to withdraw from the situation. The very intensity of group interaction that demands submission, however, also denies easy exit.

A further deterrent both to overt internal group conflict and to individual withdrawal is the thick ideological atmosphere in which the sects operate. The sects are nourished by hairsplitting ideological disputes within the broad framework of Marxism. Whatever personal or social forces may operate behind internal conflicts, they are ultimately expressed in ideological terms because that is the medium of internal communication. The same applies to individual reservations; if they cannot be translated into ideological objections, they cannot be expressed legitimately. And most personal reservations about a more extreme course of action can be summarily rejected with the insinuation that they are bourgeois. The result is that a great deal of private discomfort with the group is simply suppressed by the individual as an embarrassing personal flaw that should not be revealed. In this sense, the continuous expression and creation of ideology is itself a conflict management technique, since its function is to sustain a particular definition of the situation and to prevent potentially conflicting interpretations from being considered.

All these features—the intensity of interaction within the group,

antagonism toward close ideological allies as well as the original enemies, conflict management techniques that emphasize submission to
group consensus, and an esoteric ideological atmosphere that is per-
petually stretching to fit new situations—increase one's dependence
upon the group. Their combined effect is to leave individual members with virtually no external reference points against which to evaluate what is happening inside the group.

Even students whose daily lives take them in and out of the group
setting are unable to apply externally derived standards; they simply
compartmentalize their lives. Pharr tells of radical students who live
at home with a disapproving parent and simply do not talk about
movement activities.[16] Equally common is the parent who offers full
emotional support but does not really understand what the student is
talking about. The former situation increases the student's emotional
dependence on the sect; the latter may provide emotional support
that helps the student manage private reservations. Neither situation
offers an acceptable alternative view of reality. Students whose daily
lives are entirely conducted within the orbit of the sect are of course
even less likely to find external reference points.

The heady atmosphere of external conflict activity, combined with
the individual participant's dependence on interaction with a group
that is extremely isolated from alternative points of view, easily leads
to a psychological state which Lofland calls "encapsulation." This
state is characterized by a tremendous sense of urgency about the
immediate problem and a foreshortened time perspective with regard
to the consequences of actions. Encapsulation is precipitated by a perceived threat. While initially the frustration of failing to produce
desired change might be viewed as threatening to members, in later
stages a more immediate threat was posed by the government's pressure on the movement itself. Lofland observes;

> The state of psychosocial encapsulation is facilitative of an eventual
> deviant act not because of the characteristics of this state itself but rather
> because of the *congruence between* some features of encapsulation and
> some features of a few types of social acts, deviant ones in particular. . . .
> Put in briefest form, then, encapsulation is a heightened sensitivity to
> simple solutions. Simple solutions tend to be deviant acts. Therefore
> encapsulation heightens sensitivity to deviant acts.[17]

When an atmosphere of encapsulation pervades a small group, it is
relatively easy for decisions to be made and actions to be carried out

which would be unthinkable for the same individuals under ordinary circumstances. Sometimes these decisions and actions represent sudden, major shifts in behavior, but more often they occur in such small increments that the participant is unable to say when or where the line might have been crossed explicitly. At some point in such a seemingly inexorable progression, the acts themselves begin to burn bridges and thus fundamentally alter the person's future options. A deviant identity may therefore be acquired imperceptibly and come to be recognized only when it is too late to alter the consequences.

Not everyone, of course, slides unwittingly into deviant political identity; some embrace it quite deliberately, while many seek something which fits the externally defined label although they define it quite differently. A person the government labels a terrorist usually regards himself as a guerrilla fighter in the vanguard of the impending revolution. The issue here is not so much the fact of clashing definitions but how the Japanese university student arrived at the state in which being a guerrilla rather than a bureaucrat became his goal: a state in which the activities of a guerrilla could be carried out by someone whom life had prepared for the bureaucracy. Participation in the movement produced this transformation.

EXIT

There are a number of different ways to extricate oneself from the student movement, but they are not equally available to all participants at all times. An essential aspect of escalation into deviant identity is the fact that certain ways of leaving the movement may be foreclosed at critical junctures, so that the deeper one goes into the movement, the more difficult it may be to leave, even if one is not comfortable with the demands of further participation.

Exiting from the movement presumes that one has entered. The more tenuously one has entered, however, the easier it is simply to withdraw from participation. This is partly a question of the kinds of conflict tactics one has participated in and partly a question of the type of organization one has participated in, though the two are related. It is also much easier to withdraw when the issues themselves have diminished in salience.

Withdrawal or dropping out becomes increasingly difficult as participation extends into sectlike organizations and more violent tactics. The same pressures that make it difficult for individuals to express objections to group decisions may make it equally difficult to leave as a result of those objections. The group's demand for conformity may be fundamentally a demand that one stay and conform, while considerations of face may require that one participate in precisely the acts that one has reservations about.

Since student status is transitory, another apparently simple way to exit from the student movement is to leave the category of student. The vast majority of movement participants do complete their education and leave the movement when they leave school. Three considerations make this form of exit problematic for some.

First, some student conflicts have so thoroughly disrupted either the individual's educational career or the functioning of his educational institution that his categorical exit is delayed. This, in turn, may delay his exit from the movement. Second, some students either remain in the university as graduate students or obtain positions in the national parent organization of their student group, thereby extending their participation past the point of categorical exit. This means they have to find some other way of getting out. Third, some people become so thoroughly labeled as deviant through their student movement participation that they can no longer maintain either a student identity or an appropriate poststudent identity; the only avenue left is a professional deviant identity. This has happened to members of the Japan Red Army (a branch of the Red Army Faction) who have become professional revolutionaries abroad and can no longer return to Japan, let alone finish their education or take up legitimate white-collar employment. It has also happened to the hundreds of student movement participants with prison records. Categorical exit from the student movement is not an option available to them.

To a lesser extent, the thousands more who have arrest records or have been screened out of corporate employment for student activism have been marked by their participation and cannot extricate themselves simply by not being students anymore. They have been declared deviant and may have to take specific action or deliberately hide their pasts in order to be restored to normalcy.

A further form of exit is provided by the internal conflict management mechanisms, although again not every reluctant participant may be able to utilize them. Sometimes a group of reluctant participants can be relieved of certain obligations through a factional fight in which they take the more conservative position. Nearly every factional split in the movement's history represents one faction's refusal to go along with a more extreme course. Some individuals may in fact be spared the necessity of anguishing over the issue by being conveniently located in a group that is structurally attached to the more conservative leadership elements. By simply remaining loyal to their leaders, they can draw back to an acceptable level of commitment. The converse situation, however, is equally fortuitous and equally binding. Some participants are carried into more extreme commitments by their structural ties to a particular faction, whether or not they are comfortable with the consequences. Such a form of exit involves as much luck as it does individual judgment.

There are two related ways in which conflict management mechanisms can effect a withdrawal, but both require considerably more individual assertiveness than the passive use of a factional split. The first is for an individual to be officially purged from the organization for his actions. These fairly rare situations represent the organization's initiative in divesting itself of an intolerable member. It is not always clear who "exits" in such a procedure, however. Since the action often involves a group dissociating itself from the more extreme actions of an individual, it may be the group that exits, and not the purged individual.

Closely related is the refusal of an individual to undergo self-criticism when asked to do so by the group. As the ultimate insubordination, it represents a highly antagonistic way to withdraw, which may be related to factional division when done by someone with the power of a faction behind him. Theoretically an individual without factional support could resist a demand for self-criticism and extricate himself as a result, but he would have to have a strong personality to do so in the face of heavy collective pressure for self-criticism. The dramatic public resignation on principle found in American organizations is quite rare in Japan, and when it does occur there is often a taint of *tenkō*, or recanting under pressure, associated with it.

Ironically, arrest and imprisonment may provide the missing opportunity to exit from the movement. For many students caught up in movement activities, arrest becomes the point at which they first face the deviant labels attached to their actions by society. They have been insulated in an encapsulated milieu which concentrated so much attention on ideological justification for action that the world's understanding of those acts has completely dropped out of consideration. Arrest suddenly makes the implication clear. Some persons caught in this fashion resist acceptance of the label by expressing their apologies to the police. Such repentance is appreciated in Japan and generally results in delabeling if the student then goes home and stays out of the movement. To come back to the movement after such an episode would raise serious questions about whether one had become a police spy, as well. In any case, the immediate emotional tie to the group has been broken by the experience, and therefore it becomes a point at which a graceful exit can be achieved.

Even if a student accepts arrest and prosecution as the appropriate consequences of his actions, he may subsequently experience difficulty in maintaining his ideological commitment in isolation. Emotional and ideological commitment are so dependent upon continuous group interaction that the imprisoned member often becomes disoriented. Because he is no longer party to the intense ideology creation that underlies the group's actions, he soon finds himself unable to justify or interpret their new acts. And without the constant pressure to interpret every event ideologically, he may begin defining situations in more personal, emotional terms.

Once a student activist has been labeled deviant by arrest or imprisonment, or more informally by public notoriety, he cannot exit unless he rejects the deviant identity. How thoroughly he has to do so depends on the extent of the label. Students who have simply been picked up in a mass arrest of participants in a disturbance may exit from the threat of deviant identity by rejecting it and promising to leave the movement. While there has apparently been no formal campaign to encourage *tenkō* (recantation) among imprisoned postwar student activists, there are a number of examples of what may be termed spontaneous *tenkō* involving either an explicit change in ideology or a quiet drifting away from the movement. Others, either further radicalized by their experience or unable to re-enter the establishment, have made adult careers out of some aspect of their student movement experience.

A final mode of exit is by death. In addition to a handful of student deaths during external conflicts and over forty in internal conflicts, the movement has also experienced many suicides and attempted suicides. Just within the small Red Army Faction there have been five successful suicides and six other known attempts, most of which were precipitated by arrest or impending arrest.

Like entry, exit modes are unequally available to individual members both because of structural circumstances in the movement and because of social and psychological factors such as personality, interests, background, and social ties that color each member's responses. These factors do make a difference in whether one thinks one can leave a situation and whether one has the courage (or lack of it) to leave. Yet the situations themselves are so highly structured that the further into the movement one has entered, the more difficult it is to exit.

The effect of the simultaneous operation of these entry and exit possibilities and the quality of movement participation is to make student movement activity very much like walking through a maze. One is constantly confronted with small but critical alternatives, the ultimate consequences of which cannot be discerned. Sometimes it is possible to turn back; sometimes it is not. And some people are simply better than others at getting where they want to go. Thus, with imperfect clarity of either vision or purpose, deviant identities are created.

Consequences and Conclusions

Labeling and acceptance of deviant identity are two sides of the same coin. Their consequences are, to a certain extent, an exacerbation of the very conditions that precipitated the labeling process. This makes it nearly impossible to draw sharp cause-and-effect lines in time. Nevertheless, four interrelated consequences of the labeling process can be discerned in the Japanese student movement throughout the 1960s and into the 1970s.

First, as a result of the sharpening distinction between acceptable and unacceptable tactics, milder dissenting groups and individuals in the movement were co-opted into the labeling efforts of the government. They not only joined in rejecting the groups that lay outside the new line; they also purged themselves of any members who sympathized too openly with what was becoming a deviant or unacceptable position. This process, as noted earlier, was greatly facilitated by the internal organizational structure of the student movement, particularly its propensity to divide along vertical factional lines in the face of conflict. The process of self-policing and co-optation can be observed both within the student movement, however, and in the relations between the student movement and other groups on the left that were initially supportive.

Within the student movement, the case histories of the major factional splits and the various attempts to form new coalitions can be read as internal struggles to define the acceptable limits of dissent in the face of pressure to label the movement as deviant. In the late 1960s, the line of internal dispute often coincided with the government's definition of acceptable dissent, even though the disputes were certainly not couched in those terms. Once groups had crossed the line into the deviant category, of course, divisions involved more minute variations of policy. On the far side of the line, every conflict over labeling also became a convenient exit point for some to leave the movement entirely.

A second consequence of the labeling effort was that as the movement began to police itself and participate in the labeling, government resources could be concentrated on a much smaller, less powerful, and more acceptable target. While the civil authorities did not really have the authority to squelch all protest, even if they had wanted to, they could make a very visible and much safer attack on the most extreme expressions of discontent. Besides the effect described above, of moving the rest of the potential dissenters away from the target group, such an action also helped satisfy supporters of the government who wanted evidence that it could maintain its authority.

Had the entire body of groups and individuals who participated in the 1960 Ampo demonstrations used the tactics of the most violent Zengakuren faction, the conflict would have been a civil war rather than a contained confrontation. As violence escalated throughout the 1960s, the proportion of students involved in that violence tended to decrease, despite some large mass protests. Incidents of violence could not be prevented effectively, but they could be quite well contained by using the labeling strategy. The more government forces could contain violent tactics, the more the groups involved split over tactics, causing ever smaller splinter groups to use ever more violent tactics, against which even larger government forces could be deployed.

The third consequence of labeling may be understood as a result of the first two. The concentration of highly specialized resources on a small segment of the student movement, which was increasingly abandoned by its near neighbors as they scrambled for a safe and legal berth from which to dissent, created a psychological state of siege or encapsulation within the groups being labeled deviant. This in turn pushed the isolated groups to adopt more clandestine forms of organization and more extreme forms of protest. Labeling may have co-opted the majority, but it made the minority more radical. In this sense, it is fair to say that government actions created terrorism and other forms of urban guerrilla activity. This was accomplished by isolating the extreme groups from dialogue with other elements in the movement—forcing individual members into greater reliance on the stigmatized group and reducing their contacts with nonmembers or sympathizers—and by branding the individual members through surveillance and threats of arrest so that they could not easily give up their group affiliations and move back into normal society. The only available options became terrorism and other illegal and violent activities. The increased pressures on individuals and organizations also raised grave and genuine concerns about internal security and solidarity within the tiny groups, which in turn generated the conditions for violent purges. The increased radicalism of the groups labeled deviant, and the aberrant behavior their hunted members displayed, served as public justification for the campaign against them.

Fourth, the ultimate effect of successful labeling was in many cases the complete rejection of the new deviant label by its subjects. The immediate consequences of labeling were arrest and imprisonment in solitary confinement. Since acceptance of a deviant identity initially depended on intense group participation, loss of group contact through arrest and isolation severely impaired many students' ability to sustain such an identity.

If the deviant identity were not rejected, it would theoretically be possible for any group labeled deviant to grow in time and eventually transform itself into a social movement too large to be controlled by labeling as a conflict strategy. Lofland has pointed out that the short-run effectiveness of labeling in controlling a social or political threat is often counterbalanced by the long-run burdens of maintaining a category of deviance and an establishment trained professionally to identify and supervise that type of deviant (as in the mental health establishment or the apparatus for managing juvenile delinquency). In this particular case, the labeling process succeeded in drastically reducing the number of persons who fit the label: It had a clear deterrent effect. The unanswered question is whether the establishment designed to control that category of deviance called student activism will be similarly able to dissolve itself or whether it will instead find new definitions of conduct to which its labeling machinery can be applied. Since the fundamental issues which prompted student conflict initially have not been resolved, however, the movement itself should be regarded as dormant but not necessarily destroyed by the labeling efforts of the past two decades.

In sum, then, the application of labeling theory to student conflict in postwar Japan has provided an explanation of the movement's escalation in violence that emphasizes the structural relationship between the student movement and civil and university authorities, organizational characteristics of the movement, and the social psychological experience of participation in the movement. Conflicts at each of these levels are seen as feeding into conflict processes at other levels.

In the spirit of this volume's attempt to apply Western conflict theory to Japanese conflict phenomena, one question remains. What, if anything, is particularly Japanese about student conflict? Labeling theory was developed out of observations of conflict in American society. Although no comprehensive study of postwar American student conflict has applied this model explicitly, there seem to be many obvious parallels.

The mechanisms for conflict management that are used most commonly in the Japanese student movement can all be traced to the Marxist tradition that permeates the movement. The terms used to describe these practices are either direct translations of foreign terms —such as *chūō iinkai* (central committee), *sōkatsu* (synthesis), and *jiko-hihan* (self-criticism)—or Japanese neologisms incorporating foreign words—such as *uchi geba* (internal factional conflict), *sekuto* (member of a New Left "sect"), and *non-sekuto* (a person who may be active but is not a member of a *sekuto*).

Yet it should be obvious to any student of Japan that these mechanisms all have traditional Japanese parallels. Democratic centralism has many features in common with the notion of vertical society popularized by Nakane; *sōkatsu* looks suspiciously like traditional consensus decision-making procedures; self-criticism finds cultural roots in the tradition of formal apology and acceptance of responsibility for an error or wrong; factional division is endemic in Japanese organizations of all types.

The fact that the presence of these mechanisms in the postwar Japanese student movement can be traced to non-Japanese sources demonstrates that such features are not uniquely Japanese, as some commentators have implied. On the other hand, the acceptance of these mechanisms in the student movement was undoubtedly facilitated by the fact that they are variants of familiar social arrangements and understandings. In general, the versions of traditional Japanese conflict management mechanisms found in the student movement are noteworthy for their more explicit acceptance of direct interpersonal conflict, both between formally equal parties and between persons in hierarchical relationships.

Similarly, the vocabulary of external conflict tactics in the move-

ment is remarkably Western. Some of the terms are direct translations, such as *tōsō* (struggle), *suwarikomi* (sit-in), and *taishū dankō*
(mass bargaining—though another term for normal Western-style
collective bargaining exists). Most, however, are directly borrowed
Japanese neologisms, such as *demo* (demonstration), *gerira-sen*
(guerrilla warfare), *barikēdo* (barricade), *haijyakku* (hijacking), *suto*
(strike), and *boikotto* (boycott). Some of the movement's basic
equipment and activity also carry foreign names: *bira* (handbill),
gebabō (a neologism combining the German *Gewalt*, or struggle,
with the Japanese term for a long pole), and *kampa* (literally campaign, the term for soliciting funds directly).

Certain tactics, though foreign, were introduced into Japan by
other groups for other purposes, most notably by the labor movement. When the student movement has used a Western tactic previously introduced and adapted by another group, it is always the
Japanese variant that is used. Student strikes, for example, as pointed
out earlier, are always conducted according to Japanese rules of timing and significance. The language of the most violent tactics, however, reverts to common Japanese terms for acts which are ordinarily
regarded as criminal, though this may depend on the source using
the words.

It certainly cannot be argued that the extremity of direct conflict
practiced by the student movement is Western in origin, since the
most extreme acts are the only ones that are described in indigenous
terms. Rather, the Western contribution is in the intermediate tactics
used by a low-power group to gain the attention of authorities. The
fact that a group espousing a Western ideology chooses to use the tactics common to that tradition does not preclude the possibility that a
more traditionally Japanese set of tactics exists to cover the same situations. On the other hand, there is some indication that these tactics
are used because traditional methods either failed to work or did not
permit such direct assertions of contrary opinion. Other essays in this
volume suggest that this situation may be one for which Japanese tradition does not provide many tools for conflict expression and management.

Some of the demands and responses made in student movement
conflict, on the other hand, have a very Japanese character. The
demand that school authorities apologize for their conduct follows
the Japanese tradition of official apology as a means of redressing an
institutional wrong. The only oddity is that the students must explicitly demand and bargain for an apology which traditionally should be

offered voluntarily as an act of noblesse oblige. On occasion, officials have begun a *taishū dankō* by offering a traditional apology, but the atmosphere at the meetings is such that it can only become the starting point for further demands. Indirectly related to official apology is the sensitivity to repentance which underlies the handling of persons arrested for student movement violations of the law.

Perhaps the most fitting expression of the mélange of Western and traditional Japanese elements in student conflict is the word coined for the violent factional disputes that have so characterized the postwar student movement. *Uchi geba* fuses the alien word for conflict or struggle (German: *Gewalt*) with all the emotional loadings of *uchi* that Takeshi Ishida has described elsewhere in this volume.

Uchi geba is a contradiction in terms, by the traditional theory of Japanese harmony, yet it has pervaded the Japanese student movement for clear structural reasons within the movement and its external environment. *Uchi geba* is both a cause and an effect of labeling. It is central to an understanding of the acquisition of deviant identity. Why, when factional divisions—even violent ones—are found throughout Japanese society and can be discussed with perfectly good Japanese words, must the word for factional conflict in the student movement be coined anew with a distinctly foreign flavor? Not only because of the movement's penchant for ideological jargon, I would argue, but also because doing so helps to preserve the myth that small-group harmony is Japanese and internal conflict has to be an alien, deviant aberration.

NOTES

1. See Henry D. Smith II, *Japan's First Student Radicals* (Cambridge, Mass.: Harvard University Press, 1972).
2. Lewis Coser, *The Functions of Social Conflict* (New York: Free Press, 1976), pp. 87–95.
3. Totals are calculated from National Police Agency, *Shōten* (19 December 1972), as quoted in Donald Wheeler, "Value Politics, Student Politics and the Tokyo University Struggle," Ph.D. dissertation, Columbia University, 1974, p. 267; and "Seiji Tero—Shūmatsuteki Mirai, Tokushū," *Asahi Jānaru* (30 January 1976), p. 11.
4. The counts are based on all reported transformations of organizational name and identity, plus all reported factions with some name attached, as found in charts in Shin Sayoku Riron Zenshi Henshū Iinkai, eds., *Shinsayoku Riron Zenshi* (Tokyo: Ryūdō shuppan, 1979), p. 575; and "Seiji Tero—Shūmatsuteki Mirai," p. 17. Various sources report varying degrees of factional detail for the same organizations over the same time period, but these figures at least give some sense of the magnitude of the phenomenon.

5. Stuart Dowsey, ed., *Zengakuren: Japan's Revolutionary Students* (Berkeley: Ishi Press, 1970), p. 195.

6. "Seiji Tero—Shūmatsuteki Mirai," p. 16.

7. See the chapters by Ishida and Hanami in this volume.

8. For a detailed description of *taishū dankō*, see Yasuyuki Owada, Alan H. Gleason, and Robert W. Avery, "Taishū Dankō: Agency for Change in a Japanese University," in T. S. Lebra and W. P. Lebra, eds., *Japanese Culture and Behavior* (Honolulu: University Press of Hawaii, 1974).

9. This term is difficult to translate literally into English and has multiple connotations in Japanese. *Bōryoku* means violence or force, but a *bōryoku-dan* can be either a terrorist organization or a gang of racketeers or ruffians. *Bōryoku* revolution or politics, on the other hand, refers specifically to Bolshevik, hence communist, ideology. And the term as used in the law includes *shugi* (ideology or "ism"), thus heightening the political connotation.

10. For the complete text of the law in English, see Ministry of Justice, ed., *The Constitution of Japan and Criminal Statutes* (Tokyo: Government Printing Bureau, 1958); Hideo Tanaka, ed., *The Japanese Legal System* (Tokyo: University of Tokyo Press, 1976), contains additional commentary.

11. For a full account of the passage of the University Control Law, see T. John Pempel, *Patterns of Japanese Policy-Making: Experiences from Higher Education* (Boulder, Colo.: Westview Press, 1978).

12. Cullen Hayashida, "The *Kōshinjo* and *Tanteisha,* Institutionalized Ascription as a Response to Modernization and Stress in Japan," *Journal of Asian and African Studies* 10 (July 1975): 198–208.

13. John Lofland, *Deviance and Identity* (Englewood Cliffs, N.J.: Prentice-Hall, 1969), p. 14.

14. Ibid., p. 18.

15. Coser, *Functions of Social Conflict,* pp. 95–104.

16. Susan J. Pharr, *Political Women in Japan* (Berkeley: University of California Press, 1980).

17. Lofland, *Deviance and Identity,* pp. 53–54.

9
Status Conflict: The Rebellion of the Tea Pourers
SUSAN J. PHARR

Status-based conflict, or "status politics," arises from the efforts of persons of a given social status to adjust their status position vis-à-vis those occupying statuses above them.[1] In the broad sense in which conflicts involving social status are discussed by leading conflict theorists, status-based conflicts can occur as a result of many different types of status-related grievances, including, for example, the type dealt with by Gusfield, in which a conflict arose as an attempt to recoup the loss of achieved status suffered by a given social class.[2] The concern in this chapter, however, is with status conflicts in which the statuses of the two parties are ascribed—that is, are dictated by age, sex, caste, and other attributes that are normally beyond the powers of the individual to change.

I focus on such conflicts in recognition of their special significance in Japanese society. Status inequalities based on ascribed differences are an important locus of conflict in Japan as a result of social structural characteristics left over from Japan's feudal past and the ideological responses to those characteristics today. A hierarchically ordered feudal system ended in Japan so recently—little more than one hundred years ago—that the word "feudalistic" is still widely used pejoratively to refer to ways of behaving in which status lines are thought to be overaccentuated. The legacy of a feudal caste system in which dress and styles of speech were rigidly prescribed, and even punishment for crime was mediated by status, is a social structure in which considerations of rank and status continue to loom large despite the phenomenal changes that Japanese society has undergone since the feudal era ended in 1868.

The persistence of status inequalities as a major characteristic of the Japanese social system has been recognized in virtually every study of how the society works—from Ruth Benedict's early analysis and later social science studies to popular accounts directed at American managers hopeful of doing business in Japan.[3] Generally, these diverse analyses discuss status inequality in terms of the importance of inferior-superior, or junior-senior, relationships and other considerations of rank and status in ordering social relationships in Japan. A few years ago the prominent Japanese social anthropologist Chie Nakane drew much acclaim for work treating the pattern of Japanese status inequalities somewhat more systematically and concluding that Japan is a "vertical" society.[4] Although Nakane has been criticized for trying to explain too much with one model, few critics question the significance of the social structural characteristics that are the focus of her analysis.

Most analyses of the hierarchical features of the Japanese social order have emphasized their positive merits for promoting social integration, consensus, and harmony in Japan—for example, by showing how the smooth functioning of junior-senior relations (that is, status inequalities based on age) in the workplace contributes to workers' satisfaction and productivity.[5] It is very clear, however, that conflict or breakdown in such relationships has major consequences for the level of social conflict in Japan, for the very reason that status relationships are such a key adjunctive mechanism in the social structure.

The increasing importance of status-based conflicts may be seen as the direct outgrowth of an ideological clash in postwar Japan between democratic values and the traditional value structure mediating human relationships. Democratic values have had some impact on institutions in Japan since the modern period began in 1868 and have been available as counterideology since that time to those challenging traditionally ordered social arrangements.[6] But since World War II, as a result of the far-reaching legal, political, and social changes set in motion by the Allied Occupation (1945–1952), *demokurashi* was elevated to the status of official ideology. Democratic values have gained even further authority as Japan's contact and identification with the liberal democracies have increased in the postwar period. As a result, democratic ideology—incorporated in the postwar constitution, spread by a mass educational system, and supported both by internal socioeconomic changes and by the process of Japan's internationalization—increasingly challenges the legitimacy of the authority exercised by status superiors in social relationships and provides an ideological basis for status inferiors to engage in conflict to improve their lot. In everyday life, those attempting to exercise status-based prerogatives derived from the traditional normative system may find the legitimacy of their claim to power questioned.

Taken collectively, challenges (in the form of status-based conflicts) to the structure of power and authority have major implications for social and political arrangements in Japan and for the breakdown of Japan as a consensual society. As Weber notes, consensus in a society is possible only to the degree that the existing power structure, reflected in social relationships, is accorded legitimacy.[7] To the extent that an alternative ideology offers a competing formula for the proper distribution of power in status relationships, the basis for consensus is undermined.

Numerous conflicts over status inequalities in Japan have been reported and analyzed in recent years by scholars, but they have seldom been thought of as such. Their generic relation to one another as status-based conflicts and their common characteristics have been overlooked. Conflicts involving inequalities in authority based on age (that is, intergenerational conflict), for example, have received much attention in the literature not only for their impact on social change and their impact on youth, as manifested in the student movements of the 1960s,[8] but for their bearing on growing conflict in Japanese political parties and in organizational life more generally between Young Turks and the senior generation in whom power is concentrated.[9] Conflicts involving the efforts of women to improve their status vis-à-vis men in the family, in the workplace, and in politics have been the focus of much recent attention.[10] Similarly, conflicts involving the two to three million persons in Japan referred to as *burakumin,* who suffer discrimination in marriage, employment, and in other ways today as a result of their hereditary membership in a former outcast group, have been much studied.[11] These various conflicts, however, have been treated as discrete phenomena or else have been clumped together with other types of "protest politics" in a way that obscures their common place of origin in the social structure. Thus the significance of their collective impact on the level of social conflict has been underestimated.

Understanding status-based conflicts—their nature, their dynamics, the chances for their resolution—is thus crucial for anyone concerned with how Japanese society is changing today. Moreover, status-related issues and conflicts have a significance that extends far beyond Japan, due to the apparent rise in importance of similar conflicts in advanced industrial societies. In the past, conflict theorists from Marx and his successors to Dahrendorf have been primarily concerned with struggles over economic interests, even though their definitions of class conflict generally have been broad enough to subsume conflicts over status.[12] But it is equally clear that for Western conflict theorists, struggles over inequalities dictated by ascribed status have been hardly more than a residual category in relation to conflicts arising over the ownership, use, and distribution of material goods. Writers such as Gusfield, in singling out status-based conflicts for attention, have felt compelled to build a strong case for their significance.[13] Studies of "postindustrialism" and value change in advanced industrial societies suggest, however, that status issues may be taking on increasing significance as part of a general pattern of change in which struggles over values, meaning, and quality of life have come to take their place alongside the traditional economic conflicts in the industrial nations. Even as conflicts over shares of the economic pie continue—and, indeed, may surge to the forefront once again in the "politics of scarcity" of the 1980s—conflicts over values and life-style have come to take on major significance in affluent, industrialized societies.[14]

Japan offers a compelling example of a country in which such "struggles over meaning," taken collectively, are assuming increased importance. This trend may be observed not only in the emergence of status politics issues dealt with in this chapter but in the nature of numerous other conflicts of the 1970s and early 1980s: conflict over the human and ecological costs of industrialism; conflict over capitalist business practices and the uses of technology (debates on pollution, land use, nuclear power plants, price fixing, truth in packaging); conflict over moral and ethical issues (the Lockheed scandal, political corruption, profiteering by energy cartels); conflict over symbolic and cultural issues (the Narita airport struggle and the controversy over what calendar Japan should officially adopt); and conflict over the psychological and cultural (as well as economic) implications or problems of the aging (debate within government-sponsored study groups in the early 1970s over "the meaning of life" *(ikigai)* in the later years).[15] In the context of this trend toward conflict over meaning in Japan and elsewhere, status-related issues have a central place. Heisler, for example, notes that status issues have been of paramount significance in ethnic and regional conflicts that have emerged in European states in recent decades.[16] Indeed, it may be argued that numerous conflicts today ostensibly classified as conflicts of economic interest are as well understood, or perhaps even better understood, as status-related issues. The rising importance of noneconomic issues in collective bargaining, the issues of status and recognition that surround the efforts of middle-class and upper-middle-class working women in advanced industrial societies to better their lot, the status-related concerns that have marked student malaise—all are examples.

The focus in this study on status-based conflict is thus appropriate, not only from the standpoint of changes occurring in Japan but also in light of more general trends in all the advanced industrial nations. This chapter examines status-based conflicts in Japan with three major aims: first, to explore the nature of such conflicts which, as noted, have been neglected by Western conflict theorists; second, to study the dynamics of status-based conflicts, bringing Western conflict theory to bear in the analysis; and third, to look at the patterns of resolution (or nonresolution) of such conflicts as a way of assessing their current and potential impact on social and political arrangements in Japan.

In the case of status politics presented in the next section, what is at issue is the ascriptive attribute of sex. The case focuses on a group of female civil servants in a public bureaucracy who formed a movement to protest a specific duty assigned to them on the basis of sex—that is, the duty of making and pouring tea several times daily for the men in their respective sections of the Kyoto City Office. Intersex conflict is central to any study of status-based conflict in Japan because women, in sheer numbers, make up a vast proportion of the population who continue to be assigned positions of inferiority in numerous social contexts. The case selected for study holds particular interest because it involves conflict over an activity (the serving of tea) that is a significant symbolic act tied to their traditional status and thus provides a close look at the subtle psychological and symbolic issues that appear to characterize status-based conflicts. The conflict is also of special significance because the larger issue it raises is whether the State, speaking through the rules, regulations, and employment practices of the public bureaucracy, can continue to sanction and perpetuate status inequalities based on sex while officially upholding an ideology of meritocracy and egalitarianism. How this larger issue, which arises in the values and practices of public bureaucracies in most societies today, is resolved worldwide has profound consequences for contemporary social arrangements.[17] In this sense, the case to be analyzed in the next section has particular comparative relevance.

A Case Study of Status-Based Conflict

Social conflicts unfold in a framework and in a series of stages that are by now well analyzed.[18] Their beginning point is an objective situation that has the potential of giving rise to a conflict between parties. The objective situation involves incompatibility of goals pursued by the potential parties to the conflict. Since the conflict latent in the objective situation may or may not become manifest, one of the principal tasks of the analyst is to specify the conditions under which conflict does arise.[19] If the existence of an objective conflict situation may be considered the *first stage* of a conflict, in the *second stage* the conflict becomes manifest. This is through a process by which the parties become aware that they have incompatible goals.[20] In the *third stage* the parties initiate conflict behavior; the relevant questions to ask at this stage are what modes the parties adopt in pursuit of conflict goals (persuasion, coercion, reward), to what degree the conflict is institutionalized, and to what degree third parties play a role.[21] In the *fourth stage,* the conflict escalates and deescalates in response to changes in intensity and scope.[22] In the *fifth stage,* the conflict terminates. Although one conflict may well begin a new one, every conflict has some kind of outcome.[23] In addition to these stages in the life of a conflict, there is clearly a further stage in which the effects of the conflict feed back into the objective conditions that potentially will give rise to further conflicts. This feedback process by which social structures and values undergo adjustments provides the central dynamic of social change.[24]

Kriesberg offers a simple but useful diagram to suggest the relationship among the stages (see Figure 1).[25] While applying broadly to all types of conflict, including war, it schematically acknowledges two features of status-based conflict that are of special interest: that the "awareness process" by which conflicts become manifest is an integral part of the conflict and that termination of a conflict is itself a lengthy stage, rather than a simple end point following escalation and deescalation.

In the status-based conflict that I call the tea-pourers' rebellion, the struggle began in the objective conditions that define the status of women in the workplace in Japan and, more specifically, that defined the status of women in a particular public bureaucracy in the early 1960s. The objective basis for conflict was (and is) inherent in the tension between the official ideology of the workplace, which for-

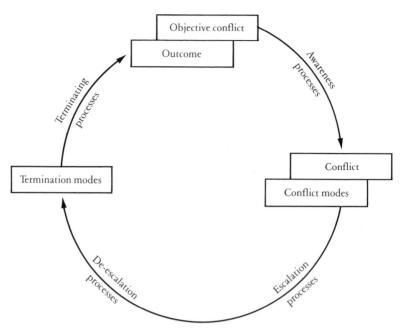

FIGURE 1   *The Five Stages of Conflict*

From Louis Kriesberg, *The Sociology of Social Conflicts,* © 1973, p. 19. Reprinted by permission of Prentice-Hall, Inc., Englewood Cliffs, N.J.

bids discrimination on the basis of sex and upholds the principle of equality of opportunity and the idea of the equal ability of women and men, and the informal ideology, derived from traditional values, which structures women's roles and opportunities in the workplace on the basis of their ascribed status as women. Tea-pouring duties, as will be shown, are a metaphor or "condensation symbol" for traditional expectations for women that run counter to the official ideology.[26] The tea-pouring rituals of a public bureaucracy thus distill the objective conditions of the workplace, which structure the lives of all working women in Japan—and, indeed, to varying degrees in all societies today—into a set of conditions closer to the daily lives of the women participating in them. In a broad sense, the objective basis for conflict in the case under study had existed throughout the postwar period in Japan. In a narrower sense, the tea-pouring rituals had been practiced in the Kyoto City Office over the same period, and thus the specific objective conditions that gave rise to the conflict had been in place over most of the postwar era.

In the second stage of the conflict, a group of women bureaucrats in one division of the Kyoto City Office developed an awareness of the objective conflict situation inherent in the duties routinely asked of them. This stage unfolded gradually over the period from the late 1950s, when officials in the union that serves the needs of City Office employees began to take up some of the problems of women workers, until the spring of 1963, by which time the participants in the conflict had begun to meet to discuss their grievances. The third stage, during which conflict behavior was actually initiated, began when the band of women, having formally organized themselves, initiated a series of demands on their male status superiors. The conflict then moved into the fourth stage, marked by escalation and then deescalation, as the women, over a period of approximately a year, moved through their plan of action and struggled to cope with the response of their status superiors to each of their initiatives.

The termination stage, consonant with the findings of other students of conflict, was a lengthy one. In fact, the end point is still the subject of debate among the participants. In general, however, the conflict may be seen as having wound down gradually after the women initiated conflict behavior to achieve the last of their series of goals. From the standpoint of this analysis, the tea-pourers' rebellion may be seen as having ended in the summer of 1964, when it became clear that despite some immediate gains the protest was not to spread beyond the one division. With the groundwork thus laid, the conflict can now be examined in more detail for what it tells us about the nature of status-based conflicts and about conflict and its resolution in Japan.

Stage One: The Objective Basis for Conflict

It is a long-established tradition in Japanese offices that tea is served to employees. Employees, even if their wages are low or the work is unsatisfactory, are generally supplied with as much tea as they wish to drink. The interesting thing about the ritual of providing tea to office members is that all the activities relating to it except the drinking—heating the water, pouring it in the teapot, pouring the tea into cups, serving the tea, remembering which cup belongs to whom (since personal cups are generally used), gathering, washing, and arranging the cups afterward, cleaning up the counter where the tea was made, buying the tea or making sure that it is bought—are assigned to women employees by virtue of their ascribed status as women. It is true that most offices hire certain women to do little other than to prepare tea. These women, however, known as *ochakumi,* are generally reserved for "up front"—that is, for serving tea to high-ranking officials who are in regular contact with the public and for their guests. Quite apart from the *ochakumi* and their duties, it is the general expectation of everyone in the office that if a woman employee is present when tea is wanted by male employees, it is she who will be responsible for its preparation.

The tea-making routines in the Kyoto City Office had been highly developed. In most sections, the women employees formed themselves into a pool and rotated the duty. In one section of the Housing Division, for example, there were four women among the seventy employees, and thus each woman's turn came once every four working days. On her tea day in the spring or fall, the woman employee came to work approximately twenty minutes early on her own time (without compensation) to get the water ready for everyone's morning cup of tea. After she had served the first morning round she went about her regular office duties, only to drop them again to prepare for rounds of tea served at shortly before noon and again at three. At the end of the day, during which she had served a total of some 210 cups of tea, the woman employee made a final round of the office to collect the cups, wash them, arrange them, tidy up around the tea preparation area, and check supplies. She then went home and was free of all tea-making responsibilities . . . until her turn came up again four days later.

In a legal or "official" sense, none of these duties existed. Nowhere did tea making appear on the women employees' job descriptions. Even the tea itself was not paid for by the City Office, but rather from a kitty for such purposes made up of money collected from the employees. A number of women interviewed for the study reported that when they had gone to their section chiefs with problems arising from the competing demands of their regular job and their tea-pouring responsibilities, they were told to manage as best they could. Since pouring tea was not their official duty, nothing could be done. They would have to be treated equally with the men, however, when it came to dividing up official duties. Occasionally, at this juncture, they were reminded that Japan is a democracy and that women must accept equal responsibilities in exchange for their rights. Meanwhile, however, a number of women employees and several high-ranking male employees told me that female job applicants, during the interview that follows successful performance on the civil service exam, were asked how they felt about serving tea to their coworkers. If they voiced objections, they said, there was little chance of getting hired. A representative of the personnel office halfheartedly denied that this practice existed, but he added that it was natural and proper for women to pour tea. Among the many male officials and employees interviewed, none could agree with the view that it was unfair for women to be required to pour tea for their male colleagues. Most repeated the phrase often heard in Japan that it is "women's duty to pour tea."

The serving of tea has profound symbolic meaning in Japanese culture. In a broad sense, it is a ceremony, a ritual activity aimed at opening and maintaining lines of communication between people.[27] But it is the asymmetry implied—indeed, ritualized—in the relationship between server and served that makes it central to this inquiry. The serving of tea fits comfortably within Goffman's definition of "status rituals" as "marks of devotion . . . in which an actor celebrates and confirms his relation to the recipient."[28] The implied relationship is reciprocal, for in the status ritual involved in pouring tea for another, the social inferior expresses deference and dependence and is rewarded by the superior's protection. The sociological and political uses of ritual forms such as tea pouring are profound, for they are transmitters of cultural formulas for what constitutes appropriate social behavior and thereby function to regulate and channel power.[29] In terms of the earlier discussion of status politics, the tea-pouring ritual evokes the traditional normative code regulating interaction between people of different statuses and thus legitimates— indeed, celebrates—the exercise of prerogatives of status superiors over status inferiors. As a ritual engaged in primarily by women, the serving of tea is a dominant symbolic act in Japan expressing the asymmetry between the sexes. Through pouring tea for men, women express their deference for them and their inferiority to them. At the same time, serving tea is a symbolic act linked to women's role as nurturer, a function assigned to women on the basis of sex in most of their social roles. In this sense, the tea-serving ritual accentuates the differences in behavioral expectations for the two sexes while ceremonially acknowledging and approving the traditional functional justification for them.

For all these reasons, the expectation that women employees will assume the duties of tea pouring clashes with the official ideology of public bureaucracies in Japan, which holds aloft the principle of achievement over that of ascription and explicitly forbids sex-based discrimination. The objective basis for conflict is thus laid.

Stage Two: From Objective Conditions to Subjective Awareness

Unfolding over the period from 1957 to 1963, the second stage, in which a small group of women in the Housing Division became aware of the objective basis for conflict inherent in their daily routines, was a long one. The chief agent of change was a man named Kawata, then in his late twenties, who had become active in the public employees' union to which all regular employees in the city bureaucracy belonged. (All names and other details have been changed to protect the anonymity of participants in the conflict.) Kawata's initial concern was the problem of young, temporary workers, male and female, and he set about organizing new "Youth and Women's Bureaus" *(seinenfujin-bu)* of the union in various divisions of the City Office to address their needs. He started a union bureau in his own division, in fact, and became its head.

Gradually Kawata's attention fell on the problems of regular women employees, who were hired on the basis of their performance on an examination administered without regard to sex, but whose careers thereafter followed a wholly different course from those of men: "The role of women was as men's assistants. They had the jobs of servants and maids—running errands for men who should have run their own errands, cleaning up the men's desks. . . . Their future was entirely different from men's. They were permanent assistants to men." It is impossible to establish to what degree Kawata held such views in the late 1950s, some twenty years before he expressed them in an interview. His efforts continued to center on issues relating to temporary workers. But the establishment of the union bureau did create a setting in which the objective terms of women's employment in the City Office were tacitly exposed to scrutiny. And, moreover, Kawata took it upon himself to stir the women employees into action.

The union bureau was being formed just at the time when Yuriko Makino, the woman who was to lead the rebellion, came to work in the Housing Division. As a new high school graduate attending college classes at night, Makino was for four years only nominally involved with the Youth and Women's Bureau of the union. Then, in 1962, soon after her graduation from college in March of that year,

Kawata came to her and asked whether she would be interested in forming a Women's Section within the union bureau to deal with the special problems of women workers. Since there were so few women in the division, he thought it would make sense for the women to form their own group as a section under the union bureau. He singled out Makino because she had just completed her college degree and was therefore in a position to take a leadership role. Kawata, both by his account and hers, went to Makino many times urging her to lead the undertaking. From his report, she was a most reluctant leader, fearful of criticism from the men in her section of the Housing Division if she asserted herself in any way. By the account of several female participants, observers to the recruitment process, however, Makino was quite willing to step forward. For these women, Kawata's role in getting the section under way figures less prominently than Kawata's own report indicated; meanwhile, Makino, while acknowledging the importance of Kawata's role, claims not to remember the details. Concretely, however, there is agreement that for a period of at least a month or so in 1962, Kawata and Makino discussed the question of how to organize a Women's Section of the bureau.

It was quite striking, in interviewing both leaders, that neither remembered discussing specific issues to be dealt with by the proposed Women's Section. Kawata explains it by stating that his primary aim was to see the new group launched; he assumed that once the group was formed, it would single out problems for its attention. Makino, who by then was eager to take the reins of leadership, reports that she did not see the need for spelling out the issues to be taken up by the women and preferred to concentrate on organizational questions. Another interpretation, based on a close reading of the accounts of both, is that the two were engaged in conflict avoidance behavior. It became obvious in the interviews that while Makino, like the other female participants, reported the later conflict as a struggle centering primarily on the women's tea-pouring duties, Kawata preferred to portray it as a conflict with larger aims; in fact, he appeared embarrassed to hear it referred to as a "tea-pourers' rebellion." There was every indication from his verbal and facial responses that he saw this designation as demeaning to the seriousness of what he had been trying to encourage. It also should be remembered that Kawata, despite the importance of his role as an agent of change and a third party and ally once the conflict commenced, was a status superior whose tea got poured every day by the women. For both these reasons, then, if Makino had been planning to make tea pouring a central issue in the conflict to come, it seems doubtful that she would have brought the matter up with Kawata. For his part, Kawata, eager to make a leader out of someone he saw as reluctant to take that role, would have had his own stake in conflict avoidance.

After a month or so of discussions with Kawata, Makino was prepared to call a meeting of women in the division to initiate discussions of what was to be done. The meeting marked the beginning of a process by which subjective awareness of the conflict situation inherent in the office setup gradually diffused from Makino herself, and a small group of fellow college graduates who soon rallied around her, to the other women. Ostensibly the meeting itself was an informal social get-together held after work at a restaurant near the City Office. Little was said about the problems of women in the Housing Division (or elsewhere, for that matter) or the possibility of organizing a Women's Section. The tone of the meeting, by Makino's description, was "let's all get to know each other."

Following this dinner, there was a long period—nearly a year—given over to what is best characterized by the Japanese expressions *nemawashi*, (preparatory activity) and *hanashiai* (exploratory talks). Although conflict theories based on Western experience take into account that long periods of time may elapse between the emergence of conflict and the initiation of conflict behavior, there is little recognition of what in Japan may be conceived of as something akin to a distinct stage preparatory to the initiation of conflict behavior in face-to-face relations. The overall goal of this stage, which is characterized by numerous meetings, often without an explicit agenda relating to the goal, seemingly is to create a sense of oneness among the participants and a sense that they agree, but the exact terms of the agreement are not necessarily spelled out. The persons interviewed for the study all had difficulty characterizing the nature or content of these meetings except to say that the end result, after approximately a year, was the formal move to seek approval from the union for the creation of a Women's Section. These meetings, taken collectively, seem to represent the search for consensus so often described as a characteristic of Japanese decision making.[30]

Following the meeting just described, approximately fourteen women from four of the five sections in the Housing Division began getting together more or less regularly. In the course of the meetings held over the years, a number of grievances relating to tea pouring began to be aired. Several distinct but related problems could be seen. One problem was the quality of the tea-making equipment, which was felt by a number of the women to be old-fashioned and dangerous. It took an extraordinarily long time to heat the water on it. Furthermore, two of the five sections in the division had no tea-making equipment of their own. The women employees in these sections had to carry heavy teapots of boiling water up a flight of stairs several times a day when their turn came, a chore that was felt by the women in these sections to be troublesome and even dangerous. A second issue was precisely what women's duties in relation to tea pouring should encompass. There appeared to be agreement that it was women's duty to make the tea for the men in the office. The points of discussion were how often each day the tea should be prepared and whether the women had a responsibility to pour and serve the tea as well as make it. There was much talk of a need to "rationalize" the tea-pouring duties, although what was meant by this term often was not spelled out in the discussions.

A final issue, central from the standpoint of this analysis, was the attitude of the men in the office. The Housing Division was one of the new divisions in the City Office, and its office routines were said to have an unsettled quality. Everyone seemed rushed and on different schedules, with builders, architects, and planners hurrying in and out of the office. A number of high-status males, particularly the architects, appeared, by all accounts, to take personal services of all kinds for granted. Often tea was set before these men without so much as a flicker or grunt of acknowledgment. The younger men, whom the women knew better through the Youth and Women's Bureau of the union, had a much better attitude in most cases. Significantly, many of the women did not mind serving these men.

These reported discussions hold much of interest to the student of status rituals. The discussions must be seen against the backdrop of changes that were occurring in the nature of the workload in the City Office in the early 1960s. In an era of high growth, the work of public bureaucracies was expanding. Divisions such as Housing, linked as it was to the construction boom of the period, were especially affected. The workload of all employees was increasing, but the men in supervisory positions were giving little thought to how these changes affected women. Assignments were handed down without regard to how their schedules might conflict with duties related to making tea. A classic example was the decision to locate two sections of the Housing Division in upstairs rooms that had no place to make the tea that all the men expected to drink.

If we think about the conditions under which status rituals would have most meaning for those performing them, then it is clear that in the Housing Division in the early 1960s many of those conditions were not being met. It can be hypothesized that status rituals are optimally performed, with greatest satisfaction for the performer, when four conditions are maximized: first, when the deference behavior is warmly rewarded by reciprocal behavior; second, when the deference behavior is felt by the one engaging in it to be well deserved (a military salute, for example, has more meaning and comes easier when the saluted is a courageous general rather than an incompetent lieutenant); third, when the behavior called for is congruent with other expected behavior; and fourth, when the status differential due to sex is reinforced by other status differences (in bureaucratic rank, socioeconomic background, age, education, seniority, and the like).[31]

Looking at the situation of women employees in the Housing Division in this light, it is apparent that there had been an erosion on all four fronts. In the hurried atmosphere of a newly established division, there was little warmth in face-to-face relations, draining deference behavior of its emotional rewards. Meanwhile, the attitude of the older male professionals—their lack of basic courtesy and generosity and their failure to acknowledge favors—made it onerous to go through the required rituals. It is also clear that the nature of the workload for which female employees were held responsible was in flux in the early 1960s. Successive waves of "rationalization" over the postwar era had increased women's share of the normal work of public bureaucracies without a corresponding decrease in the number of unofficial "women's chores" they were expected to perform. For women, there was an increasing lack of congruence between the content of the tasks expected of them as workers and those expected of them as women. Finally, the entry into the bureaucracy of better-educated women in the early 1960s had introduced status incongruities. College-educated women were more likely to see the tea-pouring duties as beneath them—that is, as inappropriate to their level of training, experience, and skills. For all these reasons, the status rituals expected of the women were losing their meaning, thus removing some of the forces that might otherwise have constrained conflict behavior.

Over the course of the many meetings preceding the formation of a Women's Section, grievances other than those relating to tea pouring were aired. The chore, unpleasant to many of the women, of cleaning the men's desks and emptying ashtrays brimming with stale cigarette butts was discussed. Another issue centered on the problem of taking their menstruation leave days each month. According to Japanese labor law, women workers are entitled to "sick days" during their menstrual period, but custom in the City Office required that employees asking for time off state the reason for the request on a publicly displayed signup sheet. Most of the women were too embarrassed to request their leave days or suffered anguish before they could bring themselves to do so. Still another problem was the women's need for a "change room." As is the custom in many Japanese offices, City Office employees, then and now, wear uniforms. The women felt the need for a place to change in and out of their uniforms, comb their hair, touch up their makeup, eat their lunch, or lie down on an off day, especially during their menstrual period or during pregnancy. There was no place for any of these activities because the restrooms in the City Office, again following Japanese custom, were for both men and women. Hypothetically the restrooms were shared, but in practice they represented male turf. A woman might scurry past men lined up at the urinals to get to a cubicle, but she was not going to tarry long enough in the restroom to comb her hair.

These various issues have common characteristics. First they reveal, in a very stark light, the terms of women's employment in the Housing Division. All the conditions—being asked to clean ashtrays, being required to request a menstrual leave before a roomful of men, being denied the right to privacy due them, they felt, in recognition of the biological differences between men and women—reflected the harsh terms of the status relations in the office, in which status inferiors were required to celebrate men's status superiority through the performance of office rituals but were themselves exposed to humiliation in return. A second characteristic is that these issues, along with the question of tea pouring itself, were all linked to the condition of status inferiority. They were so intimate, so rooted in fundamental biological and cultural differences dividing the sexes, that they necessitated collective action on the part of the status group if they were to be acted upon at all.

The discussions among the women went on for a year. Through them, as noted, the women's subjective awareness of their situation forged itself into a collective consciousness. The meetings also appear to have been an almost formal prefatory stage prior to taking action. One additional function should be mentioned. The meetings made it possible for distance to grow between the women and their male superiors. Locked into day-to-day relations with the targets of their anger, there is a necessary psychological process by which the ordinary Mr. Tanaka and Mr. Sakao of the office became cast as "the enemy." Only when status superiors are objectified, blown up into larger-than-life caricatures and viewed collectively, can the anger be released on them.[32]

Stages Three and Four: From Initiation of Conflict Behavior to Escalation and Deescalation

After a year of meetings, the women came at last to a point of declaring themselves a "Women's Section" and seeking formal recognition as such from the union. This action, figuratively speaking, drew a bright circle around the quasi group of status inferiors and thus marked the initiation of conflict behavior. By adopting the formal standing of a section attached to the union, key decisions about the style of conflict behavior were implied. Moreover, the action put the men of the office on notice that women workers had a distinct set of problems and, moreover, that those problems were worthy of attention.

The Women's Section, once formed, began to put forward a series of demands, one by one, at intervals of several months over a period of slightly more than a year. The first demand was for the change room. The request was granted, and the room became the center for the group's organizational life. Meetings were held there to plan the group's conflict strategy on other issues. The general plan of action called for sending delegations of women to relevant groups of status superiors, and the room became the staging area for these sallies out into the office and also a place to fall back to after a conflict episode.

The escalation of the conflict was reflected in an increase in the frequency of meetings held by the women. Before the formation of the Women's Section, formal meetings of the entire group had been held monthly. The get-togethers in between had been more or less informal. Now, however, the entire group met with greater frequency, and the leadership core met weekly in the change room. Additional meetings of the leaders and, occasionally, of the whole group were held whenever they were deemed necessary. As their demands intensified, it became common for the leaders to hold several meetings a week. The sequence of the issues put before the status superiors also reveals a pattern of escalation. The "easiest" issue, the desire for the change room, came first. This request was made in the spring. As women began to use the meeting room as a base, their activity increased; by summer they had made the second demand, this time on the issue of menstrual leave. They wanted not to have to explain that they were taking menstrual leave. Their request, by their accounts, was met by a strangled silence and then a confused but generally positive response from the official responsible for sick leave and other related matters, who was apparently struck dumb with embarrassment. The women interpreted his response as a victory and, as of July, began taking their menstrual leave without offering an explicit written explanation. The crescendo in the process of escalation came in the fall of 1963 when the women launched what is even now remembered in the City Office as the "tea-pourers' rebellion."

The strategy adopted by the women for bringing about change in the tea-pouring rituals reveals certain arresting features of Japanese conflict behavior. Whereas the group, until that time, had taken their demands one by one to appropriate male officials using normal channels and a mode of conflict behavior involving direct attempts at persuasion, they now changed strategies. Several factors appear to have influenced the switch. One was certainly the nature of the issue. The request for a change room required positive action from the men. The request that they be allowed to take their menstrual leave without stating the reason required that the appropriate official not bar their way when they started doing so.

Changing the terms of the tea-pouring rituals was much more complex, however. First of all, since the tea pouring was based on informal practice, there was no one formally vested with specific supervisory responsibility. There was no specific target for conflict behavior, therefore, and no one in a position to give or deny permission for the women to change the terms of their performance. Thus no normal channel even existed for handling the grievance. To merely stop serving tea without prior notice, however, was sure to arouse anger and confusion among the men that was to be avoided at all costs. It seems likely, then, that the women selected indirect means over confrontational methods at this stage as a way of containing the level and intensity of a conflict that, by other measures (such as the frequency and length of their meetings), was clearly escalating.

The goal of the women at this stage in relation to tea pouring was to end their responsibility for serving the tea, but not for making it. The actual formula was left up to the women of each of the four sections in the protest. In one section, the women wanted to stop all but the actual morning preparation of tea. In another section, the women were prepared to make tea at all the usual times, but without serving it. It is significant that the group as a whole could not agree on uniform goals. In the interest of maintaining solidarity, apparently the group tacitly agreed to disagree. The lack of solidarity, of course, may have been another factor governing the decision to select indirect, over direct, methods of conflict. Divided over the issue, in other words, the women fell back to safe tactics.

The strategy they adopted may now be examined. Essentially it involved alliance politics—the use of a third party as a go-between in the conflict. The alliance was with the younger men in the office through the Youth and Women's Bureau of the union. The bureau, it may be noted, was the only institutionalized form of contact between men and women in the division in which they were, in an institutional sense, on an equal footing. Prior to a regular meeting of the bureau, Makino met with Kawata and won approval for the plan. The group then sent a written notice to the men in the bureau announcing the new arrangements for serving tea in the office. The leadership corps of the women's group attended the bureau meeting (as was their normal practice). They left the formal announcement of the plan at the meeting to Kawata as the union bureau's head. According to all available reports, no discussion followed the announcement. Kawata had already sought and secured the members' support.

Then the next day the women put the plan into effect by making tea at agreed upon times, but then leaving it for the men to serve themselves. Key men from the Youth and Women's Bureau came forward to show the older men the way. In some cases, they carried tea for their immediate boss. Women in some of the sections reportedly did the same. The reaction of the men to the new plan is difficult to ascertain. According to Kawata and women participants interviewed long after the rebellion, the men of the office said nothing and ostensibly went along with the new arrangements. And yet we know that a number of women in the various sections were soon backsliding— that is, carrying tea as before, at least to some of the men—and meetings continued to be held by the women to bring these members in line. We can only conclude that the silence greeting the attack on the basic lines of status difference in the office was alive with anger and tension. Perhaps the most telling evidence of the climate of feeling in response to the rebellion was the reception my questions received *nine years later* when I interviewed high-ranking male officials in the City Office about the struggle. Their faces visibly darkened, and they spoke of the rebellion with a tone that can only be described as outrage.

In the overall conflict, deescalation was signaled by the women's final request, this time for new tea-making equipment for the two sections without any. In this case there was an appropriate official to approach, and the request was made directly. It was granted without ado.

Stage Five: Termination of the Conflict

The final demand by the Women's Section was made in the fall of 1963 not long after the rebellion had commenced. Over the winter months the men and women were working out, or responding to, the new routines surrounding the making and serving of tea. It seems likely that tension persisted for some time. How else are we to account for the anger on the faces of City Office officials, nine years later, when they were interviewed about the tea-pourers' rebellion?

The parties to the rebellion disagree about the outcome of the conflict. In the summer of 1964, a meeting bringing together a large number of representatives from women's groups was held in Kyoto. News of the formation of the Women's Section and of the teapourers' rebellion had spread and Makino was asked to make a brief report before the group as head of the section. In doing so, she may be seen as claiming victory for her side of the struggle over status-related issues. She and other female participants, interviewed many years later, reported the rebellion as at least a partial success, for they and the other protesters had refrained from making and pouring tea on a "business-as-usual" basis for several years after the rebellion itself—indeed, for as long as they remained in the Housing Division. Kawata, too, remembered the outcome of the conflict as a victory for the women. Male managers who had not been directly involved, however, reported that the conflict had "faded out." The fact that several of the leaders had ultimately left the City Office in order to get married was taken as a sign of the frivolity of the whole enterprise.

From the standpoint of the present analysis, the revolt of the tea pourers must be seen as a failed rebellion, but for reasons different from those given by the male managers. In the end, this rebellion failed to spark widespread social change. The failure of the revolt, in this larger sense, is revealed every working day in the City Office: Women employees continue to make and serve tea. Even in the

Housing Division, the tea-serving activities resumed once all the key women had either left the office to get married or had been transferred to other divisions in the normal rotation of personnel within the City Office.

The fate of the rebellion was sealed at the point that it failed to spread to other divisions. For a brief moment, there was the possibility that the protest would be taken up throughout the City Office. In the summer of 1964, a retreat of union representatives from the various Youth and Women's Bureaus in the City Office had been held. At the meeting Kawata, who had organized the retreat, held up the Housing Division as a model and urged representatives from the various union bureaus to go back and get the young men in them to pour their own tea. By his report, however, Kawata's suggestion got a mixed response at the meeting. At any rate, the recommendation was never implemented. Any prospect for fundamental change died then. In a real sense, then, the conflict ended at that meeting.

The critical question to ask in exploring why the movement did not become general is this: Why did the central office of the union choose not to endorse the women's efforts and urge all the divisions to follow suit? The Kyoto City Employees' Union, after all, was formally the parent of the Women's Section itself. In interviews with union officials, however, it became clear that they had avoided getting involved. They chose to regard the tea-pourers' rebellion as a shop-level struggle in a single division, without broader implications. Three reasons were given. First, because only four sections were involved in the conflict, the dispute was regarded as too localized to merit union involvement. Second, the women's grievances were not of the type dealt with by the union proper. Had the issues been equal pay for equal work or maternity benefits, the union would have gotten involved, but the issues at stake in this case were not the proper concern of the union. Third, the issues were not serious enough to receive union attention. Although officials acknowledge that most of the 2,000 women in the 8,000-member union have various tea-related duties and the union got wind of numerous complaints at the section level, the union's position had been to regard the issue as outside its domain.

Conclusions

Status-based conflicts—the stages they pass through, the modes of behavior involved in the expression of status-related grievances and the responses they evoke from status superiors, the prospects for social change inherent in the outbreak of status conflict—are as yet little understood. The study of such conflicts occurring in Japan or elsewhere is at a very preliminary stage. Based on an analysis of the case just presented, a number of possible characteristics of status-based conflicts stand out and invite further investigation.

The first of these characteristics is the intensity of feeling reflected in the expressed attitudes and the reported and observed behavior of parties engaged in status-based conflict. To illustrate, a manager may talk dispassionately about the wage level being sought by workers during the annual spring offensive and discuss ideological issues (on which he has clearly defined positions) with every appearance of composure but become visibly shaken when he talks about the protest of a small group of women workers over the requirement that they pour tea for the men in the office. Although Western conflict theory leads us to predict such intensity in cases where it is the manager's own tea that is not getting poured,[33] it is quite striking that status superiors (in this case the male managers in the central office of the City Office) were visibly upset when they described the rebellious behavior of status inferiors in a distant section of a huge public bureaucracy.

A second characteristic is the importance of both symbolic and instrumental goals in status-based conflicts, each of which may be handled and responded to quite differently in the process of conflict resolution or nonresolution. Theorists such as Edelman lead us to expect the powerful to yield on symbolic issues or, at any rate, to manipulate symbols themselves as a way of avoiding concrete concessions, but the behavior of status superiors in cases of status politics appears to be precisely the opposite.[34] The concrete goals of this conflict—the change room, the new tea-making equipment—were readily conceded while the symbolic issues linked to tea pouring in the end proved intractable. In cases involving status-based conflict, yielding on symbolic issues requires a fundamental concession from status superiors that something is amiss in the superior / inferior relationship itself, a concession that throws the very basis of social relations in Japan into question.

A third characteristic, noted before in social psychological research on conflicts in Western nations, is the importance of status within the ranks of status inferiors in establishing their role in relation to the conflict. The importance of this factor in ordering status-based conflicts in Japan is quite striking, and the case study offered here allows for a close analysis of the actual process involved as status operates in the ranks of inferiors. The role of a status superior—in this case, Kawata—in legitimizing a new interpretation of reality on the part of status inferiors stood out sharply. The role itself was not surprising. The part played by white liberals in the civil rights movement in the United States and the role played by men in the suffrage and feminist movements in America, Britain, and indeed Japan (with Arinori Mori and Yukichi Fukuzawa as famous examples from Japan's history) are reminders that this phenomenon has been widespread in other status-based conflicts. In essence, members of the superior status group lay the groundwork for the conflict by doing what they normally do in their overall pattern of interaction with status inferiors: Use their authority, but this time to legitimize the substitution of a new ideology of interstatus relations for an old one. From the standpoint of the status inferior, this act of legitimation not only lends authority to his or her own emerging view of the objective conflict situation; it also helps relieve the anxiety attendant upon contemplating hostile actions against status superiors. This anxiety, which often keeps conflicts latent, centers not only on the fear of reprisal but on the likelihood that once the conflict becomes manifest the dependency needs of status inferiors will go unmet. The intercession or show of support by a third party from the ranks of the status superiors calms this anxiety and reassures status inferiors that their new view of reality is comprehensible to at least some status superiors.

The importance of status in ordering the roles of actors in status-based conflicts also was evident in the process by which a leader emerged from the ranks of the status inferiors. For in identifying a leader to challenge the basis of one set of status relationships, Kawata had no hestitation in relying on another status attribute, education, as the basis of selection. Makino, as one of the two college-educated women in the group of status inferiors, was seen by him as the group's natural leader, and, indeed, there is no evidence that the women who followed her disagreed. It can be argued, of course, that her selection on the basis of such a criterion was justified. Numerous surveys in Japan in recent years have indicated that dissatisfaction with the status of women is highest among college-educated (as opposed to less educated) women, and thus there was a strong probability that a college-educated woman would be a good choice to lead the way in consciousness raising.[35] But in addition, the ease with which she accepted a leadership role and then exercised her prerogatives as such are a reminder of the importance of status considerations in all areas of Japanese life, including the organization of status-based conflicts.

A fourth characteristic concerns the process by which the conflict became manifest—namely, the degree to which the process was not verbalized. Both Makino and Kawata report no recollection of discussing the issues that were to be taken up by the Women's Section. It may be that their failure to address the issues was due to conflict avoidance behavior. But it is nonetheless striking that the two put their heads together to challenge the legitimacy of the basis of social arrangements all around them without attempting to agree on what their objections were. Why this was so may get to the heart of the major characteristic of status-based conflicts in Japan today, for it appears that the objective conflict situation involved in status relations is near the surface of consciousness for many people, especially better-educated people like Kawata and Makino. Thus little discussion is required for them to see the lines of conflict, even when they are not prepared to act. This appears to be especially true in the case of male-female status relations. That a fairly high percentage of Japanese people believe that women experience discrimination in the workplace is regularly borne out in survey data. Even those who declared in interviews in 1978 that "it is women's duty to pour tea" were likely to state the proposition aggressively or defensively rather than matter-of-factly.

The situation in Japan today over status relations between the sexes might be compared to race relations in the United States in the 1950s after the Supreme Court upheld the principle of equality to challenge the legitimacy of the authority traditionally exercised by whites in interracial relations. The court in dramatic fashion did precisely what the Allied Occupation (and subsequent laws in Japan) did in throwing its authority behind a set of principles meant to apply to status relations based on ascriptive characteristics. As a result, even when such conflicts do not become manifest, the objective lines of conflict are clear.

A fifth characteristic of status-based conflict, and perhaps of Japanese conflict behavior more generally, is the use of a third party at critical stages of the conflict. The true function of the alliance was the same as the function of the initial alliance between Makino and Kawata. The younger men, in effect, were asked to use their authority as status superiors to sanction the status inferiors' action. Gaining approval from the younger men also undoubtedly served to alleviate the anxiety suffered by the women in making the protest, since it represented a guarantee that the women, in protesting the terms of their dependency relationship with their status superiors, would not lose the goodwill of all the men.

A sixth characteristic is the degree to which the initiation of each conflictual act was preceded by an extraordinary amount of informal background activity that smoothed the way. Key men in the Youth and Women's Bureau were approached by the women informally well before the written announcement of the plan of action was circulated. Kawata's approval, as bureau head, had been secured in advance. In this sense, there was very little that was spontaneous about the conflict. Each step was plotted and prepared for; the difficulties ahead were anticipated. Prior research on Japanese negotiating behavior and behavior in organizational contexts alerts us to the importance of *nemawashi*, or preparatory work, in getting things done in Japan. But it is significant to find the same pattern emerging in conflict behavior. It seems likely that it is the extensive use of *nemawashi* in conflict situations in Japan that has contributed to the view among Western observers that levels of conflict are lower there than elsewhere.

A final characteristic of major significance in understanding status-based conflicts in Japan and assessing their potential impact on the social order is the finding that there appear to be few institutionalized channels for their resolution in Japan today. Established channels, after all, are maintained by persons or bodies with a vested interest in the system. The real issues in conflicts involving status inequalities cannot be taken to the unions, the courts, or other mediating agencies because these channels are not yet ready in Japan to acknowledge the legitimacy of the protest or, to put it another way, to challenge the legitimacy of the authority exercised by status superiors in the relationships that pervade Japanese life. One implication is that the gains achieved by status inferiors in specific conflict episodes have a limited chance of becoming general, as this case study has illustrated. On the other hand, the failure of structures to respond to pressures from status inferiors leads to the repetition of similar episodes. It is significant that tea-pourers' rebellions and related conflicts continue to occur today not only in the Kyoto City Office but in Japanese bureaucracies and organizations at large. These separate episodes represent a steady pressure from below for adjustments in status relations and at the same time contribute to the rise in the overall level of social conflict in Japan.

NOTES

Funding from the Japan Foundation and from the Graduate School of the University of Wisconsin-Madison made this research possible. I would like to thank Emiko

Onuki-Tierney, Patricia Steinhoff, Gary Allinson, Chalmers Johnson, T. J. Pempel, George DeVos, Takeshi Ishida, Murray Edelman, and Richard Merelman for their comments and suggestions. I am grateful to Shizuko Mori and Takako Kishima for their able research assistance.

1. Joseph R. Gusfield, *Symbolic Crusade: Status Politics and the American Temperance Movement* (Urbana: University of Illinois Press, 1966); Taketsugu Tsurutani, *Political Change in Japan* (New York: McKay, 1977).

2. Gusfield, *Symbolic Crusade*.

3. Ruth Benedict, *The Chrysanthemum and the Sword* (Boston: Houghton Mifflin, 1946). For examples of more popular works, largely directed at businessmen, that deal with this phenomenon, see William Duncan, *Doing Business with Japan*, (Epping, U.K.: Gower Press, 1976), and Herman Kahn, *The Emerging Japanese Superstate* (Englewood Cliffs, N.J.: Prentice-Hall, 1970).

4. Chie Nakane, *Japanese Society* (Berkeley and Los Angeles: University of California Press, 1970).

5. See, for example, James C. Abegglen, *The Japanese Factory* (Glencoe, Ill.: Free Press, 1958); Robert E. Cole, *Japanese Blue Collar* (Berkeley and Los Angeles: University of California Press, 1971); and Lewis Austin, ed., *Japan—The Paradox of Progress* (New Haven: Yale University Press, 1974).

6. See Susan J. Pharr, *Political Women in Japan* (Berkeley and Los Angeles: University of California Press, 1981), for further discussion of this phenomenon.

7. Max Weber, *The Theory of Social and Economic Organizations*, trans. A. M. Henderson and Talcott Parsons (New York: Oxford University Press, 1947).

8. Nobutaka Ike, "Economic Growth and Intergenerational Change in Japan," *American Political Science Review* 67 (December 1973); Ellis S. Krauss, *Japanese Radicals Revisited: Student Protest in Postwar Japan* (Berkeley and Los Angeles: University of California Press, 1974); and Akira Takahashi, "Nihon Gakusei undō no shisō to kōdō" [Thought and behavior in the Japanese student movement], *Chūō Kōron* 5 (May 1968), 6 (June 1968), 8 (August 1968), 9 (September 1968).

9. Mainichi Shimbun Sha, *Seihen* [Political change] (Tokyo: Mainichi Shimbun Sha, 1975); Susan J. Pharr, "Liberal Democrats in Disarray: Intergenerational Conflict in the Conservative Camp over the Nature of Political Leadership," in T. MacDougall, ed., *Political Leadership in Modern Japan*, Michigan Papers in Japanese Studies (Ann Arbor: University of Michigan Center for Japanese Studies, 1982).

10. See, for example, Pharr, *Political Women in Japan*, and Merry I. White and Barbara Molony, eds., *Proceedings of the Tokyo Symposium on Women* (Tokyo: International Group for the Study of Women, 1979).

11. See, for example, George DeVos and Hiroshi Wagatsuma, *Japan's Invisible Race* (Berkeley and Los Angeles: University of California Press, 1966), and Roger I. Yoshino and Sueo Murakoshi, *The Visible Invisible Minority* (Osaka: Buraku Kaiho Kenkyūsho, 1977).

12. For example, status-based conflicts fit well within Dahrendorf's definition of class conflict groups ". . . generated by the differential distribution of authority in imperatively coordinated associations." See Ralf Dahrendorf, *Class and Class Conflict in Industrial Society* (Stanford: Stanford University Press, 1959), p. 204.

13. Gusfield, *Symbolic Crusade*.

14. See Ronald Inglehart, "The Silent Revolution in Europe: Intergenerational

Change in Post-Industrial Societies," *American Political Science Review*, 65 (December 1971), and *The Silent Revolution: Changing Values and Political Styles Among Western Publics* (Princeton: Princeton University Press, 1977); Daniel Bell, *The Coming of Post-Industrial Society* (New York: Basic Books, 1973); and Leon Lindberg, *Politics and the Future of Industrial Society* (New York: McKay, 1976).

15. For an analysis and interpretation of postindustrial trends in Japan, see Tsurutani, *Political Change in Japan*.

16. Martin O. Heisler, "Political Economy Aspects of Ethnic and Regional Conflict," paper presented at the 11th World Congress of the International Political Science Association, Moscow, August 1979.

17. Alexander Szalai, *The Situation of Women in the United Nations*, Research Report 18 (New York: UNITAR, 1973), is one example of a work that has identified this larger issue. See also Rosabeth Kanter, *Women and Organization* (Englewood Cliffs, N.J.: Prentice-Hall, 1976).

18. See, for example, James S. Coleman, *Community Conflict* (New York: Free Press, 1957); Louis Kriesberg, *The Sociology of Social Conflicts* (Englewood Cliffs, N.J.: Prentice-Hall, 1973); and Lewis A. Coser, *Continuities in the Study of Social Conflict* (New York: Free Press, 1967).

19. See Coleman, *Community Conflict*, p. 4; Giuseppe DiPalma, *The Study of Conflict in Western Society* (Morristown, N.J.: General Learning Press, 1973); Kriesberg, *Sociology of Social Conflicts*, p. 24.

20. Kriesberg, *Sociology of Social Conflicts*, p. 24.

21. Ibid., p. 110; Coleman, *Community Conflict*, pp. 11–15.

22. Kriesberg, *Sociology of Social Conflicts*, pp. 155–161.

23. Coser, *Continuities*, pp. 37–39; Thomas Schelling, *The Strategy of Conflict* (Cambridge, Mass.: Harvard University Press, 1956), chaps. 2–3; Kriesberg, *Sociology of Social Conflicts*, p. 204.

24. Coser, *Continuities*, pp. 19–35.

25. Kriesberg, *Sociology of Social Conflicts*, p. 19.

26. Mary Douglas, *Natural Symbols* (New York: Vintage Press, 1973).

27. Ibid, p. 42.

28. Erving Goffman, *Interaction Ritual: Essays on Face to Face Behavior* (New York: Anchor Books, 1967), pp. 56–57.

29. Douglas, *Natural Symbols*, pp. 30, 42.

30. See Michael Blaker, *Japanese International Negotiating Style* (New York: Columbia University Press, 1977); Ezra F. Vogel, ed., *Modern Japan Organization and Decision-Making* (Berkeley and Los Angeles: University of California Press, 1975).

31. Goffman, *Interaction Ritual*; Douglas, *Natural Symbols*.

32. See Murray Edelman, *The Symbolic Uses of Politics* (Urbana: University of Illinois Press, 1964).

33. See, for example, Lewis A. Coser, *The Functions of Social Conflict* (New York: Free Press, 1956), p. 67.

34. Edelman, *Symbolic Uses of Politics*.

35. See, for example, Sumiko Iwao, "A Full Life for Modern Japanese Women," in Nihonjin Kenkyūkai, ed., *Text of Seminar on Changing Values in Modern Japan* (Tokyo: Nihonjin Kenkyūkai, 1977), and Pharr, *Political Women in Japan*, chap. 3.

PART IV

Conflict in the Political Process: Parties, Bureaucracy, and Interest Groups

Conflict in the Diet: Toward Conflict Management in Parliamentary Politics

ELLIS S. KRAUSS

The literature on most Japanese institutions and organizations has tended to portray them as relatively harmonious. By contrast, the National Diet for much of the postwar period has been seen by Western and Japanese observers as relatively conflictual. During the 1950s and 1960s, intense conflict over key social and political issues between the ruling Liberal Democratic Party (LDP) and government, on the one hand, and the opposition Japan Socialist Party (JSP), on the other, occurred frequently and represented the main focus of the sparse research on parliamentary politics in Japan.[1] These conflicts involved the government's using its large majority to force key bills through the legislative process over the obstructionist tactics of the seemingly perennial and ineffective opposition, resulting in breakdowns of parliamentary decorum and bitter, sometimes violent, confrontations between the two sides in committees and on the floor of the Diet. Vehement confrontations on major issues occurred frequently enough for some observers to question whether postwar Japanese democracy had developed the basic norms of Western parliamentarianism—regularized communication between adversaries and agreement on majority rule and minority rights reflected in institutionalized rules of the game—and whether Japanese cultural characteristics were in fact compatible with such parliamentary norms.[2]

Japan's parliament was also seen as a weak actor in the political process, a body whose major function was to legitimize policies already decided upon by the bureaucracy, cabinet, and LDP. It was viewed primarily as an arena in which the major political differences between conservative and progressive parties were expressed, and clashed, but rarely were effectively managed or resolved. The Diet seemed to be lacking in the basic institutional capacity and political function one would expect of a parliament—the ability to manage important conflicts between political parties and the interests and ideologies they represent.

The Japanese Diet during the 1970s presented a very different picture. Declining LDP majorities and increasing opposition influence in the legislative process produced the *"hakuchū jidai,"* the era of nearly equal power relations between government and opposition. Considering the postwar history of Diet conflict, this situation should have produced even greater conflict. Yet, in fact, there was a dramatic decline in both the intensity and frequency of confrontation between government and opposition. By the late 1970s rare was the successful government bill that did not receive the support of at least one opposition party, and the bitter clashes of previous decades virtually disappeared. Increasingly, government and opposition parties seemed to be resolving their differences through bargaining within normal parliamentary channels. This change in the style and role of parliamentary politics has been summed up as a transition from the "politics of confrontation to the politics of compromise."[3]

My purpose here is to analyze the development of conflict and its management in the postwar Japanese Diet. Above all I wish to describe the process of diminution of severe government-opposition conflict in the 1970s, why this transformation occurred, and the possible implications of its occurrence for Japanese politics. I contend that in responding to a changing political environment, parliamentary elites began to create new, informal rules of the parliamentary game and a new role culture within the Diet itself. These new norms and behavior represent a trend toward the institutionalization of conflict management, a development which may have major consequences for the process and stability of democratic politics in Japan. Further, I will return to the question that was raised by the intense conflicts of the 1950s and 1960s: Is there a basic disparity between Japanese cultural characteristics—in-group identification and loyalty and the absence of communication among diverse groups—and the requirements of democratic parliamentary politics? I will argue that the institutionalization of conflict management in the Diet in the 1970s also represents the adaptation of Japanese cultural patterns in the parliamentary norms necessary to bring about partisan accommodation.

Approaches to Partisan Conflict in Parliaments

Partisan political conflict frequently has been analyzed using a "mass-cleavage" approach. This approach assumes that the fundamental divisions in values and socioeconomic interests among mass publics determine the nature and intensity of conflict in national politics.[4] Clear-cut cleavages among mass publics have rarely been found, however, either in Europe or Japan, and, when found, they have not been shown to be automatically transformed into ideological, political, or partisan conflicts. Even when the mass-cleavage approach can suggest the *potential* sources of political conflicts, it neglects the crucial variable of conflict management and treats the interaction of parties as if it were unmediated by the institutional context.[5]

The political process is not just a reflection of conflict between competing societal interests and values; it is also an independent variable determining the outcome of societal conflicts. Increasingly, political scientists have noted that the behavior of political elites ultimately determines whether there is resolution or management of deep social and value conflicts, whether such conflicts are expressed without effective accommodation or resolution, or whether otherwise latent conflicts are intensified. That behavior, in turn, depends greatly on whether political elites can develop institutional role norms and informal and formal decision mechanisms that encourage conflict management and resolution.[6]

In the case of parliaments, there is an especially close connection between the development of institutional norms and decision mechanisms and the expression and effective outcomes of societal conflicts. Parliaments are established to provide a forum by which the various major interests and values of a society can be represented (more or less) through political parties and the conflict between them accommodated (more or less) to ratify binding regulations—laws—for the society as a whole. In the words of Michael Mezey:

> In a very real sense legislatures domesticate conflict. They are a structural device for keeping conflicts within the system and thus within limits acceptable to the policy-making elites. Interaction within the legislature may serve to ventilate grievances, but they also can serve to reveal areas of agreement and promote consensus.[7]

The entire body of rules, precedents, customs, and role norms that characterize the inner workings of parliaments—the formal and in-

formal rules of the game of legislative politics—exist to facilitate the
orderly ventilation of grievances and search for agreement. They aid
the management of partisan conflict. To the extent that these rules
are widely accepted and implemented, conflict management may be
said to be institutionalized.

Theorists have identified a number of basic norms and decision
mechanisms that are crucial to conflict management and its institutionalization.[8] First, there must be developed a basic consensus on
the procedures for resolving disputes. The most important consensus
is agreement on majority and minority rights in decisions. Conflict
theorists have noted that the formal principle of majority rule by
itself is an ineffective and dangerous means of resolving conflict
because it can create permanent alienated minorities and overbearing
majorities who have little motivation to engage in conflict regulation
and accommodation. Majority rule must be supplemented by other
norms that encourage the majority to respond to the interests of the
minority and that induce the minority to refrain from paralyzing
decision making.[9] Second, parliaments need a norm of "restrained
partisanship."[10] This encourages the expression of partisan interests in
a manner that does not preclude finding a basis for accommodation
of opposing interests. Third, authoritative roles and specialized organs must be developed for conflict management. And, finally, these
specialized conflict managers must have autonomy to act independently from parties and interest groups to bring about negotiated settlement of disputes.

My intent in this essay is to show how the extent of institutionalization of these role norms and decision mechanisms has resulted in different patterns of expression and regulation of conflicts between government and opposition parties in the Diet. Factors external to the
Diet are incorporated only to the extent they are relevant to institutionalization within the Diet. The research deals only with the House
of Representatives. Secondary sources in English and Japanese[11] and
interviews[12] provide the evidence for the argument.

Conflict and Its Management in the Diet: 1955–1970

The first decade after Japan's defeat and occupation was a period of
adjustment to a new political system and to the new powers and organization of the Diet under the 1947 constitution and the new Diet
Law. Numerous parties sprang up in the early years after the war, and
only during the brief period between 1948 and 1952 was one party
able to form a government.

During this early period of unstable multiparty politics, certain features that were to influence the parliamentary process for decades were introduced. Some were the result of the occupation's attempt to create a national legislature patterned after the English Parliament, but elements from the U.S. Congress were also introduced. Into a basically parliamentary form of government, for example, a congressional style of committee system organized along functional lines was instituted. In its Japanese setting of strict party discipline in voting and no seniority system for committee chairmen, the actual role and powers of these committees were left problematical. Procedural safeguards for the protection of legislative minorities were weak but great powers were given to presiding officers to prevent filibustering, a practice of American legislative minorities that was viewed with disfavor. [13]

During this early period, too, particularly with the rise to power of the former bureaucrat Yoshida, there emerged a close relationship between conservative political parties and the bureaucracy and a cabinet-bureaucrat coalition began to dominate the Diet in the formulation and introduction of legislation. [14]

It was the merger of the Liberal and Democratic parties in 1955, however, that provided the most important feature of parliamentary politics until the 1970s: a single, dominant conservative party with a large majority of seats in the Diet and thus in perpetual control of the government, Diet posts, committees, and initiation and direction of the legislative process. The Japan Socialist Party (JSP), with its approximate one-third of the seats, became the largest opposition party.

To a party system polarized around one dominant majority party and one large minority party was added the strains of an ideological polarization that reached its peak in the late 1950s. The LDP, heavily dependent on business for funds and farmers for votes, was committed to anticommunism, state power, national defense, alliance with the United States, public order, and centralized administrative control in education. The JSP, based on left-wing trade unions, was a proponent of Marxism, democratic rights, unarmed neutrality in foreign affairs, and resistance to authoritarian tendencies in civil liberties and education. These antithetical values constituted a clear basis of political conflict, causing Joji Watanuki to characterize Japanese politics of the period as "cultural politics." Every issue related to these themes was quickly escalated and generalized. [15]

In the cold war era, many LDP members and supporters viewed the leftist opposition (often strongly Marxist) as an internal security threat. Its positions against national defense and the American alliance were seen as equally dangerous to external security. Many JSP members and supporters viewed the conservatives' positions as thinly disguised attempts to put the country on a reverse course away from democracy and peace and back toward prewar authoritarianism and militarism. That the LDP was close to the two-thirds majority in the Diet which would allow it unilaterally to amend the constitution and eliminate its "no war clause" (Article IX) added to the fears of the left. The basis for polarization was not just the ideological differences between the parties but their salience and intensity in this period.

At the grass-roots level these fears and ideological tensions probably were neither prominent nor intense, and the politics of patron-client relations, vested interest, and *kankei* vote mobilization were the essence of Japanese electoral politics.[16] But polarized values and mutual suspicion were characteristic enough of party elites and activists and the politicized segments of the public to define the context of government-opposition relations until the late 1960s.

The salience of the conflicts over the major issues of foreign policy and defense, public order, and education to the two parties' elites and activists made avoidance of their injection into parliamentary politics improbable. The nature of the issues and the mistrust between the parties made their accommodation difficult. The lack of a developed consensus on procedures for handling intractable disputes in the still new politics of dominant single-party rule made their management nearly impossible. The result was almost constant confrontation in the Diet over a series of bitterly fought issues between 1958 and 1960: the Police Duties Bill (1958), the Vietnam Reparations Bill (1959), and the culminating clash of the period, the U.S.-Japan security treaty (1960).

In each of these cases there were striking similarities in the behavior of the parties and Diet members that reflected the polarization of government-opposition relations and the Diet's incapacity to manage it. On these bills, both sides violated the letter and spirit of the norms of parliamentary procedure and decorum, and total disorder, even physical violence between members, prevailed in the Diet. In each case, government and opposition could not agree on the timing or procedures for handling the bill, and no negotiated compromise was achieved within the normal legislative process. Further, the LDP and its parliamentary leaders precipitated a complete breakdown of communication by sudden closure of debate and the exercise of its majority, subjecting the government to mass protest and charges of "tyranny of the majority."[17]

These incidents, which so rapidly evolved from the issues presented by the bills to the fundamental question of the legitimate rules of the game in the Diet, caused widespread and justifiable concern in Japan and the United States about the viability of parliamentary democracy in Japan.[18]

The pattern of conflict that had alarmed supporters of democracy in Japan in the 1958–1960 period became the standard scenario for major issues through the 1960s. The government, having formulated a particular piece of controversial legislation in the bureaucracy in the LDP policy divisions, would introduce it into the Diet with little prior consultation with the JSP. The latter would then mobilize its supporters to protest outside the Diet. Within the Diet, the JSP would delay and obstruct proceedings in committees and on the floor to force the LDP to choose between extending the Diet session or shelving the objectionable piece of legislation. In this the JSP used every means possible, including "cow-walking" (extended delay in casting ballots), frequent no-confidence motions, and sometimes physical hindrance.

If the LDP were unwilling to shelve the bill, it would "snap vote" (*kyōkō saiketsu*) the measure through committee and on the floor. The committee chairman or speaker, a senior LDP politician under orders from the prime minister, would deviate from regular procedure and use his wide powers to regulate deliberations—powers that included opening sessions and altering the agenda—to shut off debate and call for a sudden vote. The LDP members, given prior notice, would then quickly exercise their majority, and the presiding officer would declare the bill passed amid the noisy protestations of opposition members. The JSP in retaliation would then boycott Diet sessions, bringing all deliberations to a complete halt, until agreement could be reached on how to normalize the session. This was usually accomplished by the speaker taking responsibility for the disorder and resigning in a face-saving gesture to the opposition.[19]

The obstruction and snap vote dramas of the 1960s took place over the same controversial issues that had caused the confrontations of the 1950s: foreign policy and defense, education, and public order. The treaty with the Republic of Korea (1965) and the University Normalization Bill (1969) for dealing with campus protest were examples.[20] But such conflicts occurred with greater frequency and concerned other issues as well under the long tenure (1964–1972) of Eisaku Satō as prime minister. The 61st Diet in 1969, for example, witnessed the longest session on record, six all-night plenary meetings, the longest plenary meeting in history, eighteen snap votes, and three committees which snap-voted all the bills before them.[21] Even such nonideological bills as one revising the National Health Insurance Law and one raising the fares on the national railways were the subject of conflictual scenarios.

And yet, simultaneous with the seeming continuation and even expansion of these confrontations, the 1960s witnessed the development of subtle changes in government-opposition interaction, changes that reflect another, less commented upon, facet of the development of the Diet as an institution. The 1960 security treaty crisis represents something of a dividing line in postwar Diet history in that it stimulated conscious concern among party leaders and members about the problem of conflict management and Diet survival. This concern provided an implicit check on a recurrence of "total conflict." As Baerwald put it: "Memories of those events have played a consequential role in delineating the kind of conduct that is permissible within the Diet and its immediate environs."[22]

Within both the LDP and the JSP, further, the 1960 crisis stimulated rethinking about basic political strategy and exacerbated differences of opinion within them as to whether a "moderate" or "hard line" toward their rival was most efficacious. In the JSP, Saburō Eda's proposals for "structural reform" were an attempt to move the party's program toward greater acceptance of the parliamentary system and more pragmatic behavior. As for the LDP, prime minister Hayato Ikeda (1960–1964), successor to Kishi who had been forced to resign as a result of the treaty crisis, adopted a low-posture strategy of patience and increased communication with the opposition parties while avoiding the introduction of legislation that would provoke total resistance from them.[23] Unfortunately, neither of these immediate consequences of the 1960 crisis was to become established permanently. Eda's pragmatic orientation was to be consistently undermined or overridden by the JSP's left wing, and Ikeda's successor, Eisaku Satō, was to return the LDP to a higher posture later in the decade. Nevertheless, the issue of making parliamentary democracy work had become more prominent and a "constituency for moderate action" had been created within both parties.[24]

More lasting than the parties' temporary diversions from their roles as overbearing majority and recalcitrant minority was the shift in conservative policy priorities after 1960. Beginning with Ikeda's "Income-Doubling Plan," the emphasis of conservative policy shifted from the areas of defense and protecting traditional values to rapid economic growth, an aim that did not provoke the ideological passion of the political left or right. Moreover, the fact that the security treaty with the United States had been automatically extended for ten years gave both sides a hiatus from the issue that had become the focal point of their extreme polarization in 1960.

Finally, as the 1960s wore on, it became obvious that both sides had reached the peak of their electoral and Diet strength in the 1958–1960 period. The LDP was not going to reach the two-thirds of Diet seats needed to amend the constitution; and the socialists had reached a "one-third barrier" in seats and votes, making the prospect of a Marxist majority remote. The worst nightmares of each side about the other's potential power, the fears that had intensified conflict in the Diet, came to appear more and more remote.

The early 1960s, then, was a time when the parties became more conscious of the need to limit the extreme consequences of their polarized ideologies and to create new strategies to deal with their now seemingly perpetual roles as government majority and opposition minority. The game of politics in Japan increasingly became a two-level process of continued intractable conflict over major ideological issues in the public arena of the Diet while communication and accommodation quietly increased.

It is interesting to note, for example, that during the same decade in which the obstruction and snap-vote scenario occurred with increasing regularity on certain types of bills, the Diet was passing about three-quarters of all cabinet-sponsored legislation.[25] This was only a slightly lower proportion of government-sponsored legislation passed than in the parliaments of Britain, West Germany, and Italy, where frequent breakdowns of procedures and decorum were not a problem.[26] And, on a great many bills, the JSP and other opposition parties ultimately voted for the government's legislation without opposition. Between 1967 and 1971, the JSP supported about two-thirds of the cabinet bills voted upon and the Komeitō and Democratic Socialist Party (DSP) supported more than three-quarters.[27]

Agreement on these noncontroversial bills was reached through a variety of methods; often the LDP agreed to minor changes in wording or other trivial concessions that did not change the basic thrust of the legislation. Substantive formal amendments incorporating the opposition's views were rare. Even the limited bargaining that did take place, it should be noted, often did not emerge from the formal legislative process itself. Rather, agreement frequently emerged from compromises made by party executives and leaders in secret deals in

restaurants and geisha houses, a type of extraparliamentary negotiating known as *"machiai seiji"* (teahouse politics).[28] "If the socialists
are a revolutionary party during the day, at night . . . they become a
parliamentary party" was the cynical Tokyo joke that indicated the
disparity between the opposition and confrontation of formal legislative sessions and the potential for minor compromise outside it.[29]
Journalists often accused the secret, extra-Diet negotiations of *machiai seiji* of having been smoothed along by the exchange of LDP cash
for opposition agreement.[30]

Even the major dramas of obstruction and snap-vote confrontation
took on a different quality. As Kosaka has pointed out, in contrast to
the total conflicts of the earlier 1958–1960 period—in which both
sides considered the stakes vital and their principles sufficiently at
stake to risk whatever necessary to pass or obstruct passage of a bill—
many snap-vote clashes of the 1960s were more like stage plays. Neither side considered certain bills important enough to risk total confrontation, and in fact there were some points of agreement between
them; nevertheless, they acted out the confrontation scenes anyway
by prior agreement. On bills which did not call into play their fundamental principles, the parties faced each other without internal unity.
Even if the leadership wanted to resolve the issue, it was under pressure from hardliners not to do so publicly: The LDP leadership could
not wait for protracted negotiations with the opposition to succeed
without appearing soft, and the JSP leadership did not wish to appear
amenable to co-optation by the conservatives. The impasse was resolved, as in the case of the revision of the National Health Insurance
Law and a bill to raise the fares on national railways in the 1969 Diet,
by a secret prior agreement between LDP and JSP leaders to pass the
bill by the "confrontation" of forced passage—that is, by a *nareai
kyōkō saiketsu* (snap vote in collusion).[31]

Consequently, the increasing use of the snap-vote format in the
1960s for the passage of bills unrelated to intractable issues represented not the widening or perpetuation of total conflict between the
camps but rather the development of a political ritual between them.
To the extent that this action helped to maintain party unity and
authority and to reaffirm party commitment to symbols of responsibility (LDP as government party) or resistance (JSP as opposition
party), it represented the development and practical use of a conflict
ritual.[32] To the extent that both adversaries knew and agreed in
advance on the way the conflict would take place, it represented the
playing of a political game. And games are played according to rules,

even if at this stage the rules were informal, implicit, and outside the framework of normal institutional procedures. The critical point is that communication between adversaries was taking place. The decade of the 1960s began with a crisis of parliamentary democracy reflecting the failure of government and opposition to develop a consensus on procedures of handling major conflicts between them. It ended with the problem still largely unresolved, but with signs that an extraparliamentary and covert process of communication and accommodation between party leaders on minor issues had begun to develop.

New Incentives for Conflict Management

Beginning in the late 1960s and reaching a peak in the middle of the 1970s, major changes in the political environment in Japan created a new party and parliamentary context encouraging the institutionalization of conflict management within the Diet. First there occurred in the mid-1960s through the mid-1970s a gradual shift in voting patterns among the Japanese electorate that eventually altered the power balance of the parties in the Diet. From a party with an overwhelming majority in the lower house, the LDP by 1976–1979 had been reduced to 49 percent of the seats and dependence on the post-election entrance into the party of successful independent conservatives just to maintain a bare majority. The decline of the LDP did not redound to the benefit of its old leftist rival, the JSP, however. The socialists' share of seats fell to 24 percent in 1976 and then to 21 percent in 1979.

Increasingly, the smaller parties that were either inconsequential or nonexistent from 1955 to the mid-1960s reaped the support that was eroding away from the major parties. The Democratic Socialists (DSP), a moderate offshoot of the JSP, maintained a consistent share of seats (about 7 percent), but to this share was now added the 11 percent (1976 and 1979) of the Kōmeitō, originally the political arm of the Buddhist Sōka Gakkai organization that ran in its first lower-house election in 1967, and the 1 percent (1979) of the New Liberal Club (NLC), a group of young conservatives who bolted from the LDP in 1976. The Japan Communist Party (JCP), with an electoral strategy emphasizing concrete benefits to voters rather than ideology, also gained seats between the late 1960s and the early 1970s.

A polarized party system of a dominant rightist party and a large leftist opposition party had thus been transformed by the mid-1970s

into a true multiparty system with five major opposition parties out-
stripping the government party in combined popular vote and nearly
equaling it in seats. This situation, the *hakuchū jidai* or "era of
nearly equal power," provided greater incentives for the resolution
and management of conflict. Compared to dominance by one side
(where leaders of that side have little incentive to seek accommodation with the minority) or bipolar balance (where intense competition
for dominance may increase conflict), a multiple-party balance not
only gives the leaders of predominant parties incentives to accommodate differences with a minority to stay in power but also gives leaders
of minority parties incentives to accommodate in order to share
power.[33]

Second, new issues were of increasing importance. Instead of the
ideological issues of defense, public order, and education, the focus
in the 1970s was on the problems created by rapid economic growth.
Specific policies to clean up the environment and improve social services became pressing demands of the electorate.[34] There was also an
increase in the number of "floating voters," highly educated citizens
in urban areas not tied into traditional party networks who were concerned with policy issues and the problems of industrialized society.[35]
The new issues cut across the traditional ideological and political divisions and created pressures within all the parties for new images and
responses.

There is direct evidence that new issues affected the priorities of
Diet members. Representatives were asked what they considered the
most important problems in Japanese society today.[36] The LDP and
opposition party representatives scored furthest apart on the problems of the reform and goals of education, the security of Japan, and
the search for a new value system. These are the very same issues that
provoked the intractable confrontations of the past. These issues,
however, were *not* the most frequently selected by either government
or opposition members of parliament. The relatively nonideological
problems of resources and energy and "clarifying and dealing with
the ills of modern society" were the issues chosen most frequently
and in approximately equal numbers by both sides. There has been a
clear decline in the salience of the ideological issues that once provoked the most bitter conflicts between government and opposition.

Third, there was a high degree of generational change and turnover in the Diet in the 1970s. We might expect that freshman representatives newly elected to the Diet during the 1970s would be more
attuned to adapting to the changing party system and political envi-

ronment compared to veteran members who had been socialized into the conflictual patterns of the past. An influential Diet member of a center party confirmed this suspicion:

> There are those people who had operated under Diet management when there was just the JSP and the other party. They know nothing but the old days and thus many of these people now say things like "There's nothing but slowness; move more rapidly!"
>
> *Q.* The younger people without experience in the previous era are more flexible?
> *A.* Yes.
> *Q.* Also in the opposition parties?
> *A.* Yes. The same.
>
> [Interview with "U," 6 September 1978]

These generational differences take on importance when one looks at the data on turnover in the Japanese House of Representatives. One-quarter of the members of the lower house were freshmen elected for the first time in the 1976 election. If one adds to this the members elected for the first time in the elections of 1972 and 1969, a full half of the house in the late 1970s were members without experience of the confrontations and two-level political game of the 1960s —much less than the earlier, more bitter ideological hostility of the late 1950s.[37] To the extent that these new members were more flexible and less encumbered by the assumptions, ideology, and norms of the past, this large turnover rate helped to create an atmosphere conducive to the development of new parliamentary roles and rules of the game.

The combined effects of the emerging competitive multiparty system, new issues, and generational turnover produced by the mid-1970s a quite new political content, one that provided strong incentives for new partisan strategies and styles of parliamentary interaction. The multiparty power balance and changing expectations of voters encouraged all the parties to develop a parliamentary strategy that shunned intense confrontation in favor of pragmatic bargaining. For the LDP, obtaining the support of at least one other party would preclude minority claims of tyranny of the majority and create an image of a responsible and effective ruling party that deserved to continue to govern. In the long run, this strategy would have the added advantage of building precedents for cooperation with smaller moderate parties in case the LDP was forced eventually to form a coalition government.

It was this very prospect of a coalition government that tempted the moderate center and right, the DSP, Komeitō, and NLC, to behave as responsible and cooperative opposition parties. As one DSP representative told me in 1978:

> It's the prologue to a coalition cabinet. We think that there will be a coalition cabinet in the future and we'll be part of it. . . . Because of that, even now though we're not a governing party and we're not in the cabinet, we're going to cooperate repeatedly on good items and make amendments to bills because we think that these are part of "the era of preparation." [Interview with "J," 4 August 1978]

In the meantime it is the same center parties that had come to have a disproportionate influence on the outcome of government-opposition conflicts. Allying themselves with the LDP on a bill could ensure its smooth passage by a solid multiparty majority that defused any rationale for obstruction by the left. Allying themselves with the opposition, they could confront the LDP with a unified multiparty opposition that discouraged crude attempts to force passage of a bill. Thus, in both their moderate ideology and their self-interested strategy, the center parties had not only a great stake in interparty accommodation but also new power to encourage the other parties to such behavior.

On the left, the confrontation strategy of the 1950s and 1960s seemed less attractive. Now that the JSP was no longer the sole major opposition party and had only one-fifth of the seats in the lower house, its unilateral obstruction would have neither the practical impact nor the symbolic value it had had in the previous era. For the JCP, indulgence in parliamentary negativism could destroy its carefully nurtured image as a legitimate democratic party responsive to the policy concerns of the voters. For both Marxist parties, the imperative problem was to avoid temporary and long-term isolation by preventing the center parties from allying with the LDP and by keeping alive the prospect of a future all-opposition coalition government.

With the declining salience of the polarizing ideological issues and a new generation of representatives unfettered by the patterns of the past, many of the prior constraints that once inhibited the requisite communication and trust necessary for developing new rules of the parliamentary game were diminished. Certainly, basic value differences between the parties remained. But as Robert Putnam has shown regarding left and right members of parliament in Britain and Italy, ideological commitment and party loyalty are not incompatible with openness to compromise, negotiation, pragmatism, and trust in dealing with opposing parties.[38]

The changing political environment in Japan by the mid-1970s had thus very much altered the value and meaning of the Diet in the political equation. Parliamentary strategy, behavior, and outcomes were now central to the parties' appeal to the mass electorate and to their present and future role in the political process. There had developed incentives for less conflictual parliamentary strategies and the prerequisite context to engage in a search for institutional mechanisms for implementing them.

Hakuchū Kokkai: Emerging Norms, Mechanisms, and Decision Rules

The Diet sessions of the 1970s, particularly from 1975 to 1979, stand in stark contrast to those of the previous era. This period witnessed a drastic decline of confrontation tactics by government and opposition and an obvious quantum leap in negotiations and compromise through normal parliamentary channels. In the late 1970s, there was only one snap vote, on the Continental Shelf Treaty with the Republic of Korea, an issue that had long been pending and on which the LDP felt enormous diplomatic pressure. One influential LDP Diet member summed up the changed attitude and behavior of the LDP by 1978:

> In past periods—when I say past periods I mean when we controlled by an absolute majority—we carried out snap votes on even nonideological matters. Now we may have to snap-vote on things based on ideology—however, we try to avoid that as much as possible—but . . . if it's a financial issue, it has become common to compromise to a certain extent, find a similar direction, and then come to an understanding and approve a law. [Interview with "S," 25 August 1978]

The behavior of the opposition parties underwent a similar dramatic change. Obstructionist tactics virtually disappeared. "Cow-walking" had ended by the late 1970s. So had the use of frequent no-confidence resolutions against the cabinet to delay proceedings. Between July 1975 and June 1980, there was not a single motion for no confidence against the entire cabinet.[39] Agreement with cabinet-sponsored legislation was also on the increase. Between 1975 and

1977, the percentage of cabinet legislation passing without opposition from a single opposition party jumped from about 43 percent to
about 68 percent.[40] Between 1970 and 1975, there was great fluctua-
tion in each opposition party's support rate for government legislation; only the DSP consistently voted for over 70 percent of government bills in any major session. In *all* the ordinary Diet sessions
between 1976 and 1979, *all* the opposition parties (DSP, JSP, Komeitō, NLC, SDL) except the Communists voted for over 70 percent (and
usually closer to 80 or 90 percent) of cabinet-sponsored legislation,
and the communists' rate had climbed from about 50 percent in the
early 1970s to consistent support for two-thirds of government bills.[41]
As one key Diet member of a center party remarked, "You can say
that the *hakuchū jidai* is certainly the age of the politics of *hanashiai*
(consultation)" [interview with "U," 6 September 1978].

How did such a dramatic change in conflict patterns in the Diet
come about? Such a development cannot simply be considered the
automatic or inevitable result of the declining majority of the LDP.
As one LDP representative involved in Diet administration ironically
noted, "When we had a real majority we ought not to have needed
snap votes; now that we are fewer, we ought to actually need them!"
[interview with "L," 11 August 1978]. Given the patterns of confrontation usual in the previous era, the new power situation conceivably
might have resulted in greater conflict, not less; yet it is the reverse
that has occurred. The changing environment discussed above provided the incentives, but it could not itself cause such an institutional
change. Conflict management depends, ultimately, on elites themselves developing and accepting "stringent procedural rules and
mechanisms that allow accommodation."[42] The explanation for the
transformation of the Diet into a less conflictual institution lies in the
creation in the 1970s of a new role culture *among Diet members* (as a
functional response to the changing environment) whose cumulative
effect was to enhance the Diet's ability to manage government-opposition conflict. This change in the parliamentary process emerged
gradually over the last decade, the result of many separate, and in
some cases subtle, adjustments of old patterns to new realities.

The Changing Power Balance and the Committee System

LDP control of committees and committee chairmanships during the
1950s and 1960s was an integral element in the conflict relationships
between government and opposition in the Diet. With an LDP chairman and majority on all committees, opposition influence on the

content of legislation before the committees was small. The LDP, on the other hand, used its monopoly on committee power to expedite its favored legislation and veto opposition demands, but in the process it also exacerbated its conflicts with its rivals. With no seniority system and their almost annual replacement as part of intra-LDP personnel shuffles, committee chairmen tended "to be viewed as agents of the governing party rather than as guardians of a committee's prerogatives."[43] The only functions the committees performed were the formal legitimation of government bills, the conferring of an honorary status on members, and the opportunity for opposition parties to embarrass the government during interpellations.[44]

The declining LDP majority during the 1970s, combined with the rules and customs of the appointment of committee members and chairmen, altered fundamentally the rule of committees in the lower house. There are sixteen standing committees in the House of Representatives—which vary in size from twenty to fifty members—plus a number of special committees. In allocating seats on committees the lower house follows a complex procedure, but its basic thrust is distribution according to a party's proportion of seats in the full house. The major factor complicating seat allocation, however, is the custom that the committee chairman does not vote in committee decisions except in the case of a tie. On the two odd-numbered (25-member) standing committees this presents no problem: With thirteen members or more the majority party is assured, given the chairman's tie-breaking vote, of always having its way. But on the remaining fourteen standing committees which are even-numbered (twenty, thirty, forty, or fifty members) this custom complicates the definition of what constitutes a majority of the committee.[45] On a forty-member committee, for example, if the ruling and opposition parties are split evenly and the LDP takes the chairmanship, it loses its voting majority on the committee. To control both the chairmanship *and* a voting majority, the LDP must have at least a majority of 21–19 on the forty-member committee of this example.

Thus to have an "effective majority" (also called in Japan a "stable majority") control of both the committee chairmanship and a voting majority on *all* standing committees, a party must have almost 53 percent (271) of the seats in the 511-seat lower house. To control all special as well as standing committees would require an even larger majority. Falling below the critical thresholds, the ruling party must choose between the chairmanship and a voting majority on specific committees.

Following the 1972 election, the LDP slipped below the requisite effective majority to control all committees, and it gave up the chairmanships of many special committees to the opposition for the first time since the formation of the LDP in 1955. It nonetheless retained control and chairmanships of all the standing committees. Following the 1976 election, however, when the LDP's majority was further reduced, it could no longer control all the standing committees either. Thus in the 1978 Diet, for example, the opposition held four of the sixteen standing, and seven of the nine special, committee chairmanships. On five standing committees, the opposition parties held a majority of voting members even though the chairman was a conservative. All told, the LDP controlled both the chairmanship and the majority of seats—the standard situation on *all* committees between 1955 and 1972—on only nine of the twenty-five committees in the lower house in 1978. And on five of these nine the LDP's majority was provided only by the votes of an independent (conservative) or by the LDP chairman casting the tie-breaking vote. A similar distribution of committee control occurred in the 1979 Diet following the LDP's failure to increase its seats to its target of 271 in the lower house elections of October 1979.[46]

By the skillful choice of committee chairmanships, the LDP between 1976 and 1979 avoided turning over a committee completely to the opposition. But the LDP was forced on many committees to yield to the opposition parties either the procedural power of the chairman or the voting power of a majority of committee members. As a result, the Japanese Diet between 1976 and 1980 represented the anomaly of a party which had a majority of seats in the full legislative assembly but which did not completely control its committee system.

It is important to note that the LDP could have used its simple majority in the full house to resist the loss of its committee power. Indeed, after the 1976 election some sentiment had been expressed within the LDP to try and change custom and allow the chairman the right to vote on all matters, not just in the case of a tie vote, a proposal that if carried out once more would have allowed the LDP to dominate most committees. This idea was never seriously attempted, however, after it met opposition party resistance.[47]

These developments had a number of important consequences for conflict management in the lower house. First, by adhering to prior custom and procedure, the LDP chose to place priority on the maintenance of parliamentary custom over pure partisan advantage, even if it meant the loss of control over committees. Had the LDP forced the issue of chairmen's voting powers, the opposition would have perceived it as a sign that the LDP intended to cling to power by riding roughshod over parliamentary norms. Instead, the values of institutional custom were chosen over pure partisan advantage and an important precedent was established about the relinquishing of power by the formerly dominant party.

Second, the attainment of committee majorities and chairmanships, each in a different way, ties the opposition parties more closely into the normal channels of the parliamentary process, diminishing the prospects of intense confrontation and extraparliamentary or obstruction methods. For the first time in postwar history, the opposition parties could use voting majorities on committees to influence the passage and process of legislation and to reject government bills. In March 1977, for example, the Local Administration Committee, on which the opposition parties had a voting majority, defeated a government proposal to reform the local tax law;[48] and in 1979, for the first time in postwar history, the crucial government draft budget bill was turned down by the opposition majority in the Budget Committee.[49] Although these committee-rejected bills were later passed in the full house by a simple LDP majority, the mere threat of such legislative difficulty provided the opposition parties with a lever to force the LDP to consider bargaining and concessions. By virtue of the new opposition power in committees, the once largely irrelevant committee system in the Diet had been transformed into an important site for cross-party discussions about legislation and policy. Moreover, the opposition parties had for the first time a visible channel to express their demands and interests through the normal parliamentary process.

The holding of committee chairmanships by the opposition parties provided an inducement to conflict management in another way. As an influential LDP politician with responsibility for Diet strategy pointedly noted, a committee chairman from the opposition parties faces role pressures that encourage him to bring about negotiated accommodations while discouraging opposition recalcitrance:

> If the LDP takes all the committees, if they take back those committees [in which the opposition holds chairmanships] now, there will be clashes again. So give them such things as commmittee chairmanships as much as possible because the committee chairman is the position of most responsibility. The opposition parties weren't in those positions until now, so there was considerable resistance. A committee chairman wants to pass as

many bills as possible in his committee. He wants to get them approved.
The chairmen from opposition parties want to get them into law too.
[Interview with "L," 11 August 1978]

This quote is a graphic illustration of the strategy of co-optation as a
means of defusing the radicalism of opposition. It also represents a
broad principle of conflict regulation: The right of a minority to
influence decisions and the decision-making process creates a responsible minority unlikely to attempt the destruction or paralysis of that
process.

TOWARD THE NORM OF "CONCURRENT MAJORITY"

Two of the most important factors exacerbating conflict between government and opposition in the Diets of the 1950s and 1960s were the
lack of regular communication between the two sides and their disagreement over the basic issue of majority rule. The two problems
were closely linked: Without regular consultation about decision outcomes or influence on them—a particularly crucial matter in Japan
given the emphasis on consensus in decision style—the opposition
perceived the LDP's quick resort to a formal vote as tyranny of the
majority. As a number of theorists have indicated, the strict application of majority-rule principles without provision of means for
minority influence exacerbates conflict relations. If accommodation
between conflicting partisan groups is to be achieved, it is necessary
to create the informal norm of "concurrent majority"—the recognition of the opposition's right "to bargain the content of decisions
and, in general, to expect decisions that take account of their central
demands."[50] There are indications that such a norm was developing
in the Diet in the 1970s.

The first stage of its development began in the early part of the
decade, motivated by the new political climate, the rise of multiparty
opposition, and the loss of LDP control over some of the special committee chairmanships. The LDP became more amenable to negotiations with the opposition and willing to modify legislation to incorporate opposition opinion. For its part, the opposition manifested an
increased concern for being responsible and constructive by taking a
greater interest in formulating and proposing legislation. Data on
legislation show these trends most clearly: There was a definite increase in amendments to government legislation. The percentage of
cabinet-sponsored bills passed with amendments in the major ses-

sions of the Diet rose from an average of about one-quarter in the
1965–1971 period to one-third between 1972 and 1976. And, during
the first half of the 1970s, a majority of amendments to bills approved by the House of Representatives were proposed by the LDP
plus at least one opposition party, rather than by the LDP alone.[51]

Thayer describes this transitional period after the 1972 election as
one of an emerging modus vivendi between government and opposition parties in which greater accommodation occurred even prior to
the consciousness of change. As an awareness developed that the two
sides were beginning to work out new rules for cooperation, he
reports that representatives were nonetheless reticent to discuss the
phenomenon and treated it as if it were not yet "public and respectable."[52] In other words, more bargaining and agreement were taking
place inside the Diet, but this activity was not yet an accepted norm
of parliamentary life.

With the reduction of LDP seats to a thin majority and the consequent loss of majority control or chairmanships of many committees
after the 1976 election, the partial and not quite respectable modus
vivendi of the early 1970s increasingly became a more generalized,
overt, and legitimate norm. Soon after the 1976 election, the late
Shinzō Tsubokawa, an elder LDP politician and the chairman of the
key Budget Committee of the lower house, publicly stated that no
longer could sessions be conducted on the basis of absolute opposition versus absolute approval. No longer was it one-way traffic: "It's
two-way traffic and somehow I'd like to create new rules to find
points of agreement."[53] During the same period, Masayoshi Ohira,
then LDP secretary-general, gave formal recognition of the right of
the other parties to be consulted on bills by adopting the LDP's new
strategy of "partial coalition" *(bubun rengo)* with the opposition in
the Diet: Although the LDP retained total control of the cabinet, it
would negotiate with the opposition parties and attempt to form coalitions with individual parties on each piece of legislation in order to
attain cooperation in its passage.[54] When he became prime minister
in 1978, it is significant that at his first press conference the new LDP
president stressed that he wanted to establish "mutual respect and
trust" between his party and the opposition to carry out Diet deliberations smoothly.[55]

How far the movement toward interparty consultation and the
concurrent majority norm had advanced was indicated by my interviews with key Diet members in the summer of the same year. The
most common change in LDP-opposition relations they cited was the

dramatic increase in *hanashiai* (consultation). A veteran socialist very involved in Diet politics described the changed style of negotiation in more detail:

> I've worked as a House Management Committee Director *(riji)* for five to six years and have experience in the Diet both before *hakuchū* and after. Comparing it to before, the number of times that the LDP has listened to the things the opposition is saying and the gentlemen of the LDP have come to this room to say "I'd like to do this, but how about it?" and to talk about various things has increased. The number of times they have tried to obtain the prior understanding of the opposition parties has increased, and when our side says "It's not good—give it up," they'll drop it at a certain stage without fighting for their claims. And there's a strong tendency for them to propose things in a form that takes into account the things the opposition parties say. [Interview with "P," 22 August 1978]

An integral element of the concurrent majority norm is the power of mutual veto—namely, that decisions have to be acceptable to both sides to be enacted.[56] The LDP with its majority in the full house always had the power to veto bills presented by the opposition. Previously the opposition's only means of checking LDP legislation was to engage in obstructionism, hoping that by postponing consideration of other important legislation it could force the LDP to shelve the offending bill. During the 1970s, the opposition parties acquired the ability to veto government legislation without engaging in obstructionist tactics or violating normal procedure. With their power on committees and the LDP's commitment to consult with other parties on legislation, there developed the informal norm that unless mutual agreement was arrived at, legislation would be deferred. One chairman of the Diet Strategy Committee of a center party characterized this norm concisely when he said, "If it's not something capable of gaining consent by both sides by consultation from beginning to end, the Diet doesn't move one step forward" [interview with "U," 6 September 1978].

There have been a number of striking examples of the enhanced ability of the opposition parties to prevent the passage of government legislation until concessions were forthcoming. One example is provided by the long history of the Nuclear Nonproliferation Treaty in the Diet, in which ratification was repeatedly put off until opposition party agreement was attained.[57] A more dramatic example occurred in 1977 when the government's draft budget bill was informally revised in the face of the united demands of the opposition parties, the first time in postwar history an LDP budget bill had been altered in the Diet because of opposition pressure. Significantly, the LDP leadership negotiated the compromise that allowed passage of the budget bill even though initial sentiment within the party and the bureaucracy was against revision.[58]

Sometimes the implicit trend toward mutual veto was made explicit in the form of a trade-off of tabled bills. A DSP representative told me:

> There are those bills passed by committees which have gone smoothly and those which are in trouble. They take these together and on a certain day they're sent to the plenary sessions. Among these, the opposition parties want this one passed and this one not passed; the government party wants this one passed, this one not. At these times it gets difficult. The "good ones" and the "bad ones" after a while, even to the final day of the Diet, are made into "continuing bills" [carried over to the next session] and are not passed by the plenary session but remain as they are. . . .
>
> *Q.* Both?
> *A.* Yes, as a set, one package. A condition of exchange to balance things.
> [Interview with "J," 4 August 1978]

This Diet member further noted that such "mutual veto" deferrals had gotten much more common in the *hakuchū* Diets of the 1970s.

The impression should not be left that the trend toward concurrent majority norms forced the government to shelve all important legislation resisted by any opposition party or that the legislative process had become paralyzed. First, these norms implied consultation and real bargaining, much of which was successful in gaining the agreement necessary for passage. Second, the norm meant that the LDP had to secure the support of *some* opposition parties, not all of them. When the opposition parties were not united in their resistance to a bill, the LDP could legitimize the passage of legislation by gaining the support of one or two of the other parties. Third, when the bill was important enough and had already been deferred over a number of Diet sessions, the tacit norm was for the opposition parties finally to allow the bill to come to a vote and be passed.[59] Fourth, on extremely vital bills that an opposition-dominated committee had rejected, the LDP could make use of its full-house majority to pass the legislation anyway, a practice referred to as "reversal passage" *(gyakuten kaketsu)* and which the LDP had recourse to a number of times after 1976.[60]

There is nothing contradictory about the continued ability of the government party to pass legislation as concurrent majority and mutual veto norms were developing. These norms are not designed to replace majority rule but merely to check its absoluteness and supplement it.[61] Indeed, the development of such norms can enhance the legitimacy of the majority-rule principle. As long as the opposition feels it participates in decisions and can influence legislation and believes that normal parliamentary procedures are followed in passage of bills and not snap votes, the opposition can accept the necessity and legitimacy of majoritarianism:

> We may have to oppose a government bill in committee, but when there's no action and the country will be paralyzed and you've already given them a bit of a hard time—you've made the government reflect—well, you've got to make laws, you've got to decide on a budget, and at those times the plenary session will pass it. [Interview with "J," 4 August 1978]

This may be the ultimate paradox to emergence of concurrent majority norms in a parliament with a single majority party: Resisting the temptation to wield power unilaterally can result in greater institutional capacity to manage conflict, facilitation of legislative process, and acceptance of majority rule.

TOWARD THE CREATION OF A NEUTRAL ARBITER:
THE SPEAKER'S ROLE

Apart from emerging norms of concurrent majority, other mechanisms for effective conflict management evolved in the Diet in the 1970s. One of these is the use of a neutral arbiter whose decisions are binding on conflicting groups. This mechanism for conflict regulation is, of course, commonly used in the settlement of labor-management conflicts and legal disputes. In the Japanese Diet, the speaker *(gichō)* clearly has developed into an institutional role for the arbitration of disputes and the facilitation of accommodation between government and opposition.

For most of the postwar period the speaker—since 1955 always a senior LDP politician—was aptly characterized as a pawn of intra-LDP factional politics, "subservient to the dictates of the LDP's leadership" with little autonomy from the prime minister.[62] It was the speaker who often used his wide powers for regulating debate and setting the agenda in the service of his party to snap-vote its legislation through the house—and then, in a ritualistic gesture to appease the boycotting opposition parties into resuming normal business, the speaker would take responsibility and resign. Each involvement of the speaker in a snap-vote confrontation further weakened the role's authority and capacity for neutral mediation. To the opposition parties the speaker was always a potential agent of LDP strategy; even in the LDP the post was substantially inferior in status to the prime ministership and was often treated like another cabinet post to be given out as a patronage plum.[63]

Turnover and tenure data on speakers in the House of Representatives in the postwar period vividly illustrate the weakly institutionalized nature of the role. There were eighteen speakers of the lower house in the postwar period up through 1972 compared, for example, to only ten prime ministers during the same period. Although the average term of an ordinary Diet member between elections was two years and seven months, the average tenure of a speaker in office was much shorter, only one year and eight months. The main reason for this rapid turnover of speakers was the conflict relations between government and opposition parties: The majority of speakers in the lower house resigned because they had to take responsibility for Diet disorder.[64]

This situation changed drastically during the 1970s. Between 1973 and 1979, there were only two speakers of the lower house, each serving terms that by far exceed the postwar average. Simultaneously, the authority of the speaker rose dramatically. One socialist Diet member I interviewed compared his judgments to "the voice of God" *(Kamisama no koe)* in the house. Attitudes toward the speaker's neutrality have also undergone a vivid transformation; he is no longer viewed as a servant of the LDP by the opposition:

> The speaker is quite neutral. From long experience and capability, he is quite above it all, so he has independent judgment. Since it is the age of *hakuchū* the desire to advance harmony as much as possible is always in his head. [Interview with "J," 4 August 1978]

The beginning of the house speaker's transformation into an authoritative neutral arbiter began with the appointment of Shigesaburo Maeo in 1973. An elder LDP politician and faction leader (former Ikeda faction) who had once held ambitions to become prime minister, Maeo was committed to raising the authority and neutrality of the speaker and the prestige of the Diet itself. Upon taking the post after the resignation of his predecessor over a purported public

insult to the opposition, he formally gave up his party affiliation to
symbolize his neutrality. This was a gesture with precedent in the
postwar period,[65] but in this case it was also emblematic of the way he
carried out his role. With the seniority and status of his long LDP and
Diet career (and lack of further ambition for a higher post), his prestige and influence were nearly equal to that of the prime minister. He
could afford to act autonomously. He used his autonomy to attempt
an even-handed administration of Diet affairs that won the respect of
the opposition parties. A socialist M.P. with an intimate knowledge
of Diet management since that period relates:

> Before [Maeo], the authority of the speaker couldn't be maintained
> because the speaker would snap-vote, then be fired, and immediately be
> replaced and because the LDP prime minister and party president was in a
> higher and the speaker in a lower position. It was no good. When we got
> a speaker who could be said to be on an equal basis with the prime minis-
> ter, it made the speaker important. When it was Mr. Maeo, not once was
> there a no-confidence vote or disorder in the Diet. In Mr. Maeo's three
> and a half years as speaker he established a record for the longest continu-
> ous term in office. [Interview with "P," 22 August 1978]

Noting Maeo's attempt to respond to the expectations of the opposition parties during the conflicts over the controversial Yasukuni
Shrine bills and Lockheed scandals, the same socialist said, "I think
he has left his imprint as a great speaker. Hasn't that become one
basis for the management of the *hakuchū* Diet?"

Maeo's successor, Shigeru Hori (1976–1979), was also an elder LDP
statesman with no further political ambitions whose status and influence in the party nearly equaled that of the prime minister. Despite
having a rather different personality and political philosophy than
Maeo, Hori continued his predecessor's impartial and suprapartisan
manner of managing house affairs. Indeed, this style seems to have
become firmly embedded in the role expectations for the speakership, transcending the particular individuals who are appointed to
the position. The speaker appointed in 1979 upon Hori's retirement,
Hirokichi Nadao, had a reputation within the LDP as something of a
hard-liner on certain issues, but on assuming the speakership he publicly committed himself to continuing the policies of his predecessors.[66] More direct evidence was provided by my interviews. There
was a nearly unanimous consensus among my interviewees of all parties concerning the role expectations for the speaker: He should be

neutral, fair, listen to the opinions of all parties without prejudice, and advance deliberations on bills.

With these new role norms, speakers came to play a major role in facilitating the accommodation of partisan conflicts in at least six specific ways. Each represents the possibility of the speaker intervening in the conflict process at a different level of escalation. First, before the actual surfacing of a conflict, he may anticipate that a projected action by the LDP will bring it into confrontation with the opposition. Using his authority as speaker and his accumulated influence within the LDP, he may then attempt to check the move in advance:

> There are times when the LDP says it wants to try to do this or that and, looking at the movement of the JSP, he puts an end to it saying, "No good. You can't go that far." [Interview with "J," 4 August 1978]

Second, once a conflict has developed on the House Management Committee, the steering committee for the Diet and the speaker's advisory organ *(shimon kikan),* he may be asked to play another behind-the-scenes role. Generally the partisan conflicts involving overall management of Diet affairs are left to the committee to handle and the speaker is not necessarily involved on a daily basis. But if a stalemate develops between government and opposition parties on this committee, a speaker's advisory decision will sometimes be solicited and his decision accepted as authoritative:

> Usually it's handled at the director's meeting *(rijikai)* of the House Management Committee, but in cases where that can't be done the speaker receives the ideas that were put forward there. When the speaker hands down a decision, as it is the speaker handing down the decision and the Diet itself wouldn't work if his authority were not recognized, when the House Management Committee accepts it each party will also accept it as unavoidable. [Interview with "A," 14 July 1978]

The House Management Committee, however, does not always solicit an advisory judgment from the speaker in such cases. It can also attempt to resolve the problem through meetings of various levels of party executives, particularly meetings of the parties' Diet Strategy Committee chairmen or, for major problems like the budget, meetings of the secretaries-general of the parties. The third way in which the speaker may manage conflict is by helping to arrange such meetings or presiding at them.

Fourth, if a stalemate develops and the two sides are at loggerheads, the speaker may attempt to exercise his influence within the LDP to add his voice to those within the party requesting a flexible attitude and further attempts at compromise. Such was the case, for example, in the 1977 budget battle when Speaker Hori played a role in convincing Prime Minister Fukuda to compromise with the opposition.[67]

Fifth, during the 1970s the speaker began to acquire a new means to deescalate already intense conflicts: the power to determine when to put legislation into effect. Thus when the LDP strongly supports a bill in committee but the opposition resists it and the committee passes it anyway, the speaker may take it upon himself to postpone plenary session consideration of the bill until tempers cool. As a member of the House Management Committee described it:

> Were he immediately to submit it to the plenary session, it would spur great party conflict, so the speaker holds onto it. Then, in a week or ten days, he sends it forward. It's a cooling-off period for awhile. Whether or not the speaker has the authority to do that sort of thing is something that really isn't covered by precedent. But this is the *hakuchū* era and so for the purpose of harmony he cools it off for awhile . . . and then in a quiet time sends it forward, saying "It's taken quite a bit of time. Isn't it all right now? Opposition is opposition and agreement is agreement. . . . "
> [Interview with "J," 4 August 1978]

In 1979 the government and opposition reached an agreement to freeze the controversial budget appropriation for the importation of Grumman E-2C aircraft but left to the speaker the decision as to when the freeze should be lifted.[68] This arrangement represents a more formal manifestation of the same device. It should be underlined again that the authority to implement these cooling-off periods for controversial bills is a new informal power developed to cope with the problems of the *hakuchū* Diet.

Finally, if no other means of conflict resolution succeeds and the unresolved conflict threatens to paralyze Diet business completely, the speaker may be asked to act as a court of last resort by arbitrating the issue formally and making a formal decision to settle the matter:

> When it comes to snap votes and that kind of stage—only when it's a case of the movement of the Diet stopping do we then entrust it to the speaker. . . . When Diet management is completely constrained, when

government party and the opposition have already collided and Diet administration isn't moving at all, then there are cases when we'll entrust it to the speaker. [Interview with "S," 25 August 1978]

The speaker's role has also developed, therefore, into that of a specialized arbiter for settling issues which none of the other channels for conflict resolution can resolve—issues that paralyze the overall legislative process and on which the authority of the Diet itself is at stake. Such cases do not occur frequently, and handing a problem over to the speaker for a formal ruling is a mechanism sparingly used; but when it is used, his judgment is considered binding on all involved.

The speaker does not become involved in every conflictual issue nor in all these ways on any particular issue. But he may become involved, or be called upon to intervene, at numerous points in the process of conflict escalation and resolution. Far from being the "pawn" of LDP leadership in the past, during the 1970s the speaker's role evolved into that of an independent, suprapartisan, and authoritative mediator and arbiter of partisan conflict.

SPECIALIZED CONFLICT MANAGERS: THE HOUSE MANAGEMENT COMMITTEE DIRECTORS

If the speaker is the final arbiter of a few highly controversial bills and stalemates that are eventually entrusted to his decision, the House Management Committee is the body that daily negotiates the overwhelming majority of issues between government and opposition so that they rarely become confrontations or have to be arbitrated. As Baerwald has noted, this committee "is the focal point for regulating the internal affairs of each chamber."[69] The Management Committee is the only house committee primarily concerned with the *process* by which bills wend their way through the house, not with their contents. As such, it is the place where each party's overall Diet strategy is most sharply focused, where the major conflicts between parties must be negotiated at each stage of a bill's passage through the chamber, and where are decided such crucial questions as how a stalemate over a certain bill might be resolved, which bills should have priority for consideration, or whether the Diet should be extended.

As the steering committee for legislation, the House Management Committee must keep its eye on all potential party conflicts over bills and determine how these questions might be resolved:

First, each party will make a "claim" about the bills that have problems —they make it bureaucratically. The bills that have claims, well, we read these as the important confrontation bills. It is these important confrontation bills that we in the Diet Management Committee consider. Until we say it is all right, they won't be explained on the floor; if they don't advance to an explanation on the floor, they can't go to committee. Therefore, everything [about that bill] is stopped here. [Interview with "J," 4 August 1978]

The House Management Committee therefore functions as the gate-keeper and conflict manager for the overall legislative process.

It is the chairman and the directors *(riji)* who are the key players. The chairman stays in close communication with the speaker since the committee, as noted earlier, acts as the speaker's agent and advisory body in managing the Diet's daily business. The chairman is usually a veteran LDP politician who is trusted by the speaker; in fact, this trust is one of the qualifications that is considered when the chairman is appointed [interview with "W," administrative aide to the speaker, 7 September 1978].

The importance of the committee, its chairman, and its directors, never negligible, has increased since the advent of the *hakuchū* situation in the Diet. One measure of the committee's enhanced significance is that the chairmanship of the committee in recent years has been given to LDP politicians with cabinet experience:

Recently, the present Defense Agency chief [and previous chairman of the committee] Kanemaru and the present House Management Committee chairman, Hosoda, are people with various types of cabinet experience. After it became the *hakuchū* Diet, the LDP tried to install people with cabinet experience in the chairmanship. To that extent, it says the committee is important. Before, the LDP Diet Strategy chairman was higher in experience and the House Management Committee chairman lower, but now they are equal or there are cases where the House Management Committee chairman has a rather higher background. [Interview with "P," 22 August 1978]

And recently, too, service as chairman of this committee has led former incumbents again into very responsible cabinet positions, a measure of the valued political skills in dealing with the opposition that such service is thought to provide.[70]

The director's job is to aid the chairman in running the committee. Appointments to the chairmanships of committees are made frequently, unlike the U.S. Congress where the seniority principle is in effect; yet some directors serve for as many as six years on the House Management Committee, thus providing crucial continuity and experience to the committee's work.

Most important, it is customary for all the directors to be one of the vice-chairmen of their party's Diet Strategy Committee, the party's organ responsible for planning and executing policy and strategy in the Diet. The House Management Committee by this simple device becomes the nexus of party organization and partisan strategy with the Diet's institutional structure and process.[71] When the chairman and *riji* meet, as they do daily when the Diet is in session, it is the coming together of the key middle-level Diet strategists of the parties for the purpose of negotiating and regulating the conflicts among the parties in order to keep Diet business running smoothly.

Since these *rijikai* (director's meetings) are closed and the interaction that takes place there is informal, all the directors I interviewed reported that real negotiating takes place. Before and after meetings directors are in continuous informal contact with each other as individuals to prepare the way for the meeting's negotiations. The decisions arrived at by these negotiations essentially become the decisions of the full committee, a tendency that has increased in recent years. With the advent of the *hakuchū* era, the full committee becomes equally split between LDP and opposition parties and the chairman is reluctant to use his vote to break ties and thus jeopardize his neutral status as facilitator of agreement:

> In former times, when the opinions on the *rijikai* were not in agreement we would immediately send it [a controversial issue] to the committee and decide it by the majority; but now, because it is a poor thing for the chairman to use his voting rights, the LDP has given ground and it has become usual to come to agreement by *hanashiai*. [Interview with "P," 22 August 1978]

Now that the directors settle disputes by informal negotiations among themselves, the full committee has increasingly become a rubber stamp, approving the items brought before it unanimously (*igi nashi*: "no dissent") in a matter of minutes.[72] The secrecy and informality provided by closed meetings of a small group of directors obviously facilitate the working out of interparty disagreements.

It is important, however, to distinguish between the secrecy and informality of *riji* meetings and the "teahouse politics" *(machiai seiji*) of the past. The latter custom, in fact, has greatly declined during the 1970s, according to many of my respondents. One cause of this change was the severe criticism by the Communist Party and the media in the late 1960s of secret deals concluded in restaurants and geisha houses which made the JSP especially hesitant to participate in such talks.[73] But some parliamentarians I interviewed asserted that the gradual disappearance of *machiai seiji* occurred for another reason. It was simply too difficult to maintain the old custom in an age of *multiparty* opposition. One DSP representative influential on the House Management Committee said:

> Now we're doing very complicated diagonal negotiations. We've got to negotiate on this side, and on that side too. You can't do all of that behind the scenes at all, either in terms of time or in terms of calculations. Therefore, they're going to come and do it here in this office; or, when a House Management Committee director's meeting *(rijikai)* opens and it isn't going so well, we'll take a break and for an hour or so I'll talk again with the LDP and JSP representatives here or talk only with the opposition party representatives. [Interview with "J," 4 August 1978]

While confidential, interpersonal bargaining is still the preferred means of handling partisan disputes, it increasingly takes place within an institutional context: in the meetings or offices of the *riji*.

That directors' negotiations are frequently successful in bringing about the accommodation of conflictual issues is due to a number of factors. One of these is the type of person appointed to these crucial "middleman" roles between party and Diet processes: They tend to be pragmatic and skilled in the interpersonal relations of bargaining and the traits of conflict managers. When asked what kind of character or attitude is most valuable for a Management Committee *riji* or a party Diet Strategy Committee vice-chairman, one LDP politician responded:

> For me, "democracy" is like Mt. Fuji—you can't try to go all the way to the top even ideally. In other words, you can agree only on going 70 percent or 80 percent of the way. Therefore, if each party tries to go 100 percent on everything, it's a mistake. At best, 70 or 80 percent. It's all right if you go over 50 percent, over half. The thinking that tries to make 100 percent for oneself is probably going to lose in more cases. . . . Thus in Diet management, and in politics, I say that if the government and opposition parties can mutually take 70 to 80 percent on various things, they ought to be satisfied with that. [Interview with "D," 11 August 1978]

Among the other characteristics mentioned as being appropriate for House Management Committee *riji* by opposition party representatives were such traits as listening to everyone without bias, being sociable, and having the ability to transcend one's own party's views. The directors' commonly held approach to interparty relations is perhaps best summed up by a phrase I heard repeatedly in my interviews with these men: One should try for *"better,* not best." Ideology, dogmatism, utopianism, unwillingness to compromise, have no place in the requirements for this role.

A second factor facilitating accommodation is the trust and friendship patterns that develop among the *riji*. A socialist representative (not a member of the House Management Committee) put it this way:

> The management of the plenary session is done in the House Management Committee and there are a small number of people on it. And among them, well, because government and opposition party members do that daily, even if government and opposition parties are in conflict, they have become good friends and they can't be unreasonable with each other. [Interview with "A," 14 July 1978]

The committee's directors I interviewed confirmed this outsider's view. Almost all of them have friends in all the other parties, almost always considering fellow *riji* among those. They invariably refer to each other as *"kun,"* a suffix denoting familiarity and intimacy. The directors feel they can trust their colleagues on the other side to keep their promises, even if they do not always agree with their opinions. An LDP *riji* indicated the expected norms of interaction and the trusting relationships that have developed among directors in recent years:

> If we talk together without deception or lying, democracy, the Japanese parliament, will operate without fail. Recently the opposition party *riji* have gotten very good. They never lie and always keep the promises they have made to us. [Interview with "Q," 24 August 1978]

Opposition party directors expressed the same feelings about their LDP counterparts.

Further, there is an overarching norm of acceptance of partisan necessities, but open communication and friendship between directors must be perpetuated regardless of party politics. As a socialist *riji* describes his experience even during the conflictual era:

At the time of Y-kun and Z-kun and others, there were snap votes many times. We had them but at those times they would tell me in advance: "It's bad, but this time we have to snap-vote no matter what." They said it was a disgraceful thing but the LDP has to defend the LDP position. . . . Because above them cabinet politics had interfered, as you'd expect. So they came to me and said they had argued in the LDP Diet Strategy Committee that a snap vote at this time would be petty, but in the end, the discussions didn't go well there and they were really sorry but it would come to a snap vote. In that sense . . . the mutual friendship continued. [Interview with "P," 22 August 1978]

Almost all the *riji* told me that in the *hakuchū* period, too, good relations among *riji* were either unaffected by highly conflictual issues of offensive partisan behavior or if temporarily damaged were soon reconstructed.

A crucial aspect of the directors' successful regulation of conflict is their feeling of responsibility for ensuring the harmonious conclusion of Diet affairs. On the basis of his observation of this committee in the 1960s, Baerwald concluded that "the members of the House Management Committee are thus not free in their negotiations but are agents of hostile—on occasion warring—camps."[74] While they are indeed such agents, this depiction of the basically partisan representative functions of the members of the committee had become only half the story by 1978. The question that elicited the most intense reaction during my interviews concerned the double roles that the *riji* play by being simultaneously representatives of their party's strategy but also responsible for smooth Diet administration. Note, for example, the words of this JSP director:

In fact, in my six years [as a *riji*] the point you stated now has been the most difficult. Well, I'm always saying it at director's meetings—we are representatives of parties. That's one thing. However, simultaneously, we are an advisory body of the speaker and increasing the authority of the Diet increases the authority of the speaker. So in that sense, we have two eyes: party representatives and advisory body of the speaker. Therefore, depending on the case, whenever we put something together in discussions in the director's meetings we have to go back to the party Diet Strategy Committee and try to persuade them to follow it and accept it. [Interview with "P," 22 August 1978]

The House Management Committee director's role by the late 1970s was not merely to function as party advocate in Diet negotiations but also to advocate Diet conflict regulation in his own party, persuading the Diet Strategy Committee to accept the compromises made in his bargainings with other *riji*.

Today directors feel the role strain of their dual mission acutely and take their responsibilities as Diet conflict managers as seriously as their role as party advocates:

> When I became a House Management Committee director, I went to my seniors in the party *(senpai)* who had been *riji* . . . and when I went to these people and asked them what I should do, they said that when you have talked to the other parties and made a promise, go back to the party and always defend it and carry through on it. Also, you absolutely must not promise things to the other parties that you will find difficult to get your own party's understanding on. I think those are the most important things. I have come to operate with those two things as principles. Especially there are times when I have talked to the other parties and earnestly tried to bring about that understanding within my own party. Therefore, I have come to operate with the intention of resigning as a House Management Committee director—I will quit at any time—in a case where I've made a promise and then go back to my own party and it is not accepted. [Interview with "P," 22 August 1978]

Usually such a drastic response to this common dilemma is not necessary. *Riji* are thoroughly familiar with the parameters set by their party's policy on a particular issue and keep in constant touch with their Diet Strategy Committee chairman, who will usually back up their actions.[75]

To summarize, the House Management Committee chairman and directors have become more important in recent years. They have evolved role norms that include informal and secret bargaining, trust, and friendship relations transcending partisan differences, and they have experienced role pressures to resolve partisan disagreements for the sake of the harmonious conduct of Diet business. The significance of these trends becomes clear in light of the classic dilemma of political party elites: the inevitable tension between partisanship and interparty accommodation.[76] Organizational and ideological pressures push party elites to partisan stands and conflict with other parties that can hamper the search for mutual accommodation of conflict in the legislature. Certainly the problem may be seen in relations between party organizations and members of parliament: the former under pressure toward partisan conflict, the latter toward accommodation within an institutional framework. One of the ways to resolve this dilemma is an overarching norm of *restrained partisanship*. This norm allows elites to maintain their partisanship and their separate goals, but it also obliges them to assume responsibility for attaining mutually satisfactory solutions with other parties through compromise and concession.[77]

The evolution of the House Management Committee suggests that it is becoming the specialized organ for the resolution of the partisan-accommodation dilemma in Japan's Diet.[78] Among its directors there has been developing the restrained partisanship necessary for the effective handling of that dilemma: suprapartisan role norms, recruitment and communication patterns, and personal relations that allow the expression of conflicting partisan demands but facilitate their accommodation.

Conclusions: Caveats and Consequences

THE DIET AND THE CONFLICT PROCESS

The trends in postwar parliamentary politics between 1955 and 1979 suggest certain insights into the dynamics of conflict. The first is that the transformation of a relatively conflictual institution into a relatively accommodative one took place in distinct stages, each building cumulatively on the preceding ones, and each representing, in part, a reaction to a specific stimulus from the political environment. The first stage was that of intense conflict between 1955 and 1960 brought about by the formation of the LDP into a large majority party and the creation of the JSP as its main, but much weaker, opposition party. Given the ideological climate of the period, this sudden shift to a power situation for which there had been no prior experience led to the major confrontations of the 1950s, culminating in the security treaty crisis of 1960. The very intensity and escalation of this latter crisis, however, brought about the first step toward conflict management: the developing of an awareness of the dangers inherent in lack of communication and mutually accepted rules of the game and the motivation to prevent a recurrence of near "total conflict."

Upon this awareness is built the second stage: the gradual development through the 1960s of an ad hoc, secret, and extrainstitutional accommodation mechanism—*machiai seiji*—by which channels of communication were opened up to keep the system from breaking down so completely again. This led, in turn, to the gradual public ritualization of conflict within the Diet. The third stage, between

1969 and 1976, witnessed real behavioral change toward accommodation within the institution itself as the legitimacy of the secret mechanism of teahouse politics was called into question and in anticipation of future electoral trends and power shifts favoring the opposition. The fourth stage began in 1976 with the near balance of power in the Diet and represented the explicit legitimation of new norms of parliamentary relations and then their implementation through the strengthening of the authority of the specialized conflict managerial roles in the Diet.

The long-term process of diminishing conflict and increasing conflict management appears to have been one of a progression with each stage building on the preceding. Awareness of the dangers of all-out confrontation motivated the behind-the-scenes communication that in turn made possible the ritualization of conflict. Secret communication and the implicit rules of the game of ritualized conflict created a foundation of trust for the behavioral changes of the next stage. And from the foundation of behavioral modus vivendi the emergence of new public norms and decision mechanisms was facilitated. Although these stages represent a logical progression, the sequences were neither inevitable nor predictable. They proved, however, to be a highly functional set of adaptations to the changing political environment resulting in the effective management of partisan conflict.

Postwar Diet politics also sheds new light on the relationship between cultural patterns and conflict relations. In most approaches to the study of Japan, traditional cultural norms and values are viewed as contributing, or even directly causing, the lack of conflict perceived as characterizing that society. Seniority norms of leadership, the consensual style of decision making in small personal groups, strong in-group identification and loyalty—all have been seen as Japanese cultural characteristics which explained the stability and coherence of their organizations.[79] Interestingly, the Diet was one of the few institutions in which some observers of the 1950s and 1960s saw these norms as exacerbating conflict because of the disparity between the principles of democratic parliamentary politics and Japanese culture:

> Such an institution as the Diet is sufficiently Western in its concept to demand rules drawn from that context if it is to bear any relation in function to its name. There is a certain premium upon direct debate, for instance, and the capacity to communicate with the opposition; hence

there is the necessity to protect minority rights and accept majority decisions. Without these principles, no democratic parliament can function.
And yet, in Japan, the historic principles of organization and decision
making were different: not direct debate, but indirect negotiation; not
communication with the opposition, but aloofness or struggle. Communication was reserved for one's in-group, and *political* commitment to this
group was only a part of one's total commitment to it. Moreover, decision
making within the group, and between it and other groups, was based
upon consensus, not majoritarianism.[80]

And yet the conflict-regulating mechanisms and norms that emerged
in the Diet in the 1970s owe much to Japanese cultural characteristics. Concurrent majority and mutual veto norms, for example, are
merely different terms for "consensus" applied across all parties.
Their acceptance was undoubtedly facilitated by the tradition of consensual decision making. Respect for seniority and for leaders who listen sympathetically to all sides and act as go-betweens in producing
accommodation shaped the evolution of the speaker's role. Identification with one's group and group loyalty has proved compatible
with cross-party communication and has contributed to the increasing acceptance of another loyalty—to the Diet as an institution. The
preference for intimate, face-to-face relations based on mutual trust
is manifested in the House Management Committee's style of operation.

Thus there may be nothing inherently antithetical between Japanese cultural values and effective conflict management in a parliamentary context. Cultural styles may help create conflict *or*
accommodation, depending on how they are integrated with the
institutional, ideological, and power context.[81] It appears that the
1970s witnessed the gradual, successful adaptation and incorporation
of such indigenous values with the requirements of partisan accommodation in a formal legislative body.

PARLIAMENTARY CONFLICT MANAGEMENT AND JAPANESE
DEMOCRATIC POLITICS

The process of transformation described here is by no means irreversible, and the mechanisms for conflict regulation that appeared in the
1970s are not completely established. In the words of one of my interviewees, "It's very new, so it is at a stage of mutual 'test' and 'trial'
. . . and there hasn't been enough time yet to be able to say that

something's been established and this is a 'rule.' " Some conflict theorists hypothesize that such an institutionalization period requires at least one or two generations in a situation in which no single conflict group predominates.[82]

If the firm establishment of the new conflict management norms and decision mechanisms were problematic before, after mid-1980 they became even more so. In the election of 1980, the LDP scored a surprising major victory, reversing the electoral trends of a decade by capturing 286 seats in the lower house and a firm majority in the upper house. Once again the LDP controlled both the chairmanships and the voting majorities on most standing committees in the House of Representatives. The election that many expected would usher in Japan's first coalition cabinet in thirty years instead produced a reversion to the situation of the late 1960s.

With one of the major incentives toward conflict management in the 1970s—the nearly equal power balance and opposition influence on committees—now gone, a new set of questions arises. Will the other environmental contributions to conflict management—the decline in ideological hostility, new voter expectations, and generational change—provide enough incentive to keep the parties acting responsibly in the parliamentary process? Above all, have the practices of communication and consultation and the authority of conflict managers become firmly enough established to prevent a reversion to the intense conflicts characteristic of the past, those between an overbearing majority and a recalcitrant minority? Many of the conflict management norms emerging in the 1970s were the result of self-interested strategic and tactical responses by the parties to the contemporary and anticipated power situation. This may in fact be a universal first stage in the institutionalization process prior to norms becoming valued for their own sake and internalized: "The transition from instrumental to intrinsic commitment is a familiar pattern in the evolution of norms."[83] But it remains to be seen whether that critical transition from pragmatic necessity to adopt values has taken place in the norms that emerged in the 1970s. The answer may well determine the nature of Japanese politics in the 1980s.[84]

If the progress made toward the institutionalization of conflict management survives (or declines and is then revived at a later date) during the coming decade, what would be the positive and negative consequences for democratic politics in Japan?[85] On the positive side, the norms, skills, and legislative leadership developed in the process of parliamentary conflict management can be considered the training ground of a political elite that may one day have to make the transition to multiparty coalition cabinets. Such experience in interparty negotiation and accommodation can provide an underlying stability to the otherwise complex and sometimes protean relationships of parliamentary coalition government.

Moreover, the trend toward conflict management may give the leftist opposition parties a greater stake in the democratic system. One of the main factors contributing to the JSP's willingness to engage in confrontation tactics in the Diet and "parliamentarianism plus" mobilization tactics outside it in the 1950s and 1960s was the dilemma of the perennial opposition described by T. J. Pempel.[86] Its only choices were, on the one hand, secret compromises and behind-the-scenes influence on policy for which it would receive no public credit, or, on the other, public confrontation which might at least succeed in preventing or delaying offending government legislation. To the extent that the leftist opposition parties can influence legislation and policy through bargaining in normal parliamentary channels, there is a third alternative, one which gives the left a vested interest in the preservation of parliamentary democracy. This option, in turn, may strengthen the hand of leaders within the Marxist parties who are committed to parliamentary democracy and to taking power through the ballot box rather than through protest and rebellion. The conversion of the left into unalterable prosystem parties may provide a more fundamental stability to the democratic polity in Japan than the apparent stability provided by continual one-party rule.

To the extent that leftist and center opposition is more fully incorporated into the system and has some influence on legislation, a wider variety of societal interests may be aggregated in the parliamentary process and reflected in public policy. The long-term rule of the LDP and its resilience have been due in great part to its accommodating within it a wide variety of interest groups and their demands.[87] But because of the nature of Japanese parties' support bases, certain elements of society have had their demands and interests less consistently represented in government policy—especially labor, intellectuals, parts of the urban white-collar class supporting the JSP and to a lesser extent the DSP, and the marginal classes from whom the Komeitō and the JCP derive much of their vote.

Finally, the changes outlined here might alleviate some of the sources of the public's alienation from government. Survey research has shown that the belief that government is unresponsive to the electorate and run primarily for the benefit of big business is widespread, as are negative evaluations of the cabinet and Diet. Opposition party supporters especially are likely to be distrustful of government and reluctant to support the political system, in part because they develop "ambivalent attitudes toward the political institutions that keep their party locked out of power."[88] The most frequent response to an *Asahi Shimbun* poll asking what was lacking in politics was "the feeling of responsibility."[89] With a wider variety of interests more obviously reflected in policy, a leftist opposition more closely tied to the system, the Diet playing a more important political role, and government and opposition managing their conflicts more responsibly, democratic government in general becomes more legitimized to a wider segment of the public and the incidence of political disaffection from the system declines.

For almost all of these promising long-range consequences of the institutionalization of legislative conflict management, there are parallel pitfalls or costs. Greater ability to manage conflicts within the legislative process may intensify conflicts elsewhere in the political system. Thus the need to respond to, and compromise with, rival party leaders can create greater conflict within parties as rival factions resent the leadership's concessions to opponents and use the issue against them in intraparty struggles. Party ideologues too may feel increasing dissatisfaction over the selling out of party principle for pragmatic gains in the passage of legislation, while those who wish to cater to party support groups may resist the attempts of parliamentary conflict managers to bring about legislative tranquility.

If parliamentary conflict management becomes "overinstitutionalized,"[90] conflict between elite and masses may intensify even as it diminishes among competing elites. The integration of legislative party elites having a strong mutual concern for compromise and conflict regulation may become so intimate that demands of supporters and nonelite groups come to be seen as disruptive to the elites' relations with each other and are therefore ignored. The overinstitutionalization of elite rules of the game can thus lead to less, not more, responsiveness to mass publics. It is here that the insights of Michels' "iron law of oligarchy" and Dahrendorf's warnings about the consequences of conflict regulation become relevant. The result may be the increasing alienation and extremist behavior of followers who begin to feel that their representatives and leaders are all part of a ruling class who disregard their grievances and bargain away their interests for the preservation of their own status or advantage.[91]

In a related vein, the distinction between conflict *management* and conflict *avoidance* should be stressed. The temporary delay or tactical postponement of decision making on controversial issues is a legitimate conflict management device. When the issues are largely symbolic, perhaps the indefinite deferral of final choices may be warranted. If even the raising of such issues is inhibited, however, or if the evasion of responsibility for dealing with pressing social needs assumes a consistent pattern, conflict management becomes conflict avoidance. Such a pattern seems to have characterized the Italian parliament in the 1960s. The title of Giuseppe Di Palma's book analyzing this phenomenon is instructive: *Surviving Without Governing*.[92]

The LDP government may have adopted a different conflict avoidance technique, one that still enabled them to govern: quietly implementing bills without parliamentary approval. During the *hakuchū* era of the late 1970s it is significant that the number of bills introduced into the Diet by the cabinet consistently declined—from an average of about 110 per session in the five years between 1970 and 1974 to an average of about 73 per session in the five yeare between 1975 and 1979.[93] This may be the normal result of the LDP, for the first time in the postwar era, realistically having to take into account the more time-consuming, complex process of negotiation required for passage and the necessity of concentrating its attention on high-priority legislation given its diminished majority. But it may also represent a conscious strategy of shunting issues away from the parliamentary process to bureaucratic fiat in order to avoid conflict or bargaining with the opposition. A knowledgeable young bureaucrat in an influential Japanese ministry I interviewed in the United States in 1979 indicated this possibility. Asked about the drastic decline in bills introduced into the Diet by the government during the *hakuchū* era, he said:

> It's basically a strategy of the bureaucracy too. We'll introduce a law only when it's absolutely necessary to pass it in the form of a law. When it can be done in the form of an administrative order or a cabinet order, etc., we prefer to do that.
>
> *Q.* Since *hakuchū* . . . has there been an increase in administrative guidance?
> *A.* Yes. It should certainly increase the role of administrative guidance.
> [Interview with "Z," 29 May 1979]

Rather than creating a greater role for the parliament in the political process, a Diet in which the government adopts such conflict avoidance strategies may find itself with more influence, but over less.[94]

On the other extreme from avoidance is the danger of immobilism. In this case so many conflictual issues are raised and such a plethora of demands is catered to in the negotiating process that it becomes impossible to resolve them and the legislature becomes paralyzed. It is worth remembering too that conflict *management* is not synonymous with conflict *resolution*. Conflict management means only that issues upon which there is disagreement are handled by agreed-upon procedures so that conflict does not escalate beyond acceptable limits. This policy often may facilitate, but does not guarantee, the resolution of an issue. The legislative passage rate for cabinet-sponsored bills was very high, for example, in the first few years of the *hakuchū* Diets with their new norms of conflict management. The passage rate rose from 84.1 percent in the 80th Diet of 1977 to a remarkable 90.2 percent in the 84th Diet of 1978. But then the 87th Diet (1979) saw that rate suddenly fall to 61.8 percent, the lowest rate in ten years. Although observers noted that it was a generally quiet session with many extremely controversial bills handled peacefully and without forced passage or obstruction, negotiated resolution of many disagreements could not be reached before the end of the session.[95]

If the necessity for negotiating compromise with opposition parties inevitably means responding to more societal interests, what may be the consequences for Japan's political economy? Not only, for example, do functional groups like labor suddenly have more bargaining power through the enhanced influence of the opposition parties in the legislative process, but opposition party representatives also have more leverage to gain distributive benefits for their districts. Support for the passage of government bills may have to be secured through "side payments" in the form of trade-offs, pork-barrel projects, and deferment of economically rational but unpopular programs. The governing party itself needs to firm up its support base or try to expand it by increasing rewards to its supporters if it is to stay in power in the age of competitive multiparty politics and diminished voting majorities.

Surprisingly Japan, known for its closely managed economy and conservative fiscal policies, quadrupled its budget deficits in the late 1970s. Deficit financing rose from slightly over 10 percent of the budget in 1974 to almost 40 percent in 1978.[96] One economist has directly connected government spending patterns to the political pressures of declining LDP majorities and increasing opposition voting strength.[97] My bureaucratic informant too linked the political pressures and the fiscal situation:

In the case of *hakuchū kokkai*, since everybody wants something but nobody wants to sacrifice anything the total budget should increase. Otherwise there is no alternative to solve this situation. [Interview with "Z," 29 May 1979]

And at least one Western journalist reports that bureaucrats are very worried about the "corrupt" and inconsistent policies that will be produced by the demands emanating from the politics of any future coalition government.[98] Whether the trends toward the institutionalization of conflict management reflect a permanent transformation in Japanese politics or a temporary interlude, and whether their consequences will be viewed as a boon or a bane for the democratic process and policymaking in Japan, remains to be seen. In the meantime, for at least a short time in the 1970s, the view of Japan as an "open society of closed components," lacking in cross-party communication and negotiation,[99] was no longer applicable. Political elites responded to a changing environment with greater communication across party lines than at any other time in the postwar era, and they created new rules of the parliamentary game for managing the conflicts between them. Further comparative study of the decline of formerly dominant parties and its impact on government-opposition relations in parliament would reveal the uniqueness of the Japanese experience or, conversely, its universality.[100]

NOTES

I would like to thank some of the many individuals and organizations that made this research possible. In Japan, I wish to thank the many Diet members who gave of their scarce time to respond to my long interviews and Makoto Hoshi, Shichirō Matsukata, Konnosuke Sakane, and Hideo Okada for aid in making contacts with key respondents. I am grateful to the University of Tokyo Liberal Arts faculty and to Professor Seizaburō Sato for providing me with a professional affiliation while in Japan.

Field research and writing of various drafts were supported by grants from Fulbright-Hays/HEW Faculty Research Abroad, JCJS of the Social Science Research Council, and a sabbatical leave from Western Washington University, as well as by affiliation as an honorary research associate at the Japan Institute, Harvard University. Kumiko Terazawa and WWU's Bureau for Faculty Research have my gratitude for various transcription and typing services during the research.

I owe a particular debt of gratitude to Terry MacDougall and Mike Mochizuki, of Harvard, for their stimulating advice and comments on many stages of my work, and to Professors T. J. Pempel, Edwin O. Reischauer, Thomas Rohlen, and Gerald Curtis for their suggestions and criticisms of an earlier version of this essay. The comments of Makaha workshop participants, particularly Dan Okimoto, were also most helpful. Only I am responsible for this study's content.

1. My description of the history, structure, and legislative process of the Diet prior to the 1970s relies heavily on the work of Hans H. Baerwald, our foremost expert on that institution. See his *Japan's Parliament: An Introduction* (London and New York: Cambridge University Press, 1974); "Nikkan Kokkai: The Japan-Korea Treaty Diet," in Lucian W. Pye, ed., *Cases in Comparative Politics: Asia* (Boston: Little, Brown, 1970); "Parliament and Parliamentarians in Japan," *Pacific Affairs* 28 (3) (Fall 1962). See also Young C. Kim, "The Committee System in the Japanese Diet: Recruitment, Orientation, and Behavior," in G. R. Boynton and Chong Lim Kim, eds., *Legislative Systems in Developing Countries* (Durham: Duke University Press, 1975).

2. Robert A. Scalapino and Junnosuke Masumi, *Parties and Politics in Contemporary Japan* (Berkeley: University of California Press, 1962), especially pp. 5–6; also George R. Packard III, *Protest in Tokyo* (Princeton: Princeton University Press, 1966), p. 347.

3. Tsuneo Watanabe, *Shinseiji no Jōshiki* (Tokyo: Kodansha, 1977), pp. 17–18.

4. See Erik Allardt and Stein Rokkan, eds., *Mass Politics: Studies in Political Sociology* (New York: Free Press, 1970); Seymour Martin Lipset, *Political Man* (Garden City: Anchor Books, 1963); Seymour M. Lipset and Stein Rokkan, eds., *Party Systems and Voter Alignments: Cross-National Perspectives* (New York: Free Press, 1967), among others for examples of this approach.

5. Giuseppe Di Palma, *The Study of Conflict in Western Society: A Critique of the End of Ideology*, (Morristown, N.J.: General Learning Corporation, 1973); also Eric A. Nordlinger, "Conflict Regulation in Divided Societies," Occasional Papers in International Affairs, No. 29 (January, 1972), Center for International Affairs, Harvard University. See, too, my "Political Opposition and Conflict in Postwar Japan," paper presented to the first workshop of this project, Lake Wilderness, Washington, 1977.

6. Ibid. The classic statement of the elite role in conflict and its escalation or regulation is that of E. E. Schattschneider, *The Semi-Sovereign People* (New York: Holt, Rinehart and Winston, 1960); see also Peter B. Merkl, "Political Cleavages and Party Systems," *World Politics* 21 (3) (April 1969).

7. Michael L. Mezey, *Comparative Legislatures* (Durham: Duke University Press, 1979), p. 10.

8. See Di Palma, *The Study of Conflict*, and Nordlinger, "Conflict Regulation." The most frequently used framework for the study of institutionalization is that of Samuel Huntington, *Political Order in Changing Societies* (New Haven: Yale University Press, 1968), pp. 12–24, in which institutionalization is indicated by an organization's increasing coherence, complexity, autonomy, and adaptability. As *adaptability* is merely the organization's ability to take on new functions and survive over the course of time, usually a given for most complex modern organizations, it is the first three elements that are most important. My consensus on procedures and "restrained partisanship" norms are integral parts of developing institutional *coherence*; developing authoritative subunits and roles is an aspect of *complexity*; and acting independently from other groups is the *autonomy* dimension. For other studies of institutionalization and conflict management in legislatures see Robert Leonardi,

Raffaella Nanetti, and Gianfranco Pasquino, "Institutionalization of Parliament and Parliamentarization of Parties in Italy," *Legislative Studies Quarterly* 3 (1) (February 1978); Nelson W. Polsby, "The Institutionalization of the U.S. House of Representatives," *American Political Science Review* 62 (1) (March 1968); Allan Kornberg, "The Rules of the Game in the Canadian House of Commons," *Journal of Politics* 26 (May 1964).

9. Di Palma, *The Study of Conflict*, pp. 10–11, and Nordlinger, "Conflict Regulation," pp. 33–36.

10. The term is from Di Palma, *The Study of Conflict*, p. 15.

11. One finds an enormous production of materials by Japanese scholars on laws, but little on the legislative process that produces them. For an encyclopedic reference on the committee system and its structure and procedures, see Masazo Tsuchiya, *Iinkai Seido* (Tokyo: Kyōiku Shuppan, 1969). Legal journals such as *Hōritsu Jihō* occasionally have articles on the legislative process; see, for example, its vol. 41, no. 12 (October 1969). Popular intellectual journals such as *Chūō Kōron* and journalists rediscover the Diet periodically at times of severe crisis or change; specific works in the latter category are cited as appropriate below.

12. A total of twenty-four interviews were conducted between 14 July 1978 and 8 September 1978. Nineteen were with members of the lower house, three with members of the House of Councillors, one with an aide *(hisho)* to the speaker of the lower house, and one with a journalist for one of Japan's leading newspapers. The sample of Diet members was chosen to emphasize those in key positions for overall Diet strategy and interaction with other parties and thus consisted primarily of present or former House Management Committee chairmen and directors, party Diet Strategy Committee chairmen and vice-chairmen, as well as chairmen or directors of other committees in the Diet and party top executives. Interviews included at least one with a dietman in these roles from all seven political parties: five LDP, two NLC, four CGP, four DSP, one SDL, five JSP, one JCP. The interviews used primarily open-ended questions; a certain number of them were repeated in all the interviews to ascertain variability of response within and across parties; others were geared to the specific role of the respondent in his party or in the Diet. Most interviews lasted an hour to an hour and a half; the shortest was forty minutes and the longest two hours. To ensure frank responses all interviewees were promised anonymity, although many assured me this was not necessary. I have adhered to that promise in this study: All respondents are referred to by a letter assigned to them based on the order in which they were interviewed.

13. Baerwald, *Japan's Parliament*, pp. 15–16, 88–89.

14. T. J. Pempel, "Can Responsible Parties Cope with Social Change?: The Japanese Experience," in Louis Maisel and Joseph Cooper, eds., *The Development of Political Parties* (Berkeley: Sage Publications, 1979), pp. 23–24.

15. Joji Watanuki, "Patterns of Politics in Present-Day Japan'" in Lipset and Rokkan, *Party Systems and Voter Alignments*; see also Michael Leiserson, "Political Opposition and Development in Japan," in Robert A. Dahl, ed., *Regimes and Oppositions* (New Haven: Yale University Press, 1973), pp. 388–390.

16. See Scott C. Flanagan, "The Japanese Party System in Transition," *Comparative Politics* 3 (2) (January 1971); Gerald Curtis, *Election Campaigning, Japanese Style* (New York: Columbia University Press, 1971).

17. See Packard, *Protest in Tokyo*, pp. 101–104, 155–156, and chaps. 6–8. The dilemma of the opposition in these circumstances, and the fact that such confronta-

tions could sometimes be effective, is perceptively discussed in T. J. Pempel, "The Dilemma of Parliamentary Opposition in Japan," *Polity* 8 (1) (Fall 1975).

18. Scalapino and Masumi, *Parties and Politics*, p. 145.

19. See Baerwald, *Japan's Parliament*, chap. 4; "Parliament and Parliamentarians"; and "Nikkan Kokkai." See also Masataka Kosaka, "Kyōkō Saiketsu no Seijigaku," *Chūō Kōron* (November 1965); Izumi Hosojima, "Yo-Yatō Gekitotsu Hoanshi," *Chūō Kōron* (January 1976).

20. For the University Normalization Bill see Baerwald, "Nikkan Kokkai'" and *Japan's Parliament*, p. 105.

21. Takeshi Hatakeyama, "Seiryoku Taihendōki no Kakkai Un'ei," *Chūō Kōron* (February 1977), p. 117.

22. Baerwald, *Japan's Parliament*, p. 112.

23. See J. A. A. Stockwin, *Japan: Divided Politics in a Growth Economy* (New York: Norton, 1975), pp. 66 and 154.

24. The term is from Louis Kriesberg, *The Sociology of Social Conflicts* (Englewood Cliffs, N.J.: Prentice-Hall, 1973), p. 164.

25. T. J. Pempel, "The Bureaucratization of Policymaking in Postwar Japan," *American Journal of Political Science* 18 (November 1974): 650.

26. Mike Mochizuki, data handout for presentation on "Perspectives on Japan's National Diet," June 1978, table 2, provided by the author. Hereafter cited as "Mochizuki data." For further details, see his subsequent, excellent Ph.D. dissertation for Harvard University, "Managing and Influencing the Japanese Legislative Process: The Role of Parties and the National Diet."

27. Pempel, "The Dilemma," p. 74.

28. Baerwald, *Japan's Parliament*, p. 84.

29. Frank Gibney, *Japan: The Fragile Super Power* (Tokyo: Charles E. Tuttle, 1975), p. 277.

30. Nathaniel B. Thayer, *How the Conservatives Rule Japan* (Princeton: Princeton University Press, 1969), pp. 289–290.

31. See Kosaka, "Kyōkō Saiketsu," especially pp. 51–56; on the railroad fares and health insurance bills' staged snap votes in 1969, see Toshiaki Adachi, *Kokkai Kaizōron* (Tokyo: Mizuto Shobo, 1974), pp. 92–96.

32. Murray Edelman, *Politics as Symbolic Action* (Chicago: Markham, 1971), p. 142, identifies the main elements in the ritualization of political conflict in discussing labor-management relations: a high measure of agreement between leaders of both sides about their relative vulnerability and bargaining resources, stylized procedures that signal aggression yet also reassure the antagonists that conflict will be held within acceptable limits, and mobilizing the support of rank and file and publics for the leadership. All these elements were apparent in the ritualization of the snap vote in the Diet in the late 1960s.

33. Di Palma, "The Study of Conflict," p. 14; Nordlinger, "Conflict Regulation," p. 50.

34. See Kurt Steiner, Ellis S. Krauss, and Scott C. Flanagan, eds., *Political Opposition and Local Politics in Japan* (Princeton: Princeton University Press, 1980).

35. Gary D. Allinson, "Japan's Independent Voters: Dilemma or Opportunity?", *Japan Interpreter* 11 (1) (Spring 1976).

36. Michio Muramatsu, "Seijika to Gyōsei Kanryō," *Jichi Kenkyū* 54 (9) (September 1978): 12.

37. Based on data in Seiji Kōhō Sentā, *Seiji Handobukku*, no. 8 (February 1978),

pp. 163–167. After the 1976 election, there were 125 freshmen, 77 members in their second term (elected first in 1972), and 70 members in their third term (elected first in 1969)—a total of 272 of the 511 members of the lower house elected since 1969. Over half of the House of Councillors also were freshmen elected in 1974 or 1977.

38. Robert D. Putnam, "Studying Elite Political Culture: The Case of 'Ideology,' " *American Political Science Review* 65 (3)(September 1971).

39. *New York Times*, Saturday, 17 May 1980, p. 24.

40. Mochizuki data, table 5.

41. *Asahi Shimbun*, 16 June 1979, p. 4.

42. Di Palma, *The Study of Conflict*, p. 10.

43. Baerwald, *Japan's Parliament*, p. 100.

44. Kim, "The Committee System in the Japanese Diet," pp. 83–84.

45. See Nathaniel B. Thayer, "The Mathematics of an Effective Majority in the Japanese Diet," unpublished manuscript, June 1976; Watanabe, *Shinseiji no Joshiki*, pp. 239–240.

46. Seiji Kōhō Sentā, *Seiji Handobukku*, no. 8 (1978), p. 148; no. 10 (1980), p. 146.

47. Mainichi Shinbunsha, eds., *Seikyoku—Rengo Jidai* (Tokyo: Mainichi Shinbunsha, 1977), pp. 77–79. My interviews in 1978, however, revealed that support for changing the custom still exists in some quarters within the LDP.

48. Ibid., pp. 73–74.

49. *Japan Times Weekly*, 17 March 1979, p. 1.

50. Di Palma, *The Study of Conflict*, p. 12; Nordlinger, "Conflict Regulation," pp. 22–24.

51. Mochizuki data, table 1 (averaged by the author) and table 4 on sources of amendments for 1971–1977 period.

52. Thayer, "Mathematics of Effective Majority," pp. 11–12, 29–35.

53. Quoted in Mainichi Shimbunsha, *Seikyoku—Rengo Jidai*, p. 72.

54. See Takayoshi Wada, "Seiken-arasoi ni Miru Saishō no Jōken," *Asahi Ja-naru* 20 (34) (1 September 1978): 14–15; see also Uchida Kenzō, "Our New Prime Minister, Masayoshi Ōhira," *Japan Echo* 6 (1) (Spring 1979): 33.

55. *Japan Times Weekly*, 9 December 1978, p. 1.

56. See Nordlinger, "Conflict Regulation," pp. 24–26.

57. John E. Endicott, "The 1975–76 Debate over Ratification of the NPT in Japan," *Asian Survey* 17 (3) (March 1977): 286–288.

58. On the 1977 budget bill, see Mainichi Shinbunsha, *Seikyoku—Rengo Jidai*, pp. 119–170. Government-prepared budgets had been altered in the Diet only twice before: once in the pre-LDP multiparty era under the Ashida Cabinet and once at government instigation under the Sato Cabinet.

59. See Kōji Kakizawa, "Nagatachō wa Shinde Iru: Taikenteki Kokkai Hihan," *Gendai* (September 1978): 99.

60. Watanabe, *Shinseiji no Jōshiki*, pp. 267–269.

61. See Di Palma, *The Study of Conflict*, pp. 12–13.

62. Baerwald, *Japan's Parliament*, pp. 82–83.

63. Kōichi Kishimoto, "Shūsan Gichō no Isu no Nukumori'" *Chūō Kōron* (February 1977), especially pp. 176–179 and 181.

64. Ibid., pp. 177 and 180.

65. Baerwald, *Japan's Parliament*, p. 77.

66. On Hori, Nadao, and the priority of the new role norms over the incumbent's background and private political beliefs, see Minoru Shimizu, "The New and Former House Speakers," *Japan Times Weekly*, 17 February 1979, p. 4.

67. Ibid.

68. *Japan Times Weekly*, 10 March 1979, p. 1.

69. Baerwald, *Japan's Parliament*, p. 83.

70. For a discussion of how recruitment and later career patterns of the chairman and *riji* of this committee and other "Diet strategy types" clearly showed greater status and influence within the parties during the *hakuchū* era, see my "Japanese Parties and Parliament: Changing Leadership Roles and Role Conflicts," in Terry Edward MacDougall, ed., *Political Leadership in Modern Japan*, Michigan Papers in Japanese Studies (Ann Arbor: University of Michigan Center for Japanese Studies, 1982); see also Tadao Koike, *Seiji Kiji ni Tsuyoku Naru Hon* (Tokyo: E-ru Shuppansha, 1977), p. 23, and Watanabe, *Shineiji no Jōshiki*, p. 259.

71. Baerwald, *Japan's Parliament*, p. 84. In 1978 there were nine directors among the twenty-four members of the committee aside from the chairman, apportioned roughly according to party strength in the house. Parties with fewer than twenty members in the house by custom do not receive a directorship and usually just send an "observer" to meetings.

72. Interviewees admitted this and a check of the minutes *(Gijiroku)* confirmed it. Most full committee meetings in the 84th Diet lasted less than ten minutes, some for as little as two or three minutes, and almost every item was approved "without dissent."

73. See Watanabe, *Shinseiji no Jōshiki*, pp. 260–261; see also Richard Halloran, "Chaotic Sessions Raise Doubts About Japan's Legislative Body," *New York Times*, 23 September 1973, and Baerwald, *Japan's Parliament*, p. 86.

74. Baerwald, *Japan's Parliament*, p. 85.

75. The difficulty that a *riji* will have in this regard probably varies by party. LDP directors should have the least difficulty because bills and strategy have already been thoroughly debated within the party before a bill is introduced; thus the parameters within which a director can negotiate are known far in advance.

76. Di Palma, *The Study of Conflict*, p. 15, cites Michels and Duverger in his discussion of the dilemma.

77. Ibid., p. 11. The "norm of restrained partisanship" seems to have been discussed first by John F. Manley in his intriguing account of an American congressional committee whose norms are strikingly similar to some of those described here. See his "House Committee on Ways and Means: Conflict Management in a Congressional Committee," *American Political Science Review* 59 (4) (December 1965).

78. Strict party discipline and the authority of directors to make binding decisions in negotiations decreases the need for this norm to be shared among all representatives in the case of the Diet.

79. See, for example, Chie Nakane's influential book, *Japanese Society* (Berkeley: University of California Press, 1970), and much of the popular and academic literature on Japanese corporate enterprise.

80. Scalapino and Masumi, *Parties and Politics*, pp. 5–6; see also Nobutaka Ike, *Japanese Politics: Patron-Client Democracy*, 2nd ed. (New York: Knopf, 1972), p. 114, and Packard, *Protest in Tokyo*, p. 347.

81. See my "Japanese Diet in Transition: 'Traditional' Cultural Norms in Postwar

Parliamentary Politics," paper presented to the 2nd International Conference of the European Association for Japanese Studies, Florence, Italy, 20–22 September 1979.

82. Nordlinger, "Conflict Regulation," p. 59.

83. Robert A. Putnam, "The Italian Communist Politician," in Donald L. M. Blackmer and Sidney Tarrow, eds., *Communism in Italy and France* (Princeton: Princeton University Press, 1975), p. 200.

84. Even at this writing, nearly three years after the LDP's overwhelming victory in the 1980 election, no definite answer to the questions can be given. In the immediate aftermath of that election, there were hopeful initial signs that *hakuchū* patterns would continue (see, for example, "Shūin Fuku-Gichō, Yatō ni: Jimintō ga Hōshin Tenkan," *Yomiuri Shimbun*, (27 July 1980). On the other hand, the first budget of the 1980s was snap-voted through the Budget Committee, the first snap vote in a number of years and the first time in decades that the budget had been pushed through the committee in that manner. Yet this latter event seems to have been a relatively rare one, with no reversion to pre-*hakuchū* patterns. Rather, there seems to be a continuation of the *hakuchū* consultations but with greater tension and greater potential for a breakdown of conflict management.

85. For a similar view forecasting that opposition participation in policymaking in the Diet would have both merits and demerits, see Yukio Suzuki, "Uō-saō no Keizai Seisaku de Keiki wa Dō Naru," *Chūō Kōron* (February 1977).

86. Pempel, "The Dilemma of Parliamentary Opposition in Japan."

87. Michael Crozier, Samuel Huntington, and Joji Watanuki, *The Crisis of Democracy: Report on the Governability of Democracies to the Trilateral Commission* (New York: New York University Press, 1975), pp. 126–127, emphasize the wide-ranging interest articulation and aggregation functions performed by LDP politicians, *koenkai*, and factions.

88. Scott C. Flanagan and Bradley M. Richardson, "Political Disaffection and Political Stability: A Comparison of Japanese and Western Findings," in Richard F. Tomasson, ed., *Comparative Social Research* (Greenwich, Conn.: JAI Press, 1980), vol. 3, draft ms. pp. 10, 32–33, and Ichiro Miyake, "Trust in Government and Political Cleavages: A Cross-National Comparison," unpublished manuscript, Doshisha University, pp. 27–34.

89. Wada, "Seiken-arosoi ni Miru Saishō no Jōken," p. 12.

90. See Mark Kesselman, "Overinstitutionalization and Political Constraint: The Case of France," *Comparative Politics* 3 (1) (October 1970). See also Nelson W. Polsby, ed., *Governmental Institutions and Processes*, vol. 5 of *Handbook of Political Science* (Reading, Mass.: Addison-Wesley, 1975), pp. 197 and 290.

91. Ralf Dahrendorf, *Class and Class Conflict in Industrial Society* (Stanford: Stanford University Press, 1959), pp. 308–311.

92. Giuseppe Di Palma, *Surviving Without Governing: The Italian Parties in Parliament* (Berkeley: University of California Press, 1977).

93. *Asahi Shimbun*, 16 June 1979, p. 4; averaging by author.

94. Suzuki, "Uō-saō no Keizai Seisaku," p. 129, predicts the possibility of bureaucratic leadership being strengthened in an era of no dominant party because of the need for some agency to play "the coordinator role" in policy.

95. *Asahi Shimbun*, 16 June 1979, p. 4.

96. See *Nihon Kokusei-Zue* (Tokyo: Kokuseisha, 1979), p. 442.

97. Kozo Yamamura, "The Cost of Rapid Growth and Capitalist Democracy: A

Political-Economic Analysis of Japanese Inflation," unpublished manuscript, 1981, pp. 19–26, 34–43, 54–59, 66.

98. Norman Macrae, "Must Japan Slow?," *The Economist: Japan Survey 3*, p. 23. For the governability of political economy and the possibility of Japan catching "the English disease," see Suzuki, "Uō-saō no Keizai Seisaku," pp. 131–133.

99. Scalapino and Masumi, *Parties and Politics*, p. 145.

100. The author (with Prof. Jon Pierre, University of Lund) is currently engaged in a comparative study of Japanese and Swedish parliaments in the 1970s. In Sweden a leftist party, the Social Democrats, which had ruled for nearly forty years, confronted a nearly equal opposition for the first time in the early 1970s before actually losing power in 1976.

II

Policy Conflict
and Its Resolution
within the
Governmental System

JOHN CREIGHTON CAMPBELL

Much writing on the Japanese policy process has been dominated, positively or negatively, by the consensus model. Some writers argue that decisions are made with unique harmony in Japan; others seek examples of conflict and dissensus to demonstrate that the model is invalid. This latter group is likely to see Japanese decision making (and other social phenomena) as quite understandable without much recourse to cultural explanations.[1]

This essay falls between these two poles. My aim is neither to portray the Japanese decision-making system as predominantly consensual, and therefore culturally determined, nor to argue that because conflict is rife we can ignore "Japaneseness" and describe Japan quite as we would any other advanced nation. My view is that the consensus model must be taken into account precisely because Japanese themselves—the officials and politicians who make up the decision-making system—think it is important. My interest is in seeing how that model is applied in real decision making, what its limitations are, and what happens when consensus does not work.

What is the consensus model? It can be seen as either structure or process. The structural argument, at its simplest, holds that because of cultural homogeneity or other reasons Japanese tend to agree with each other and hence few disputes occur. Journalistic versions of "Japan Incorporated" are of this sort: The bureaucracy, the majority party, and big business have so many interests in common, and dominate the governmental system to such an extent, that policymaking is basically cooperative rather than conflictual.

What we might call the "consensus process model" is more sophisticated. It concedes that differences of interest do occur in Japan but, perhaps because of the need to live together under crowded conditions, a set of norms has developed to control conflict and prevent social disruption. The rules for reaching decisions are fundamentally cooperative rather than competitive.[2]

If these models were framed as hypotheses for comparative research, the structural version would predict that the incidence of conflict would be lower, and the process version that similar disputes would be handled in less conflictual ways, in Japan than in the West. One could imagine direct and empirical tests of such propositions by comparing small social systems, say villages or work groups, in Japan and the United States. For a social system as large and complicated as the national decision-making system, however, I must rely on indirect inferences from the available evidence, mostly case studies of particular decisions or institutions. The first part of this essay is about structure—specifically, the pattern of cleavages within the system—and the second part about how a consensus process model might help us understand how policy conflicts are resolved.

A word on scope: My interest is limited to conflicts that are directly relevant to public policy, so disputes about, for example, who will be chosen vice-minister or Liberal Democratic Party (LDP) president are not included. Moreover, I discuss only conflict *within* the decision-making system, defined as the government bureaucracy and the majority party organization, plus the prime minister and cabinet spanning the two. The Diet, the opposition parties, big business and other interest groups, the press, and so forth are defined as outside the system because, although they are important influences on public policy, they typically do not participate directly in its formulation. Since they may be seen as providing mostly inputs and constraints for the decision-making system, conflicts within the Diet or between the opposition parties and the LDP are not discussed here. This formulation is somewhat less justifiable for the late 1970s, when the LDP's slim majority allowed more amendments in the Diet and forced more consultation with the opposition, but generally it is a useful simplification for making sense of the post-1955 policymaking process.

Structure: Policy Cleavages

Some conflicts occur at random, but most fall into patterns so that certain groupings of individuals repeatedly conflict with other groupings. Such groupings are seen as divided by a "cleavage." The nature of a particular cleavage is defined by the characteristics that unite those on either side and accordingly differentiate one side from the other. Individuals within a social system usually identify with several different groupings that become salient to them with regard to different disputes. To the extent that the boundaries of these groupings are congruent, so that the individual usually has the same allies and opponents, cleavages are said to reinforce each other or "overlap." Variegated boundaries, so that opponents on one issue become allies on another, produce "crosscutting" cleavage patterns. Other things being equal, overlapping cleavages lead to permanent, bitter divisions whereas crosscutting cleavages result in greater cohesiveness within a social system.[3] Analyzing the structure of conflict in a social system means discovering the bases of the main cleavages, how clear-cut and deep they are, the issues for which they are salient, and how they overlap and crosscut.

The American decision-making system, comprised of the Congress, the bureaucracy, and the presidency, provides a quick example. There are important cleavages between Congress and the entire executive branch, between the presidency and bureaucratic agencies, between political parties within Congress, between agencies, between higher-level political appointees and lower-level civil servants within agencies, between representatives of various interests (urban-rural, rich-poor, frostbelt-sunbelt, and so on), between people with different ideologies or opinions, between people united by bonds of friendship, and so forth. Many of these cleavages crosscut, but when for example different parties control Congress and the presidency— an institutional cleavage reinforced by a partisan cleavage—conflict is likely to be bitter and intense.

This example indicates that some types of conflict that are important in the United States do not occur within the Japanese decision-making system as defined here. First, because the Japanese constitution is based on the "unitary" parliamentary system rather than the American "separation of powers" doctrine, the institutional cleavage between the legislative and executive branch, with its legal checks and balances, does not exist. Second, in Japan, except perhaps for that brief period in the 1970s, the partisan cleavage is not directly relevant to the formulation of public policy, while in the United States many policies are actively negotiated between the Democrats and Republicans. In a broader sense the "progressive forces" in general have been continuously excluded from Japan's decision-making system for nearly the entire postwar era, so the ideological range of issues actually considered within the system is much narrower than in many European countries and perhaps the United States.[4] An additional factor is simple agreement on goals. In the immediate postwar period most Japanese agreed that the highest national priority was economic reconstruction, and such LDP leaders as Hayato Ikeda succeeded in sustaining this sense of national purpose at least into the 1960s.[5]

For these reasons, we would expect to find somewhat fewer cases of policy conflict in the Japanese decision-making system. Three points should be noted, however. First, none of these factors seem to have much to do with any cultural proclivities toward "harmony"—they are the products of the constitutional framework, of voters' preferences for conservatives, of Japan's postwar economic situation, and perhaps of certain LDP leaders' skill in advantageously defining the national agenda. Second, the agreement about growth was never total—it did not obviate disagreements over secondary goals or the means for attaining prosperity, and in any event the consensus began to crack by the mid-1960s. Third, such ideological, partisan, and institutional cleavages are not the only nor necessarily the most important cleavages relevant to the policymaking process in Japan, the United States, or anywhere.

To progress further we need a general scheme of potentially important cleavages to set against the reality of decision making in Japan. Here is a plausible list, drawn from a variety of sources:

1. Formal organization cleavages
2. Interest-representation cleavages
3. Informal cleavages
4. Hierarchical cleavages

The salience of each type for the bureaucracy, the LDP organization, and the decision-making system as a whole is assessed in the following paragraphs. I will then return to a discussion of the impact of "culture" before discussing the conflict resolution process.

FORMAL ORGANIZATION CLEAVAGES

Much of the process of policymaking in Japan goes on within the governmental bureaucracy, usually involving conflicts between bureaus or ministries, groupings primarily defined by the formal organizational structure. This type of cleavage is not as dominant in the LDP or for the decision-making system as a whole, but it offers a good place to start our analysis of policy conflict patterns.

A long tradition in organization theory has explored how subunits of complex organizations inevitably develop their own goals and come into conflict with other subunits.[6] Common sources of conflict between organizational subunits include incompatability of goals, overlapping jurisdictions, interdependencies (the outputs of one are inputs for another), and competition for scarce resources. Variations in organizational design can affect these patterns of cleavages considerably.[7] The Japanese bureaucracy is generally organized on the "line" model, seen as rather old-fashioned in the West. This means that units in the regular hierarchy (ministry-bureau-section) are relatively self-sufficient, in that they do not depend much either on staff units of specialists providing organization-wide services (the "staff-line" model) or on task-defined subunits in other lines (the "matrix" model).[8] Within ministries and bureaus (though not within sections) responsibilities are specified in great detail so that jurisdictions overlap as little as possible. By reducing overlaps and interdependencies, the frequency of interaction, and therefore conflict, among subunits is lower than in comparable Western organizations. On the other hand, the lack of contact means that cleavages between these relatively self-contained subunits are likely to be deep, so that conflicts should be more intense when they do occur.

These are theoretical hypotheses which I cannot test with real comparative data, but various impressionistic evidence suggests that "sectionalism" or conflict among organizational units at the same level is often quite intense in the Japanese bureaucracy. It varies considerably by level, however. Within a particular bureau, the sections are more interdependent than is true at higher levels; a higher proportion of its officials are engaged in bureau-wide coordination functions; and bureaus usually share the same floor of a ministry building so that its officials rub shoulders daily. These factors mitigate against deep rifts emerging.[9] Nonetheless, one often hears anecdotes of individual sections hoarding information or refusing to cooperate with other sections, even within the same bureau.

Cleavages between bureaus in many ministries run deeper. The Finance Ministry, for example, is often characterized as "all bureaus no ministry"—that is, extreme sectionalism. The hostility accompanying cross-bureau interactions was well expressed by the remark of the Financial Bureau chief after one incident: "The Budget Bureau is always cleaning up its own garden first and throwing all the garbage into ours."[10] The Ministry of International Trade and Industry (MITI) is perhaps the most integrated, particularly since reorganizing its bureaus from a vertical or industrial-sector basis toward a more horizontal task-oriented structure, but even there longstanding policy arguments among bureaus are significant.[11] Such cleavages are prevented from getting too deep by the Japanese personnel system, which rotates higher civil servants among the bureaus within a ministry rather rapidly, and by intense efforts to socialize officials into a sense of loyalty and identification with the ministry organization.[12]

Such constraints are conspicuously absent when one examines relationships among ministries, and indeed accounts of battles between ministerial feudal domains are the staple of Japanese bureaucratic folklore. For example, MITI has had persisting arguments with the Finance Ministry over macroeconomic policy, with the Foreign Ministry over export promotion and foreign aid, with the Welfare Ministry over pollution, and with Agriculture over protectionism—every ministry provides several such examples. Negotiations among ministry representatives—the weekly cabinet or vice-ministers' conference meetings, for instance, or lower-level liaison committees—often resemble the United Nations Security Council at a tense moment.

These differences between levels suggest that, other things being equal, the broader the scope of an issue (defined by the number of subunit jurisdictions it touches), the greater the likelihood that conflict will be intense. This relationship probably works in all governments, but it is unusually strong in Japan. Crossing ministry lines is particularly crucial. As Daniel Okimoto has remarked, "Here is a stage at which rational factors, reasonably well safeguarded at the level of the individual ministry, tend to be overwhelmed by the free-for-all that sets loose potentially irrational forces."[13] The scholars who point to sectionalism as the major bureaucratic pathology of Japan mainly have in mind the inability to coordinate—to resolve policy conflict—across ministerial boundaries.[14]

INTEREST-REPRESENTATION CLEAVAGES

If the conflicts between ministries and bureaus were purely bureaucratic—jurisdictional squabbles and the like—they would be interesting only to public administration specialists worried about "efficiency" and such minor virtues. But in fact one function of government is to manage the conflicts among competing interests in society at large, and in advanced democracies this is accomplished largely by the representation of those interests, directly or indirectly, within the decision-making system. Not only ministries but the bureaus within them often deal with, and become the voice for, quite specific clienteles—the division of the Transport Ministry into the bureaus of Shipping, Ships, Seafarers, Ports and Harbors, Railway Supervision, Road Transport, and Highways is a good illustration. Cleavages of interest between social sectors thus reinforce the formal organizational cleavages of the bureaucracy, and clientele groups provide both stimulus and resources for conflict within and between ministries.

Interest cleavages are also important within the Liberal Democratic Party. A dietman may come to represent particular interests for various reasons—if his constituents are farmers, he will support agricultural subsidies; he may receive campaign contributions or other electoral support from some interest group; his previous occupation or experiences as a politician may have engendered a special concern for some aspect of policy. Interest groupings within the LDP range from loose, transitory forms like so-called tribes of enthusiasts, through Dietmen's Leagues (actually little more than names on a petition), temporary or semipermanent special committees or investigative commissions (purportedly established to look into a problem, but actually most often sponsors of a single viewpoint), to the seventeen highly institutionalized divisions *(bukai)* of the Policy Affairs Research Council.[15] The policy concerns of these groupings overlap in innumerable ways, but although jurisdictional disputes sometimes occur, one does not really find formal organization cleavages as important as in the bureaucracy. Individual politicians usually do not see these organizational boundaries—and, indeed, often public policy itself—as relevant to their main concerns of getting reelected and moving up in the party. Interest representation conflicts in the bureaucracy are stabilized by the organization chart, but in the LDP they are amorphous, fluid, and often hard to predict.

Over the decades that the Liberal Democrats have been in power, however, some rather stable groupings have developed within the decision-making system. The most important are the alliances between Policy Affairs Research Council (PARC) divisions and the ministries they are supposed to oversee. Because of self-recruitment and the relationships that develop naturally over years of frequent interaction, divisions are usually dominated by LDP dietmen who are quite sympathetic to ministry views (often they have served in the ministry as an official or as minister or parliamentary vice-minister). Clientele groups seek to develop ties not only with the ministry but with dietmen in the appropriate division. The resulting three-way alliances closely resemble the famous American "subgovernments" or "iron triangles" (an agency, one or more congressional commit-tees, and a set of supporting interest groups) which dominate many policy areas. In Japan as in the United States, the bureaucrats, politi-cians, and interest group staff who make up a subgovernment may well disagree on the details of many policy issues, but they usually share a belief that their policy area is not getting its proper proportion of national attention or resources and that most problems are better negotiated within the subgovernment than left to less sympathetic outsiders.[16]

Subgovernments thus constitute a set of interest-based cleavages that divide the entire decision-making system. These cleavages are crucially reinforced by the deep formal-organization cleavages be-tween the ministries. Interactions *within* subgovernments must be taken into account in analyzing the conflict patterns of nearly all pol-icy issues, and moreover the relationships *between* subgovernments are the key to understanding most issues that are broader than the jurisdiction of a single ministry.

The nature of within-subgovernment relationships depends mainly on how directly the policy area in question bears on the immediate interests—especially the electoral interests—of LDP dietmen. Agri-culture and public works are at the high extreme and foreign affairs at the other extreme. When dietman interest is intense, the usual split is between the LDP's constituency orientation and the bureaucrats' preference for more "rational" policy: In public works, dietmen push small, election-district-sized projects while bureaucrats favor larger enterprises; the Commerce and Industry Division was more interested in protecting small business in the 1960s than in MITI's highest prior-ity, promotion of exports; rural dietmen demand high rice prices while the Agriculture Ministry presses for comprehensive reform. In some cases, notably that of the Education Ministry, interested diet-men may have a very ideological orientation in contrast to more cau-tious and moderate bureaucrats.[17]

Despite these differences, there is a strong tendency for the PARC division itself to be sympathetic to ministry views, even when the dominant opinion in the rest of the party is somewhat hostile. This situation sometimes results in institutionalizing an interest cleavage within the LDP organization. The Japan Medical Association (JMA), for example, pushing for high health insurance fees for doctors, is well represented in the LDP. The Welfare Ministry Insurance Bureau and the ministry leadership oppose these demands and are supported, at least nominally, by the PARC Social Affairs Division. This cleavage resulted in the creation of the Medical Care Basic Problems Investigation Commission within the PARC, which served as the voice of the JMA and often battled with the Social Affairs Division in various party arenas.[18]

More common than conflicts among LDP dietmen within a particular policy area is competition among supporters of different policy areas. Quite frequently cross-ministerial battles in the bureaucracy will be paralleled by cross-divisional battles inside the LDP; since the bureaucrats and politicians (and interest groups) frequently cooperate in their strategies, these struggles should be seen as essentially cross-subgovernment conflicts. The weight of LDP support in the agriculture, fishery, construction, and small-business subgovernments largely accounts for their consistent success in many policy disputes.

Of course, support within the LDP is not the only significant political resource.[19] Before 1970 the main reason why MITI consistently defeated or watered down the Welfare Ministry's attempts to strengthen environmental legislation was its disproportionate support in the LDP, but then the weight of public opinion and a resulting intervention by political leaders tipped the balance the other way.[20] Similarly, in the tough interministerial negotiations over Japan's position in the GATT talks, the Ministry of Agriculture and Forestry's opposition to lowering farm tariffs had much more LDP support than free-traders in the Foreign Ministry and elsewhere could muster. However, great international pressure, transmitted by the prime minister, finally succeeded in extracting concessions.[21] In short, the permutations on the basic pattern are many and various, but in general one form or another of intersubgovernmental cleavages dominate most important domestic policymaking in Japan. In fact, since foreign policy issues today have increasingly significant domestic aspects, these sorts of policy conflicts shape Japan's international behavior as well.[22]

The final interest cleavage to be considered is that between the LDP and the bureaucracy as a whole. This relationship is crucial in all advanced democracies—"at the levers of power in the modern state stand those two uncertain partners, the elected party politician and the professional state bureaucrats"—and has been the subject of innumerable studies in the West.[23] In Japan as well, the question of whether it is the LDP or the bureaucracy which dominates the post-1955 political system has been a central concern of many political scientists.[24]

In my view, this question is unanswerable, and in any case it is beyond the purposes of this essay.[25] My concern is where and how this cleavage impinges on the policy process. It is clear, on the one hand, that each side needs the other—almost no policy of any importance can be adopted without both LDP and ministerial approval—and on the other hand that there is considerable basis for conflict. Politicians are oriented toward voters and bureaucrats toward their own organizational concerns.[26] LDP dietmen tend to see bureaucrats as obsessed with rules and details, unimaginative, and arrogant. Officials often view politicians as irresponsible, quick to pander to special interests, and, at the extreme, stupid or corrupt. These attitudes color bureaucrat-LDP interactions at all levels, although the intimacy of long one-party rule and the fact that some one-third of LDP dietmen are ex-bureaucrats ameliorate such tensions.

Organizationally speaking, despite the many newspaper stories that refer to battles or negotiations between "the party" and "the government," cases of the LDP confronting the bureaucracy as a whole are relatively rare. The closest approximation occurs when issues are advanced by a constituency with substantial support in the LDP but no ties to any government agency. In the cases of postwar repatriates seeking compensation for their overseas property, and the movement to nationalize the Yasukuni Shrine, large numbers of LDP backbenchers were strongly in favor (with little open opposition) and at least one government agency was opposed. The rest of the bureaucracy was indifferent.[27] More generally, nearly every year at budget time there are strong pressures from rank-and-file LDP dietmen for more government spending, opposed by the Finance Ministry. In most disputes, however, the bureaucracy and often enough the LDP are internally divided and conflict more closely resembles the subgovernment type.

Formal-organizational and interest-representation cleavages make up the basic structure of most major conflicts over public policy in the Japanese decision-making system. But when one examines day-to-day decision making rather than big controversial issues, more subtle cleavages are also important. Two types are worth brief accounts: informal cleavages and hierarchical cleavages.

INFORMAL CLEAVAGES

It is a commonplace of organization theory that the social structure of a complex organization is never completely determined by the lines on a formal organizational chart. Since Japanese are often seen as particularly prone to factionalism, the impact of informal groupings on decisions must be assessed for both the bureaucracy and the LDP.

Several such groupings have been described by observers of the Japanese bureaucracy. One is the "university clique" *(gakubatsu)*: Graduates of the same school—especially the Law Faculty at Tokyo University—are commonly alleged to aid each other and discriminate against outsiders.[28] Second, whether or not because of their university ties, younger officials are sometimes drawn together by friendship and similar viewpoints into evening discussion or study groups, even across ministry lines.[29] Third, "vertical cliques" of basically paternalistic *(sempai-kōhai)* relationships from senior to junior levels of higher civil servants often develop within single ministries. They serve to advance members' careers and influence and can be self-perpetuating—the clique of Finance Ministry officials founded by Hayato Ikeda in the 1950s is a well-known and long-running example.[30]

These various informal groups provide psychological satisfactions as well as more concrete benefits for their members, and they play an indirect role in policymaking by providing channels for exchanging opinions and information. It is doubtful, however, that they are often sufficiently organized, or identified with particular ideologies or viewpoints, to be actual contenders in policy conflicts.[31] Vaguely defined cleavages between opinion groupings within ministries can often be discerned—MITI has its "international trade" versus "industry" factions, and the Education Ministry has been described as divided between "modernists" and "moralists."[32] Selecting a new vice-minister from one side of such a cleavage can signify a ministry policy shift. Of course, on big issues there is likely to be a fair range of opinions within a ministry, and building a winning coalition among officials is an important component of bureaucratic policy conflict.[33]

One type of intrabureaucratic cleavage is rather conspicuous by its minor importance in Japan. Many American organization theorists have stressed the importance of tension between specialists and managers, which amounts to a conflict between authority based on knowledge and authority based on hierarchy.[34] Moreover, in American administration specific professional groups—doctors, social workers, foresters—have often been able to maintain their autonomy within an organization or oppose leadership goals because they can draw on outside resources, including a professional association, its code of ethics, and sometimes allied professionals in other departments.[35]

Such conflicts are less characteristic of the Japanese than the American bureaucracy—partly because professional groups are less institutionalized in Japanese society generally and partly by organizational design. In Japan, most specialists are automatically relegated to a second-class status defined by the Middle Examination Certificate. Others take professional examinations theoretically equal to the general-administration Higher Civil Service Examination, but in practice they tend to be subordinate to generalist officials. In many ministries certain section chief or bureau chief positions are reserved for professionals, although only in the Construction Ministry can a professional (an engineer) reach the vice-ministership, and then on an alternating basis with generalist bureaucrats. Such frozen allocations of posts should be seen as a means of minimizing specialist-generalist competition. Since the need for special expertise is growing in the Japanese government as elsewhere, professionals have gained in influence and these cleavages are probably becoming more important, but as yet they do not approach American levels.[36]

The LDP has been divided by many sorts of informal cleavages apart from the interest-based cleavages described above: ex-Liberal Party versus ex-Democratic Party, for example, and ex-bureaucrats versus ex-local politicians. These cleavages are not usually directly relevant to policymaking, except insofar as they complicate various disputes, but opinion groups can matter. Japan's China policy has been severely constrained by the long-standing argument between pro-Peking and pro-Taiwan LDP dietmen, crystalized into two competing "study groups."[37] This pattern of relatively open polarization of opinion seems to appear mainly with regard to foreign policy: Somewhat less institutionalized splits have complicated decisions on relations with the Soviet Union and South Korea and the security relationship with the United States. Moreover, anticommunism was the main concern of the younger right-wingers who organized the Seirankai, an ideological party-within-a-party of the 1970s.[38] Foreign affairs offers more scope for ideas and opinions than domestic policy, which inevitably becomes entangled in interest-representation politics.[39]

The most famous informal cleavages in the LDP are of course its factions, which are based on a mixture of personalistic bonds and mutual benefit—members support the leader's political ambitions in exchange for financial aid and access to jobs. Ideology or common policy positions are more a nuance or tinge than a raison d'être for LDP factions. The factions dominate many important party functions, and they have been held by some scholars to determine public policy as well; certainly factions were active in such key decisions as the 1955 normalization of relations with the Soviet Union or the 1960 security treaty dispute.⁴⁰ These cases seem somewhat exceptional, however. Generally, rather than factions becoming activated because of some policy dispute, it is when factional cleavages are *already* activated—most often, because the prime ministership is somehow in doubt—that those opposed to the incumbent leadership will search around for likely issues and make them controversial. In this sense, much of what is usually interpreted as policy conflict among the various factions is really a much simpler pattern: conflict between the "ins" and "outs," the "mainstream" and "antimainstream," that occurs in all political organizations. As such, it properly belongs to the next category.

HIERARCHICAL CLEAVAGES

Ralf Dahrendorf has argued that the most fundamental cleavage in modern society is between those with power and those without.⁴¹ A similar perspective runs through American organization theory, from the standpoint of either the leader attempting to control fractious underlings or the worker oppressed by often ignorant orders from higher-ups.⁴² This concern is lacking in Japanese writing on public administration, perhaps because of a cultural assumption that vertical relationships are fundamentally close and harmonious.⁴³ In fact, the organization of Japanese ministries does tend to minimize hierarchical cleavages in two respects.

First, there is no natural cleavage line in a Japanese ministry that corresponds to the split between political appointees and permanent officials in an American department. Status divisions are instead many and small. Indeed, the continuous line of promotion from bottom to top—a new higher civil servant just out of college can envision himself becoming vice-minister and the vice-minister can well remember his days as a junior official—helps to create a sense of identity among all higher civil servants in each ministry.⁴⁴ There is a real cleavage between higher civil servants and those who enter through the middle-level examination, who can rise no higher than a low-status section chief post before retirement. Looking at the Foreign Ministry, which includes many middle-level area specialists, Fukui has called this discrimination "the most obvious and probably the most fundamental source of tension" in the organization.⁴⁵ However, this cleavage may be less important in other ministries (where middle-level officials are more likely to be clerks) and usually does not appear to impinge on policymaking very much.

Second, as has often been noted, the Japanese leadership style tends to be passive and reactive, at least on the surface.[46] There are fewer bold programmatic initiatives from the top and little value is attached to firm control of underlings. Organizationally, ministry-level officials lack the staff resources to develop policy on their own and so must defer to the bureaus on most substantive matters. Occasionally an activist cabinet minister will attempt to shake up an organization, such as Yasuhiro Nakasone's attempt to rejuvenate the Defense Agency, but these seem the exceptions that prove the rule.[47]

It seems to be true that ministries, like large Japanese firms, do display less conflict and a greater sense of solidarity between leaders and subordinates than their American counterparts, but this characteristic is not necessarily a direct outcome of cultural tendencies. Kenneth Skinner's case study of a public corporation demonstrates that Japanese bureaucratic organizations can be split by a deep cleavage between the managerial and working levels, with unremitting vertical conflict. The main reason is that the managers are *amakudari* officials from the ministries that supervise the corporation, and they tend to look down on lower-level employees as well as to block their chances for promotion.[48]

Another contrary example is in fact the Liberal Democratic Party, which has many attributes of a Japanese-style organization but is nevertheless quite subject to vertical conflict. The struggles of the anti-mainstream factions to depose the leadership represent one example; another is the resentment of younger dietmen against elderly members occupying all the positions of influence.[49] Moreover, an implicit or explicit cleavage between the party's rank and file and the leadership is a major factor in many policy issues. Backbenchers are easily enlisted in expensive or ideologically extreme causes that the party leaders, who must help govern the nation responsibly, cannot tolerate.[50] The LDP and the national ministries, though products of a common cultural setting, thus appear opposite in terms of conflict patterns: The bureaucracy is dominated by various horizontal conflicts; the party is split to a large extent by vertical conflicts.

PATTERNS OF CONFLICT

The tasks of this section have been to describe the cleavages within the decision-making system that are relevant to conflicts over public policy. We are interested in discovering whether Japanese culture—a preference for "harmony"—has an impact on either the quantity of policy conflict or the patterns of whom is likely to quarrel with whom.

No definitive assessment of the amount of policy conflict is possible without an empirical cross-national comparison, a project with formidable problems of definition and measurement that certainly has not been attempted here. We did observe that many sorts of conflict found within the American decision-making system are absent, external, or less frequent in Japan, but this difference has much less to do with culture in any sense than with constitutional arrangements, the continual reelection of one party, and the objective economic situation that produced (at least for a time) agreement on growth as the top priority. On the other hand, my analysis and the case-study evidence on which it rests indicate that policy issues do cause significant conflict among the members of the Japanese decision-making system, for the most part in rather regular patterns.

These patterns were described above. Formal-organizational cleavages between ministries, and to a lesser extent bureaus, dominate policy conflict within the bureaucracy; they are reinforced by cleavages based on interest representation. Both informal cleavages (with the possible exception of "vertical cliques") and cleavages between leaders and subordinates appear markedly less important in Japanese than in American bureaucratic policymaking. Within the LDP, formal-organizational lines matter little, interest-representation and informal cleavages (especially factions) are important, and various hierarchical cleavages—ins versus outs, leaders versus rank and file—are more prevalent than the vertical-society model would lead us to expect. For the decision-making system as a whole, the policy process is dominated by subgovernmental conflict: disputes among the interest-based alliances of a ministry supported by connected politicians and interest groups. That this pattern appears so prominently is not because it is unique to Japan—in fact something like it can be found everywhere—but because in Japan it is more nearly the only game in town. Lacking fights between political parties during the formulation process, or strong chief executives trying to impose their will on recalcitrant bureaucrats and legislators, the ministries and their entourages loom up as the most conspicuous contenders in the field.

This general line of argument does not take "culture" as a major direct explanation of these Japanese peculiarities. But this subject is worth exploring a little further. I noted that in the Japanese bureaucracy "horizontal" conflict is unusually intense and "vertical" conflict muted, and while the immediate explanations seem to be structural features such as the personnel system, one can also ask *why* these structures in particular were chosen and preserved in Japan. That is, these organizational forms were chosen in the Meiji period from among several possible foreign models, and historical research akin to that on the origins of private firm organization might reveal whether certain distinctive values predisposed Japanese leaders to favor one over another.[51] Still more to the point, one wonders why Japanese line ministry organization has been so stable for so long, sacrificing the advantages of organizational forms regarded as much more modern elsewhere in the world. Either the staff-line or matrix style of organization would seem to allow more effective use of special expertise, increase the capability of ministry leaders to make policy, and inhibit sectionalist horizontal conflict—all highly regarded organizational values in the West. It may not be going too far to suggest that the Japanese originally chose and still maintain their rather old-fashioned bureaucratic forms precisely in order to preserve vertical solidarity.[52]

In other words, my analysis of cleavages in the LDP and Skinner's description of a strife-ridden public corporation demonstrate that a cultural tendency toward vertical organization (Nakane's argument) does not automatically preclude conflict along the vertical dimension. Deep cleavages between superiors and subordinates can and do develop. But the Japanese do think that vertical solidarity is important, more important for the effectiveness of an organization than other characteristics (strong leadership, coordination, scientific expertise) more highly valued in the West, and thus they are willing to accept certain costs so that devices to inhibit hierarchical conflict and promote solidarity can be designed into the organizations regarded as crucial in Japanese society. These include the central government ministries and—as so many American writers on management have been pointing out recently—the large private firms.[53] Some public corporations may lack these design features because they are not high-priority institutions.[54] In my view, this *belief* that structural vertical solidarity is the key to effective organization can properly be seen as culturally derived.

Process: Conflict Resolution

Once policy conflicts arise, how are they handled in Japan? Probably most are dealt with as in other advanced nations, but Japan does have some distinctive styles. Our next task is to identify these styles and assess whether they are due mainly to cultural traits.

A cultural approach to conflict resolution in Japan might begin with Takie Lebra's suggestion that the Japanese are "socially preoccupied"—oriented toward people rather than physical or symbolic objects (including "rationality" itself).[55] It is not that desirable social relationships are the only ends for Japanese, but that "in order to attain an end—whether social or nonsocial—the creation, maintenance, or manipulation of a relevant social relationship is a foremost and indispensible means." Lebra's example is that "elaborate codrinking and codining . . . precede a business transaction," more generally, an empathetic human relationship is seen as necessary to solving most problems. The highest moral value is "trustworthiness" (shinyō).[56] Lewis Austin's comparative study of Japanese and American executives demonstrates that cultural traits of this sort have a major impact on behavior in a modern organizational setting.[57]

In a decision-making situation, these values are manifested in the celebrated Japanese consensual model: Participants take a cooperative attitude, all contribute to the discussion without putting forth a strong opinion, and eventually a solution that is at least acceptable to everyone emerges. This pattern contrasts with the competitive or adversarial decision-making model, where participants advance specific proposals and argue for them strongly, winding up in a choice by majority vote.[58] Japanese prefer the consensual model for two reasons: By avoiding open conflict it preserves the social fabric of the group; and it is likely to produce substantively better outcomes—decisions which are certainly more implementable and probably more rational.[59]

Let us assume without further discussion that this distinction captures a real difference between the way small groups function in Japan and the United States. The implications of this difference for resolving policy conflict in the national decision-making system are not at all clear, however. Too many people are involved, the information required is too complex, and the volume of decisions too great to leave policymaking up to a group of officials and politicians meeting in a small room. A critical problem is goal differentiation: Each component of a large and complicated system tends to develop and pursue its own goals. March and Simon have argued that this point is crucial to conflict resolution, because when goals are shared, decisions can be reached through "fact-finding" or "persuasion"—roughly similar to the consensus model—but when goals differ "bargaining" or "political" methods are required.[60] Thus we cannot expect the pure consensus model to apply *directly* to all policy conflict resolution.

Yet the model may still be important. The Japanese officials and politicians who inhabit the system have been brought up to value harmony as an ideal and to regard accommodation to group process as the way to achieve it. Americans in contrast are more likely to value independence, self-assertion, and rationality. It would be surprising if such fundamental views did not have an effect on the norms and expectations that govern how people approach their jobs, which in this case are decision-making roles. Japanese, then, will attempt to translate the small-group ideals noted above into the decision-making system to the extent possible. But what extent *is* possible?

My interpretation is that officials and politicians carry around a distinctively Japanese "implicit theory" of decision making and conflict resolution. In brief, this implicit theory holds that a pure consensus model, when it can work, will produce the best output: decisions that not only satisfy all relevant participants but are speedily reached and appropriate to the problem. When the pure consensus model will not work, the alternatives are to devise an approximation which we can call "contrived consensus" or to apply a related strategy of "mediation from above." When none of these stratagems work, Japanese decision makers are likely to give up on real conflict resolution altogether and employ various techniques of conflict avoidance.

THE PURE CONSENSUS MODEL

Takeshi Ishida observes that the distinction between *uchi* (inside) and *soto* (outside) runs deeply through Japanese society.[61] Individuals must feel themselves within an *uchi* relationship for the pure consensus model to operate; only then can they be fully open and "human" with one another. A component of this feeling is a shared commitment to the group, which means at least an underlying common goal. It is important to recognize, in terms of the Simon and March hypothesis mentioned above, that the *subjective* sense of sharing a goal may be more important in determining the mode of conflict resolution than whether or not the participants objectively (as perceived from outside) have common interests.

Within the contemporary decision-making system, what sets of decision makers are likely to be in a natural *uchi* relationship? One case is perhaps the inner circle of an intraparty faction, politicians who have associated together for many years. Another is the bureaucratic section whose members typically belong for only two years but work together intimately every day. We lack detailed studies of internal processes within governmental sections, but there is good reason to believe that they resemble those described by Rohlen and McLendon for sections within a Japanese bank and trading company: informal, human, and basically consensual.[62] As implied in the previous section, Japanese also tend to assume that the consensus model can operate rather naturally in vertical, hierarchical relationships. That is, they believe that people feel more connected and more comfortable with someone either above or below them in status than with an equal.[63]

Given at least the subjective sense of shared goals in the *uchi* relationship, it will be presumed that any differences of opinion can be worked out by fact-finding or persuasion—in other words, by encouraging more communication between the contenders. This in fact is the normal response in Japanese organizations to conflict in the vertical dimension. Within the bureaucracy, for example, we note that section chiefs work in the same room with their subordinates so they can talk easily; frequent meetings between section and bureau chiefs, and between bureau chiefs and the vice-minister, are heavily emphasized. My observation of the decision-making process within the Budget Bureau seems to hold for the bureaucracy as a whole:

> According to participants, the tone of the various budget conferences is informal and cooperative. The examiner does not simply submit his written recommendations up through channels for decision. Rather, he and the director (or vice-director) communicate face to face, repeatedly talking over how budget problems should be handled. This accounts for the vast amount of time consumed by meetings. . . . [The examiner] intuits the opinions of the director and vice-director by watching their reactions to his suggestions.[64]

Clearly a high degree of sympathy and shared goals is needed for such processes to be effective in problem solving.

In the more volatile LDP too the key to resolving differences between leaders and backbenchers is seen as communication and participation. The leadership will encourage everyone to express his opinions fully and will see that they are listened to by someone in authority. Fractious backbenchers will often be drawn into some sort of committee to talk the problem out. The belief is that so long as everyone feels they have been taken seriously (and, just as important, have been able to demonstrate their commitment to some constituency group) they will go along with even an unfavorable decision.[65]

Note that I am speaking mainly of assumptions about what should work—the "implicit theory"—and not necessarily what does work. Improving communication and participation resolves conflict only when there really is an underlying sense of agreement on goals and common interests; otherwise it may well exacerbate a dispute. The Japanese implicit theory does not provide good guidance for dealing with such basic hierarchical cleavages as the generation gap in the LDP, the ideological dispute between senior and junior officials in the Education Ministry, the tension between higher "generalists" and middle-level "specialist" officials in the Foreign Ministry, or the mutual resentment and suspicion between *amakudari* superiors and the permanent lower-level staff of a public corporation. Such antagonistic conflicts might well be handled better in an American context, where the likelihood of vertical conflict is recognized and ways to cope with it are better understood. Moreover, Vogel and others who celebrate the Japanese genius for consensual decision making notwithstanding, fact-finding and persuasion cannot easily be used to resolve horizontal conflicts such as those between formal organizational units, where goals are unlikely to be shared.[66]

CONTRIVED CONSENSUS

Most policy conflicts arise among contenders who do not naturally feel a community of interest or share an *uchi*-type relationship. Because of the high value attached to the consensus model, and the expectation that such processes produce better decisions, Japanese officials and politicians often attempt to simulate its necessary conditions, consciously constructing informal bonds and a sense of common interest—a "pseudo-*uchi*" relationship. The extreme expression of this tendency is the remark sometimes heard in the midst of a long and complicated negotiation that all would come out well if only everyone could sit in a bath together and really talk.

Several organizational devices are used in attempts to establish enough *uchi* feeling for the consensus model to operate. One is the interagency committee or "project team" created to grapple with a policy problem that spans several jurisdictions. Such liaison committees tend to be ineffective in all governments and particularly so in Japan.[67] The rare successful example is therefore instructive.

In 1973, a section chiefs' conference of representatives from five ministries was established to develop the Japanese position for the General Agreement on Tariffs and Trade (GATT) Tokyo Round talks.

It worked very well: except when ministry positions were diametrically opposed, the conference managed to devise compromises which were acceptable all around. Keys to its success were holding meetings weekly and running them informally, with no minutes taken, along with the obvious importance of the problem and the strong pressure for a solution coming from the prime minister. All these elements encouraged an *uchi* sense of common endeavor. Haruhiro Fukui observed that each member

> was, of course, the advocate and delegate of his ministry and its clients. But at the same time he was a member of an interministry team in search of a group consensus. This dual role demands much creativity and flexibility from each participant. The decision-making process here was one of improvisation, adaptation, and mutual compromise, while its guiding spirit, as one participant phrased it, was one of "creative gameplaying."[68]

This degree of *uchi* is difficult to contrive, though, and most interagency committees accomplish much less.

Interestingly, committees of representatives of conflicting groups are more likely to be effective within the LDP than in the bureaucracy. As noted above, dietmen are less likely than bureaucrats to feel strongly attached to an organizational policy position—at least in private—or indeed to rules and procedures in general. Moreover, the politician's craft encourages, in a sense, the ability to create quasi-*uchi* relationships quite easily. Since LDP leaders know that interests which are too divergent cannot be reconciled through small-group dynamics, often a series of ad hoc committees will be established—so that, for example, an impossibly large backbencher demand can be watered down by degrees until small enough for serious negotiations with the government.[69]

Such processes may substitute for or supplement the more formal Policy Affairs Research Council structure, which shares some of the rigidities of organizational representation seen in the bureaucracy (for example, the annual sessions in which the Policy Affairs Deliberation Council draws up the party's official budget compilation policy more often papers over real policy conflicts than resolves them). It is the LDP's ability to bypass formal organization for more flexible forms that sometimes allows unsolvable bureaucratic deadlocks to be settled, for better or worse in terms of rational policy, within the party's policymaking process.[70]

Often enough the price of achieving a sense of *uchi* within a coordinating body, so that its members can work well together, is a loss of effectiveness because the parent organizations refuse to accept the resulting compromises. Within the bureaucracy, the difficulty of coordinating policy through part-time liaison committees has led to a widespread practice of assigning officials full-time to some "office" or "headquarters" in the Prime Minister's Office. The Policy Office for the Aged was established in 1973, for example, partly because several ministries resented the tendency of Welfare Ministry officials to make policy suggestions beyond their jurisdictional boundaries. The staff is largely made up of low-level officials on temporary assignment from various ministries. In theory, this office is supposed to develop comprehensive policies and coordinate agency programs, but in practice, because the ministries do not take it seriously, it has been limited to conducting surveys and symposia and compiling information. The various deliberative councils *(shingikai)* in the Prime Minister's Office, which often indirectly represent several ministries, have also not been very effective in conflict resolution, although they perform other useful functions.[71]

The Councillors' Office (Shingishitsu) of the Cabinet Secretariat is a more significant attempt to coordinate policy on a broader scale. It too is made up of seconded ministry officials, but they are usually up-and-coming bureaucrats at the section-chief level and are more likely to be listened to at home. Judging from interviews with members, the operating ideology of the Councillors' Office is aimed at counteracting tendencies toward sectionalism in which each official simply represents his own ministry. Group cohesion, cooperation among councillors, and a "national" viewpoint are heavily emphasized. It appears that when the chief cabinet secretary is particularly powerful and energetic, or when the issues are of high priority to the prime minister, this body can be an effective mechanism for resolving conflicts among ministries or subgovernments. In day-to-day routine, however, it is most common for a councillor to communicate directly only with his own ministry and to be wary of compromising its policies.[72] The "contrived consensus" strategy is thus partially effective here.

AGENCIES AND MINISTRIES AS "PSEUDO-*UCHI*"

Permanent or recurring problems that cross ministerial jurisdictions are sometimes dealt with by establishing an entire new agency, a *chō* within the Prime Minister's Office. Leadership positions (down to the section-chief level) are allocated on a permanent basis among the concerned ministries, who regard them as regular slots in their personnel systems. Of the twenty-eight leadership positions in the Environmental Agency, for example, eleven are filled by Welfare Ministry officials, four by MITI, three by the Agriculture Ministry, and the remainder by eight other ministries or agencies.[73] Since these officials return home after two years or so, they are ministry representatives in a real sense, but they must work with officials from other ministries on a day-to-day basis and are expected to internalize the distinctive mission of the agency. These agencies thus have enough cohesion to resolve many policy disputes, though generally not those of highest intensity. For example, conflicts over macroeconomic policy, in which the primary contenders are usually the Ministry of Finance and MITI, are worked out with the Economic Planning Agency.[74] Such agencies provide at least an arena for policy conflict resolution, and at best a mechanism for creating a real consensus.

I might also suggest that the ministry itself can be seen as a "contrived consensus" in a sense, even though it (along with the firm) has often been cited as the prototypical Japanese family-style organization. It is contrived in that the institutional loyalty and sense of agreement on goals shared by its members are, first, created by an intense effort at socialization into ministry values and norms and, second, maintained by a tightly controlled personnel system. If Japanese "naturally"—because of cultural preconditioning—were prepared to give up their egos to a large organization, the organization would not have to work so hard to instill loyalty and identification. It is in the Ministry of Finance, where largely because of the nature of its tasks the bureaus perhaps are most autonomous, that the greatest stress is placed on socialization to ministry traditions and ideology and on the "Finance Ministry family" *(Okuraikka)* idea. Note also the extent to which Japanese ministries are willing to accept costs (such as the loss of specialized knowledge and experience) in order to rotate its officials so rapidly among bureaus; a major reason is to inhibit the tendencies toward sectionalism which are perceived as inherently very powerful.

Certainly conflict resolution among bureaus even within one ministry does not *naturally* fall into a pure consensus model. When the Welfare Ministry set up a "project team" to work out a response to the growing pressure for free medical care for old people, the best it could produce was four alternative drafts, representing the long-held views of the four bureaus participating.[75] The Welfare Ministry was forced by the Ministry of Finance to deal with the consequences of this expensive program in 1980: With a greater sense of urgency, it established not another "project team" but a "countermeasures headquarters" at the ministry level. The key difference was that representatives from each bureau were assigned to work full-time in the same room until they could come up with a policy.[76]

Japanese place high value on resolving conflicts by consensus procedures, but they realize that for these procedures to work, participants must share (or *think* they share) an underlying agreement on goals and a sense of group cohesion. Except for the case of real work groups such as a bureaucratic section, and perhaps in hierarchical relationships, these conditions are not natural within and between complex organizations, as the many failures of interagency committees indicate. Therefore, when the policy issue is serious, or is constantly recurring and annoying, it is worth spending time and energy to construct a pseudo-*uchi* relationship between contenders that will allow some semblance of consensus-style decision making to work. At the extreme, we may infer that the enormous attention to socialization and to combating sectionalism within a ministry indicates that even this hallowed pillar of Japanese government is less a natural group than a continuous attempt to contrive a working consensus.

MEDIATION FROM ABOVE

When contrived consensus will not work, particularly for nonrecurring policy conflicts, the next-best method is to employ a go-between. This style of conflict resolution is not emphasized in the American organizational literature except in the field of labor-management relations, but it is quite common in Japan. Unlike the labor mediator, the Japanese middleman should be higher in status than the contending parties, ideally the hierarchical superior to both sides. There are many correspondences of this sort of mediation in Japanese society at large, including the *nakōdo* who brings two households together to arrange a marriage as well as conciliation processes in both traditional and contemporary Japanese legal practice.[77]

Mediation from above rests on the same set of assumptions that makes the consensus model work: The go-between makes a point of talking over the problem exhaustively with both contending groups, so that each side is confident that the mediator has heard and understood its point of view. When the go-between comes up with a possible solution, he then has considerable leverage to persuade each side that it is the best he can do given the situation. The relationship between each contender and the go-between should therefore be *uchi* rather than *soto*, an important limitation, but as we have seen Japanese are prone to regard vertical relationships as more naturally *uchi*.

Several roles in the governmental system are well suited to mediation from above. For battles between bureaus within a ministry, the vice-minister usually plays this part easily, since he should have an appropriately close relationship (one of *senpai-kōhai*, senior-junior, as well as formal superior) with each bureau chief.[78] Intraparty battles of various sorts are often mediated by a party elder who enjoys general esteem and is not himself deeply involved in factional leadership struggles. For systemwide conflicts between party and government or between subgovernments, it is only the prime minister, aided by the chief cabinet secretary on the government side and the secretary-general and other leaders on the party side, who can be the go-between.[79]

It has often been observed that the Japanese leadership style is predominantly mediative, but it is less often noticed that this style actually can encompass a wide range of behavior and need not be passive. We might see a spectrum, for instance. At one end is the truly passive leader who lets conflicts develop on their own and simply serves as a neutral channel of communication. Perhaps he will be called in at the last moment to make a final, tiny choice that brings the conflict to an end. This pattern is often found in budgeting, where the prime minister normally just ratifies solutions actually worked out elsewhere. At the other end of the spectrum is the leader who is trying to carry out specific policy goals of his own but in effect pretends to be mediating a battle among subordinates because that style is more acceptable in Japan than a forthright top-down leadership style. Such strategies are especially characteristic of influential vice-ministers.[80]

Most interesting are the two types in between. One occurs when a leader intervenes in a dispute actively but has less interest in any substantive outcome than simply in ending the conflict. This priority is not surprising: In most organizations leaders prefer quiet to contentiousness, if only because conflict threatens the status quo from which they benefit.[81] Japanese leaders pursue this end by devoting enormous energy to rules, procedures, and schedules. Early in a dispute the leader will often urge procedures aimed at slowing things down, in hopes the contenders will eventually lose interest. If that does not work he may well switch to speeding the process along by actively arranging meetings and setting deadlines. This sort of mediator must avoid making public comments about the merits of the case; he retains leverage with both sides over procedural matters by not getting into arguments about substance. The importance of this strategy helps account for the reluctance of Japanese leaders to venture opinions on policy matters.

The other intermediate case occurs when a leader wants action of some sort but is not particularly concerned with its content. This pattern is probably crucial in the few cases when effective policy coordination is achieved. As noted above, for example, the government often responds to heavy public pressure on some issue which spans several subgovernments by establishing a coordinating body, usually in the Prime Minister's Office. Normally these bodies are not very effective, but if the prime minister is sufficiently eager to break bureaucratic inertia and achieve results, he can actively support the coordinating body and put pressure on the contending ministries and their supporters within the LDP to negotiate sincerely and reach an acceptable compromise. Tsunao Imamura's excellent study of environmental policy reveals that because of Prime Minister Satō's active involvement, the Public Nuisance Countermeasures Headquarters, which had weak formal authority and was made up of personnel drawn from the interested ministries, was actually able to establish control over ministerial press releases on pollution and ultimately helped bring about a set of legislative proposals (passed by the 1970 "Pollution Diet") that gave Japan some of the toughest environmental programs in the world.[82] These policies were not imposed unilaterally—indeed, MITI and its associated LDP dietmen, representing business, substantially modified the more radical first drafts—but the fact that so comprehensive a plan could be agreed upon so quickly is quite noteworthy.[83]

Which mediative role will be assumed depends on the personality of the leader and on the situation.[84] Prime ministers cannot be very active in many policy areas simultaneously because their time and energy are limited, and accomplishing positive results by manipulation of the go-between's role requires maintaining a close relationship with all contenders. This personal touch is hard to delegate to underlings, though a chief cabinet secretary or LDP secretary-general who is known to be close to the prime minister is very helpful. One might doubt, incidentally, if this role is likely to be institutionalized on a broader scale, along the lines of the American White House staff, since lower-level assistants would be unlikely to have sufficient clout with either officials or politicians to intervene very successfully.

Moreover, as the repeated failures to strengthen the prime minister's or cabinet's capacity to coordinate policy indicate, the ministries so far have been powerful enough to prevent even experiments which might interfere with their ability to fight their own battles.[85]

CONFLICT AVOIDANCE

The picture which emerges is that of a system with considerable conflict over policy and a rather limited capacity to resolve it: Japanese tend to rely on a set of culturally derived techniques which can be effective but have severe limitations. What happens when these are inapplicable? Again, to an appreciable though undeterminable extent, many conflicts in Japan are handled much as in other governments. One approach, found everywhere but in my view particularly prevalent in Japan, is to leave conflicts unresolved—ignored, papered over, postponed in hopes they will go away, or arbitrarily settled by imposing some mechanical and therefore acceptable decision-making rule.[86] Several strategies of conflict avoidance are especially important in Japan. I will describe them briefly.

Overlaps. Contradictions in policy and overlaps or duplications in ministerial jurisdictions and programs are often tolerated. While such overlaps occur in all governments, they appear particularly frequent in Japan, and moreover in other countries usually some sort of liaison committee is established for at least minimal coordination among the agencies involved. In Japan, often the agencies do not communicate at all—once a Welfare Ministry official asked me, as a foreign scholar, to go over to the Construction Ministry and find out what the officials there were thinking about housing for old people.[87]

Stability. Changes in policy are avoided because new initiatives arouse more controversy than leaving things as they are. That changing policy in Japan takes a long time is a journalistic commonplace, but Alan Rix, in his study of decision making in foreign aid, goes beyond this point to demonstrate how the unwillingness to risk policy conflict among the several ministries concerned in effect froze foreign aid policy into an increasingly inappropriate pattern.[88] As I have argued elsewhere, public policy as measured by the distribution of expenditures has been unusually stable in Japan. Conflict avoidance within the decision-making system is one of the major reasons.[89]

Slack. "Buying off" contenders helps to evade hard choices and reduce hostility. This has been a relatively easy tactic in Japan because high economic growth has produced large increments of governmental revenue almost every year; the decision-making system thus has a great amount of slack.[90] All ministries have been able to increase their budgets, including starting new programs even if they may be somewhat redundant, and the government has been able to indulge many demands from groups within the LDP.

Negative Coordination. As Mayantz and Scharpf observed in a study of German bureaucracy, a minimal degree of horizontal coordination can be attained without causing real conflict over goals through a lowest-common-denominator procedure.[91] Within Japanese ministries, this process has been institutionalized as the *ringisei* system, under which a policy document must be stamped as approved by each affected unit before a final decision is made.[92] Between ministries, negative coordination is even more pronounced: A ministry will often propose its new policies in the form of a report by one of its advisory councils, for example; these reports are routinely sent around to all other ministries concerned with that policy area before final approval. In both cases, the normal response to objections—or often enough to *anticipated* objections—is simply to drop the affected passage or water it down beyond recognition. References to policies or programs beyond the initiating unit's jurisdiction thus become either general platitudes or endorsements of existing policy —the result not of direct discussion but of bureaucratic paper shuffling.

Vagueness. A related point is that, as Wildavsky and Lindblom have pointed out, being any more specific about goals and policies than necessary brings "useless" conflict and delay.[93] As will be appreciated by any reader of economic plans, ministerial white papers, and LDP election platforms, Japanese bureaucrats and politicians have learned this lesson well. Sometimes the vagueness is precautionary and sometimes it is the result of earlier conflicts. As early as 1956 and at several later points, for example, the Economic Planning Agency threatened to preempt much of budgeting by specifying year-by-year sectoral government spending totals in its medium-range plans, but after brisk defensive campaigns by the Finance Ministry, the principle that only five-year aggregate projections could be included was established.[94] Within the LDP, the intensity of conflicts among groups of dietmen who support various special interests has led to policy "decisions" so general that real contradictions are often papered over; in effect, the party trades off influence over policy, which would require specific directives, in order to avoid intraparty arguments.

Encapsulation. As noted in the discussion of structure, Japanese "line" bureaucratic organization emphasizes self-reliance and precise divisions of responsibility among bureaus and sections. Conflict is avoided by minimizing interdependence and jurisdictional overlap (*within* ministries, not between). This approach extends to many problem-solving situations. Both Fukui and Okimoto have observed that when the Foreign Ministry needs a quick decision on an important issue, it organizes a "vertical work group" limited to one line of the ministry.[95] Typically its members are the vice-minister, a councillor (the ministry-level senior specialist in that policy area), a bureau chief, a section chief (plus sometimes another section chief from the same bureau), and perhaps an assistant section chief. Faced with a similar policy problem, an American department would be likelier to organize a team with members from all the bureaus concerned (and probably from other departments as well), but as the Welfare Ministry "project team" example mentioned above shows, Japanese officials believe with good reason that too much horizontal coordination will delay or even prevent decisions. Again, their assumption is that superiors and subordinates can cooperate effectively—such vertical work groups are described as informal and flexible, indicating *uchi*-style relationships—while officials of equal status from different subunits cannot. Coordination with other bureaus is usually minimal and takes place only after the basic decisions have been reached. Both useful information and consensus building are thus sacrificed in the interest of speed.

Budgeting. The most important mechanism for avoiding real conflict over policy is the budgeting system. The rules of the policy game in Japan are written to push as many decisions as possible into the budgeting routine. For example, new program initiations, major sources of policy conflict, in Japan must first be approved during the budget process. As Daichi Itō has observed, "The rules of the budget compilation process have, as they stand, necessarily come to substitute for the rules of policy decision making."[96] In other words, conflicts which in other governments would be resolved by more direct and perhaps confrontational means are defined as budgetary issues and are therefore forced into a highly institutionalized process that appears almost deliberately designed to fragment, mute, and control policy conflict.

As Wildavsky and others have demonstrated, budgeting defuses conflict by focusing attention on marginal changes, transforming issues of principle into haggling over money, encouraging horsetrading or side-payments of concessions among unrelated matters, stimulating politicians to think in terms of fragmented constituency issues, developing a network of long-term trustful relationships among contenders, and breeding a variety of mechanical decision-making rules. Particularly in Japan one also notices how the largely workaday allocation process is overlaid by a highly publicized ritual of conflict—of ministries and politicians battering at the walls of the Finance Ministry castle, defended by austere samurai examiners, to carry off some attractive program. Such ritualized conflict seems to provide psychological satisfaction (including just blowing off steam) for participants; it also allows them to gain credit with their constituencies.[97]

Budget processes actually operate quite similarly everywhere, but there is a telling difference in the way they are thought of in Japan and at least in the United States. For decades the American budgeting system has been the target of reformers trying to make decision making more rational. Cost/benefit analysis, program budgeting, the planning-programming-budgeting-system (PPBS), and more recently zero-based budgeting differ in details, but they share the objective of requiring decision makers to develop alternatives and choose among them on the basis of which contributes most to some explicit hierarchy of policy goals.[98] Since both goals and the various means for attaining them are backed by different organizational and political interests, this emphasis on rationality inevitably increases conflict over policy; indeed, in a sense that is its objective.

Japanese too worry about getting the most "bang for the buck," and they certainly have not been reluctant to experiment with new management technologies from the United States. PPBS in particular attracted attention from public administration specialists and a few Finance Ministry officials in the 1960s. There have been no serious attempts to implement any of these budget reforms, however. In fact, most adjustments to the budget process have been in the opposite direction: more widespread use of mechanical rules (such as across-the-board ceilings on requests) and decision-making criteria like "balance" that reduce the scope for real choice and therefore minimize the likelihood of conflict.

So in Japan a large proportion of policy decisions are made through budgeting, and the natural tendencies of budgetary systems to limit conflict have been institutionalized and protected, rather than attacked. These observations reinforce my point that the Japanese governmental system has been arranged in a fashion that tends to avoid direct policy conflicts which cannot be resolved by strategies of consensus or mediation.

Conclusions

The picture I have drawn of the limitations of effective conflict resolution or coordination mechanisms and the strong tendency toward
conflict avoidance in the Japanese decision-making system contrasts
sharply with the prevailing view among American scholars that Japanese policymaking is unusually well coordinated. Ezra Vogel, for
example, in *Japan as Number One*, makes much of the Japanese skill
at building consensus and resolving conflict by information gathering, *nemawashi*, and other techniques.[99] Still more recently, T. J.
Pempel, in his excellent analysis of six policy areas in comparative
perspective, concludes that "Japan emerges as having far greater consistency and continuity in its policies than other countries. Although
the primary goals of one policy have occasionally conflicted with
those of another, the Japanese experience rarely reveals the bureaucratic infighting and consequent policy disjunctures of France or Britain."[100] The reader may well be puzzled about whether the Japanese
decision-making system is, relatively speaking, quite fragmented or
unusually well coordinated.

Two caveats are needed before addressing this problem. First, in
my view the available evidence does not yet permit conclusive judgments: Comparing either decision-making processes or substantive
policy across nations is extremely difficult, and political science theory does not provide much guidance. Second, as noted above, it is
indeed true that because of constitutional arrangements, continued
conservative rule, and the high priority on economic growth, the
ideological scope and quite possibly the sheer quantity of policy conflict in Japan is lower than in other advanced nations.

Nonetheless, I maintain that significant policy conflict does occur,
and when it does there is considerably less conflict resolution than
meets the eye. Much of the appearance of consensus is precisely
because of widespread conflict avoidance, a native Japanese tendency
which had been carried to extremes because revenue growth provided
so much slack in the system. When conflict cannot be avoided, unless
one of the culturally derived techniques described above can be
brought into play, the likelihood of delay and deadlock is even
greater than in Western countries. The Japanese consensual *style* of
preferring ambiguity or silence to sharp, open argument should not
obscure real underlying conflicts in many policy processes.

Vogel, Pempel, and others maintain that effective coordination is
achieved in Japan through a variety of means—social traits like
homogeneity and personal connections within the establishment, for

example, or organizational mechanisms like the Cabinet Legislation Bureau, the Vice-Minister's Conference, and the LDP Executive Council. In surveying the literature on Japanese decision making, it is striking that such assertions are rarely supported by systematic and detailed research; in fact, most case studies indicate that coordination among agencies or conflicting interests is absent or ineffective. At the time of this writing, the inability of the government, despite intense foreign pressure and the commitment of the political leadership, to dismantle the many barriers against imports (regulations, inspection procedures) maintained by various ministries and their LDP and interest-group backers is providing yet another good example. Moreover, Japanese students of public administration have long pointed to the lack of coordination and the inability to make comprehensive policy as the most serious defects of the Japanese government. In the absence of specific process studies demonstrating successful coordination, one is disinclined to take general assertions about how well the Japanese government works at face value.

It is of course undeniable that the Japanese policymaking process has been effective in the sense that it has produced relatively good policy—national goals have consistently been achieved to a much greater extent than in other advanced nations. Can this observation be squared with my picture of creaky decision making? One answer, for which considerable support could be gathered, is that Japan's policy environment has been sufficiently benign that a good many dysfunctions do not much matter.[101] Another answer might be a speculative argument that good coordination and other characteristics of "rational" policymaking simply are not as important as Americans think.

That is to say, Japanese tend to see a policy "decision" as emerging from a complex network of relationships among individuals or institutions with conflicting interests; in their eyes the process of getting them all together to accomplish something is extraordinarily difficult. Unless one is willing to pour considerable energy into manipulating these social relationships, it is often more sensible to avoid the decision somehow. The normal American view is quite different: We see decisions as choices among sharply drawn alternatives (think of policy memoranda with the inevitable three options or those agonizing choices in the Oval Office immortalized in so many presidential memoirs); as the result of rationally organized decision-making procedures (PPBS and the like); or as the outcome of an open conflict (either the prize of total victory or a bargained compromise).

But a recent strain of American organization theory—one so far not taken very seriously by practical people—actually seems much more compatible with the Japanese than the American viewpoint on organizational process. This school includes Cyert and March's ideas about organizations as coalitions, decision-making costs, and the "quasi resolution of conflict" and perhaps even March and Olsen's "garbage can model" of decision making in "organized anarchies."[102] If this approach does offer a more realistic picture than the conventional American understanding of how organizations really work, and if Japanese managers are culturally predisposed toward this way of thinking, we have another attractive explanation of Japanese policy success, one worthy of more study.[103] The hypothesis might be that Japanese are more realistic about the limitations of complex organizations and design their processes accordingly.

This argument probably raises more questions than it settles. I can mention only a few of the most important here. First, how significant are the patterns described above? As noted above, many decision-making processes are common to all advanced nations, and it is hard to estimate what proportion of policy issues in Japan are handled by those mechanisms rather than the Japanese-style processes emphasized here. Second, to what extent is the Japanese approach to organizational conflict resolution applicable only inside Japan? Has it emerged because Japanese find vertical relationships easier than horizontal relationships, for example, or because Japanese are more willing to identify with organizations than Americans would find comfortable? Finally, are these phenomena time-bound? It might be argued that they could persist only when participation in the decision-making system is very restricted and a great deal of slack is available—that is, the period of LDP domination and high economic growth in the 1960s, from when much of my evidence is drawn.

With regard to the first two questions, I believe that the Japanese "implicit theory" is not only relevant to a fairly large proportion of policy decisions in Japan but also applicable in other cultural settings as well, though I cannot provide much empirical support for these positions. The third question, however, was tested to some extent in the late 1970s, when economic growth was much slower and the opposition parties began to penetrate the decision-making system via legislative amendments and Diet committee processes. In effect, the resources for conflict management were reduced at the same time that the likelihood of conflict was rising and its ideological range broadened. The response to these trends was interesting. First, the government borrowed money in breathtaking amounts, partly for macroeconomic reasons but also to avoid making hard policy choices. Even the highly publicized "administrative reform" campaigns of the early 1980s were more notable for an even-handed, rather mechanical approach to restraining expenditures than for anything like the highly selective budget cuts of the Reagan administration. Second, when the LDP had to deal with the opposition parties in order to get legislation through the Diet, the techniques it adopted were quite similar to those I have described—for example, considerable energy was devoted to turning the House Management Committee into a "contrived consensus."[104] These developments should increase our confidence that the Japanese approach to policy conflict is actually quite robust.

In this essay I have outlined the basic cleavage structure of the Japanese decision-making system and described some of the ways that conflicts over public policy are managed. I have not tried to provide a comprehensive picture of the Japanese policy process—that would require a discussion of additional decision-making mechanisms, consideration of the many links between the decision-making system and the broader society that I have virtually ignored here, and a dynamic analysis of the sources of policy change. I hope to take on that large project someday. Here my main concern has been with the old Japanologists' question: "What difference does 'Japaneseness' make?" My answer is that it makes considerable difference in the process of how decisions are made and, therefore, also in the substance of public policy. Moreover, although the lessons Americans learn are not always the right ones, I think that sophisticated studies of these Japanese processes can enlarge our understanding of how complex policymaking organizations work, and perhaps how they might work better.

NOTES

This study draws on research conducted in Japan under the auspices of the Fulbright Program and the Japan Foundation. It was written with support from the Center for Japanese Studies, University of Michigan, and partly during my tenure as a fellow of the Woodrow Wilson International Center for Scholars. These institutions are not responsible for my opinions. This study has been revised roughly once a year since 1976, and along the way I have benefited from suggestions by Michael Donnelly, Haruhiro Fukui, Fritz Gaenslen, Tsunao Imamura, Ellis Krauss, T. J. Pempel, Steven Reed, Michael Reich, Alan Rix, and Richard Samuels.

1. See, for example, James White, "Tradition and Politics in Studies of Contemporary Japan," *World Politics* 26 (April 1974): 400–417.

2. The formulation is by Morton Deutsch, *The Resolution of Conflict: Constructive and Destructive Processes* (New Haven: Yale University Press, 1973). Chalmers Johnson remarks that "norms of consensus have developed primarily as a way of overcoming the ever-present dangers of deadlock among Japan's highly competitive groups"; see "MITI and Japanese International Economic Policy," in Robert A. Scalapino, ed., *The Foreign Policy of Modern Japan* (Berkeley: University of California Press, 1977), p. 231.

3. See Lewis Coser, *The Functions of Social Conflict* (New York: Free Press, 1956).

4. A major theme of T. J. Pempel, *Policy and Politics in Japan: Creative Conservatism* (Philadelphia: Temple University Press, 1982).

5. See chap. 10 of my *Contemporary Japanese Budget Politics* (Berkeley: University of California Press, 1977) for the importance of goal consensus inside and outside the decision-making system.

6. Philip Selznick, *TVA and the Grass Roots* (Berkeley: University of California Press, 1949), is an early source; since then organizational conflict has been variously emphasized by James G. March and Herbert A. Simon, *Organizations* (New York: Wiley, 1958); Richard Cyert and James G. March, *A Behavioral Theory of the Firm* (Englewood Cliffs, N.J.: Prentice-Hall, 1963); Victor Thompson, *Modern Organization* (New York: Knopf, 1964); James D. Thompson, *Organizations in Action* (New York: McGraw-Hill, 1967); Lewis Gawthorpe, *Bureaucratic Behavior in the Executive Branch* (New York: Free Press, 1969); P. R. Lawrence and J. W. Lorsch, *Organization and Environment: Managing Differentiation and Integration* (Homewood, Ill.: Irwin, 1969); Meyer N. Zald, ed., *Power in Organizations* (Nashville: Vanderbilt University Press, 1970); Koya Azumi and Jerald Hage, eds., *Organizational Systems* (Lexington, Mass.: Heath, 1972); and Robert Presthus, *The Organizational Society*, rev. ed. (New York: St. Martin's Press, 1978).

7. See James D. Thompson, "Organizational Management of Conflict," *Administrative Science Quarterly* 4 (March 1960): 391–403.

8. Akira Kimimura, "Sutaffu to Rainu," in Kiyoaki Tsuji, ed., *Gyōseigaku Kōza*, vol. 2, *Gyōsei to Soshiki* (Tokyo: Tokyo University Press, 1976), pp. 83–125.

9. The importance of physical propinquity is emphasized by Cyril Sofer, *Organizations in Theory and Practice* (New York: Basic Books, 1972), p. 359.

10. See Campbell, *Budget Politics*, pp. 47–49, for several citations.

11. Johnson, "MITI."

12. For Japanese personnel practices see Akira Kubota, *Higher Civil Servants in Postwar Japan* (Princeton: Princeton University Press, 1969); for the importance of socialization in Japanese organizations, see Thomas P. Rohlen, *For Harmony and Strength* (Berkeley: University of California Press, 1974); and for socialization in governmental bureaucracies generally, see Gawthorpe, *Bureaucratic Behavior*, chap. 6.

13. Daniel I. Okimoto, "Ideas, Intellectuals and Institutions: National Security and the Question of Nuclear Armament in Japan," Ph.D. dissertation, Department of Political Science, University of Michigan, 1978, p. 418.

14. See, for example, Michio Muramatsu, *Gyōseigaku Kōgi* (Tokyo: Aobayashi, 1977), p. 16.

15. For more details see Nathaniel B. Thayer, *How the Conservatives Rule Japan* (Princeton: Princeton University Press, 1969); Haruhiro Fukui, *Party in Power: The Liberal Democrats and Policy Making* (Berkeley: University of California Press, 1970); and Campbell, *Budget Politics*, chap. 5.

16. Standard treatments of American subgovernments include J. Leiper Freeman,

The Policy Process: Executive Bureau-Legislative Committee Relations, rev. ed. (New York: Random House, 1965); and Randall B. Ripley and Grace A. Franklin, *Congress, the Bureaucracy and Public Policy* (Homewood, Ill.: Dorsey Press, 1976). See also the critical treatment by Hugh Heclo, "Issue Networks and the Executive Establishment," in Anthony King, ed., *The New American Political System* (Washington, D.C.: American Enterprise Institute, 1978), pp. 87–124, and a rebuttal by H. Brinton Milward and Gary T. Wamsley, "Policy Networks: Key Concept at a Critical Juncture," paper delivered to the annual meeting of the Midwest Political Science Association, Chicago, 19–21 April 1979.

17. Yung H. Park, "Party-Bureaucratic Relations in Japan: The Case of the Ministry of Education," *Waseda Journal of Asian Studies* 1 (1979). For an account of ministerial variation in contact with parties and groups, see Michio Muramatsu, "Gyōsei Kanryō no Katsudō Taiyō," *Kikan Gyōsei Kanri Kenkyū* 12 (4) (1978): 10–23.

18. See William E. Steslicke, *Doctors in Politics: The Political Life of the Japan Medical Association* (New York: Praeger, 1973).

19. Note that during the period of near parity between the LDP and opposition in the Diet, differential support from opposition parties became an important factor— for example, in advancing housing policy (particularly public housing) compared with LDP-supported river and highway projects. Interviews in the Ministry of Construction, 1980.

20. Margaret A. McKean, "Pollution and Policymaking," in T. J. Pempel, ed., *Policymaking in Contemporary Japan* (Ithaca: Cornell University Press, 1976), pp. 201–238.

21. Haruhiro Fukui, "The GATT Tokyo Round: The Bureaucratic Politics of Multilateral Diplomacy," in Michael Blaker, ed., *The Politics of Trade* (New York: Occasional Papers of the East Asian Institute, Columbia University, 1978), pp. 75–169.

22. See I. M. Destler et al., *Managing an Alliance* (Washington, D.C.: Brookings Institution, 1978).

23. Joel D. Aberbach, Robert D. Putnam, and Bert A. Rockman, *Bureaucrats and Politicians in Western Democracies* (Cambridge, Mass.: Harvard University Press, 1981), p. 3, and many citations therein.

24. See Haruhiro Fukui, "Studies in Policymaking: A Review of the Literature," in Pempel, *Policymaking*, pp. 22–59.

25. However, the *relative* power balance between bureaucrats and politicians can usefully be compared both across nations and across time; for the latter, see my *Budget Politics*, chap. 9.

26. Aberbach, Putnam, and Rockman, *Bureaucrats*, discuss the implications of such differences for Western Europe and the United States; Michio Muramatsu does so for Japan in *Sengo Nihon no Kanryōsei* (Tokyo: Tōyō Keizai Shinbunsha, 1981).

27. One such case is described in my "Compensation for Repatriates," in Pempel, *Policymaking*, pp. 103–142.

28. Kubota, *Higher Civil Servants*, p. 85.

29. Richard Samuels and Michael Reich pointed out the increasing importance of such groupings in personal communications.

30. Albert M. Craig, "Functional and Dysfunctional Aspects of Japanese Bureaucracy," in Ezra Vogel, ed., *Modern Japanese Organization and Decision Making* (Berkeley: University of California Press, 1976), pp. 3–32; Yasuharu Honda, *Nihon Neokanryōron* (Tokyo: Kodansha, 1975), p. 95.

31. That was not the case in prewar Japan, when the cross-ministerial faction of

revisionist "new bureaucrats" had a substantial impact on policymaking. See Robert M. Spaulding, "The Bureaucracy as a Political Force," in James William Morley, ed., *Dilemmas of Growth in Prewar Japan* (Princeton: Princeton University Press, 1971), pp. 33–80.

32. Johnson, "MITI"; T. J. Pempel, *Patterns in Japanese Policymaking: Experiences from Higher Education* (Boulder, Colo.: Westview, 1978), pp. 117–118.

33. The process is called *nemawashi*, which an American bureaucrat would call "getting his ducks in a row." See Ezra Vogel, *Japan as Number One* (Cambridge, Mass.: Harvard University Press, 1979), pp. 93–96. For a theoretical account of such coalition formation, see Samuel B. Bacharach and Edward J. Lawler, *Power and Politics in Organizations* (San Francisco: Jossey-Bass, 1980).

34. See, for example, Presthus, *Organizational Society*, p. 21.

35. J. Thompson, *Action*, p. 139ff.

36. Yasuo Watanabe, "Kōmuin to Kyaria," in Tsuji, *Gyōsei to Soshiki*, pp. 189–207.

37. Fukui, *Party in Power*, and "Tanaka Goes to Peking," in Pempel, *Policymaking*, pp. 80–102.

38. J. Victor Koschmann, "Hawks on the Defensive: The Seirankai," *Japan Interpreter* 8 (4) (Winter 1978): 467–475.

39. Note, however, that the Taiwan and South Korea debates in the LDP are flavored by interest representation as well, and the economic foreign policy process often resembles that for domestic policy.

40. Donald C. Hellmann, *Japan in East Asia: The New International Order* (New York: Praeger, 1972), and *Japanese Foreign Policy and Domestic Politics* (Berkeley: University of California Press, 1969); George R. Packard III, *Protest in Tokyo* (Princeton: Princeton University Press. 1966).

41. Ralf Dahrendorf, *Class and Class Conflict in Industrial Society* (Stanford: Stanford University Press, 1959).

42. See particularly V. Thompson, *Modern Organization*, pp. 92–101, and Gawthorpe, *Bureaucratic Behavior*.

43. Chie Nakane, *Japanese Society* (Berkeley: University of California Press, 1970).

44. For the American cleavage, see Hugh Heclo, *Government of Strangers* (Washington, D.C.: Brookings Institution, 1977). Anthony Downs emphasizes the importance of the promotion system in defining organizational loyalty: *Inside Bureaucracy* (Boston: Little, Brown, 1967), pp. 211–212.

45. Haruhiro Fukui, "Policy Making in the Japanese Foreign Ministry," in Scalapino, *Foreign Policy*, p. 28.

46. However, see also Terry MacDougall, ed., *Leadership in Contemporary Japan* (Ann Arbor: Michigan Papers in Japanese Studies, 1982).

47. In fact, Nakasone's intervention was seen as heavy-handed by officials and he did not have much impact; Okimoto, "Ideas," p. 400.

48. Kenneth A. Skinner, "Conflict and Command in a Public Corporation in Japan," *Journal of Japanese Studies* 6 (Summer 1980): 301–330.

49. As Susan Pharr points out, the secession of the New Liberal Club was a product of this cleavage, overlapped by a gap in values; see "Liberal Democrats in Disarray: Intergenerational Conflict in the Conservative Camp over the Nature of Political Leadership," in MacDougall, *Leadership*.

50. Backbencher campaigns to support rice farmers, expropriated landlords, and repatriates are three cases in point. See Michael Donnelly's essay in this volume; see also Fukui, *Party in Power*, chap. 7, and Campbell, "Compensation."

51. See Robert E. Cole, "The Theory of Institutionalization: Permanent Employment and Tradition in Japan," *Economic Development and Cultural Change* 20 (October 1971): 47–70; and *Work, Mobility and Participation* (Berkeley: University of California Press, 1979), chap. 1. Cole's analysis of the manipulation of cultural symbols to legitimate management power is probably also relevant to the development of bureaucratic organization. Although Eleanor Westney's current research on Meiji-period organizational borrowing does not include the central government ministries and does not explicitly address the "cultural hypothesis," its case studies offer fascinating starting points for analysis along these lines.

52. Simple inertia is another explanation, but in other contexts the Japanese have been quick to adopt organizational innovations; see Cole, *Work*, chap. 5.

53. A major theme of this literature is the stress on close identification of "members" with the firm and participatory management: "We saw how the boss-subordinate relationship encourages a degree of effective coordination that we might envy"; Richard Tanner Pascale and Anthony G. Astos, *The Art of Japanese Management* (New York: Simon and Schuster, 1981), p. 204.

54. That is, they serve the interests of the superior ministries and as such might be compared with suppliers and subsidiaries of large firms as dependent or even exploited organizations. See Rodney Clark, *The Japanese Company* (New Haven: Yale University Press, 1979), pp. 64–73.

55. Takie Sugiyama Lebra, *Japanese Patterns of Behavior* (Honolulu: University Press of Hawaii, 1976), p. 3. As she notes, this observation pervades the literature on Japanese national character. The threefold typology is from Talcott Partsons, *The Social System* (Glencoe, Ill.: Free Press, 1951).

56. Lebra, *Patterns*, pp. 4, 14, 38–43. Robert Marshall provides a provocative exchange-theory explanation for these traits in "Collective Decision Making in Rural Japan," Ph.D. dissertation, Department of Anthropology, University of Pittsburgh, 1981.

57. *Saints and Samurai* (New Haven: Yale University Press, 1965). Austin's observations are too extensive and subtle to summarize easily, but many relate interestingly to my arguments.

58. See, for example, Robert E. Ward, "Japan: The Continuity of Modernization," in Lucian Pye, ed., *Political Culture and Political Development*, (Princeton: Princeton University Press, 1965), pp. 61–62.

59. Austin, *Saints*, pp. 131–135. Social-psychological small-group research provides experimental support for this view. For an interesting discussion that refers briefly to Japan, see Fritz Gaenslen, "Democracy vs. Efficiency: The Consensual-Adversarial Dimension of Small Group Decision-Making," *Political Psychology* 1 (1980).

60. March and Simon, *Organizations*, pp. 129–130.

61. See his essay in this volume. Chie Nakane's notion of "frame" *(ba)* is an institutionalized manifestation of *uchi*; see *Society*, chap. 1, and Lebra, *Patterns*, chap. 2.

62. Which is not at all to say that hierarchy and tensions are absent. See Rohlen, *For Harmony and Strength*, chap. 4, and Hiram James McLendon, "Sōgō Shosha:

Social Structure and Sociocultural Process and Change in a Japanese General Trading Company," Ph.D. dissertation, Department of Anthropology, Harvard University, 1979.

63. Compare Austin, *Saints*, p. 34: "In Japanese political culture, the relation of superior and subordinate is ideally no more formal and no less intimate than the relationship of friends, lovers, or members of a family."

64. Campbell, *Budget Politics*, pp. 53, 61. For a similar analysis of vertical relations in Japanese firms, see Richard Pascale and William Ouchi, "Made in America (Under Japanese Management)," *Harvard Business Review* 5 (1974): 61–69; but see also Pascale's "Communication and Decision Making Across Cultures: Japanese and American Comparisons," *Administrative Science Quarterly* 23 (April 1978): 91–110.

65. Some theorists have made similar points in criticizing American organizational practice. See, for example, Gawthorpe (quoting Murray Horowitz): "As long as the individual is satisfied that a proper degree of deference has been granted to his point of view by organizational superiors, his hostility reaction will, in all probability, be minimal if his superiors do not accept his judgement"; *Bureaucratic Behavior*, p. 42.

66. Vogel, *Number One*. Many examples of blocked or conflictive horizontal communication in private firms, Rohlen, *Harmony*, and especially McLendon, "Sōgō Shosha."

67. Take, for example, the report of the Rinji Gyōsei Chōsakai in 1964; see the discussion in Muramatsu, *Gyōseigaku*, p. 167ff.

68. Fukui, "GATT," p. 119.

69. Campbell, "Repatriates," gives an example of this process, which stems from the fact that heavy constituency pressure, or high "accountability" of representatives, tends to reduce flexibility in negotiations. See Deutsch, *Resolution*, and J. A. Rubin and B. R. Brown, *The Social Psychology of Bargaining and Negotiation* (New York: Academic Press, 1975).

70. See Michael Donnelly's essay in this volume.

71. Young Ho Park, "The Governmental Advisory System in Japan," *Journal of Comparative Administration* 3 (February 1972): 435–467.

72. Note that the American White House staff, which has similar functions, is much larger and therefore more capable of devising and analyzing policy on its own. Also most of its members are not subject to the personnel systems of the departments they are supposed to be coordinating.

73. Watanabe, "Kōmuin." However, control over posts in these agencies can become a bone of contention between ministries—as, for example, the MITI and Finance Ministry disputes over the EPA in the 1960s. See Johnson, "MITI," pp. 237–244.

74. This agency is old enough for its own officials (the "agency economists") to be reaching leadership seniority, giving them an increasing voice in policy disputes and creating tricky personnel problems. See "Keikichō Tekunokuraato no Ishiki to Kōdō," *Tōyō Keizai* (25 July 1970): 31–35.

75. The result was to leave the decision up to the LDP, which resulted in a decision more generous than any of the four bureaus wanted. See my article, "The 'Old People Boom' and Japanese Policy Making," *Journal of Japanese Studies* 5 (Summer 1979): 321–357.

76. Interviews in the Ministry of Health and Welfare, 1980.

77. See Dan Fenno Henderson, *Conciliation and Japanese Law: Tokugawa and Modern* (Seattle: University of Washington Press, 1965).

78. His go-between role is more difficult if the ministry is split by personal or ideological cleavages. For a similar analysis of management as mediation using *sempai-kōhai* relationships, see McLendon, "Sōgō Shosha," p. 312ff.

79. When two ministries are involved in a conflict of insufficient importance to draw in the prime minister, their two ministers can often get together and work out the problem, particularly if they are members of the same LDP faction or have some other personal tie.

80. When Yoshihisa Ojimi became vice-minister of MITI, he set three goals: reformulating trade and industry policy, reforming the patent system, and establishing the information industry. He said that all three were accomplished. See his "A Government Ministry: The Case of the Ministry of International Trade and Industry," in Vogel, *Organization*, pp. 101–112.

81. Presthus, *Organizational Society*, p. 43.

82. Tsunao Imamura, "Soshiki no Bunka to Kōsō," in Tsuji, *Gyōsei to Soshiki*, pp. 183–187.

83. Also see Steven R. Reed, "Environmental Politics: Some Reflections Based on the Japanese Case," *Comparative Politics* (April 1981): 253–270. It is interesting that the later Environmental Agency, which had far greater formal authority than the Countermeasures Headquarters but was less enthusiastically supported by the prime minister, was much less effective in overcoming ministry resistence and coordinating antipollution policy. See Imamura, "Soshiki."

84. For "brokerage" by two Japanese prime ministers, see Kent Calder, "Kanryō vs. Shomin: Contrasting Dynamics of Conservative Leadership in Postwar Japan," in MacDougall, *Leadership*.

85. Toyoharu Ikeda, *Gyōsei Kaikaku no Rekishi to Kadai* (Tokyo: Kyōikusha, 1979).

86. See Ide Yoshinori, "Gyōsei Kokka to Tekunokurashii," in Masamichi Inoki and Nobuhiko Kamikawa, eds., *Gendai Nihon no Seiji* (Tokyo: Ushio Shuppansha, 1969), pp. 276–303. See also Austin, *Saints*, p. 134.

87. I should note that "slivered administration" *(tatewari gyōsei)* at the national level is often balanced by reasonably effective coordination at the local level, where governments are somewhat less fragmented (partly due to a unified personnel system). See Steven R. Reed, "Is Japanese Government Really Centralized?," *Journal of Japanese Studies* 8 (1) (Winter 1982): 133–164; and Richard J. Samuels, *Localities Incorporated? The Politics of Regional Policy in Japan* (Princeton: Princeton University Press, 1983).

88. Alan Rix, *Japanese Economic Aid* (New York: St. Martin's Press, 1980).

89. See my "Japanese Budget *Baransu*," in Vogel, *Organization*, pp. 71–100.

90. See Cyert and March, *Behavioral Theory*, and, more generally, Lester Thurow, *The Zero-Sum Society* (New York: Basic Books, 1980).

91. Renete Mayantz and Fritz W. Scharpf, *Policy Making in the German Federal Bureaucracy* (Amsterdam: Elsevier, 1975), p. 147.

92. See Kiyoaki Tsuji, "Decision-making in the Japanese Government," in Ward, *Political Development*, pp. 457–476, and Austin, *Saints*, pp. 127–128. *Ringisei* is not a mechanism for making major decisions; see Vogel's "Introduction" to his *Organization*, pp. xvii–xviii, and Muramatsu, *Gyōseigaku*, pp. 183–187.

93. Aaron Wildavsky, *Budgeting: A Comparative Theory of Budgetary Processes* (Boston: Little, Brown, 1975); Charles Lindblom, *The Intelligence of Democracy* (New York: Free Press, 1965).

94. Similar battles over five-year work plans were fought with several ministries; see Campbell, *Budget Politics*, chap. 8.

95. Fukui, "Foreign Ministry"; Okimoto, "Ideas," p. 377ff.

96. Daichi Itō, "The Bureaucracy: Its Attitudes and Behavior," *Developing Economics* 6 (December 1968): 446–467.

97. Wildavsky, *Budgeting*; Campbell, *Budget Politics*, chap. 7; Thomas J. Anton, "Roles and Symbols in the Determinance of State Expenditures," in James W. Davis, ed., *Politics, Programs and Budgets*, (Englewood Cliffs, N.J.: Prentice-Hall, 1969); and Akira Kojima, "Gendai Yosan Seiji Shiron," in Ken Taniuchi et al., eds., *Gendai Gyōsei to Kanryosei* (Tokyo: Tokyo Daigaku Shuppankai, 1974), vol. 2.

98. The literature on PPBS and such reforms is extensive; see Robert D. Lee, Jr., and Ronald W. Johnson, *Public Budgeting Systems* (Baltimore: University Park Press, 1973).

99. Vogel, *Number One*, chaps. 3–5.

100. Pempel, *Policy and Politics*, p. 306.

101. This theme ran through much of the writing on Japan before it was seen as "number one"; see, for example, White, "Tradition and Politics," and Zbigniew Brzezinski, *The Fragile Blossom* (New York: Harper & Row, 1972).

102. The seminal work is Cyert and March, *Behavioral Theory*; see also James March and Johan Olsen, eds., *Ambiguity and Choice* (Bergen: Universitetsforlaget, 1976). The implications of this approach for political decision making at the national level have not been fully explored, but Lindblom's critiques of the "syncretic" model and the "bureaucratic politics" approach to foreign policy are suggestive. See Lindblom, *Intelligence*, and Graham Allison, *Essence of Decision* (Boston: Little, Brown, 1971).

103. Rodney Clark similarly observes that "the decision-making process in Japanese companies probably recognizes the existence of such a [Cyert and March-type] coalition, and the need for a variable and politically determined set of aims, rather more clearly than in the American and British company." See *The Japanese Company* (New Haven: Yale University Press, 1979), p. 136.

104. See Ellis Krauss's essay in this volume. Incidentally, Krauss's observation that this Japanese behavior is compatible with recent, nonconventional political science theories of parliamentary conflict management is parallel to my argument about Japanese organizational behavior and recent organizational theory.

12

*Conflict over
Government Authority
and Markets:
Japan's Rice Economy*

MICHAEL W. DONNELLY

Of all the divisive issues in Japanese agricultural policy, the most persistent and fundamental in this century have been those related to
state involvement in the rice economy. The country's most important
agricultural commodity has been too closely linked to income standards, national power, and political order to permit exclusion of the
rice trade from some kind of public control. Rice has rarely flowed
from producer to consumer simply in accordance with the whimsy
and free play of unregulated markets. Indeed, except for a rare period
following the Meiji Restoration (1868), the rice economy has been
tangled in a web of government rules and requirements since at least
1600.[1] The nature of this web has rarely failed to prompt some kind
of political conflict—that is, "a struggle over values or claims to
power and resources."[2]

This study investigates the issue of conflict in Japan by examining
aspects of rice politics which represent specific instances of a more
fundamental subject in political economy: conflict generated by
simultaneous attempts to employ political and economic ways of
organizing market activities.[3] Government is important in the rice
economy because of the economic activities it engages in—the prices
it sets, the regulations it promulgates, the subsidies it provides, the
controls it exerts, and thus the conflict it can create.

The Rice Economy Through the Prism of Conflict

The essential division concerning rice policies has been a collision of
views concerning the purpose and functioning of the food-control
system *(shokuryō kanri seido)* during a period of surplus production.
Control for many years meant protection of consumers at the expense

of producers. Rice farmers were "coerced" into selling to the government at cheap prices. By the 1960s, however, food control had come
to mean subsidies, administrative privileges, income security, social
welfare, and general economic support for the most important sector
of the rural economy. The regulated had gained control over the regulatory process. Stated differently, rice farmers and agricultural cooperatives had become political wards of the state.[4]

According to most standards of judgment, organization of the rice
economy through state authority had become highly irrational and
excessively costly by the late 1960s. Japan's farmers were producing
an unprecedented surplus at a time when aggregate and per capita
demand were falling. Official deficits connected with control costs
and inventories reached record levels. High producer prices fostered
marginal farming and discouraged part-time producers from leaving
agriculture, a necessary development in a period of agricultural surplus and rapid industrial growth. The "controlled market" was in
disarray—a "free market" flourished outside the law and official
direction. High producer prices had provided a stable source of
income to farmers during a period of rapid economic growth which
began in 1955. But government generosity had also imposed a serious
maladjustment in the country's agricultural sector.[5]

Abundance and associated economic problems thus produced new
dimensions of economic and political feasibility. Many of the premises of control no longer existed. The long-term outlook for production was favorable. A national capacity to maintain self-sufficiency in
rice was no longer in doubt. If supply and demand were brought into
a rough balance, then prices would stabilize without excessive government interference. Experts believed that a well-ordered, indirectly
controlled market was more appropriate than meddlesome interference and unenforced laws. The international outlook for food was
good, the country had funds to pay for necessary imports, precious
land was needed for industrial development, and there was no danger
of war in the Far East. The time seemed propitious to start reducing
the size of a huge administrative system and to let the market rather
than government provide proper economic signals to a client farm
group benefiting substantially from artificially inflated agricultural
prices.[6]

Rice farmers and organized agriculture did not willingly accept the
notion that a desirable mode of carrying out economic activities could
be created outside a network of government control. Farm groups
and their political allies strongly opposed any move toward unfet-

tered commerce based on marketplace ideologies. They preferred to take their chances on political conflicts within controlled markets to commercial competition prompted by an unregulated market. Moreover, few farmers were prepared to abandon production of the country's most profitable agricultural commodity in favor of uncertain ventures in commercial farming. In such a way, then, the conflict was joined.

The food-control system was not abolished after 1968. The rice market did not suddenly become a natural and self-adjusting economy, working providentially without official aid and concern. Considerable effort was made by state officials to modify the political market in the direction of economic competition. Nonetheless, after a decade of tinkering and adjustment, the problem of what to do about rice remains on the political agenda. Government deficits generated by market operations are still substantial, prices remain extremely high despite a decline in demand and an abundance of supply, and other agricultural programs are consequently distorted. The rural economy is still maladjusted and many critics argue that the source of the dilemma remains the irrational, ill-advised, and opportunistic use of government authority by farm groups and their political allies within the Liberal Democratic Party (LDP) and elsewhere.[7]

The old aphorism that "the more things change, the more they stay the same" would therefore seem apt. But such an assumption is misleading. Procedures of government intervention have changed. Subsidies are being spent for new purposes. Fewer farmers are cultivating rice. More commercial interests are involved in the rice trade. The government is less involved and purchases less rice. A smaller proportion of the budget for agriculture goes now to "rice control." For two decades rice politics and conflict had been linked most essentially to pricing disputes within a controlled market. Now politics and policy are fractionated into new patterns of control and conflict. The period under examination thus marks a transition between different rule structures and economic relationships and therefore a new pattern of political tension and conflict management in agrarian politics.

Policy has involved three somewhat overlapping areas of decision and political interaction which will be used here as comparative cases for analysis:

1. Annual income adjustments through *price fixing*
2. Regulation by means of *market* programs
3. Industrial restructuring through *land diversion*

The task, then, is to explain the ebb and flow of conflict and cooperation in the three issue areas—the visibility, intensity, and extent of
conflict; the site for major political encounters; and the interplay of
political and economic conflict.

We lack an integrated theoretical model for explaining a conflict or
the policymaking process in which economic and political goals are
contradictory, although there are lots of tentative, middle-range hypotheses.[8] The premise of this study is that a limited number of structural and behavioral elements go a long way toward explaining not
only why there is so much disagreement in Japan about rice programs
but, more important, how conflict in these three cases can best be
understood. These elements are:

1. *The economic setting:* the nature of rural transformation and the
   public issues created by a "crisis of abundance" within a weak
   and declining economic sector
2. *General relations among the major actors:* their numbers, institutional positions, political resources, vested interests, and goals
3. *The nature of the three issues:* costs and benefits to the parties
   involved and the intensity of disagreement about them
4. *Complexity of choice and implementation:* the possibilities for
   political and economic trade-offs and the character of public
   authority required to implement a decision or program
5. *The decision process:* incentives for encouraging or discouraging
   conflict, tactics for thwarting or controlling the behavior of
   others, and different ways of handling conflict
6. *Conflict consequences:* the content of major decisions terminating the conflict, the perception of winners and losers, and the
   effect of the decision on the rice economy and subsequent political decisions

Since these elements are interrelated in complex ways, assessing
their importance in a specific case is extremely difficult. In all cases,
however, conflict has been produced by the threat of government-
sponsored change. Thus the interplay of conflict and cooperation
found in each of the policy areas is principally, but not completely,
determined by the manner and degree to which government officials
and politicians have sought to force the rice economy into a new patterned system reflecting the theoretical logic of economic competition. I begin, then, with discussion of the first two elements involved
in agrarian political conflict; thereafter I take up the other aspects of

the conflict process in a brief case study of each of the three subareas of rice policy. The final section offers some broad judgments based on the cases at hand.

Economic Environment and the Issues at Stake

Conflict around rice programs must first be placed against the background of an overall decline in the importance of the agrarian sector. The economic position of agriculture in all advanced economies, relative to other economic sectors, has deteriorated over the past twenty years. Agriculture is a declining sector in the sense that it provides a diminishing percentage of total national employment opportunities for national resources including land, labor, and capital. The resulting deterioration has been defined variously as the farm problem, price problem, income problem, or size problem.[9] These all represent facets of a general inability of the sector as a whole, or of individual farm households, to adjust to new economic, social, and even political conditions.

A few statistics of the most routine kind can sketch the picture of change in Japanese agriculture during the past three decades.[10] Agriculture's contribution to net national product fell from 17.4 percent in 1955 to 5.0 percent in 1975. The number of people engaged in agriculture within the total working population dropped from 33.8 to 11 percent in the same period. In 1955 about 260,000 new school graduates (the main source of farm labor) turned to farming. In 1975 only 10,000 graduates selected agriculture as a vocation. The number of farm households dropped from 6,176,000 in 1950 to 4,835,000 in 1977. Thus the ratio of rural to urban dwellers almost reversed during the same period from about 62.38 to 30.70. In 1950 about 50 percent of all farm households were classified as full-time. In 1977 only about 13 percent were full-time.

The proportion of full-time agricultural households has declined steadily because small farms do not provide adequate incomes in a wealthy society. About 9 percent of all households are considered "viable" in the sense of providing the family with an adequate agricultural income. In 1977 about 67 percent of all farm households earned over half their total income from nonagricultural employment. This category of part-time households cultivates about 40 percent of all agricultural land. In 1975 more than 70 percent of those engaged in farming were either men over sixty years of age or women. Women make up over 50 percent of the total labor force. Most part-time farms are run by grandparents, wives, and children. This part-time farm structure has clearly limited productivity gains, impeded the enlargement of farm scale, and created grave doubts about the core work force in the future.

A dramatic change in food demand occurred during the country's recent period of unprecedented economic expansion. Consumption of meat, eggs, fruit, and dairy products rose while consumption of staples such as rice declined. Requirements for livestock feed almost quadrupled within two decades. Domestic production did not keep up with this increase and change in demand. Some agricultural land was swallowed up by urban sprawl. The total amount of cultivated land thus fell from 6,004,000 hectares in 1965 to 5,515,000 in 1977. Gross cultivated land decreased ever more drastically as farmers all but abandoned second-cropping in favor of work outside agriculture. The cropping ratio of cultivated land dropped from 123 percent in 1965 to 103 percent in 1976. According to Fred Sanderson, Japan's food self-sufficiency, measured in terms of original food energy, was 80 percent in 1955 and 51 percent in 1972.[11] There has been no improvement since then. Agricultural products account for about 15 percent of all imports. Japan is the world's largest single importer of food and takes more seafood from the world's oceans than any other country.

Statistics just begin to tell the story of a very complex period of economic and social change.[12] Farmers in Japan are as skillful and resourceful as any in the world. Overall standards of living have improved markedly in most rural areas. Unprecedented achievements have been made in improving rice cultivation. But new technology has not been accompanied by an enlargement of the scale of management. Production costs have not declined. Agricultural production and productivity have improved for many commodities, but overall improvement has not matched that achieved in other sectors of the economy.

It is hard to find an economist or other professional commentator who is especially optimistic about the viability of Japanese agriculture. The dominant and recurring themes suggest that farms are too small, land is insufficient, the population is too large, incomes are uncertain and unpredictable, food prices are the highest in the world, growth in food production is unbalanced, pollution in many rural areas has become a major problem, and the country is excessively dependent on foreign sources of supply.

What the government has been able to do about the future has been directly connected to the rice economy since the structure of agriculture and the content of policies, including especially income-support programs, are so strongly linked to the country's most important agricultural commodity. The debate over the food-control system has been circumscribed. No important voice has been heard advocating complete government withdrawal from the marketplace. Price and market stability are too crucial to rural well-being to permit any massive infusion of free market forces. An adequate supply of rice is also considered a public responsibility, like provision of education or creation of a public transportation system. Moreover, the prices of all food commodities in Japan are subject to some kind of official intervention in the form of deficiency payments, subsidies, or direct purchase.[13] Nevertheless, debate has led to considerable disagreement since several generic issues are present which easily foster sharp social and political differences.

Government decisions prompt disagreement, discontent, and anger because they impinge on various political and economic values in different ways. The following contradictory, but valid, arguments are given varying importance by those participating in decisions or by individuals and groups who exert influence inside or outside the government:[14]

1. High producer prices enhance farm equity; but high prices mean the consumer will pay more, place heavy demands on the public treasury, add to inflation, encourage a surplus but discourage consumption, and distort the priorities of other agricultural policies.
2. Import restrictions help protect a vulnerable domestic industry and enhance national self-sufficiency; but protection can be costly and discourages appropriate trade policies based on theories of free trade and comparative advantages.
3. A "cheap rice" policy for consumers can aid economic growth by providing a necessary product at low prices; but cheap prices go against values of farm equity, discourage production of high-quality rice, anger farmers and farm-group leaders, and provide the opposition political parties with an issue at the next election.
4. Less regulation in markets pleases cost-conscious officials in the Ministry of Finance and permits more private profit in trade; but an open market weakens the bargaining power of small-scale

farmers, makes rice an object of speculation, and restricts the Ministry of Agriculture in its efforts to assure stable and reasonable prices.

Government actions thus flow in different directions. The scope, substance, and impact of various actions are usually different. Conflict can occur because a diversity of goals and values must be reconciled before a policy decision is reached. Conflict comes to the fore also because of disagreement about (1) the effects of various programs for achieving goals or values, (2) the sacrifices required from different individuals and groups, (3) the allocation of benefits, and (4) the rules for economic and political competition. Contending individuals and groups thus make claims for public action or inaction which are perceived in some way as advancing their interests over others.

General Relations Among the Antagonists

The character of conflict depends also on the number, location, and relations of individuals and groups who are connected by interest or who hold specific views. Conflicts intensify to the extent that institutions and political relations force people into antagonistic camps. In fact, political arrangements in connection with rice policies are somewhat loose; individuals and groups have not concentrated around two poles, even though the bias of general arrangements does favor producers. For purposes of analysis, the antagonists are divided into three groups: producers and consumers, petitioners and advisers, and the proximate decision makers.

PRODUCERS AND CONSUMERS

Of Japan's 4.8 million farm households, about 4 million produce some rice,[15] and about three-quarters of these market at least part of their crop. According to the 1977 white paper on agriculture, 60 percent of all farm households producing rice are classified as part-time and depend mainly on nonagricultural income.

Rice farmers are well organized, maintain regular communication among themselves, and share a high sense of solidarity because of their essential homogeneity. They also believe that they share a common fate because the government is their most reliable customer: The food-control system gives them a collective identity which an open market would never provide. Consumers, on the other hand, are weakly organized, have no strong collective identity, and experience the problem of high rice prices only as part of more general issues like inflation and wage levels.

PETITIONERS AND ADVISERS

Between producers and consumers of rice and proximate decision makers is an intervening structure of individuals and groups who claim to express the economic and political interests of various segments of the rice economy.[16] They do not make government decisions, but their petitions and advice are taken into account.

Farm Groups. The most important farm group connected with the food-control system is the Association of Agricultural Cooperatives (Nōgyō Kyōdō Kumiai, hereafter Nōgyō).[17] In structural terms the cooperative system displays many institutional traits characteristic of corporatist ties which link interest groups and government in capitalist societies.[18] Over ten thousand separate unit cooperatives throughout the countryside handle 94 percent of all rice marketed each year and are organized roughly in a pyramidlike fashion into a number of hierarchically arranged economic and administrative federations at the prefectural and national level. The cooperative system is fundamentally a creature of the government and retains political rights to "functional representation" in national policymaking. The relationship between the nation's most significant farm group and state officials is one of reciprocal influence since government ministries rely heavily on the cooperatives as an administrative mechanism and political means to organize the rural sector behind national policy. The rice lobby *(beika undō)* is directed by the National Central Union of the Agricultural Cooperatives (Zenkoku Nōgyō Kyōdō Kumiai Chūōkai, hereafter Central Union) which sits uneasily at the apex of the system and makes its headquarters in the middle of Tokyo's business section. It is widely accepted that the agricultural cooperatives represent one of the nation's most powerful pressure groups.

Consumer Organizations. Not all advice to government officials and LDP leaders favors rice producers. Consumer interests are also represented. There are federations of housewives and consumer organizations involved in rice politics. Representatives from these groups sit on government advisory councils and testify at LDP hearings. Consumer groups, however, do not have the organizational strength and political clout brandished by farm groups.

Opposition Camp. Interest group alignments in Japan have been characterized as a "perpendicular, party-aligned system of pressure groups."[19] Politics has been polarized by conflict between the LDP and various opposition parties. Rice farmers receive support from all camps. No political party has been willing to champion the cause of urban consumers at the expense of rural producers.

The organizational infrastructure which is part of the opposition camp also provides allies. Every farm organization connected to the opposition supports continued state control of the rice economy as a means to subsidize and protect farming. The All-Japan Federation of Farmers' Union (Zennihon Nōmin Kumiai Rengōkai) is closely aligned with the Japan Socialist Party (JSP) and to some extent with the Japan Communist Party (JCP). Federation officials sit on various government advisory committees. Farm unions are generally more radical than the agricultural cooperatives in their demands and more aggressive in their actions. Other farm organizations linked with both camps also support the interests of rice farmers.

Organized labor too has supported farm demands. All three major labor federations (Sōhyō, Dōmei, and Shinsabetsu) have called for support of rice farmers on different occasions. Sōhyō, the largest, most leftist, and very politically active federation, has even organized a National Liaison Council to protect the Food-Control System. While supporting the producers, opposition parties and labor unions also attempt to avoid alienating the consumer. Many labor officials believe that the government should support both consumers and producers as part of a comprehensive social policy.

Big Business. The big four economic federations have all issued statements over the years calling for less control and more free-market rationality.[20] Representatives from economic federations sit on various advisory councils dealing with agricultural policy. But it should be noted that, with varying degrees of seriousness, big business has been exhorting the government for almost three decades to restore market rationality in the rice business.

"Neutral Advisers." Detached and unbiased advice is supposed to be provided by "people of learning and experience" who serve on various advisory committees including the Rice Council (Beika Shingikai).[21] Those who fall into this category include ex-officials, specialists of various kinds, and sometimes local officials including prefectural governors. Few of these individuals are appointed to serve on a committee because of their neutral, unbiased beliefs, however. Most appointments are made because individual views in some way repre-

sent broader interests connected with the politics and economics of the issue under examination.

The Press. A fundamental aspect of every political conflict is the degree to which concerned parties and spectators are aware that an incompatibility exists. The press plays a major role in defining and intensifying conflicts in rice politics by heavy coverage of the issue and the differences between players. Usually farm groups are criticized for their "submissive begging for alms" while the LDP is blasted for its political exploitation of the food-control system. The press keeps rice politics in the news, and the content of most reporting supports the widespread belief that consumers and taxpayers are bilked, exploited, and clearly cheated.

PROXIMATE DECISION MAKERS

Civil servants and members of the LDP have been the closest to the making of actual decisions. They constitute the proximate decision makers.[22] The Ministry of Agriculture, Forestry, and Fisheries (MAFF) is at the heart of the rice controversy. It is widely recognized that the ministry represents the interests of farmers and will work to assure that agriculture retains its political and economic viability. In this sense, the MAFF is a clientele ministry within the Japanese government.

The electoral strength of the cooperatives helps the ministry vis-à-vis the ruling party and other government agencies. Many high-ranking officials in the ministry have taken up postretirement careers in the LDP or in part of the rice-related commercial industry. The ministry is also important for the rural-rooted LDP. Subsidies comprise about 60 percent of the ministry's annual budget—bits and pieces of state aid which can be distributed as small favors throughout the countryside.

The Food Agency is a slight exception to this generally paternalistic orientation in favor or farming.[23] The agency, through its twenty thousand employees at the local level, gathers data, estimates costs, and directs the flow of distribution. At the national level, it does most of the basic research and drafting of policy proposals. Although its management of the rice economy involves a close partnership with agricultural cooperatives, in the functioning of the Rice Council (for which it has administrative responsibility) it makes an effort to balance the interests of producers and cooperatives with the interests of consumers and market organizations.

Two other government agencies are among the proximate decision makers. The Ministry of Finance (MOF) stands at the center of political activity because of its responsibility for government expenditures. MOF officials have regarded the food-control system as a nettlesome if not disastrous program because it threatens a number of central objectives pursued by the ministry. First, decisions about rice are often made outside the annual budgetary process and financial aspects of the control program are freqently at odds with the ministry's version of "correct" fiscal policies at a given time. Thus rice issues can be seen as encroaching on MOF's autonomy, jurisdiction, and power. Second, rice-related programs represent a violation of the norm of program "balance" operating in Japanese budgetary politics. Third, rice policies violate the ministry's sense of national priorities and fiscal responsibility: deficits in the food-control account are higher than what the ministry considers sound or fair.[24] The Economic Planning Agency (EPA) is less directly involved in politics but supports the MOF on most issues.

As the bureaucracy, represented by MAFF and MOF, does not take a unified approach to rice policies, the role of the governing party, the LDP, becomes crucial. The allocation of seats in the lower house favors the countryside, and voter turnout has been much higher in these areas than in metropolitan districts. Many leaders and cabinet ministers have been elected from rural constituencies. All the postwar prime ministers have had farmers in their districts. Probably every LDP member elected from a rural or semirural constituency has had rice producers among his supporters. The party has also been under constant pressure from farm groups, with great surges occurring whenever an important departure or decision has been considered. But the nature of the relationship between the ruling party and the countryside has changed in recent years just as industrialization has proceeded.[25]

The LDP has been in substantial disagreement concerning what should be done about rice farming. There are a number of unofficial groups in the party which get together at certain times to press a cause or seek a special demand. Among these various "Dietmen's Leagues" (Giin Renmei) one of the most successful has been the informal group organized each year to support farm groups during the rice-pricing season. Most recently they have called themselves the "Conference of Diet Members to Consider Countermeasures to the Producer's Rice Price" (Seisansha Beika Taisaku Kyōgikai, hereafter Producer's Rice Conference).

Some dietmen see participation in the group as merely a necessary action to show allegiance to the agricultural cooperatives. But few party members dare to refuse to enroll since cooperative activists are quite careful about recording the movements of LDP politicians whenever major decisions are made by the party. About 275 LDP members supported farm group demands when the producer's price was set in 1976.[26] By contrast, a league of dietmen from urban constituencies which attempts to represent the interests of consumers on price issues can usually muster only about forty members of the LDP.

The most important official coordinating body in the party involved in rice decisions is the Research Council for Comprehensive Agricultural Policies (Sōgō Nōsei Chōsakai, hereafter Agricultural Research Council). The council was established in 1968 when it was decided that something had to be done about the rice surplus. Its members mobilize, support, test, and probe the political winds and help resolve conflicts within the party by consulting with as many individuals and groups as possible, including fellow LDP politicians, government officials, and interest groups.

Backstage conversations outside of formal party structure accompany formal hearings of the Agricultural Research Council. But informal *hanashiai* (discussions) are rarely enough. When controversial issues are brought to the formal agenda for decision, it indicates that informal, teahouse politics has not succeeded. Continuing debate and sharp confrontations at formal hearings mean that the vaunted Japanese style of informal, heart-to-heart talks does not always work.

Two aggregating units are charged with approving decisions reached by PARC divisions or councils such as the Agricultural Research Council: the Policy Deliberation Commission and the Executive Council. Considerable effort is made to reconcile party differences before these bodies are convened. Meetings are frequently rescheduled until differences within the Agricultural Research Council are reconciled. When this proves impossible, the sessions of both bodies can be lively and rancorous. Recommendations from below do not always get a free pass. If there is agreement below, approval by the Executive Council seems to be more pro forma. After an internal party consensus is reached, several party leaders—the secretary-general, PARC chairman, Executive Council chairman, vice-president, and the chairman of the Agricultural Research Council—will then represent the LDP in final negotiations with the government. This summit meeting of party leaders and cabinet officials is a frequent necessity before an authoritative cabinet decision on rice is announced. The government side is usually represented by the minister of finance, minister of agriculture, and the director-general of the EPA. The prime minister does not participate in government-party meetings. But they are usually held at his residence and he is at the apex of the formal decision-making process which brings the two sides together.

CONFLICT AND DECISION MAKING IN RICE POLITICS

The issues related to rice control are thus far from trivial. The scope of conflict is also quite broad, as measured by the number of people directly or indirectly involved. The complexity of the issues at stake prompts conflict, but intermingling views prevent polarized disagreements. The cabinet might wish to restore market relations in the rice economy. But government leaders do not want to threaten the unity of the LDP, pose a severe economic threat to the agricultural cooperatives, or lose votes in rural constituencies. Backbench politicians in the LDP work hard to support their constituents. But rural politicians also recognize that something must be done about a surplus, deficits, and agricultural adjustment. Rural members of the LDP also want their party to win in urban areas. MAFF and MOF officials are not eager to see an end to LDP rule. They recognize the need to make political adjustments in rationally designed policies. The Central Union openly solicits the support of the opposition political parties. But Central Union officials also recognize that effective power still rests with bureaucratic officials and the LDP. Participants inside and outside the government thus do not hold opposing views on all issues. Areas exist for compromise and negotiation.

While there is a high degree of organization in rice politics, organizational roles and boundaries are permeable. People shift back and forth between groups with different approaches to the issues. LDP politicians who leave the cabinet are free to join in the support of rice farmers. A newly appointed cabinet minister from a rural constituency will become more cautious about prices in adjusting to the expectations of his new role. Agricultural cooperative officials elected to the Diet are also members of the LDP caucus. Former officials from the MAFF do not completely sever their ties with the ministry. There are even cases of the same individual serving simultaneously in intra-LDP farm lobby groups and in party organs designed to determine price policy.[27]

The degree of subordination and authority is also uncertain at times. Setting prices is an administrative responsibility, but no cabinet or prime minister can avoid consulting with the LDP. Cabinet officials and prime ministers reluctantly compromise their public views because of pressures from the LDP. The MAFF must be responsive to the agricultural cooperatives just as the Central Union has to compromise with local pressures.

But power relations are not totally unstructured. Parliamentary institutions like those in Japan concentrate political power in the hands of political executives. The key relationships are between the government and its backbench and between the party in power and the political opposition. The political logic of parliamentary politics requires that members of the ruling party be united in their support of the cabinet in parliamentary debate and actions. Only in a limited sense can competing policy factions be tolerated within the ruling party. At some point, debate within the ruling party has to be terminated. Legislative proposals must be drawn up and receive party blessing. Rank-and-file members fall behind the party leadership. Parliamentarians, unlike American senators and representatives, do not have the political leverage or bargaining resources to subvert their leaders. Concentrated political power in the dominant party fosters unity but also requires party leaders and cabinet officials to make difficult decisions on competing values.

The need for a decision via party and governmental unity is further reinforced by the presence of the opposition parties. Never having had to face the complexities and cross-pressures of rice politics as a governing party, they are quick to try to exploit these issues to partisan advantage, often criticizing the government and LDP in inflammatory and exaggerated language.

If an issue is controversial, then, the political strategy of the cabinet, prime minister, and high-ranking civil servant will be to limit participation of competing policy factions within the LDP and to privatize the conflict even further by avoiding the parliament altogether. If agreement can be reached at the top, policymaking will become bureaucratic rules, regulations, ordinances, and orders. The food-control system is ambiguous and hence provides the opportunity for very loose interpretation by government legal experts. Rice politics thus tends to become bureaucratic adaptation approved by cabinet rather than Diet debate, formal amendment to the law, and thus radical departure.[28] But, as we will see, there are differences.

Rice Pricing: The Question of Income Maintenance

Price fixing as a political and economic issue centers on efforts by a coalition of farm groups and politicians to maintain farm incomes during a period of rapid industrial growth. These annual decisions to set producer prices are among the most "institutionalized" decisions in agricultural policy, supported by long-developed and widely understood rules of the game and marked by complex bargaining and negotiations. The cast of characters has been fairly stable, although their interactions are marked by considerable tension and conflict. Indeed, the political tactics adopted by some participants cast into doubt easy generalizations which suggest that Japanese place special value in maintaining harmony and that decisions are more the product of a delicate process of unanimous consent than the results of an open clash among competing adversaries.[29]

An open clash makes sense. For example, a recent study of agricultural policy in the United Kingdom suggests that secrecy and the lack of political trouble during annual pricing reviews has weakened the political and economic position of farmers.[30] In striking contrast, farm groups in Japan have deliberately exacerbated conflict in order to strengthen their hand. The politics of producer prices reveals the positive benefits which can accrue to an interest coalition when conflict is open. Pricing also helps crystallize the economic irrationalities of government control.

Producer prices doubled in the period 1960–1968. They were frozen in 1969 and 1970. In the next seven years they doubled again. Since 1970 producer prices have exceeded the government sales price to dealers and consumer rice prices, and they have risen faster than the agricultural parity index and the Bank of Japan wholesale price index. Producer prices have not, however, kept up with the national wage index in manufacturing. But clearly prices are too high in a condition of surplus. In 1977 the government absorbed about a 5,500-yen loss on every 60 kilos of rice it purchased from cultivators. Losses connected with rice control and the budget for diversion of paddy fields together amounted to 863.9 billion yen in 1977. This was 33 percent of the total budget for the MAFF.[31]

The Japanese government has been setting rice prices for five decades—in conditions of economic depression, war, military occupation, postwar industrial recovery, and in times of prosperity. The manner and character of decisions has changed considerably during this extended time span. But annual allocation decisions force some kind of continuity in political and administrative practice. Durable bonds of institutional arrangements developed after the formation of the LDP in 1955 and the beginning of one-party domination. Formal laws do not provide clear directions for reaching a politically viable decision. According to the food-control law, the cabinet is authorized to determine producer prices "at a level so as to ensure the production of rice, and with consideration to costs of production, other commodity prices, and general economic conditions."[32] The selling price to distributors is to be set "at a level to stabilize general household expenditures, and with consideration to costs of living, other commodity prices, and general economic conditions."[33] The two prices do not have to be fixed at the same time. The Rice Council, created in 1949, must be consulted by the minister of agriculture before the cabinet makes an official decision.

THE PRICING PROCESS

In practice, producer rice pricing has become a thoroughly institutionalized process of staged conflict involving a complex, almost ritualized, sequence of events. The process, which varies somewhat each year, is summarized in the following paragraphs.

Gathering Information and Building an Agenda. Government officials and farm-group technicians define the situation by analyzing economic constraints and establishing initial expectations. Differing agendas and statistical formulations emerge because of competing economic, political, and "moral" ideas concerning the purposes of food-control and the conditions of the economy.

Defining an Acceptable Price. This process involves sounding out the views of others in order to create internal cohesion and political alliances. The central question for all parties at this stage is: What price is possible this year and how do we get it? Politicians, civil servants, and farm groups are all involved in this process of evaluating their bargaining positions and guessing how they can best sell their arguments to others.

Disseminating Information and Organizing Political Advocacy. Farm groups announce their demands and prepare for human-wave sorties on government ministries and political party headquarters in Tokyo. High-ranking officials in the government make basic decisions concerning the research and drafting of proposals done by subordinates. Government economic reports on the rice economy are sometimes released. Articles in the press focus on differences by communicating the bids and other signals from adversary parties.

Narrowing Choices by Decision Elites. At this stage, coordination and agreement between the MOF, EPA, and the MAFF are completed. The government's position is determined and the Rice Council is convened in the midst of demonstrations and rallies held by farm organizations. Serious formal and informal discussions begin with the LDP. The narrowed range between minimum and maximum "bids" is clear.

Final Politics of Choice. An LDP target price is usually determined after the Rice Council has made its report to the minister of agriculture. Sometimes the party cannot agree and so, without taking a united stand, the Executive Council defers to party leaders. The process of accommodation reaches a conclusion when LDP leaders and cabinet ministers negotiate a settlement which includes the amount of subsidies to be offered to rice cultivators.

THE POLITICS OF PRICING

The politics of pricing tends to be pluralistic. The most noteworthy characteristics, which have continued for some time now, are worth examining here. First, fundamental disagreements exist over why the government is in the rice business and over what administered prices should accomplish. Second, the major units participating in the decision process are roughly equal in power and hence must bargain with each other. Third, clientele groups are consulted and their representatives participate in the process of decision. Fourth, the process of decision is open and there is a great awareness of conflict among spectators and participants. Fifth, the conflict over prices touches upon the concerns of many bureaucratic, political, and economic interests. And sixth, technical pricing adjustments, subsidies, and changes in the pricing formulas help provide a number of small concessions to satisfy different participants at least partly.[34]

Different participants try to push outcomes favorable to themselves —by shaping the bargaining environment to their own objectives, persuading others to alter their point of view, and, if persuasion fails, then controlling the bargaining environment so that others are forced to go along. Bargaining moves thus dampen or exacerbate the scope and intensity of conflict. In many years, for example, conflict was generated by attempts to control the timing and manner in which decisions were made. Efforts to broaden or narrow the range of economic conditions considered relevant to decisions often exacerbated differences. All sides to the issue sought to exploit the political and economic climate each year to get their own way.

PRICING DECISIONS

Table 1 is a rather crude way of describing a small part of what happened during the period 1969–1976. In percentage form, it shows farm-group demands, the initial government offer, the LDP target price (when the party could agree) before party-government negotiations, and the final pricing decision. Internal differences within the government are not shown, nor is it certain how many rural-based politicans within the LDP actually took the Nōkyō demands as serious. My impression is that very few did. The problem of anticipated reactions makes it difficult to assess the real intentions of different parties. There is always a gap between formal demand and what an interest group hopes to get. Rice politics is marked by considerable role playing. What is clear is that farm groups have never approached getting what they have demanded in public. Nor has the government side, represented by the MOF and MAFF, capitulated very far.

In the case of pricing decisions, the results are more or less calculable and thus one can readily see how well farmers have done. The results are not buried in a ponderous government budget. They are announced in newspaper headlines throughout the country. Since the

TABLE 1   *Producer Rice Prices: Demands, Offers, and Final Decisions*

Year	Nōkyō Demand	Zennichi Demand	Initial Government Offer	Percentage Increase over Previous Year	
				LDP	Final
1969	16	33	0	2	0
1970	20	45	0	2	0
1971	30	57	0	stalemate (0–15)	3.0
1972	39	73	3	5	5.0
1973	46	80	9	stalemate (15–20)	15.0
1974	62	96	25	37	32.1
1975	48	80	13	14.3	14.3
1976	31	62	5	6.4	6.4

Source: Computed from various newspapers and *Shokuryō Kanri Geppō* (various issues).

place of decision is open and visible, it provides an arena for conflicts to flare. And since the demands or recommendations of various antagonists are well known, decisions imply that there are winners and losers. Official actions invite recriminations and also affirm that different parties to the dispute hold incompatible interests and competing claims to scarce resources. On the other hand, a complex system of subsidies facilitates an easier decision and softens rural resentment. Subsidies have been added to basic producer prices since state control was imposed on the rice economy during wartime. The character and size of these subsidies are negotiated each year. Special subsidies to encourage improvement in rice varieties raised prices by 2 percent in 1969 and 1970. The economic rationale for these subsidies is sometimes quite dubious. The MOF is usually disgruntled. Still, an artful use of subsidies helps to dampen conflict and reconcile political differences.

There are other ways to reduce the magnitude of concessions or mitigate the size of the triumph. Technical elements in the pricing formula are often modified, recordkeeping practices are revised, and the unit used for costing has been changed. Informal promises are made by LDP leaders or MAFF officials that new subsidies and support will be available in the future to help facilitate production. New committees have been set up and a subcommittee of the Rice Council is occasionally appointed to review pricing practices and other rice-related matters.

Pricing decisions are budgeted each year according to various demands and pressures. They are thus subject to renegotiation if not reversal from one year to the next. All parties are able to claim that "great efforts were made this year" but unfortunately the results "cannot be helped." Few negotiators will take personal blame, although the chairman of the Central Union once resigned following a pricing decision. Many participants are willing to shift the blame elsewhere. All participants agree that termination of debate is conditional and that they will confront each other again on another day.

Competitive and Protective Regulation: Risk in Marketing

Pricing decisions are repeated each year. A decision to partially withdraw from the market is a different matter since it involves a challenge to the basic structure of the food-control system and a redefinition of government responsibilities which might not be easily reversed. The rationale behind the attempt to introduce the market mechanism is straightforward. Economic competition is expected to make commercial transactions less costly, the allocation of resources more efficient, supply and demand more balanced, and the government less constrained by political demands springing from the entrenched tradition of clientelist politics established in pricing decisions. Government officials and the LDP are, in effect, attempting to restructure the economic and political rules of the game by transforming public conflict into private, economic competition. In a period of abundance, free markets would encourage prices to fall.

Regulatory adjustment began in the late 1960s under the direction of Prime Minister Satō. His strategy, in the face of farm-group resistance, was to displace conflict by restructuring the debate along different lines and by moving decisions outside the price-fixing stream of political interaction. The subsequent workings of rice markets became part of the routines of politics and economic markets once the new autonomous market *(jishu ryūtsū)* was adopted.[35] Within a few years quotas were established on government purchases, consumer prices were decontrolled, and regulations on participation of new retailers were modified so that supermarkets, department stores, and other merchants could compete in commercial sales. By 1978 about 25 percent of all commercially marketed rice for direct food consumption was decontrolled but substantially subsidized.[36]

At first glance, government marketing programs would seem to be a case of deregulation. The rice market has been partially decontrolled. But decontrol has not meant removal of the web of government. Official actions have moved in two directions. Competitive regulatory policy has aimed at fostering market competition. Protective regulations have been designed simultaneously to protect farmers, rice traders, and even consumers from excessive competition by setting the conditions under which various private activities can be undertaken. The result has been state-supported commerce.

DISPLACEMENT OF POLITICAL CONFLICT

Some uncontrolled commerce has always existed outside the restrictions of bureaucratic surveillance. When collection quotas were modified in the early 1950s, the illicit trade in rice became open and obvious. One government study estimated that about half of all marketed rice in the mid-1950s was flowing through unauthorized channels.[37] No sensible politician or civil servant was ready to prevent these exchanges by waging an all-out war on consumers and producers.

Besides, a free exchange also relieved the public treasury of additional financial burdens. The amount of black-marketed rice varied from year to year, but even rising official prices in the 1960s did not diminish illicit trade. According to government surveys, about 40 percent of all households purchased on the black market in 1967. A study of Osaka in 1968 showed that almost 50 percent of all households surveyed purchased only "free rice."[38] Abundance persuaded government officials and the Satō Cabinet that surreptitious commercial practice could be legalized.

Following elections held for the House of Councillors in the summer of 1968 the Satō Cabinet moved toward decontrol, despite an earlier pledge from the prime minister to "maintain the nucleus of the food-control system."[39] Political practice during the pricing season works most often to prevent any single individual or group from being decisive and hence provides opportunities for high-price advocates to prevent or inhibit government actions. Irreversible decisions which aim at changing not just policies or prices but also institutional arrangements are generally fought over harder than reversible ones. On the question of markets, then, the prime minister and his allies in the cabinet and the LDP sought to broaden the debate while concentrating the ability to determine outcomes to a more limited number of officials and politicians. The issue was defined as being broader than just farm incomes while the site of decisions was shifted to normal, party-government practices by certain maneuvers described in the following paragraphs.

A Restructured Rice Council. Since 1949 politicians had served on the Rice Council along with representatives from consumer and farm groups. Functional representation was suspended in 1968 and all politicians were permanently removed. A "neutral" Rice Council thereafter recommended radical changes: joint determination of producer and consumer prices, revision of pricing formulas to reflect general prices and supply conditions, elimination of controls on consumer prices, reform of marketing and distribution, and more attention to "integration" of agricultural policies. Never before had the Rice Council made such strong recommendations along these lines. Functional representation, on a reduced scale, was restored only after the new market was under way and a small-scale crop diversion program had begun.

Mobilization of Nonagrarian Advice. Advisory councils in the EPA and the MOF, including the prestigious Fiscal Systems Council (Zaisei Shingikai), advised the government to restrict rice purchases, freeze or lower prices, introduce the "market mechanism," and make supply and demand a central pricing consideration. The prime minister also turned to the Deliberation Council on Agricultural Policies (Nōsei Shingikai), lodged in the office of the prime minister, to advise him on future agricultural policies. The president of the Central Union was appointed to this advisory committee along with three other representatives of farm groups; but farm interests were outnumbered.

Restructured LDP Committees. In the middle of the pricing season in 1968 Naomi Nishimura, minister of agriculture, called for "integrated agricultural policies." The new catch phrase meant that something had to be done about rice. In the early fall, the Agricultural Research Council replaced two existing party committees, including one which had concerned itself mostly with rice prices. Masayoshi Ohira, a former official of the MOF, was appointed the first chairman. He was replaced in December by Nishimura.

Broadening the Issue. Price fixing exists separate from other national priorities established in the annual government budget. A move to create a new market or a crop diversion program modified some of this comfortable independence enjoyed by producers and agricultural cooperatives. Rice programs were linked to overall agricultural policies. An intraministry committee headed by the administrative vice-minister was set up in the MAFF to work out ways of integrating rice programs into the overall priorities of the ministry. MOF officials also participated in working out the scope and details of the new market and crop diversion programs. Appropriation requirements for new departures were made along with other annual budgetary decisions so that the interests of rice farmers were placed in competition with other considerations.

Bureaucratic Discretion. The Satō Cabinet decided that changes could be made in the form of new regulations or by cabinet and ministerial ordinance rather than by formal amendment which required approval by the Diet. The cabinet could thus claim that the system had been preserved while the opposition parties were effectively removed from participation in decisions. In fact, coping with abundance was a task willingly avoided by the opposition parties.[40]

Briefly this is what happened. The MOF used the advice offered by its own advisory committees to favor the most radical departures, including price setting in December when the general account budget is usually determined by the cabinet. The MAFF was much more cautious than the Rice Council and more divided than the MOF about decontrol. Agricultural officials were quite ready to cope with abundance and deficits. But they did not want to jeopardize the Food

Agency's capacity to manipulate supply and demand or threaten the cooperative system which is a crucial element in agricultural administration and closely connected to the political prestige and power of the ministry.

THE POLITICAL RESPONSE

Decisions were not left to the accumulated expertise of civil servants or to the expert advice of "men of learning and experience" serving on advisory committees. A subcommittee of the party's Agricultural Research Council heard testimony and examined evidence provided by government officials and agricultural cooperative officials. The party unit relied heavily on the information and proposals provided by the MAFF while MOF bureaucrats, politicians, and cooperative officials met with each other and discussed technical matters in measured tones, trial balloons appeared in the media, and academic experts were consulted and wrote articles. Participants quickly discovered which areas permitted innovation and which decisions seemed politically impossible.

The agricultural cooperatives had the most difficult time. Like a prime minister, the president of the Central Union needs advice and political allies to meet new challenges. Asao Miyawaki appointed an advisory committee to deliberate on rice problems. In most circumstances, recommendations by Central Union executives require consent at a meeting with prefectural union chairmen. Among the prefectural chairmen at this time seven were LDP dietmen. Seven more were LDP members in prefectural assemblies.[41] Central Union executives were publicly opposed to modifications in the controlled market; in private, many were reconciled. The real task of the cooperative leadership was to preserve the income commitment of the government and to protect the privileged economic position enjoyed by the cooperatives in market operations.

It took almost two months before national and local officials of the cooperatives could reach agreement. In the end, the nation's largest farm organization decided that the rice problem was essentially one of inadequate demand. Cooperative officials refused to endorse any form of decontrol and rejected any land diversion program.[42]

A winter version of the pricing season took place in December 1968. The issue this time was decontrol. LDP leaders and MAFF officials tried hard to persuade cooperative officials to declare some kind of qualified approval of a modified free market. The farm leaders refused. The challenge of demonstrating farmers, however, did not prevent structural changes. In late December the Executive Council of the LDP approved creation of the autonomous market by cabinet ordinance. A small-scale land adjustment program was also authorized. A meeting of cabinet officials and party leaders confirmed the new decisions.[43]

Thus, through the leadership of top party executives and by administrative fiat, commercial capitalism was introduced, but on an extremely modest scale. Special financial arrangements were worked out by MAFF and MOF officials so that local cooperatives were able to purchase nongovernment rice from producers. The bulk of annual production would continue to be purchased by the government. Only two years later did the government begin to limit its official purchases. Generous subsidies were provided to producers and dealers to facilitate the easy introduction of commercial competition. Funds were also pledged for a new program of "integrated agricultural policies" to help enable farmers to convert paddy fields to production of other agricultural commodities.

The LDP prevented radical departures. The MOF had wanted more substantial change but the LDP opposed lowered producer prices, quantitative limits on official rice purchases, forced diversion of paddy fields, and price setting in December. Political parties normally do not undertake policies which tend to threaten their electoral foundations. Given the emotional as well as economic importance of control in rural areas the lack of major change should not be surprising: Government regulation significantly benefits a well-organized constituency dispersed among a great number of electoral districts and thus generates substantial political support. LDP leaders in this case did not have to be reminded of these facts by demonstrations, warnings, and threats. On the other hand, what resentment did exist among farmers for even the limited changes introduced could be defused by subsidies, special administrative privileges, and other benefits to farm groups as incentives to cooperate.

In early 1969 the national and prefectural officials of the cooperatives issued an enthusiastic challenge to all the nation's unit cooperatives that an all-out effort be made to capture the new commercial market. The cooperative system remained the organizational mechanism through which government officials could be sure that their decisions would be accepted.[44]

Farm unions aligned with the opposition political parties viewed the matter differently. Union activists met in Tokyo in February under the slogans of "destroy the new market" and "overcome the dangers to agriculture." Some two thousand participants marched to the headquarters of the Central Union to register their protest and demand that the cooperatives withdraw their willingness to go along with new marketing rules. After a long day of acrimonious discussion, the Central Union agreed to "reconsider" their commitment to work with the government. The ambiguous promise ended the sit-in.[45]

STATE-SUPPORTED COMMERCE

Commerce within the new, more autonomous economic arrangements has not become totally free. The market has remained regulated by a complex set of rules, licensing requirements, and purchasing regulations which link the autonomous flow with more strictly controlled distribution. Thus allocation plans for all commercially marketed rice are drawn up by food bureaucrats in Tokyo and issued to collection agents, dealers, and producers by prefectural and local governments. Consumers are still required to retain their ration book for purchases, although few families are able to produce it.[46]

There are really two systems of marketing: an officially approved system of designated collection agents and dealers for both autonomous and government rice, on the one hand, and a "free" (technically black market) market on the other. Unit cooperatives handle over 90 percent of government and autonomous rice. In the case of government rice, the local cooperative acts as a collection agent for official purchases, at prices determined during the annual "pricing season." Special financial arrangements with the government also provide unit cooperatives with capital to finance purchase of autonomous rice at market-determined prices. Early each year the MOF and the MAFF decide the total amount of rice to be purchased. Farmers are no longer under compulsion to sell to the government: An elaborate formula linked to land diversion programs is used to calculate the maximum amount of rice each farmer *can* sell to the government, and a sales contract with the government is made each year through the unit cooperative. In 1977, for example, the government purchased about 2 metric tons for every ton designated as autonomous rice. Whereas the initial decision in 1971 to limit government purchases caused considerable resentment and protest,[47] now these purchase quotas do not prompt significant political trouble or even special attention beyond interested parties.

The consequences of this semicontrolled, semifree, market system in rice include the continuation, even expansion, of subsidies, profiteering, and speculation. Farmers who sell on the autonomous market are partially subsidized in order to encourage production of high-quality rice. The particular kind and amount of subsidies is negotiated during the annual pricing season, and the politics of the pricing season has helped keep the rice market well subsidized. Control remains a deficit-producing enterprise amounting to about 5,000 yen per 60 kilos in 1978. Furthermore, because the new autonomous market is threatened by cheap government rice, commercial dealers argue that they cannot compete with government rice without some kind of aid; they too are subsidized.

Leaks in the system and profiteering exist. What happens to rice after it leaves the farm is still a matter of no small mystery, and officials of the Food Agency are extremely guarded in their responses to questions concerning possible leaks in the official distribution system. Farmers and local retail dealers selling directly to the consumer are more open about the problem and delight in explaining how government and cooperative officials can be outwitted. There have been cases when free rice, which has been purchased from a grower, is later resold to the government. On the other hand, a lot of lower-priced government rice is converted somewhere in the great grinding machine of the rice market into high-priced, tasty rice. What is certain is that profits are being made, some of it because of government subsidies and some of it through leaks in the system.[48]

Speculation also returned to the rice market. When the autonomous market was announced in 1969, large trading companies like Marubeni and Mitsui, which had participated in the rice trade in prewar Japan, immediately set out to lay the foundations of a new distribution route. They expected that the rice market would be almost completely decontrolled within a few years. Other private dealers, who had been handling free rice for years in a twilight zone of illegality, began a more public campaign to restructure the market and cope with the threat posed by the large trading companies.[49]

The expansion of private commercial dealings in the rice market has led to at least one highly publicized example of speculation in the form of *kaishime*: buying up a basic commodity in order to corner the market, raise the price, and then make a quick handsome profit.

Land Diversion: Reallocation of Resources and Avoidance of Conflict

An autonomous market is a program of deregulation and thus a loosening of bureaucratic chains in order to foster commercial competition and a new, market-driven economy in agriculture. The third stream of decisions represents new forms of bureaucratic intervention not only to displace private decisions on the use of resources with government decisions but also to restructure the rural economy substantially. Land diversion is a fight over surplus production and inefficient use of a resource in short supply: agricultural land. The problem has been intractable for the government and threatening to individual producers because more is involved than simply reduction of an unwanted surplus. Supply management has also been linked to broad attempts to redefine landownership, diversify and enlarge farm size, and push resources in agriculture into a pattern more closely in line with domestic needs.[50]

Decisions in this area are consequently more complex than in pricing and marketing matters. Goals and objectives must be derived, realistic and acceptable programs on how to achieve them must be designed, funds must be allocated, and extensive cooperation within a complex network of reciprocal links must be achieved in order to secure implementation.

MAJOR LAND PROGRAMS

Five different programs, costing billions of yen, have been tried since 1969 as a way to coax, facilitate, and encourage a movement away from rice.[51] Results have been mixed. Rice production reached an all-time peak with 14.5 million metric tons in 1967. By 1978 production had dropped to 12.6 million metric tons. Paddy fields were reduced from 3.2 million hectares to 2.5 million hectares during the same period.[52] Nonetheless, abundance persists. Demand for rice declined faster than official projections—despite a growth in national population, an enthusiastic campaign to encourage consumption, and an augmented school lunch program. Remarkable gains in productivity kept overall production high while mechanization and other advances cut required labor time almost in half in a decade.[53] No other crop in Japanese agriculture so successfully encourages part-time farming on marginal land. Government stocks of old rice in the late seventies were almost as large as they had been a decade earlier.

This situation might suggest that government programs to rationalize production had failed because intense conflicts of interest were involved and people who were expected to cooperate were at loggerheads. We might investigate how political conflict was used by farm groups to prevent policy success. The record, however, is more complex. In a narrow sense, government programs did not fail. Overall reduction targets were met or exceeded in all but two years during the period 1970–1977. Experience confirmed the conventional wisdom that it is not easy to calibrate supply and demand. Conditions change unpredictably. For example, enormous efforts have been made to lessen the dependence of rice production on the vicissitudes of nature. But nature remains the master. Supply and demand were roughly in balance in 1974. At that time the international food and energy crises exacerbated fear about national "food security." Producer prices went up during raging inflation, land diversion programs were considerably modified, and a new effort was started to increase national self-sufficiency in food. Dreadful weather in 1976 helped reduce production below domestic needs. Thereafter, weather conditions improved and abundance followed.

The problem of calibration becomes even more complex and convoluted when such matters are considered as the number of participants whose preferences have to be taken into account, the variety of separate decisions which are part of a single program, and the intricate interdependencies which are created when a government seeks to persuade and encourage rather than to impose firmly from above.

The results of government programs thus are quite ambiguous when judged in terms beyond reduction targets. Many problems remain unsolved: regional specialization, permanent diversion of paddy fields to production of other food crops, enlargement of farm scale, improvement in rice qualities, and some restoration of full-time farming.

What about conflict? Continuous contact and extensive discussions between government and private interests are usually considered of key importance in the formulation and implementation of successful public policy in Japan. The argument in this section is that consensus politics, consultative overload, the complexity of policy implementation, and deliberate avoidance of conflict all worked to prevent policy from becoming too ambitious. This is not to suggest that there was no protest against government actions or that political power was unimportant. Within the political community of consultation, the LDP stimulated change but also worked hard to moderate its consequences. Politicians did not move cautiously in the face of persistent political threats. The LDP is simply reluctant to move in an open, direct way because politicians believe that sudden policy change in an uncertain rural environment will foster social anxieties and political confusion. Agriculture can be ignored but not unnecessarily threatened. The watchword in the party is thus to "speed down" the plans of task-oriented bureaucrats and theoretically trained academic advisers.[54] As a consequence, the process of decision was weighted on the side of restraint. Insufficient political incentives existed for cooperative leaders to make special trouble; generous subsidies, preservation of the food-control program, and other financial and administrative concessions made it somewhat easier for them to go along.

INCREMENTALISM AND DECISION CYCLES

The five major land programs have developed in an incremental pattern of trial and error.[55] During the first few years land programs were conducted with only casual concern about the totality of the nation's agricultural system, despite a new rhetoric of "integrated agricultural policies." Land was fallowed for compensation and some farmers were encouraged to sell their plots for industrial purposes. The international food crisis prompted more explicit attention to the interplay of major agricultural policies—that is, commodity prices, land structure and ownership, regionalization, self-sufficiency in food, and social welfare. By 1978 programs had become less voluntary and more compulsory, based on an authoritative process of administrative sanctions.

Most of these programs did not require parliamentary action. Nonetheless, the process of adopting a new measure was hardly closed and narrow. Politics involved three overlapping tasks: designation of programs, commitment of funds, and implementation. Issues generally moved from shadows to the hustle and bustle of consultation, advisory committee hearings, and political debate in the light and then back to the twilight areas of bureaucratic routine. Different types of decisions were required, throughout the year, at various levels of governmental organization.

Debate and decisions clearly exemplified close, reciprocal ties among political, administrative, and interest-group elites. Everyone did not agree. There were sharp programmatic differences separating the MOF and the agricultural cooperatives. Tactical maneuvers sometimes surprised the other side. Nonetheless, personal compatibility among key personnel, general agreement on the necessity for cooperation, and broad participation in decisions fostered mutual understanding and moderation.

Political bargaining is facilitated when participants agree on the premises that define their relationships; conflict and protest are more likely when agreement is absent. Land diversion programs are potentially the source of protest since government officials have sought to redefine somewhat the relation of rice farmers and the state. None-theless, as we will see, a number of structural factors related to the process and content of decisions discouraged protest tactics and delib-erate exacerbation of differences.

Prior Consultation. The government's responsibility for guiding and initiating economic change in the rice economy has given rise to an intricate network of consultative relationships. In order to realize its economic purposes, the MAFF has entered into a contractual rela-tion with farm groups, local governments, and individual farmers. Cooperation is the desirable norm; without it, public purposes can-not be achieved. Consultation encourages the mutual exchange of information and makes possible the articulation and reconciliation of demands. In this sense, practical problems of governing can better explain the propensity to consult in Japanese politics than references to vague notions about cultural predispositions to seek consensus.

Drafting various land programs involved a broad, time-consuming process of participation, advice, and consent. Politicians, civil ser-vants, and farm group officials met constantly, formally and infor-mally, to maintain mutual understanding on issues related to diver-sion targets, subsidies, administrative routine, and the like. Rural backbenchers did not disrupt party routine because they were con-sulted from the start. Cooperative officials were usually given ample advance notice by politicians and bureaucrats concerning what to expect.

Still, "voluntary" cooperation was not always assured through con-sultation because farm groups were not convinced that the MAFF was interested primarily in rural welfare. The contrast with the Ministry of Trade and Industry and its clients is striking.[56] Advice about specific aspects of agricultural policy came consistently and forcefully from committees and advisory groups representing industrial and other nonagricultural interests. Consultation helped avoid conflict; but the very breadth of the advice offered to officialdom created a persistent tension between farmers and the state since farm groups wanted the issue narrowly defined to suit their interests.

Concessions. Research by social psychologists has demonstrated that the number of concessions made by a party in a bargaining situa-tion is significantly affected by the number of concessions made by the other side; frequent compromises by one side will elicit reciprocal moves from opponents across the table.[57] A strategy of making an ini-tial proposal and remaining firm thereafter does not seem politically reasonable in a policy area involving many decisions and reciprocal ties. Indeed, the evidence in rice politics suggests that the likelihood of compromise is positively related to the occurrence of concessions by another party. There is little scope for concessions in pricing decisions. On the other hand, a complex program of land diversion permitted trade-offs, compromises, mutual face saving, and even the postponement of decisions. Room for concessions provides the possibility for avoidance of conflict.

The Force of Political Empathy. Settlements in rice politics are rarely imposed by domination or command because power is not concentrated in the hands of a few. Pure persuasion has also been impossible because of the conflicting interests at stake. The game of politics thus resembles an elaborate bargaining process of mutual manipulation. Successful bargaining requires that participants understand the position of others, including their schedule of acceptable costs and preferences. Only when the other fellow's point of view is understood is it possible to formulate a realistic strategy concerning a specific goal. The complexity and permanent character of the administrative and political relations involved in land diversion programs fostered bargaining. Political empathy thus facilitated the creation of a workable consensus about the outer limits of feasible actions, even if it did not guarantee ultimate unanimity.

Small to Big Changes and Big to Small Changes as Techniques. A time-honored technique for inducing compliance to a controversial government program in the absence of coercive power is to begin by enacting a minimal departure which will get compliance and then to advance to bigger changes in subsequent years. Land diversion programs were first introduced in 1969 through this "foot-in-the-door" technique and broadened in an incremental way thereafter.

An equally effective method for getting compliance has been an opposite procedure: an extreme threat or request sure to be rejected followed by a more moderate proposal which proves to be efficacious in producing compliance. Invariably, whenever land reduction programs were under consideration, the MOF proposed radical measures sure to cause considerable anger and probably substantial conflict in rural areas if they were arbitrarily imposed: lowered producer prices, compulsory land diversion according to government plans, minimal subsidies, substantial revisions of the food-control law, more liberalized agricultural trade, and so forth. Actions along such lines were uniformly rejected by farm groups as excessive and outrageous. The LDP then intervened unambiguously with a more moderate set of proposals which seemed like reasonable concessions in the light of initial possibilities. Threatening farmers with initial MOF formulations thus enhanced subsequent compliance to smaller changes while the LDP probably received some political credit for standing-up to MOF bureaucrats.

Sensitivity to Long-Term Relations. Bargaining and compromise were also facilitated because of reciprocal ties and a high level of interaction, especially among cooperative leaders, MAFF officials, and conservative politicians. Excessive conflict on one issue could threaten to reduce the chances of collaborative action in the future on matters that tended to unite, for example, cooperative officials and government bureaucrats. Because the parties to the conflict over land had relationships beyond the issue of the moment (subsidies, targets, administrative practice, and the like) there was a built-in pressure to work out a compromise somehow. Politics was therefore marked by an intensive search for agreement prior to official government decisions. The LDP did not want to impose a solution whereas the Central Union wanted to make the government back down publicly. Unity was rarely achieved; the cooperatives did not get all they wanted. But substantial effort was made by those involved to work out an acceptable deal. Some of the bargaining was open, involving public denunciations, displays of solidarity, and occasional political showmanship by a prime minister or a high-ranking cooperative official. Public discussions were also accompanied by private meetings, mutual modifications of positions, and a search for agreement.

Side Payments as Incentives. Bargaining is usually facilitated when the conflict at issue is divisible—that is, when it is a matter of "more or less" rather than a question of "all or nothing." Rice pricing is essentially a divisible issue. Land diversion programs have tended to be less divisible since they threatened eventually to put some farmers out of the rice business. But land programs were also somewhat compromised by side payments—that is, incentives to make it easier for farmers to go along. These incentives included promises for future support ("integrated agricultural policies," "coordinated food policies"), voluntarism, participation in decisions, subsidies, retention of the food-control system, and the granting of various administrative preferments and prerequisites to the agricultural cooperatives. Some critics, of course, argue that these incentives compromised and weakened the content of a program crucial to restructuring the agricultural economy. It can also be argued that, with no side payments, bargaining would have been supplemented with, if not replaced by, more political conflict.

Conclusion

The functions of government and the role of markets in the rice economy have changed considerably during the period under study. Government authority is no longer the only coordinating device used to connect decisions influencing production, incomes, distribution, and consumption. State policy is less supportive of farmers whereas the market has gained importance in terms of providing information, allocating resources, and coordinating economic decisions. But, for all this change, commerce is not anywhere near being totally free. Government officials still exert indirect control over transactions: through subsidies, licensing requirements, distribution plans, inspection, financial accounting and reporting requirements, and, of course, by means of buying and selling operations. The introduction of land diversion quotas in 1978 represented a significant imposition of government authority and another indication that the marketplace will not be used to solve important policy problems.

Debate concerning the relative merits and demerits of government authority and economic markets thus endures. Conflict persists in the rice economy not only as a narrowly conceived process of social interaction but, more broadly, as part of a deep-rooted structural tension in a society undergoing rapid economic change. An unwanted surplus prompts specific problems in a weak economy dominated by small-scale, part-time farmers, many of whom are unwilling and unable to adapt to new conditions. There are still wide differences concerning what to do about rice, although institutional arrangements and the distribution of power allow for ultimate accommodation. Situations rarely develop in which there is no basis for reconciliation. Antagonisms and cooperation have subtly interacted in various ways depending on the nature of the issue, the complexity of choice and implementation, the process of decision, and the way in which conflict has been terminated.

The struggle over values or claims to power and resources has differed within the same policy area and also among the three issues. What generalizations can be made? Conflict is more likely than cooperation when the policy involves an unavoidable commitment by the government to negotiate an annual income settlement, deadlines are part of the process, and implementation is simple, thereby limiting political flexibility for trade-offs and mutual concessions. Price fixing demonstrates that the resort to pressure and conflict is favored when there are multiple contenders for power, a lack of accepted hierarchy, and an ambiguous structure of representation and decision. Conflict also seems inevitable if government officials or elements within the ruling political party try to impose a change inimical to the interests of a major voting bloc without the promise of adequate side payments, and the proposal can be significantly influenced by the activities of informal party groups and interest groups affected by the threatening action.

E. E. Schattschneider's view that the scope of conflict is related to political outcomes is also partially confirmed by rice pricing.[58] A lack of secrecy tends to promote conflict, especially if there is a watchful audience. In this sense, broadening the scope of conflict is a rational political strategy for weak, vulnerable groups which do not enjoy the support of top officials and politicians. But the critical aspect of changing the scope and intensity of conflict is not so much the character of publicity as the support of a large number of elected politicians who cannot avoid taking sides on the issue. That the results are widely understood in terms of winners and losers also tends to exacerbate antagonism.

The significance of who controls the scope of conflict is further underscored by the shape of politics and decisions concerning market programs. Since a move toward free markets was theoretically more threatening to the rice lobby than a temporary wage freeze, introduction of risk into marketing was possible only because the prime minister and party leaders were able to exploit the economic environment and their political resources. Price controversies were partially redefined as market dilemmas, and some of the politics of rice programs was moved into regular channels of decision within the LDP and the government. These decisions were accepted by the rice lobby because they were modest departures and seemed inevitable.

From the government's viewpoint, a freer exchange in rice thereafter helped reduce political conflict by diverting some economic decisions to the obscure and opaque workings of the marketplace. Marketplace arrangements reduce the need for official decisions. They permit producers and consumers, wholesalers and retailers, to deal with each other on a voluntary basis of mutual advantage rather than along the lines established by government authority. Open markets disperse responsibility, obscure winners and losers, and reduce the official burden of seeking out and evaluating hard-to-get information. Less regulation also eliminates the need for the government to make so many public choices and thereby reduces some of the conflict over the complex details of price fixing and other nettlesome decisions.

The character of conflict in marketing politics was thus quite different from that seen in price fixing. Indeed, rice farmers and the agricultural cooperatives viewed open, unregulated economic conflict as a condition to be avoided. Regulatory policies which aimed at fostering competition were thus accompanied by protective regulations, less than complete enforcement of the law, and a variety of generous subsidies. Spreading subsidies among intermediaries is an important way for politicians and government officials to build support for controversial programs. Rather than having to convince everyone of the value of a new departure, politicians can preside over the scramble for new benefits. Side payments are a major conflict-management device: In pricing, these payments were used primarily to soften the blow for losing a public struggle; in marketing, they were used more as incentives for cooperation after a decision had been made by administrative fiat.

Land diversion programs involved an attempt to change the structure of the rice economy through more regulations. The question of land use is probably the most intractable of all agrarian problems, made all the more complex by the intricacies of implementation which require extensive delegation and widespread cooperation. This study suggests that the sheer difficulty of a public problem and the number of issues perceived as relevant are significantly related to how conflict is handled and terminated. Programs can be more artfully disaggregated as the number of land-related issues expands and thus the likelihood increases that parties involved will be willing to negotiate the compromise. In this case, side payments have been used as a bargaining chip to go along with a program worked out as a result of negotiated compromises.

Decisions about land use tended to be handled within "proper" channels in which conflict and cooperation ran in several directions. Political conflict is much less centralized than in the case of price fixing. The evidence suggests also that the greater the number of continuing interactions which link interest groups, politicians, and government officials, the more likely that cooperation will ensue. This is especially so if one party provides "resources" or "institutional means" required by others. For example, the MAFF and the LDP need cooperation from the agricultural cooperatives. Symbiotic relations among a number of parties, who are connected in complex ways, will tend to keep conflict low, unless one party decides to act in a completely arbitrary way.

The scope and intensity of conflict was also determined by the manner in which the three issues are related. Substitutability in policy permits the government to achieve similar objectives in different ways. Rice farmers still receive support from the government, but it has taken different forms: price support in the 1960s evolved into a varied array of subsidies and administrative arrangements a decade later. Conflict has often been reduced and policy options broadened to the extent that there have been many ways of doing the same thing: Farm incomes can be supported by marketing subsidies rather than higher prices or by production subsidies rather than through direct government purchases. Of course substitutability in policy also provides the opportunity for farm groups to push for concession in one area in exchange for cooperation elsewhere. The issues have frequently been joined in this way.

Finally, the question of conflict is related to the sheer difficulty of getting new policies adopted in agriculture when compared to other areas of policy concern. Only a tentative conclusion is possible since the study of policymaking in Japan is relatively undeveloped and few studies have looked at politics in that country systematically through the prism of conflict.[59] It can be argued, nonetheless, that because the political structure of policymaking in agriculture is relatively complex and pluralized, because the process of decision is broad and less disciplined than in other areas, because the LDP and government ministries are weak as integrating mechanisms while the points of potential veto are numerous, and because there is no real policy consensus or intense commitment by the political leadership to move too quickly, only a narrow range of innovation has been attempted thus far. The status quo tends to prevail until economic circumstances force new considerations and new possibilities. Rice farmers are certainly still protected even if they did lose some of their privileges.

NOTES

The author would like to thank the following individuals who provided helpful comments on earlier drafts of this essay: Ellis Krauss, Takekazu Ogura, T. J. Pempel, and Michael Blaker. Part of the research for this study was supported by a fellowship from the Social Science Research Council.

1. See Michael W. Donnelly, "Political Management of Japan's Rice Economy," Ph.D. dissertation, Columbia University, 1978.

2. Among the various discussions on conflict I have found the following to be most useful: Louis Kriesberg, *The Sociology of Conflicts* (Englewood Cliffs, N.J.: Prentice-Hall, 1973); Clinton F. Fink, "Some Conceptual Difficulties in the Theory of Conflict," *Journal of Conflict Resolution* 12 (1968): 412–460; Raymond W. Mack

and Richard C. Snyder, "The Analysis of Social Conflict—Toward an Overview and Synthesis," *Journal of Conflict Resolution* 1 (1957): 313–448; A. Rapoport, *Fights, Games and Debates* (Ann Arbor: University of Michigan Press, 1960); Philip Brickman, ed., *Social Conflict: Readings in Rule Structures and Conflict Relationships* (Lexington, Mass.: Heath, 1974).

3. These are classic dilemmas emphasized most frequently by economists. For a useful discussion see Charles E. Lindblom, *Politics and Markets* (New York: Basic Books, 1977).

4. The official history of the food-control system is *Shokuryō Kanrishi* [History of food control] (Tokyo: Ministry of Agriculture and Forestry, Food Agency, 1972). I–IX. For a unique historical approach see Takekazo Ogura, *Can Japanese Agriculture Survive?* (Tokyo: Agricultural Policy Research Center, 1979).

5. Michael W. Donnelly, "Setting the Price of Rice," in T. J. Pempel, ed., *Policymaking in Contemporary Japan* (Ithaca and London: Cornell University Press, 1977), pp. 143–200.

6. Toyotoshi Tanaka, *Nihon no Nōkyō* [Japan's Association of Agricultural Cooperatives] (Tokyo: Nōkyō Kyōkai, 1971); Tetsumaru Otani, *Nōkyō no Ryūtsū Senryaku* [The market strategy of Nokyo] (Tokyo: Nihon Keizai Shimbunsha, 1973); and Makoto Sakurai, *Beika Seisaku to Baika Undo* [Rice prices and the rice-price movement] (Tokyo: Zenkoku Nōgyō Kyōdō Kumiai Chūōkai, 1975).

7. Yasuhiko Yuize, "Truth About Japanese Agriculture," *Japan Quarterly* 30 (July–September): 264–297.

8. A good deal of "politics" involves bargaining situations such as those described in this essay. The theoretical literature cited in note 2 substantially shaped the manner in which the subject of this study has been formulated. The conditions needed to explain the shape of conflict are included in most studies of conflict. The analysis does not seek to test a single generalization or hypothesis, however. A single proposition simply does not hold within its own terms the possibilities of a complete or adequate description of the three policy areas. I have also drawn some ideas from Robert A. Dahl, *Democracy in the United States* (Chicago: Rand McNally, 1976), a book not often mentioned among the plethora of discussions about conflict. Another useful volume is Robert A. Dahl, *Political Oppositions in Western Democracies* (New Haven: Yale University Press, 1966).

9. James Gwyn, *Agricultural Policy in Wealthy Countries* (Sydney: Angus and Robertson, 1971); Lee R. Martin, ed., *A Survey of Agricultural Economics Literature* (Minneapolis: University of Minnesota Press, 1977).

10. The various statistics on Japanese agriculture are taken from the following sources: *Nōrin Suisan Geppō* [Monthly statistics of Agriculture, Forestry, and Fisheries], various issues; *Nōgyō Hakusho* [Agricultural white paper], 1978. Two recent studies which trace recent changes in rural Japan are Robert J. Smith, *Kurusu: The Price of Progress in a Japanese Village, 1951–1975* (Stanford: Stanford University Press, 1978), and Ronald Dore, *Shinohata: A Portrait of a Japanese Village* (London: Allen Lane, 1978).

11. Fred H. Sanderson, *Japan's Food Prospects and Policies* (Washington, D.C.: Brookings Institution, 1978), chap. 2.

12. See Ogura, *Can Japanese Agriculture Survive?*

13. Organization for Economic Cooperation and Development, *Agricultural Policy in Japan* (Paris: OECD, 1974).

14. I. M. Destler, "United States Food Policy 1972–1976: Reconciling Domestic and International Objectives," *International Organization* 32 (Summer 1978): 618–619.

15. Statistics on rice farming, including government costs, are from Ministry of Agriculture, Forestry, and Fisheries (MAFF), Food Agency, *Shokuryō Kanri no Genjō* [Current conditions in the control of food] (1979) and MAFF, Food Agency, *Beika ni Kansuru Shiryō* [Materials concerning rice prices] (1979).

16. David B. Truman refers to this outer ring of policymaking as the "intermediate structure." See his *Governmental Process*, 2nd ed. (New York: Knopf, 1971).

17. Tanaka, *Nihon no Nōkyō*; Otani, *Nōkyō no Ryūtsū Sanryaku*; Suda Yuji, *Nōkyō* [Association of Agricultural Cooperatives] (Tokyo: Kyoikusha, 1978).

18. Philippe C. Schmitter, "Modes of Interest Intermediation and Models of Societal Change in Western Europe," *Comparative Political Studies* (October 1977): 7–38.

19. Fukuji Taguchi, *Shakai Shūdan no Seiji Kinō* [The political functions of social groups] (Tokyo: Miraisha, 1969), pp. 137–157.

20. Some of these statements can be found in Nōsei Janarisuto, ed., *Nihon Nōgyō no Ugoki* [Trends in Japanese agriculture], various issues.

21. On the role of advisory councils see Yung Ho Park, "The Governmental Advisory Commission System in Japan," *Journal of Comparative Administration* 3 (February 1972): 435–467; Ehud Harari, "Japanese Politics of Advice in Comparative Perspective," *Public Policy* 22 (Fall 1974): 537–577.

22. A term coined by Charles E. Lindblom, *The Policy-Making Process* (Englewood Cliffs, N.J.: Prentice-Hall, 1968).

23. For a history of the Food Agency see *Shokuryō Kanrishi*, passim.

24. John Creighton Campbell, *Contemporary Japanese Budget Politics* (Berkeley: University of California Press, 1977), p. 111.

25. Akiyoshi Takahashi, "Jimintō no Nōson Shihai" [The rural support of the Liberal Democratic Party], in Rei Shiratori, ed., *Hoshu Taisei* [The conservative system] (Tokyo: Tōyō Keizai Shimposha, 1977), vol. 1, pp. 128–167.

26. *Nōgyō Kyōdō Kumiai Nenkan* [Yearbook of the Agriculture Cooperative Associations], 1977.

27. *Nōgyō Kyōdō Kumiai Nenkan* (1973), pp. 67–69.

28. An observation also made recently by T. J. Pempel, "The Bureaucratization of Policymaking in Postwar Japan," *American Journal of Political Science* 18 (November 1974): 647–664.

29. For a recent discussion which emphasizes the nonconflictual aspects of decision making in Japan, see Robert E. Ward, *Japan's Political System*, 2nd ed. (Englewood Cliffs, N.J.: Prentice-Hall, 1978), p. 71.

30. Graham Wilson, *Special Interests and Policymaking: Agricultural Policies and Politics in Britain and the United States of America 1956–1970* (New York: Wiley, 1977).

31. Based on calculations in *Beika ni Kensuru Shiryō* (1979).

32. Food-Control Law, article 3.

33. Ibid., article 4.

34. A slightly different description of this process of decision is contained in Donnelly, "Setting the Price."

35. For the most definitive study of rice markets and the food-control law in recent

years, see Shokuryō Kanri Saido Kenkyūkai, ed., *Shokuryō Kanrihō no Kaisetsu* [A commentary on the Food-Control Law] (Tokyo: Taisei Shuppansha, 1978). Also useful are Toyotoshi, *Nihon no Nōkyō*; Sakurai, *Beika Seisaku*; Kokuritsu Kokkai Toshokan, *Shinkyokuman ni Tatsu Shokkan Seido to Jishu Ryūtsūmai* [New aspects of the food-control system and the autonomous rice market] (Tokyo, 1970); and *Nihon Nōgyō no Ugoki*, various issues.

36. See *Shokuryō Kanrihō no Kaisetsu.*

37. Masanobu Kuwabara, et al., *Shokuryō Kanri Seido to Kome no Ryūtsū* [The food-control system and rice distribution] (Tokyo: Ie no Hikari, 1969), p. 318.

38. Yomiuri Shimbunsha, *Kome: Sono Hiryoku o Saguru* [Rice: a search for its appeal] (Tokyo: Yomiuri Shimbunsha, 1975), p. 196.

39. See *Shinkyokuman ni Tatsu* for a detailed discussion of this period.

40. A tactic adopted often by the political opposition in any country whenever an unpopular decision seems unavoidable.

41. Asahi Shimbunsha, *Jimintō* [The Liberal Democratic Party] (Tokyo: Asahi Shimbunsha, 1970), pp. 59–61.

42. Sakurai, *Beika Seisaku*, pp. 230–231.

43. Ibid., pp. 235–237.

44. See Otani, *Nōkyō no Ryūtsū*, pp. 22–53.

45. Sakurai, *Beika Seisaku*, pp. 233–238.

46. For a recent account of the autonomous market see Risuke Hinodo, "Kome: Ryūtsū no Genjō to Mondaiten" [Rice: current conditions and problems in the market], *Nōgyō to Keizai* (February 1977): 25–31.

47. See Sakurai, *Beika Seisaku*, pp. 254–263.

48. Otani, *Nōkyō no Ryūtsū*, p. 35.

49. *Asahi Evening News*, 23 April 1973.

50. Rice diversion programs during the period 1969–1978 are described in Kiyoshi Oshima, ed., *Kome no Seisan Chōsei* [Adjustment of rice production] (Tokyo: Ochanomizu Shobo, 1975); Sakurai, *Beika Seisaku*; *Nihon Nōgyō Nenkan*, 1976 and 1979; *Nihon Nōgyō Kennō* [Annual report on Japanese agriculture] 27 (1979); and *Nihon Nōgyō no Ugoki* 45 (1978).

51. A useful discussion of these programs is in *Nihon Nōgyō Nenkan* (1979).

52. For statistics on rice production and related matters in this section, see *Shokuryō Kanri no Genjō* (1979) and *Beika ni Kansuru Shiryo* (1979).

53. See *Nihon Nōgyō Nenkan* (1979), p. 92.

54. See Campbell, *Contemporary*, p. 141.

55. The chronological outline is based on materials cited in note 50.

56. Chalmers Johnson, "MITI and Japanese International Economic Policy," in Robert A. Scalapino, ed., *The Foreign Policy of Modern Japan* (Berkeley: University of California Press, 1977), pp. 227–279.

57. A. W. Gouldner, "The Norm of Reciprocity: A Preliminary Statement," *American Sociological Review* 25 (1960): 161–178.

58. E. E. Schattschneider, *The Semisovereign People* (Hinsdale, Ill.: Dryden Press, 1975).

59. See the annotated bibliography in Pempel, *Policymaking.*

PART V:
Conclusion

13
Conflict and Its Resolution in Postwar Japan

ELLIS S. KRAUSS
THOMAS P. ROHLEN
PATRICIA G. STEINHOFF

The foregoing essays have presented sharply drawn analyses of conflict and its resolution in many areas of Japanese life. Their approach and results raise two general questions: What do these studies tell us about models of harmony and models of conflict as applied to postwar Japan? And what do they tell us about postwar Japanese society and its similarities and differences in conflict patterns with Western societies?

Models of Harmony and Conflict

The effort to perfect our understanding of a society is an effort to build more adequate models of its structures and basic processes. In this regard the dominant model so far has had a marked inclination toward explaining Japan as relatively harmonious. The studies in this volume highlight a number of weaknesses in this harmony model.

First, the harmony model is based on a limited number of studies of situations in which small-group solidarity and the ideal of community have been particularly strong, but it ignores areas of Japanese society in which internal conflict has been a persistent problem. The first generation of foreign social scientists, whose research first imprinted the harmony model on Japanese studies, were few in number and tended to study the most tightly knit Japanese social organizations: small groups, villages, and single firms and factories.[1] The studies in this volume have shown that when a wider variety of institutions and settings, particularly larger and more complex organizations, are included as research sites, there is much more conflict in Japan than the harmony model recognizes.

Second, the harmony model often confuses cultural ideals with reality. Many of the pioneer researchers on Japan were anthropolgists primarily concerned with the cultural differences that made Japan unique. Their interpretations reflected this cultural determinism, explaining behavior as a product of Japanese cultural ideals such as prizing harmony and ignoring contention. Our conflict-oriented studies have shown, however, that when values are treated as merely ideals not always implemented in practice, and as but one factor influencing behavior, a more realistic perspective of the extent of harmony in Japan emerges.

Third, earlier studies of Japan tended to generalize from the small solidary groups studied to society as whole. One of the most important results of our authors' conflict studies has been to demonstrate how much the extent, frequency, and type of conflict varies at different levels of society.

Fourth, political contexts were rarely studied and thus the harmony model fails to recognize the distinction between such situations, which may be ideologically polarized, and private situations, which can be relatively impervious to political tensions. The studies of politics in this volume reveal that the public institutions of Japanese society have neither a solid structure nor inevitably harmonious process.

Finally, the harmony emphasis in Japanese studies tends to offer a static image of that society. The stress on culture and social structure, treated as relatively persistent through time, ignores the dynamics and complexities of Japanese social processes. Our studies, by taking a process-oriented approach, reveal the role of conflict in bringing about change and demonstrate that the harmony which does exist is best understood in terms of unceasing efforts to avoid and resolve very real conflicts within and between groups.

We enumerate the weaknesses of the harmony model not to condemn it but rather to benefit from its strengths and move on to a more comprehensive and dynamic approach to Japanese society. It is thanks to the insights of those scholars who shaped the solidarity model that many of the distinctive qualities of Japanese society have been recognized. Indeed, the studies in this volume do confirm the harmony model's utility in highlighting certain key characteristics of Japanese society. The authors agree unanimously that the ideal of harmony is still strong at the interpersonal level. They find individuals attempting to avoid conflict and open confrontation, and while this may be true to a degree in all societies, the Japanese case is more notable. Within their organizations, furthermore, Japanese seem especially sensitive to the dangers of conflict, to anticipate them, and to make greater efforts to contain and manage them. When social scientists in search of conflict report such findings, these results are impressive. Finally, the lines of overall social cleavage—class conflict, urban-rural conflict, sex-role conflict—seem less salient, intense, or widespread in Japan than in many Western societies.

But these studies also indicate that the harmony model alone is insufficient. It highlights but part of a larger picture. Japan may not be as conflict prone as Western societies, but the fact remains that postwar Japanese society has witnessed a great deal of conflict, whether or not it is always obvious to Western observers. As Takie Lebra in particular points out, people who avoid expressing conflict continue to feel hostility. People may use less direct means of communicating antagonisms, but they do communicate them. Teigo Yoshida shows how villagers who repress their differences within the confines of their tight-knit community, subconsciously displace their feelings in other ways. Tadashi Hanami, Thomas Rohlen, John Campbell, Ellis Krauss, and Michael Donnelly reveal various organizations experiencing significant conflict along predictable structural lines, and Susan Pharr shows that sex-role conflict can occur in Japanese organizations, too. Workers do make demands on managers, albeit in different ways than in the West, and once expressed openly, the intensity of the struggle can be greater than the West. The contest of parochial interests is very real, and certain institutions have witnessed more salient and intense struggle than their Western counterparts. These include the parliament, the student movement, the machinery of agricultural policy, and the educational system. Many other areas of Japanese life are equally prone to severe political conflict.

How do we reconcile the seeming contradiction between harmony and conflict? Obviously this is one of the major challenges in attempting to construct a more sophisticated and comprehensive model of Japanese society. What follows is our initial attempt to outline such a model. Even as we argue that Japan does not lack conflict and can be analyzed using conflict theory, we seek in this model to identify what is distinctive about those patterns of conflict and the way the Japanese try to manage them. As with all models, it rests on sweeping generalizations to which there are known exceptions. Yet we believe it to be more accurate than the prevalent harmony model, in the sense that it recognizes the ubiquitous conflict that does exist, and to be a more realistic foundation for understanding contemporary Japan, in the sense that it does not seek to portray Japanese patterns of conflict and its resolution as immutable, as without elements of individual and social costs, or as somehow better than Western patterns. The model emphasizes the link between conflict at different levels of society and between conflict tendencies and patterns of conflict resolution.

Toward a Conflict Model of Japan

THE IDEAL OF HARMONY AND INTERPERSONAL CONFLICT

Conflict is neither desired nor idealized by most Westerners, but it is legitimate, accepted, and expected in the West more than in Japan. The emphasis on individualism and individualistic expression in Western culture, especially where Protestant and utilitarian traditions have been strong, for many centuries provided a powerful moral counterforce to the personal desire to avoid conflict. All the leading social theories of the last few hundred years postulate and encourage one or another expression of self-interest. This has not been the case in Japan, where collective unity and the attainment of group goals have dominated both practical and moral thinking. During the very long Tokugawa period Confucian values and a national ideology of order and unity were deeply implanted. As the Meiji leaders continued to emphasize this tradition, national unity and selfless devotion to the collective good became even more explicit. Their emperor-centered ideology took Confucian family ethics and applied them on a nationwide scale. When modernization and the importation of Western values challenged this ideology, Japanese society experienced strains of class and occupational divisions, secularization, rationalism, and so forth, but the ideal of harmony in interpersonal relations remained. With the militarist regime of the 1930s and mobilization for war, unity and general harmony were once more emphasized as the national ideology.

Defeat and the Allied Occupation removed Confucianism from public life, but the new democratic values and perspectives filtered down to the organizational and interpersonal levels rather slowly. Perhaps because it was a time of national breakdown and rapid change, many Japanese retreated even more into the close-knit relationships of family and small group. In these relationships the old cultural values remained strong. Harmony too remained a latent norm in organizational life. Many companies actually promoted a Confucian perspective. Ideological continuity in the private sphere did not

mean, however, the absence of conflict. It meant that conflict continued to be expressed and handled in ways different from those anticipated by Western theories. Takie Lebra, Agnes Niyekawa, and Teigo
Yoshida make this clear in their essays. Their point is that a surface of
interpersonal harmony is generally maintained not by the absence of
conflict but by its transference, introjection, and very great efforts at
management.

Avoidance, displacement, and repression are not necessarily functional for the maintenance of interpersonal and small-group relations. Coser, for example, says the expression of conflict is healthy
when it allows for the identification of real differences within a group
and thus opens the possibility of adjusting relations accordingly. In
Japan explicit identification and overt adjustment seem less common
than a process of anticipation and response that may manage conflict
but only partially resolve its deeper origins. As a consequence, the
group's norms and structure are preserved, and the dissatisfied individual has been catered to, but there is no fundamental readjustment
of relationships. The great sensitivity of Japanese in small groups to
linguistic and behavioral cues indicating dissatisfaction is a crucial
part of this approach. Then leaders and other group members may
make strenuous efforts to respond to the internal dissatisfactions.
Much of this is symbolic reassurance, but it creates an obligation to
respond with a more conciliatory stance. Compromises emerge as the
need to conform for the sake of the group is underscored.

When such anticipation and response do not occur, however, the
result is alienation and growing hostility, just as in the West. Latent
tensions and dissatisfaction may actually be more prevalent in Japanese small groups than in Western societies, precisely because of the
inhibitions on conflict expression. Japanese, furthermore, rarely feel
they have the option to leave a relationship. Without the options of
either exit or expression, the lack of cathartic resolution and fundamental adjustment in the relationship may produce a deep and persistent sense of malaise. This outcome implies that it is the individual, rather than the group or society, who bears the cost of conflict in
Japan.

CONFLICT WITHIN ORGANIZATIONS

An ideology of harmony applied within formal organization can lead
to the oft-noted Japanese tendency toward constructing organizations
that resemble total communities. The individual, particularly the

male, is expected to identify strongly with an organization and to derive both professional and personal fulfillment from it. Relations with other members involve the total personality, not just formal roles, and whole lives are committed to a common goal. Many Japanese social organizations strike Western observers as quasi-religious, or even totalitarian, in the way they promote solidarity and loyalty.

To create a homogeneous organization that perpetuates a common culture and smooth interpersonal relations, Japanese organizations are inclined to recruit pliable youth without too much concern for their specialized skills and then to socialize them intensively. This tendency too contrasts to the ideal Western organization, conceived of as a functional entity for the accomplishment of narrowly prescribed tasks. The Western emphasis is on functional differentiation and specialization; recruitment and training center on technical skills. Once again, the contrast between Japanese and Western types does not imply conflict versus no conflict, but merely different patterns of conflict. March and Simon indicate that intergroup conflict within organizations may occur for two reasons.[2] First, conflict may occur because of differences in goals or in perceptions of reality. Second, it may occur because of the felt need for joint decision making—that is, the greater the sense of interdependence, the greater the potential for conflict. The first notion fits Western economic, ideological, and rational explanations for conflict. The second is less classically Western in the case of modern organizations because it postulates belonging and common interests as fundamental. We would hypothesize that the difference in norms already discussed results in more conflict created by the first source in the West and more conflict created by the second in Japan.

Western organizations recruit individuals from more heterogeneous populations in terms of race, religion, and ethnicity. The result is greater diversity among members and less receptivity to the notion of a singular organizational culture. The emphasis on specialization and technical expertise within the organization creates a further layer of diverse perceptions based on functional task. In Japan, a relatively homogeneous society and a very uniform educational system establish a basis of common socialization experience that greatly enhances the efforts of organizational leaders to mold a common identification and set of values. The priority given to personal relations over technical expertise further lessens diversity of values.

Yet if conflicts based on differences in personal attributes are less common in Japanese organizations, the very intensity of small-group orientations creates the basis for other conflicts less notable in the West. A serious problem in many Japanese organizations is inadequate coordination and communication between subunits because of the strong personal relations among members of the same subunit. Divisional and unit conflict is ubiquitous in formal organizations, but it is more acute where group ties are strong. Nakane has pointed to this general tendency within Japanese organizations, but she did not view its implications as part of the larger picture of conflict patterns.[3] As Mack and Snyder have hypothesized, "a high degree of intimacy between the parties, as contrasted with a high degree of functional interdependence, will intensify conflict."[4]

We would expect conflict within Japanese organizations to be no less prevalent than in the West, but for somewhat different reasons. The expression and resolution of conflict within organizations will vary greatly between Japan and the West following these general lines of difference in organizational recruitment, socialization, and identifications. In each type of organization, conflicts can also be minimized by managerial intervention, but again in somewhat different ways. In Western organizations, subunits can be granted relative autonomy of decision making within their own specialized areas, thus lessening joint decision making and its conflict potential except at the very top of the organization (where conflict over coordination can be intense). In Japanese organizations, frequent transfer of middle-level officials (which often occurs in fact in Japan) and constant top-level supervision can mitigate development of personal factions and isolation of small groups from each other. Simply put, Western organizations can lessen intergroup conflict by granting more autonomy to subunits whereas Japanese organizations can do so only by granting less. John Campbell's analysis of the coordination of policymaking in Japan and his account of the special efforts government leaders must make to overcome the in-group norms of each ministry created by their recruitment and socialization processes is a vivid illustration of this problem.

The ideology of harmony raised to an organizational principle also creates other special circumstances. Because Japanese organizations incorporate aspects of community, all members are conceived as intimately interdependent with common vested interests. Expectations that joint (and consensual) decision making will take place throughout the organization are high. A basis of trust is expected, and if it is indeed present, the settlement of many issues is smooth by Western standards. This quality has made Japanese companies the envy of their Western counterparts in labor-management relations. It also means, however, that should an issue arise that cannot be settled by normal processes, or should the basis of trust be lost, conflict is likely to involve the entire organization and become particularly intense, even violent. As Tadashi Hanami indicates, in order to overcome the inhibitions on conflict expression imposed by the norms of organizational harmony, and to force officials to take their demands seriously enough to bargain with them, labor union leaders on occasion must try to destroy the normally close and dependent relationships between employee and management. Susan Pharr also indicates that the women tea pourers had to objectify their male coworkers and come to see them as the enemy before they actually took collective action to express their grievances. These phenomena, incidentally, conform closely to Coser's proposition that aggression and hatred are not inevitable aspects of all conflict; rather, it is often *useful* to hate the opponent.[5]

Thus Japanese unions engage in slowdowns, plant occupations, symbolic gestures, and strikes at an early stage in their struggle, rather than as a weapon of last resort once negotiations have broken down as in the West. If these actions are not appropriately responded to by management, then all basis for further communication and trust is destroyed and the conflict will escalate explosively. The issue at stake seems rapidly to become, in addition to the grievances themselves, the dispute's destruction of the values of harmony and community by the union's actions and management's failure to anticipate and respond to dissatisfaction. It is also difficult to avoid wondering whether the intense and explosive release of aggression in such situations may not also be the result of long pent-up frustrations because of the inability to express conflict in daily work life—that is, whether such labor-management relations in Japan contain greater elements of the release of tension.[6]

Finally, even the vaunted Japanese penchant for *nemawashi* (literally, "root-binding") in organizations—the special attention given to preliminary discussions and emergence of common views prior to decision making—can become a factor in conflict as well as in integration. As the case of Pharr's tea pourers indicates, conflict groups can engage in such practices to unify themselves internally, laying the groundwork of solidarity necessary to confront others in the organizations. Strong ideals of harmony and the expectation of joint decision making through consensus can contribute to organizational solidarity, but they can exacerbate conflict as well.

CONFLICT BETWEEN ORGANIZATIONS AND POLITICAL CONFLICT

Characteristics of interorganizational conflict stem directly from the structure and dynamics of interpersonal and intraorganizational conflict. In Western societies the prevalence of interpersonal and intraorganizational conflict means that much of the conflict between organizations begins at the grass roots and bubbles upward when higher levels of organization cannot manage it. Further, lower-level and intraorganizational conflicts are fairly easy to universalize beyond a particular group or organization because of the heterogeneity of values and interests found in Western society. Within every organization and institution there are individuals who have more values and interests in common with others in different organizations and institutions than with many of their fellow members. (Nakane calls these ties horizontal relations based on "attribute.")[7] This is one reason why class (trade unions), profession, race, and other identifications and associations that cut across organizational and community membership play such a major role in our social and political conflicts.

Because a conflict within one organization can often be duplicated in many others, widening in scope and significance, leaders of dissatisfied groups within an organization readily see the possibilities in broadening their struggle by appealing to those outside. Such universalized conflicts cut across vertical organizational bounds and are a counterforce to interorganizational conflict. Their likelihood gives organizational and political elites in the West a common interest in preventing grass-roots conflict in one organization from spreading. Elite common interests are often stronger than those between members of a particular organization. These qualities, of course, create a vicious circle of continuing grass-roots dissension.

In Japan, the nature of interpersonal and group relations within organizations and the ideology of community mean that conflicts rarely bubble up from the grass roots. Rather, conflict more frequently occurs between whole organizations. Elites, as leaders of Japanese organizations, have less in common with each other than with their own members and more often they are in conflict. Those in authority often act as conflict managers within their organization, but it is also their role to *express* conflict in representing their organization outside. This is one reason why a third party trusted by all sides often must be brought in to encourage a resolution of differences. What we are describing here, of course, are relative tendencies in comparison to the West, not absolute characteristics, but the Japanese pattern seems to conform to Deutsch's proposition that internally homogeneous conflict groups different from each other (in the Japanese case, primarily in organizational subculture and socialization) are more likely to engage in competition than organizations which are internally heterogeneous and have overlapping characteristics (the Western pattern).[8]

Because the conflicts that do arise within Japanese organizations become intense due to the very intimacy and emotional aspects of relations, they are not readily universalized beyond the organization's boundaries; when they do transcend a particular organization, they lose their intensity. Dissatisfied groups have a hard time broadening their struggles, as Tadashi Hanami points out in the case of labor disputes and Susan Pharr shows in the failure of the tea pourers' revolt to spread beyond the first division involved. And as Thomas Rohlen reports about education, although disputes between the union and educational authorities do become most intense in certain schools, they rarely become generalized, whereas conflicts at the national level which are universalistic in character rarely reach the intensity of school-level confrontations.

Conflict in postwar Japan has occurred frequently between organizations holding different ideals. Many such conflicts can be traced to the Allied Occupation's attempt to transform Japanese values and ideology. As Takeshi Ishida points out, the occupation destroyed the prewar ideology of national unity and harmony and substituted a democratic ideology that legitimized opposition conflict within the bounds of law. The polarization of values that followed fed political conflict, especially around such issues as foreign policy, defense, public order, and education.

These political issues and values cut across institutional boundaries and created major conflicts, especially in public institutions, that involved differences of value as well as of interest. The loss of a common principle of community at the national level meant conflict resolution was very difficult. The constitution was itself at the heart of the struggles rather than serving as a legitimized means for resolving conflicts. In the early postwar period, these political struggles were especially frequent and difficult to manage. Ellis Krauss's description of party politics in the Diet and Thomas Rohlen's discussion of the politics of education give a feel for how the polarity of values has exacerbated conflict in public entities. The political conflicts between left and right quite naturally seemed aberrant to the general Japanese pattern, for they were universal and intraorganizational.

In contrast to the West, however, the universalization of these conflicts in Japan did not proceed from the bottom up but from the top down. Their continuity and intensity centered on the national level. The further down the levels of society, the more entrenched the old norms of harmony and organizational community. These differences in norms at varying levels help explain some of the paradoxes and contradictions of Japanese politics and society implicit in the writings of many observers. While conflict was the chief focus of attention of observers of political parties in the Diet, and of unions in public bureaucracies, analysts were describing local-level politics and electoral mobilization as replete with strong community norms, patron-client relations, and interpersonal relations that accepted the ideals of unity and harmony.[9] Rohlen's analysis of education, because it embraces both aspects, is an almost unique attempt to explain these contradictions and show in detail how the top-down political conflicts of the postwar period lose their impetus at the grass-roots level where norms of interpersonal cooperation still prevail.

The shape of conflict at the interorganizational level, in other words, reflects a specific historical mixture, one that the harmony model fails to take into account. The model we propose does not ignore the areas of organizational solidarity that exist, but it also recognizes the many areas and intersections between organizations where the harmony model does not work.

CLASS CONFLICT?

The reader may note that there is no explicit emphasis on class conflict in our model. Depending on one's definition of class, one may see or not see implicit class divisions as fundamental to many of the conflicts described in these pages. None of the authors, however, have put their subjects into such a mold. We believe there are a number of reasons for this.

First, there are two types of actors that could fit a wide definition of class conflict: economic interest groups such as unions and farmers' associations seeking better conditions, on the one hand, and, on the other, advocates of radical social change such as students, the Communist or Socialist parties, and even citizens' protest groups, which seek egalitarian ends. Yet many of these groups themselves do not advocate an ideology based on class consciousness. Some of those that do, such as the leftist parties, especially in recent years have downplayed such consciousness as part of their appeal to the electorate.

Second, unions in the private sector, where economic interest should be divisive, express very little concern with class issues and are not oriented to the wider concerns of a working class. Public sector unions most certainly have leaders who are so oriented and who regularly use class rhetoric, but the fact is that political, not economic, issues are the fundamental source of their disputes with the government. One would be hard put to create a theory that views well-paid public servants as the vanguard of class conflict.

Third, the most keen advocates of a class perspective in Japan all belong to the intelligentsia. They are privileged students and professionals, not members of oppressed economic groups, and their relative, and perhaps increasing, isolation in Japan may say much about the difficulties that an ideology based on class conflict faces when confronted with Japanese patterns of social organization.

Japan is indeed a society with hierarchical structure, strong group consciousness, economic inequalities, and social conflicts; but as these studies reveal, their combination in postwar Japan has produced surprisingly little class conflict in the traditional Marxian sense. Here we are in general agreement with the harmony model in noting that ideologies of community and the focus of vertical loyalties in organizations have discouraged the awareness and organization of economic class interests. We would suggest that a conflict theory such as Ralf Dahrendorf's, which argues that general relationships of domination and authority in social organizations are more important than a strict class struggle in determining patterns of conflict and coalition, may be more relevant to a society such as Japan's.[10] If one broadens the focus of "class" conflict to become the relations between authority and "subordinate groups in the social structure," as Sugimoto does, then one may find evidence of substantial "class" conflict.[11]

CONFLICT MANAGEMENT

Conflict management techniques all have a common characteristic—to bring together the opposing parties in a legitimized forum under a set of norms encouraging compromise or an acceptance (however reluctant) of a solution. The actual techniques used and their frequency, however, depend on the typical patterns of conflict in each society.

In the West, the preferred, the most frequent, and probably the most effective conflict management techniques are impersonal and formal. This pattern is a function of the universalistic approach to conflict in the West and the need to regulate people of diverse goals and interests. Conflict management typically means shifting the problem to some impersonal authority, either at a higher organizational level or outside altogether. Since the same type of conflict may be duplicated in other organizations, conflict must be managed by general principles that can be applied in all situations and organizations. Thus, in the West, the most frequent, legitimate, and effective conflict-management mechanisms are the generalizable and formal ones of law, contract, arbitration, unilateral decision by the highest authority, and majority rule voting (even within small groups).

Contrast this case to Japan, where the most legitimate, effective, and frequent conflict-management mechanisms are the informal and personal ones of small-group discussion, personal communication, and the use of go-betweens. These techniques keep the conflict localized and centered on the original parties. Wherever the norms of harmony are still strong, conflict can best be handled by personalizing it —by bringing together the leaders of conflict groups and invoking the norms of interpersonal relations. We have seen the penchant of Japanese for attempting such personal conflict-management techniques in conflicts between formal organizations in many of the essays in this volume—in Ellis Krauss's description of informal relations among partisan directors of Diet committees and the use of the speaker of the house as a go-between, in John Campbell's discussion of the strenuous efforts that political authorities make to construct artificial interpersonal settings in order to resolve interministerial disputes, in Tadashi Hanami's description of labor dispute resolution, and in Michael Donnelly's analysis of conflict management in agricultural politics.

Another apparent difference between Japan and the West lies in the frequency and location of bargaining compared with persuasion. March and Simon indicate that bargaining is likely to take place where disagreement over goals is assumed.[12] Persuasion and joint problem solving are expected where common objectives are readily acknowledged. Since the assumption of conflict and disagreement over goals is more common within Western organizations and the ideology of community is more common within Japanese organizations, it follows that bargaining is the prevalent mode in the West, whereas problem solving and persuasion are more common in Japan when it comes to serious internal conflicts. Many observers have praised the Japanese inclination to resolve issues through an intensive search for information leading to the creation of alternatives within a narrow range of reason followed by the gradual formation of consensus through mutual persuasion.[13] Such processes within Japanese organizations are not the magical product of cultural uniqueness; they are the logical derivatives of organizational conflict patterns. On the other hand, between organizations in Japan, because common goals are not assumed, bargaining is as common and as hard-nosed as in the West.

We can also ask which conflicts are the most difficult to manage. In the West, because of the high reliance on formal and impersonal mechanisms, the most problematic conflicts are those in which the mechanisms themselves become part of the struggle or in some other manner lose legitimacy—as when the equity and fairness of the law or the courts are questioned, for example, or when favoritism or corruption is reported in high office. Around the established formal mechanisms are fought the greatest symbolic battles. The very survival of established society often appears to hinge on the preservation of impartiality in the institutions of conflict resolution. Naturally, the elites seek to preserve their legitimacy whereas those out of power aim to challenge the notion of equitable justice. Here lies the ultimate forum for conflict in Western society.

In Japan, the most unmanageable conflicts are the ones unresponsive to personal conflict management. Among conflicts of this type we include those involving ideological extremists, mass protests, and situations with a history of interpersonal hostility. In such circumstances, face-to-face resolutions and go-betweens are not very effective. These struggles too have almost by definition a high symbolic component, because they are waged impersonally. Furthermore, symbolism is heightened because one or both parties must first symbolically destroy the framework of personal relationships which up to a point inhibited the expression of hostility. Tadashi Hanami's portrait of union struggles within individual enterprises and Patricia Steinhoff's account of the mass bargaining sessions against faculty and administrators conducted by student radicals both fit this expectation. Authorities, on the other hand, must try to isolate the dissidents as definitionally outside the community altogether; this occurred in both cases. Westerners would turn such situations over to legal mechanisms, just as Japanese would attempt to handle many problems internal to organizations without recourse to formal means.

Some of these essays also make it clear that personalized conflict resolution has its limitations and costs. John Campbell, for example, indicates that attempts to resolve deep-rooted differences in organizational interests between ministries by bringing bureaucrats together in personal settings often does not succeed. And Susan Pharr reminds us that when universal and formal resolution mechanisms are lacking, any changes accomplished by conflict are less likely to be generalized beyond the specific group involved.

Finally, we should note one universal device of conflict management that seems to be used widely in Japan but has not received very much attention and also has its costs. The desire to avoid and manage overt conflict frequently leads Japanese leaders to use material "side payments" to antagonists to smooth over conflicts intractable to resolution by the preferred small-group and interpersonal techniques. As Michael Donnelly indicates, the government attempted to gain compliance with the new rationalization of the food distribution system, many aspects of which were unpopular with their supporting farmer interest groups, by raising the material rewards to farmers in other elements of the program. The LDP's decision to risk high debt financing to maintain the amount of divisible rewards available to its supporters and to make concessions to the opposition at a time of economic contraction and political threat, as described by Ellis Krauss, is another example. This device, perhaps used frequently in Japan as part of the more general tendency to structure situations in order to avoid the appearance of zero-sum outcomes, may help alleviate confrontation by buying off intense opposition, but it definitely has its disadvantages in terms of producing rational policy.

JAPAN IN TRANSITION

Our authors suggest that the most salient conflicts and lines of cleavage in Japanese society during the postwar period have occurred in public arenas between organizations polarized along left-right political dimensions. In the immediate postwar period, all of Japanese society was liable to such conflict, but by the mid-1950s private organizations had reasserted traditional values internally. The Allied Occupation set the stage for this situation by removing the legitimacy of traditional ideology at the highest level. Public policies and institutions subsequently have been vulnerable to conflict of a highly symbolic kind, and interpersonal means of resolution have often proved difficult in these politicized conflicts. Nevertheless, our authors also seem to have discovered new patterns of conflict and new lines of cleavage in Japan during the last decade, suggesting the need for considering how the patterns we have described may be changing.

One important source of change is the gradual institutionalization of left-right political conflict. Clearly there are moments when a general atmosphere of left-right conflict still exists, when microlevel events are seen in the light of national political issues, but these moments are much less frequent than during the period 1945–1960 and they are often followed by phases of construction and stability during which the issues are worked out at lower levels. Conflicts have led to permanent changes in most public institutions. In some cases, the institutionalization of conflict involves the development of rather passionless, ritualized struggles following implicit rules of the game. Party relations in the Diet in the 1960s, the spring labor offensive, farmers' annual rice price demonstrations, and certain aspects of student demonstrations—all are examples of this ritual drama. In other cases, long-term conflict relationships, as in education and recent Diet sessions, have led to quasi-informal mechanisms of conflict management, many quite personalized, that have gradually achieved institutional status. As a result, many of the most serious value conflicts of the occupation and immediate postwar period have been reduced in intensity and brought into routinized channels of bargaining, negotiation, and daily communication and interaction in specific institutions.

If conflict has lessened in some areas, however, it has increased in others. Particularly striking in recent years has been the extent to which egalitarian and democratic values have finally been accepted and internalized at the individual, grass-roots level, becoming intertwined with the problems of economic affluence and advanced industrialization. New issues and new patterns of conflict have emerged. The most salient issues of the 1970s centered on pollution and quality of life, Japan's low level of welfare services, and the expansion of rights for low-status groups such as women and *burakumin*. These new sources of protest did not arise from the established opposition of unions and leftist parties and often pushed the older left-right national-level conflicts into a secondary place in the pantheon of public controversy. The new issues cut across conventional organizational lines; they were mostly grass roots in origin and quite capable of becoming universal in terms of the principles enunciated. A white-collar worker could share the community norms of his firm but in his free time join as a citizen with his counterparts from other companies to organize a neighborhood residents' movement to confront local authorities about some environmental problems. Socialist and conservative politicians who continued to squabble with each other over foreign affairs or school textbooks found themselves under the same pressure from their constituents to be more responsive to local concern about day care, pensions for the aged, noise, smog, or other industrial disruptions.[14]

The resulting conflicts centered on local communities, as when residents demanded compensation from a polluting factory, or they arose in organizations as when women or *burakumin* demanded an adjustment of relations within their offices or schools. Clearly these new sources of conflict bubbling up from below and involving heterogeneous collections of citizens are reminiscent of the type of conflict most prevalent in the West. As we would predict, these new conflicts brought with them a shift toward conflict management methods that depended on the formal authority of the law and courts.[15] The issues and participants cut across too many organizational boundaries for informal means dependent on interpersonal ties to succeed.

The new conflicts may still encounter the old norms of organizational harmony. As in Susan Pharr's study of status conflict in a bureaucratic office, the proponents of the new values may fail to overcome the strength of old practices and attitudes. But merely the fact that such universal values now penetrate organizations from outside is notable as it indicates a weakening of the ideology of organization-as-community. As the norm of harmony is challenged from within, the character of conflict and its management must change too.

Other new patterns of conflict have been forming closer to the top, among elites who previously shared the common goals of either the leftist or conservative camps. One example is the greater complexity of conflicts within the government today. No longer can the LDP, the bureaucracy, and conservative interests be described as a monolithic bloc completely sharing common interests. Japanese national politics has simultaneously become less polarized and more complex. Elements of the conservative coalition are no longer in fixed coalition on all matters; rather, they may shift alliances with the issues more than previously, meaning that conflicts are less predictable and conflict management more flexible. John Campbell's description of the fluidity of alliances and the crosscutting of conflicts involving "subgovernments" is a most instructive case in point. Another vivid example of this changed situation is Michael Donnelly's account of agricultural politics since 1968. As the prime minister and elements of the bureaucracy emphasized the goals of fiscal responsibility and economic rationalization above the older aims of national food self-sufficiency and politically expedient subsidies to farmers, the highly routinized ritual of rice price demonstrations gave way to less predictable, "real" conflict. Old allies became potential antagonists and old enemies potential friends on this policy issue. The result of the simultaneous trends toward ideological depolarization and new and variable cleavages within the camps has been the movement of Japanese politics away from a pattern of basic consensus within an established in-group but conflict with perpetual antagonists outside it. The move is now toward more complex bargaining within and between partisan and ideological groupings.

For Further Research

We conceive of this volume as an initial attempt to apply a conflict approach to Japanese society and politics. Far from believing that this book is in any way the definitive word on the subject, we hope that the efforts of our contributors will stimulate further rethinking of the social science paradigm of Japan, more research on Japan with attention to conflict, and the testing of the hypotheses and propositions contained in our findings. In conclusion, we would like to indicate a few of the directions such future research might take.

First, in this endeavor we were able to look at conflict and its resolution in only a selected number of institutions and contexts. There are many others that have yet to be analyzed from a conflict perspective. For example, we need much more empirical research on the dynamics of interaction in the small group in Japan. What are the typical dynamics of conflict and its resolution between generations in the family, in the workplace peer group, in neighborhood friendship groups, and in local community organizations? How does a large organizational structure mold conflict patterns in primary groups? What is the interface between the patterns of conflict and its resolution in small groups and the structure of authority in an organization? Despite the importance of the primary group in Japanese society, we have surprisingly little systematic research on its internal interactions and its external relationships to larger organizations.

Although Tadashi Hanami's work has given us major insights into conflict between labor unions and management and Thomas Rohlen's into conflict at different levels of the teachers' union, we know very little about the high levels of conflict within most other unions and union federations and between labor unions and the socialist parties or the consequences of these conflicts. For that matter, we probably know much more today about the patterns of conflict within the LDP, the bureaucracy, and conservative interest groups than we do about conflict within and among the opposition camp members and how it affects the politics of opposition and the decision making of government.

This is not to say that research on the conservative elite has been exhausted. If John Campbell's description of the importance of "sub-governments" is correct, then one of the most promising approaches to study of the ruling elite would be to concentrate on policy conflicts within specific issue areas that involve party, interest groups, and bureaucracy, much as Michael Donnelly has done in this volume, rather than only on conflict within and between institutions.

Another topic that requires greater attention is that of the law and other formal mechanisms of conflict resolution. If such methods are becoming somewhat more prevalent than in the past, they should be studied more thoroughly for the functions they perform in managing and resolving conflict. It would be especially interesting, for example, to investigate the psychology and motivations, and the costs and benefits, involved in invoking impersonal and formal conflict-resolution mechanisms in Japan rather than the typical personal means.

Second, apart from researching institutions and groups that could not be dealt with in this volume, we would encourage future conflict studies to adopt a wider diversity of theoretical and methodological approaches. It would be an interesting experiment, for example, to take one conflict theory, say Dahrendorf's, and apply it consistently throughout Japanese society. And the vast resources of available quantitative data on Japan should be examined from a conflict perspective.

Third, we believe that the groundwork laid by our contributors must be expanded by more explicitly comparative work on conflict in Japan—comparison both across time and across societies. We have indicated how conflict patterns in Japanese society and in specific institutions have shifted, but we need many more studies that analyze with depth the adjustment of one organization or institution to changing conflict patterns internally and externally. And if our volume serves any purpose at all, it should be to prove that even if certain patterns of conflict and its resolution in Japan are distinctive, Japan and its institutions experience many of the same conflicts we find in other societies. Thus comparative research should be undertaken that directly examines how the same type of institution in North America or Europe or Japan handles conflict over similar issues.

Finally, Japan may have much to teach theorists of conflict in the

West. Takeshi Ishida's introductory essay, for example, contains a number of concepts familiar to Japanese, such as the distinction between *omote* and *ura*, that might also prove useful for analyzing Western societies. Further, because of the lack of direct research on conflict in Japan, we have been content here primarily to use the insights and propositions of theories derived from the structure and experience of Western societies and apply them to Japan. It may be, however, that many of those theories will have to be modified to account for the Japanese case if they are to have universal applicability.

The ideas of vested interest and rationality as causes of conflict behavior, for example, so heavily emphasized in Western conflict theory, may be too narrowly defined. The Japanese case shows that vested interest need not necessarily mean material interest; it can also mean social interest. Especially in a context like the Japanese (but also perhaps more universally than has been recognized in the West), such factors as preservation of the relationship, nonspecific trust, and the desire to conform to the norms of a group from whom satisfaction is derived may weigh quite heavily in the complex equation that determines whether and how an individual engages in conflict. What seems like irrational conflict behavior—such as the passivity of Japanese unions in pushing for economic benefits and then sudden intense confrontation out of proportion to the bargaining issues immediately involved—may in fact be quite logical given the history and context of the symbolic relationships involved.

If this volume stimulates even a small part of the reconceptualization and new research we have suggested, it will have served its purpose.

NOTES

1. For example, see Ruth Benedict, *The Chrysanthemum and the Sword: Patterns of Japanese Culture* (Cleveland and New York: Meridian Books, 1967); John F. Embree, *Suye Mura: A Japanese Village* (Chicago: University of Chicago Press, 1939; Phoenix edition, 1964, especially chap. 4; James G. Abegglen, *The Japanese Factory: Aspects of Its Social Organization* (Glencoe, Ill.: Free Press, 1958), especially pp. 129–135.

2. James G. March and Herbert A. Simon, *Organizations* (New York: Wiley, 1958), p. 121.

3. Chie Nakane, *Japanese Society* (Berkeley: University of California Press, 1970), pp. 53–54, 57.

4. Raymond W. Mack and Richard C. Snyder, "The Analysis of Social Conflict—

Toward an Overview and a Synthesis," in Clagett G. Smith, ed., *Conflict Resolution: Contributions of the Behavioral Sciences* (Notre Dame: University of Notre Dame Press, 1971), p. 14; also reprinted in Fred E. Jandt, ed., *Conflict Resolution Through Communication* (New York: Harper & Row, 1973). The essay originally appeared in the *Journal of Conflict Resolution* 1 (1957).

5. Lewis A. Coser, *The Functions of Social Conflict* (New York: Free Press, 1956), p. 59.

6. Ibid., pp. 47–55.

7. Nakane, *Japanese Society*, pp. 1–3.

8. Morton K. Deutsch, "Conflict and Its Resolution," in Smith, *Conflict Resolution*, pp. 45–46.

9. For examples of political scientists who saw great conflict at the national level, see many of the references in note 2 of our introductory essay; for examples of political scientists who saw patron-client relations and fairly consensual processes at the small-group and electoral mobilization levels, see Gerald Curtis, *Election Campaigning, Japanese Style* (New York: Columbia University Press, 1971); Nathaniel Thayer, *How the Conservatives Rule Japan* (Princeton: Princeton University Press, 1969), especially chap. 4; Nobutaka Ike, *Japanese Politics: An Introductory Survey* (New York: Knopf, 1957), especially pp. 25–36; Chitoshi Yanaga, *Japanese People and Politics* (New York: Wiley, 1956), pp. 293–298.

10. Ralf Dahrendorf, *Class and Class Conflict in Industrial Society* (Stanford: Stanford University Press, 1959). Evidence from survey research indicates that the relationship between class and party support and between class and voting behavior is not strong, but membership in an organization or social network does have an impact on political attitudes and behavior. See Nobutaka Ike, *A Theory of Japanese Democracy* (Boulder, Colo.: Westview Press, 1978), chap. 4; Scott C. Flanagan and Bradley Richardson, *Japanese Electoral Behavior: Social Cleavages, Social Networks, and Partisanship* (Beverly Hills: Sage Professional Papers, 1977).

11. Yoshio Sugimoto, *Popular Disturbance in Postwar Japan* (Hong Kong: Asian Research Service), especially pp. 191–194.

12. March and Simon, *Organizations*, pp. 129–130.

13. Ezra Vogel, *Japan as Number 1: Lessons for America* (Cambridge, Mass.: Harvard University Press, 1979), especially chaps. 1–3.

14. On the new issues of the 1970s cutting across old ideological lines, giving rise to demands for more pragmatic and concrete policy responses from parties and politicians, see Taketsugu Tsurutani, *Political Change in Modern Japan* (New York: David McKay Co., 1977), pp. 47–69; Kurt Steiner, Ellis S. Krauss, and Scott C. Flanagan, eds., *Political Opposition and Local Politics in Japan* (Princeton: Princeton University Press, 1980), especially pp. 20–23, 223–224, 267–270.

15. See Margaret McKean, *Environmental Protest and Citizen Politics in Japan* (Berkeley: University of California Press, 1981), chap. 2.

Contributors

John Creighton Campbell is associate professor of political science at the University of Michigan and directs its Center for Japanese Studies. He received his Ph.D. from Columbia University. The author of *Contemporary Budget Politics,* he is currently writing a book on policy change in Japan, focusing on policy toward the elderly.

Michael W. Donnelly is associate professor of political science at the University of Toronto, having also been visiting professor at Keio University and visiting research fellow at the Institute of Developing Economies in Tokyo. He has published a number of articles on Japanese agriculture and Canadian-Japanese trade relations and is currently writing about nuclear power in Japan.

Tadashi A. Hanami is professor of labor law and dean of the law school at Sophia University in Tokyo. The author of numerous articles on industrial and labor relations and law in both English and Japanese journals, and books in Japanese, he has also published two books in English: *Labor Relations in Japan Today* and *Labour Law and Industrial Relations in Japan.* He has served as a public commissioner of the Tokyo Metropolitan Labor Relations Commission (1968–1979) and has been a visiting scholar at the University of California (Berkeley), the Catholic University of Leuven (Belgium), and Cornell University.

Takeshi Ishida is professor of political science at the Institute of Social Sciences, University of Tokyo, and former director of the institute (1970–1980). He has been a research associate at Harvard, a senior specialist at the East-West Center in Honolulu, and a visiting professor at El Colegio de Mexico, Oxford University, University of Arizona, Dar-es Salaam University, and Free University (Berlin). His publications include *Japanese Society* and *Japanese Political Culture: Change and Continuity* in English, thirteen books in Japanese, and many contributions to professional journals. His current research is on Japanese political culture in comparative perspective.

Ellis S. Krauss is professor of political science at Western Washington University and has been a visiting researcher at Tokyo, Kyoto, Sophia, and Harvard universities. He is the author of *Japanese Radicals Revisited: Student Protest in Postwar Japan* and numerous articles; he is also coeditor of *Political Opposition and Local Politics in Japan*. His current research interests are elites in the policy process, politics and media, and the state and opposition in Japan.

Takie Sugiyama Lebra is professor of anthropology at the University of Hawaii at Manoa. She has received grant awards from the National Science Foundation and the Japan Society for the Promotion of Science; she is the author of *Japanese Patterns of Behavior, Japanese Women: Constraint and Fulfillment,* and various articles. Her current research interests focus on Japanese upper-class and career women and on Japanese culture and mental health.

Agnes M. Niyekawa is professor of Japanese at the University of Hawaii at Manoa, having received her Ph.D. in social psychology from New York University and postdoctoral training in linguistics at Columbia University and M.I.T. She spent her childhood in Vienna speaking German and learned the language and culture of Japan only later, an experience to which she attributes her research interests in cross-cultural and bilingual education and in Japanese psycholinguistics and sociolinguistics. Her publications include *A Study of Second Language Learning—The Influence of First Language on Perception, Cognition, and Second Language Learning,* "Authoritarianism in an Authoritarian Culture: The Case of Japan," and *Cross-Cultural Learning and Self-Growth,* of which she was coauthor.

Susan J. Pharr is associate professor of political science at the University of Wisconsin-Madison and for the past year has also been a senior research analyst for the Agency for International Development, U.S. Department of State. She is the author of *Political Women in Japan,* numerous articles in professional journals, and a forthcoming book on the status politics of minorities, women, and younger-generation politicians in Japan. Her current research interests are politics and media and the state and opposition in Japan.

Thomas P. Rohlen is a business consultant and research associate at Stanford University and formerly a member of the faculty of the University of California, Santa Cruz (1970–1979). An anthropologist, he is the author of *For Harmony and Strength,* a participant-observation study of a Japanese bank, of the recently published *Japan's High Schools,* and of numerous articles in professional journals.

Patricia G. Steinhoff is professor of sociology at the University of Hawaii at Manoa, where she teaches courses on conflict theory as well as on Japanese society. She holds a B.A. in Japanese language and literature from the University of Michigan and a doctorate in sociology from Harvard University. Her major research interest in Japan is ideological commitment and coercion, which she has examined through studies of ideological defection *(tenkō)* in the prewar Japanese communist movement and internal violence in the postwar New Left student movement. She is also the author or coauthor of two books and more than thirty articles on abortion in the United States.

Teigo Yoshida is a professor of cultural anthropology at the University of Tokyo. He is the author of *Nihon no Tsukimono* [Japanese spirit possession] and *Masho no Bunkashi* [The cultural analysis of evil]. He has also published over sixty articles in various journals, including *The American Anthropologist* and *Ethnology*. His current research interests include the analysis of Japanese traditional cosmology in the Anami and Okinawa islands and the comparative study of curing rituals in Japan, Bali, Mexico, and Micronesia.

Index

acceptance, 54–55, 56. *See also* Fatalism;
Innen
accommodation, 251, 263; of government
and opposition and House Management
Committee, 271–278; of majority and
minority parties, 254, 256, 262, 282; and
party politics, 248, 251, 253, 256, 262; in
rice pricing, 352, 354; in schools, 156–157;
and Speaker, 266, 269. *See also* Consensus;
Mutual Veto Power
adjudication, labor and courts, 118–
119
administrative authority: and dependent
revolts, 19–20; and principle of participation, 154
adversaries, political, 253, 261–262. *See also*
Japan Communist Party; Japan Socialist
Party; Liberal Democratic Party; Opposition party; Parliament; Sōhyō
agencies and ministries, 315–317. *See also*
Ministries
aging, 63, 78–80
agrarian, Japan as, 18–19, 24–25
agreement: and multiparty system, 264–265;
in Parliament, 245–246; snap vote as, 248–
249, 252–253. *See also* Conflict management; Consensus
agricultural cooperatives, 28–29, 31–32, 34,
344; and Agricultural Research Council,
358–359; and Ministry of Forestry and
Fisheries, 345, 349; *omote* and *ura*, of, 31;
relationship with government, 29, 31, 343,
346–347, 358–359, 360
Agricultural Cooperative Union, 28–29
agricultural land, 340, 364. *See also* Land
diversion programs
agricultural policy, 349. *See also* Agricultural
cooperatives; Rice pricing
Agricultural Research Council, of LDP, 347,
357, 358–359

akirame (resignation), 54. *See also* Fatalism;
Innen
alienation, 4
alliance politics, and tea pourers, 232
All-Japan Federation of Farmers' union, and
Japan Communist Party, 344
allocentric worry, 51
amae (emotional dependence), 19, 68. *See
also* Conflict; *Uchi-soto*
amakudari superiors, and hierarchical cleavage, 307, 313
ambivalent feelings, and dependent revolt,
19–20
American Occupation Authority: and
changes, 8, 189, 215, 380, 386, 391, 392;
democratic values and Japanese society,
137–138, 380, 386, 391; influence on government, 27, 29, 137–138, 246–247; and
unions, 28–29, 137, 139. *See also* West;
Western and Japanese comparison
American speech, compared to Japanese, 72
American system, 323; and cleavages, 296,
308; and independence, 311; and vertical
conflict resolution, 313. *See also* Western
and Japanese comparison
amnesty, and student position, 186, 188. *See
also* Student conflict; Student movement
Ampo demonstrations, 1960, 208
ancestor worship, and displacement, 47
animal-spirit holders, and political divisions,
98–99
animal-spirit possession, 86, 88–93. *See also*
Spirit possession
antagonisms, 9, 10–11, 60
anticipatory management, 42–43, 55
anticommunism, in LPD, 305
antimainstream, 161; factions in LPD, 306–
307; Japan Communist Party as, 141–142.
See also Mainstream
apathy, and IRAA, 27

vocational and night schools, 155. *See also* Sakura High School; Schools

wage campaigns, 30, 32, 173 n. 36. *See also* Strikes
Watanuki, Jōji, 247
Weber, Max, 5, 7, 18, 216
West, Western, 380, 382, 389, 390; and conflict management, 388–391; government models of, 246–247; and grass-roots conflict, 385; intraorganizational conflict, 385. *See also* Western and Japanese compared
Western and Japanese, compared, 45, 61, 72, 243, 379–380, 383–386, 388–391; conflict and managerial intervention, 383, 385–386; conflict management, 388–391; formality and respect, 72; goals, 389–390; grass roots, 385; interpersonal conflict, 380; parliamentarism, 243; recruitment of youth, 382; sex-role conflict, 379; social behavior, 61; spirit beliefs, 100; union strikes, 108–110, 114–115, 384; vicarious responsibility, 45
Western democratic models, and Japanese, 176–177, 210
Western parliamentarism, 243, 247, 262, 279–280

wildcat strikes, 134–135 n. 36
witchcraft, 96, 100
withdrawal from group, 201, 203–205
women: college educated, 236; and older men, 228–229, 232–233, 237; status of, 220, 215; tea pourers, 228. *See also* Status; Tea-pourers' rebellion
workshop, 24, 26. See also *Buraku;* Hamlet; Village

Yama Commercial High School, 147–150. *See also* Kōbe schools; Schools; Union castles
yami (black market), 22. See also *Ura*
Yoshida, Teigo, 85–104, 379
Youth's and Women's Bureaus *(seinen fujinbu)* 224–225, 226, 230, 230–231. *See also* Unions

Zengakuren, 177, 178, 190, 197; factionalism in, 182; internal conflict, 177; and *jichikai,* 178–180; as vertical, 179; versus Zenkyōtō, 179. *See also* Student activist; Student conflict; Student movement; Zenkyōtō
Zenkyōtō, 179, 198. *See also* Student activists; Student conflict; Student movement; Zengakuren

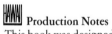 **Production Notes**
This book was designed by Roger Eggers. Composition and paging were done on the Quadex Composing System and typesetting on the Compugraphic 8400 by the design and production staff of University of Hawaii Press.

The text and display typeface is Garamond No. 49.

Offset presswork and binding were done by Vail-Ballou Press, Inc. Text paper is Glatfelter Hi-Brite Offset Vellum, basis 55.

Social and political conflict in postwar Japan is the subject of this volume, which draws together a series of field-based studies by North American and Japanese sociologists, anthropologists, and political scientists. It focuses attention on the sources of conflict and the ways in which conflict is expressed and managed. This book challenges the widely held theories stressing the harmony and vertical structure of social relations in Japan, which imply that conflict is only of minimal importance. Not only does the research presented here force recognition of the existence and complexity of conflict patterns in Japan, its approach to conflict provides a dynamic, empirical, and interdisciplinary focus on social and political processes in the postwar period.

The editors' theoretical introduction is followed by a general conceptual piece by one of Japan's foremost sociologists. Ten empirical studies, each offering both new data and new insights on known data about Japanese social and political systems, analyze conflict and conflict resolution in interpersonal relations, industrial relations, education, rural villages, government bureaucracy, parliament, political parties, and interest groups, including how they are manifested in women's and student protest movements and portrayed in the mass media. Western social science conflict theories are applied to enhance our understanding of both the universal and the unique elements in Japanese social and political institutions.

This book offers fresh perspectives on Japanese society. It should appeal to scholars and students of Japan and to those interested in the comparative application of social science theory to non-Western settings.

ELLIS S. KRAUSS is professor of political science at Western Washington University. THOMAS P. ROHLEN, anthropologist and business consultant, is a research associate at Stanford University. PATRICIA G. STEINHOFF is professor of sociology at the University of Hawaii at Manoa.

University of Hawaii Press
Honolulu, Hawaii 96822

ISBN 0-8248-0867-